Praise for *Driving Terror*

"Few objects can encapsulate the history of twentieth-century Argentina as perfectly as the Ford Falcon, and Robert uses it effectively as a connecting thread to write a multilayered story of the company, the car, the workers, the military repression of labor, and the search for justice after the fall of the last dictatorship."—Natalia Milanesio, author of *Destape: Sex, Democracy, and Freedom in Postdictatorial Argentina*

"*Driving Terror* is a groundbreaking social and political history of the Ford Falcon, a vehicle that epitomized mid-twentieth-century promises of prosperity and development and became an enduring symbol of state terror in Argentina. Karen Robert's fine-grained analysis draws on an impressive range of sources and newly declassified records to reconstruct the contradictory meanings of the Falcon, moving from the factory floor to the corporate boardroom and the halls of justice. This is an essential book about a notorious chapter in Latin America's long Cold War and its legacies."—Jennifer Adair, author of *In Search of the Lost Decade: Everyday Rights in Post-Dictatorship Argentina*

"Before the darkened-windowed SUV became the preferred vehicle of the world's death squads, there was the green Ford Falcon. Karen Robert's extraordinary *Driving Terror* tells the story of how Argentina's anticommunist military regime of the 1970s turned an object associated with middle-class pleasure and working-class pride into an instrument of terror. A wonderful, creatively and thoroughly researched book that details how the Cold War was, in places like Argentina, a class war."—Greg Grandin, author of *Fordlandia: The Rise and Fall of Henry Ford's Forgotten Jungle City*

Driving Terror

Understanding Latin America demands dialogue, deep exploration, and frank discussion of key topics. Founded by Lyman L. Johnson in 1992 and edited since 2013 by Kris Lane, the Diálogos Series focuses on innovative scholarship in Latin American history and related fields. The series, the most successful of its type, includes specialist works accessible to a wide readership and a variety of thematic titles, all ideally suited for classroom adoption by university and college teachers.

Also available in the Diálogos Series:

Frontier Justice: State, Law, and Society in Patagonia, 1880–1940 by Javier Cikota

Anti-Catholicism in the Mexican Revolution, 1913–1940 edited by Jürgen Buchenau and David S. Dalton

The Struggle for Natural Resources: Findings from Bolivian History edited by Carmen Soliz and Rossana Barragán

Viceroy Güemes's Mexico: Rituals, Religion, and Revenue by Christoph Rosenmüller

At the Heart of the Borderlands: Africans and Afro-Descendants on the Edges of Colonial Spanish America edited by Cameron D. Jones and Jay T. Harrison

The Age of Dissent: Revolution and the Power of Communication in Chile, 1780–1833 by Martín Bowen

From Sea-Bathing to Beach-Going: A Social History of the Beach in Rio de Janeiro, Brazil by B. J. Barickman

Gamboa's World: Justice, Silver Mining, and Imperial Reform in New Spain by Christopher Albi

The Conquest of the Desert: Argentina's Indigenous Peoples and the Battle for History edited by Carolyne R. Larson

From the Galleons to the Highlands: Slave Trade Routes in the Spanish Americas edited by Alex Borucki, David Eltis, and David Wheat

For additional titles in the Diálogos Series, please visit unmpress.com.

Diálogos Series

KRIS LANE, *Series Editor*

Driving Terror

Labor, Violence, and Justice in Cold War Argentina

Karen Robert

University of New Mexico Press *Albuquerque*

© 2025 by the University of New Mexico Press
All rights reserved. Published 2025
Printed in the United States of America

Library of Congress Cataloging-in-Publication Data
Names: Robert, Karen, 1966– author.
Title: Driving terror: labor, violence, and justice in Cold War Argentina / Karen Robert.
Other titles: Diálogos (Albuquerque, N.M.)
Description: Albuquerque: University of New Mexico Press, 2025. | Series: Diálogos series | Includes bibliographical references and index.
Identifiers: LCCN 2024024223 (print) | LCCN 2024024224 (ebook) | ISBN 9780826367600 (cloth) | ISBN 9780826367617 (paperback) | ISBN 9780826367624 (epub) | ISBN 9780826367631 (pdf)
Subjects: LCSH: Dictatorship—Argentina—History—20th century. | Ford Falcon automobile. | Argentina—Politics and government—History—20th century.
Classification: LCC F2849.2 .F59174 2025 (print) | LCC F2849.2 (ebook) | DDC 982.06—dc23/eng/20240626
LC record available at https://lccn.loc.gov/2024024223
LC ebook record available at https://lccn.loc.gov/2024024224

Founded in 1889, the University of New Mexico sits on the traditional homelands of the Pueblo of Sandia. The original peoples of New Mexico—Pueblo, Navajo, and Apache—since time immemorial have deep connections to the land and have made significant contributions to the broader community statewide. We honor the land itself and those who remain stewards of this land throughout the generations and also acknowledge our committed relationship to Indigenous peoples. We gratefully recognize our history.

Cover image courtesy of Fernando Gutiérrez
Designed by Isaac Morris
Composed in Avant Garde Gothic Pro, Beowolf, and Scala Pro

To the memory of
Beverley Robert (1931–2019)
and Pedro Troiani (1941–2021)

An experience that traumatic needed to be located somewhere, poured into an object whose existence might one day form the basis of a meaningful story.

—GRACIELA B. GUTIÉRREZ, "Falcon Verde"

Contents

LIST OF ILLUSTRATIONS — xi

ACKNOWLEDGMENTS — xiii

INTRODUCTION.
A Cold War Model T — 1

CHAPTER ONE.
The Falcon Family — 22

CHAPTER TWO.
From Aristocracy to Insurgency — 51

CHAPTER THREE.
"It Was Like a War" — 79

CHAPTER FOUR.
Driving Terror — 109

CHAPTER FIVE.
Survivors and Citizens — 135

CHAPTER SIX.
History, Justice, Memory — 165

CONCLUSION.
Endurance — 207

NOTES — 215

REFERENCES — 259

INDEX — 285

Illustrations

Figure 1. Ford Motors assembly plant in La Boca, Buenos Aires (ca. 1925) · 25

Figure 2. Workers at the Ford Argentina factory (1960s) · 52

Figure 3. Pedro Troiani at the Ford Argentina factory, General Pacheco (1960s) · 53

Figure 4. Pedro Troiani and Elisa Charlín on their honeymoon in Mar del Plata · 54

Figure 5. Map of the Zona Norte · 61

Figure 6. Ford Falcon in Bariloche, Argentina (2018) · 171

Figure 7. Detail from *Secuela* by Fernando Gutiérrez (2004) · 174

Figure 8. *El Broche*, Plaza de la Independencia, Tandil, Argentina (2004) · 197

Figure 9. Ford plaintiffs, Federal Criminal Court of San Martín, Argentina (2018) · 202

Acknowledgments

My first thanks must go to Pedro Troiani, Elisa Charlín, Carlos Alberto Propato, Ismael Portillo, Arcelia Luján, Tomás Ojea Quintana, and Victoria Basualdo, who answered my questions, shared resources, and kept me connected with the Ford case over many years, even during long periods when I was unable to travel to Argentina. Pedro and Elisa invited me into their home, both in person and virtually, on multiple occasions, and Victoria never forgot to update me about important conferences, reports, and publications. I was especially touched that she called me the day of the final verdict so that we could debrief about its significance right away. I also thank sculptor José Rossanigo for sharing his time generously during my visit to his studio in Tandil.

I am indebted to library and archival staff at Memoria Abierta, the Archivo Intermedio, the Comisión Provincial por la Memoria, CeDInCI, the Hartman Center at Duke University, the Benson Ford Research Center, the Detroit Public Library, and the University of New Brunswick. Several booksellers in Buenos Aires also helped me track down rare materials that I could not easily find in libraries. Research funding came from St. Thomas University in Fredericton, New Brunswick, the National Film Board of Canada, Telefilm Canada, and Duke University.

One blessing of taking far too many years to complete a book project like this one is that I was able to learn so much along the way from countless other scholars. My oldest debts are to Catherine LeGrand and George Lovell, who sparked my passion for Latin America in my undergraduate days at Queen's University in Kingston, Ontario. Rebecca Scott, Fernando Coronil, and David Scobey were my closest mentors at the University of Michigan. Though not directly involved in this project, they modeled curiosity, tenacity, intellectual rigor, and the highest ethical standards in their research, and I continue to be in their debt.

In Argentina, I thank the many scholars, journalists, archivists, lawyers, and activists who have worked so hard to reconstruct the stories of labor activists and working-class communities who came under attack during that country's last period of military rule. That body of work expanded exponentially during the long years I spent on this manuscript, and it brought into focus questions that seemed unanswerable when I began to think about the project in 2005.

Aside from Victoria Basualdo, I also received helpful guidance in Buenos Aires from scholars Dhan Zunino Singh, Emilio Crenzel, Ezequiel Adamovsky, and the many guest instructors in Emilio Crenzel's graduate seminars.

In North America, I have benefited from feedback and encouragement from Jennifer Adair, Lindsay DuBois, Greg Grandin, Naomi Klein, Avi Lewis, Shawn Miller, Jorge Nallim, Carlos Osorio, Max Page, David Sheinin, Kirsten Weld, and Joel Wolfe. Jeff Schuhrke generously shared resources on the American Institute for Free Labor Development (AIFLD)'s ties to the Argentine Sindicato de Mecánicos y Afines del Transporte (SMATA) union. I was able to workshop the project very early on at Columbia University's Oral History Summer Institute, where I had the privilege of learning from Alessandro Portelli, Mary Marshall Clark, and other brilliant figures in the field. Although distance, money, and other challenges reduced the scope of my interviews, I still found that learning experience invaluable. Several wonderful colleagues at St. Thomas University and the University of New Brunswick also provided feedback on chapter drafts and research presentations.

The first spark of this project came to me in my undergraduate classroom because of questions asked by inquisitive students about whether Ford Motors could be held accountable for supplying the Falcon sedans that were used by the Argentine death squads. Over the years, my students have continued to inspire me with their questions and passion about the world, and they have served as first readers of chapter drafts to help me keep this story accessible and engaging. Several research assistants have also helped me along the way, including Pablo Costa, Abby Herrington, Kristy Martin, Anna White-Nockleby, Austin Miller, and Magdalena la Porta. Doug Vipond and Norman Ware provided meticulous copyediting support, and editor Michael Millman at the University of New Mexico Press and series editor Kris Lane were unfailingly encouraging and supportive. I also appreciate the helpful feedback provided by the anonymous external reviewer engaged by the press.

I owe a great deal to the moral support of friends and family in North America and Argentina. Sadly, my parents, Beverley and Elston Robert, did not live to see the book finished, but they were always supportive of the strange adventures and ambitions that took me so far from home. My second set of parents, Beatriz Hermelo and Nestor Gutiérrez, welcomed me into their family with open arms many years ago. We have shared countless meals and rounds of yerba mate over the years, and Nestor even helped me with some of my archival work. My brother-in-law, Fernando Gutiérrez, also provided some of the earliest inspiration for this project with his moving photographs of Falcons, which are discussed in chapter 6.

Thank you to the dear friends who always make me feel at home in Buenos Aires: Rubén, Martín, Guillermo, Elena, Sergio, and Alicia. Thank you to dear Carol, who has been my virtual writing buddy, friend, and informal coach for several years. I also treasure my supportive community of friends in Fredericton, New Brunswick, who are too many to name. The deepest gratitude must go to my beloved Rodrigo, Lucas, and Sofía, who stuck with me and provided love, affection, and much-needed laughs along the way.

INTRODUCTION

A Cold War Model T

When the last Ford Falcon taxi was officially retired from the streets of Buenos Aires in 2004, most of the major news media took notice. Television crews and print journalists were in attendance as members of the local Falcon fan club honored the taxi's owner, Alberto Lucas, with a party and a plaque. Lucas then led a caravan of twenty vintage Falcons on a tour of downtown Buenos Aires, culminating in a spin around the large obelisk that stands at the intersection of Avenida Corrientes and Avenida 9 de Julio: the sixteen-lane boulevard that cuts through the city's core. This veteran driver described his taxi as "a member of the family," and he cited the more than three hundred thousand miles on its odometer as proof of the Falcon's legendary endurance. The daily newspaper *Clarín* quoted his sentimental remarks the following day: "This is the last Falcon taxi to be touched by the nostalgia of forty-three years of shared stories in Buenos Aires."[1]

Two weeks later, celebrated playwright and psychotherapist Eduardo "Tato" Pavlovsky published his own ambivalent reaction to this media coverage. On the one hand, he could not help but be touched by Lucas's affection for the machine that had supported his livelihood for so many years. On the other hand, Pavlovsky could not forget his own very different memories of the Ford Falcon as one of the "emblems" of Argentina's last military dictatorship, which had ruled the country from 1976 to 1983. "Whenever a Falcon passed or slowed down, we knew there would be kidnappings, disappearances, torture, or murder," noted Pavlovsky, referring to the military regime's widespread use of extrajudicial kidnapping, or "disappearance," as a tool of state terrorism. For him, the unmarked Ford Falcons typically driven by the military's fearsome *grupos de tarea* (task groups) became "the symbolic expression of terror. Death-mobiles."[2] Both Lucas and Pavlovsky evoked their personal memories of the Ford Falcon as collective memories shared by their broader society, but their associations could not have been more different. For one man, the car signified family and security. For the other: terror and traumatic violence.

Introduction

It might seem surprising that a simple Kennedy-era sedan could stir up such powerful emotions, especially as late as 2004: fully thirteen years after the end of Falcon manufacturing in Argentina and more than two decades after the generals had relinquished power to civilian politicians. Yet Argentine society remained deeply divided over the legacies of those years. In the country's long post-transition era, different groups—political and military leaders, human rights activists, former guerrilla fighters, intellectuals, and lawyers—had articulated distinct and often conflicting narratives of the dictatorship and the political and social conflicts that had preceded the coup of March 1976.[3] The Ford Falcon occupied a symbolic place in such debates over memory and human rights because of its close associations with the state terror system imposed by the military juntas. In fact, Lucas and Pavlovsky framed their distinct memories of the car around the binary of trust and betrayal, which anthropologist Antonius Robben has proposed as an explanatory framework for understanding this issue of contested memory in Argentina.

Robben argues that the Argentine military's systematic use of extrajudicial kidnapping and torture represented an extreme betrayal of social and political trust "by creating an uncertain environment in which the state [could] strike unawares."[4] The ensuing culture of "suspicion and mistrust" that gripped Argentine society carried forward into the democratic era, revived again and again as new revelations of human rights abuses came to light and as military officials sought to defend themselves against prosecution. Opposing groups in Argentine society put forth competing accounts to make sense of new information, and they repeatedly framed these stories around experiences of trust and betrayal. As a result, Argentine society remained fragmented over the country's recent history. Robben's framework captures the tensions between the very different Falcon memories put forth by Alberto Lucas and Tato Pavlovsky. Lucas framed his relationship with his taxi in personal, not political terms. He valued his Falcon because of its endurance and reliability: qualities that had made the car a huge hit with Argentine consumers since the 1960s. The taxi that had supported his family's economic security over many years signified for him trust and stability. While acknowledging the sincerity of Lucas's feelings, Pavlovsky could not separate the car from its traumatic associations with military violence and betrayal. His response spoke to the visceral emotions that the Ford Falcon could still provoke in some members of Argentine society.

The year 2004 brought forth yet another set of Falcon memories, though these did not immediately register in Argentine public consciousness. In January of that year, American human rights attorneys Paul Hoffman and Benjamin Schonbrun submitted a civil claim against the Ford Motor Company in US courts on behalf of sixteen former autoworkers and union activists at Ford's manufacturing plant in Argentina: men who had spent their careers on the assembly line building Falcon sedans. The claim demanded redress for damages the men had suffered in 1976 "as a result of arbitrary arrest and detention, torture, 'forced disappearances,' and other human rights violations." It alleged that Ford's Argentine subsidiary had

> actively cooperated with military authorities and allowed them to operate a detention facility on Ford premises and willingly allowed the military to utilize Ford's facilities to perpetrate these human rights violations. The purpose of the detention center was to capture and detain Ford workers who participated in union activities. To this end, Ford actively assisted the military authorities by providing information on union delegates and actively cooperating and facilitating in the military's actions against these plaintiffs and others at the plant. The company did so in order to suppress trade union activity at the Ford plant.[5]

Here was another story of betrayal: this one perpetrated not only by military authorities but by corporate executives who had allegedly blacklisted union activists and delivered them into the terror apparatus. The plaintiffs in the claim, who had somehow survived their detentions, also represented a perspective that had largely been missing from Argentina's memory debates up to that point: the collective experiences of the dictatorship's working-class victims. The Ford workers' accusations added a new layer of complexity to the narratives of the dictatorship era, raising questions about the role played by business leaders in military repression against grassroots union activists. Many similar stories came to light in these early years of the twenty-first century, with other cases launched against both national and multinational corporations in Argentina for their role in attacks on shop-floor unionists.[6]

The Ford survivors had been forced to turn to the US courts in 2004 because a set of amnesty laws passed in Argentina in the 1980s blocked judicial channels for human rights prosecutions in their own country. Unfortunately, this strategy was unsuccessful in the short term because a precedent set in an unrelated case forced their American attorneys to drop the claim. However, the workers soon found a way to move their case forward in Argentina after the country overturned its amnesty laws in 2005. Their legal struggle dragged on for years, suffering multiple setbacks, until in 2018 a federal criminal court issued a landmark decision, finding two former Ford executives and one military commander guilty of crimes against humanity for their role in the workers' illegal detention and torture.[7] Though appealed, that decision was upheld by Argentina's Federal Criminal Appeals Court on September 30, 2021.[8] The ruling set a new precedent in corporate human rights law, with both national and international implications.[9]

Driving Terror aims to reconstruct the Falcon's contradictory history in Argentina and to bring the remarkable story of the Ford survivors to a wider audience. It starts from two premises: first, that the Falcon's symbolic endurance and ambivalence point the way to unresolved questions about the nature and origins of the violence that so deeply marked Argentina's contemporary history; and second, that it is possible to take that symbolic life seriously while also bringing the Falcon out of the realm of pure abstraction and rooting its history in the lived political struggles of the Cold War era. Drawing on a wide variety of sources including declassified documents, corporate archives, film, advertising, art, and interviews, the book situates the Falcon's history within the broader social history of grassroots activism, violence, and the pursuit of justice in Cold War Latin America.

COLD WAR CONTEXT

The years of Falcon manufacturing in Argentina, from 1963 to 1991, coincided with key turning points in the Latin American Cold War, from the aftermath of the Cuban Missile Crisis to the dissolution of the Soviet Union. Scholars have identified this era as one of the most tumultuous periods in the continent's history. There, as in other regions of the Global South, geopolitical competition between the United States and the Soviet Union manifested in "hot" and violent escalations of local conflicts. The period was characterized by utopian political and economic projects, mass mobilizations for change, and atrocious acts of violence unleashed mainly by military governments with material and moral support from the United States. The Falcon itself was a perfect emblem of that era's dreams and nightmares, from its early association with midcentury promises of development and prosperity to its role as a tool of state terrorism in the 1970s and early 1980s. The car's contradictory afterlives, and the dogged pursuit of redress by the Ford survivors, illuminate the long struggles over truth, memory, and justice that have animated Argentine society in the post–Cold War era. My purpose here is to bring this compelling story to an audience beyond Argentina. Its broad periodization, spanning from the Falcon sedan's origins in the early 1960s to the resolution of the Ford survivors' human rights case against their former employers in 2018, provides a unique window on the creative ways that Argentines have sought to contend with the legacies of the Cold War era over the long term. It also puts the emphasis on working-class activism in the arenas of both labor and human rights, a story that is not well known beyond Argentina's borders.

Argentina has sometimes fit awkwardly into the Cold War historiography, at least in more traditional works that focus on superpower struggles in the realms of diplomacy, military strategy, and intelligence.[10] Although declassification projects have revealed the tacit support offered to the Argentine dictatorship by top US foreign policy officials, American power was far less overt there than it was in countries like Cuba, Nicaragua, and Chile.[11] The newer Cold War literature, however, has put greater emphasis on the historical agency of Latin Americans themselves and traced the more complex patterns of influence that shaped Latin American societies in these decades. It has moved beyond a dichotomy between imperial domination and local resistance to examine the lived experiences of a far broader range of historical actors: from radical priests to peasant activists, technical experts to union organizers, democratic reformers to neofascist ideologues.[12] These studies have demonstrated that while ordinary Latin Americans had to contend with the polarizing dynamics of the Cold War, and with the overt and covert power of the United States, they articulated their own ideals and asserted their own political projects in these years. This literature interprets the decades spanning from the end of World War II to the fall of the Soviet Union as an extended "age of revolutions" in which different groups within

Latin American society struggled over the boundaries and meanings of citizenship, rights, and political power.[13] The Ford workers' story of labor activism, persecution, survival, and the pursuit of justice during Argentina's long democratic transition offers a ground-level perspective on these issues.

Scholars have also begun to reassess the political economy of the Cold War era with interdisciplinary studies of labor and business history, policy making, investment, and corporate complicity with authoritarian regimes.[14] These years brought wrenching transformations to the continent's larger economies, like Argentina's, which experienced an industrial boom and bust in the span of forty years. From the 1940s through the early 1970s, both civilian and military governments in Argentina promoted economic development through rapid industrialization, which in turn boosted the size and relative power of the industrial working class. They did so largely by attracting investment from foreign multinationals, especially from the United States.[15] Whereas American businesses had mainly extracted raw materials from Latin America at the beginning of the century, corporations like Ford and Coca-Cola increasingly did business directly with Latin Americans after World War II by setting up branch plants and selling consumer goods on a much larger scale.[16]

US multinationals also began to play a more active role in shaping local cultures by undertaking what economic historian Thomas O'Brien calls "herculean efforts to create broad-based consumer societies" across Latin America.[17] Argentina, with its relatively large middle class, offered one of the continent's most promising markets. This influx of foreign capital, technology, and popular culture provoked mixed feelings among many Latin Americans. The late 1960s and early 1970s saw an outpouring of influential books that denounced and satirized the power of foreign corporations, including Gabriel García Márquez's *One Hundred Years of Solitude*, Eduardo Galeano's *The Open Veins of Latin America*, and Ariel Dorfman and Armand Mattelart's *How to Read Donald Duck*.[18] Leftist guerrilla groups also targeted executives from national and multinational firms, including Ford Argentina, whom they decried as exploiters and imperialists.[19] However, the Falcon's huge popularity in Argentina offers just one example of the way Latin American consumers also embraced new products and made them their own.[20]

In fact, the Ford Motor Company had a long history and special status in the region as a corporation that seemed to represent the best the United

States had to offer. Henry Ford had enjoyed celebrity status throughout the continent in the 1920s because of the production innovations that made his Model T the world's first mass-produced and relatively affordable automobile.[21] As he revolutionized capitalism, Ford inspired such unlikely admirers as Mexican muralist and Communist Party member Diego Rivera, who celebrated Ford's huge River Rouge plant on an epic scale in his Detroit Industry Murals, depicting it as the embodiment of technological modernity and human dignity through work.[22] When Henry Ford bought up a vast tract of land in the Amazon rainforest to produce rubber for car tires, prospective laborers flocked to the estate, known as Fordlandia, expecting to earn Ford's famous five-dollar-a-day wage.[23] In fact, as historian Joel Wolfe has argued, many Brazilians came to view the affordable Model T and its rival, the Chevy, as ambassadors of American democracy itself.[24] Latin Americans were therefore thrilled to share in the material progress and dynamism associated with modern car manufacturing in the postwar period, when Ford and other multinational automakers built their first full-scale automotive plants in Brazil, Mexico, and Argentina.[25]

Even the workers detained and tortured at Ford's factory outside Buenos Aires in 1976 remained proud of the work they had done building Falcons and trucks at Ford, regardless of their later determination to expose the corporation's complicity in their ordeal. In the 1960s, the men and their families had embraced the promise of financial security that came with employment at a modern automotive plant like Ford's, and they had taken pride in contributing to the Falcon's runaway success with Argentine consumers. However, their story illustrates how the midcentury dreams of industrial progress foundered in the political battles and global economic recession of the early 1970s. After the coup of 1976, Argentina's military regime aggressively dismantled the import substitution industrialization policies that had created thousands of jobs in the automotive sector and other heavy industries. As soldiers and paramilitary "task groups" rounded up labor organizers like the men from Ford, the ruling junta deregulated the economy and reoriented it toward financial speculation, provoking mass unemployment and a collapse in real wages. In Argentina, as in neighboring Chile, this authoritarian drive to restructure the economic and social order had clear winners and losers, as the story of the Ford workers will demonstrate.[26]

Introduction

ORIGIN STORY

Before embarking on the history of Ford's manufacturing operations in Argentina, it is worth tracing the Falcon's genealogy back to its origins in the United States to better grasp the car's significance as an artifact of the Cold War era. The Ford Motor Company launched its "new-style Ford Falcon" in 1959 as an economy compact designed to compete with the Volkswagen Beetle. Though later overshadowed by the Mustang in American pop culture and memory, the Falcon's success showcased Ford's revitalization after the end of World War II, when the firm had been on the brink of collapse. When the founder's grandson, Henry Ford II, took charge of the company in 1945, he lured staff away from Ford's main rival, General Motors, and engaged a group of college-educated army veterans who brought with them new methods of statistical analysis and planning, which they had learned at Harvard Business School and honed within the battle campaigns of World War II. These young men, known at Ford as the "whiz kids," were typical examples of the broader skills transfer between the military and expanding American corporations in the early years of the Cold War.[27]

Ford began turning a profit in 1949 and modernized 95 percent of its plants in the following decade.[28] However, all the Big Three American automakers (Ford, General Motors, and Chrysler) faced new challenges by the late 1950s, as the US economy slid into recession and European imports began to challenge their domination of the domestic market. The biggest competition came from the Volkswagen Beetle, the antithesis of that era's American dreamboats, with their luxury features and stylized fins. The Beetle embodied simple design, and Volkswagen ads targeted first-time buyers by emphasizing the car's affordability and reliability.[29] Its success was especially humiliating for Ford Motors, which had lost over $350 million in the failed launch of its 1957 Edsel, an overpriced model weighted down with heavy chrome.[30] That same year, the Big Three began to work on their own affordable cars with the hopes of opening up new markets among second-car buyers in the United States and emerging middle-class consumers around the world. Ford's version would be the Falcon.

The person behind the Falcon design project was none other than Robert McNamara, that quintessential Cold War technocrat who would move on from Ford Motors to become a key architect of US Cold War policy under the Kennedy and Johnson administrations and later oversee the World

Bank. Raised in a modest household that valued both science and ambition, McNamara became a champion of statistics-based management while studying economics at Berkeley and then business at Harvard during the Depression years. During World War II, he applied his learning in the Pacific arena by helping to design an elaborate statistical control system to track thousands of airplanes, parts, and crew members for the rapidly growing US Air Force. The American role in the Allied victory brought home to him "the power of information, the importance of data, the need for control and analysis," lessons that he would carry with him to Ford Motors and infuse into the Falcon's design.[31]

McNamara's austere and bookish manner made him an oddball in Detroit. When he was put in charge of the Falcon design project, he decided to break with recent trends and revive the principles of simplicity and durability that Henry Ford himself had brought to the original Model T.[32] Using an autocratic management style, he pushed Ford engineers to cut 1,500 pounds out of the design of their typical six-person sedan by removing nearly all the chrome ornamentation and cutting the frame down to a bare minimum of components. The Falcon would embody the smaller size and economy associated with European compacts like the Beetle, but its straight lines, expansive windows, and ample seating would still offer the feel of a big American car. McNamara had such faith in rational progress that he believed the car's austere design might even serve the broader social good by teaching American consumers to value efficiency over flash.[33] Early promotional materials described the Falcon's components as "so simply designed that a competent backyard mechanic can take them apart with hand tools."[34] Ads highlighted the car's seating room for "six (not five) big people," as well as its large trunk space and wide doors.[35] The 1960 catalog claimed that it was "sized to handle and park like a 'small' car, powered to drive in turnpike traffic and climb hills like a 'big' car ... built to save you trouble and money like no other car."[36] Henry Ford II reputedly hated the design, but *Car and Driver* magazine declared the Falcon to be "the best-looking Ford since the Thirties," and *Road and Track* likened it to the Model A: "good, solid, honest transportation."[37]

Like most commercial advertising of the late 1950s, early promotional campaigns for the Falcon were barely distinguishable from official Cold War propaganda materials, "filled with the ... orthodoxy of prosperity, progress, and consumer satisfaction."[38] Ford launched the car in the United States with a lavish, three-minute television advertisement that freely mixed space-age kitsch with edifying ad copy.³⁹ It begins with a shot of an observatory roof opening to reveal a night sky, as the voice-over tells viewers they are "about to know the thrill of seeing that which has never been seen before: the wonderful world of 1960!" A crowd of onlookers in evening gowns and tuxedos watches as three cars descend from the heavens like shooting stars: the Galaxie, the Thunderbird, and finally the Falcon. The guests admire each vehicle while choir voices sing about the "beautiful, wonderful new world of Fords," finally introducing the "car everyone has been waiting for: the new-size Ford Falcon, the easiest car in the wide world to own!"

American car ads were especially hyperbolic in these years, which saw the US government embark on the largest public works project in history: the National System of Interstate and Defense Highways. From 1956 to 1975, it spent over $100 billion to connect the continental states with a unified system of paved highways, a project that cultural historian Cotten Seiler has described as a "massive piece of propaganda" about American Cold War values.⁴⁰ A whole host of US opinion makers lobbied for this enormous investment by identifying the act of driving itself as a crucial feature of American freedom. "The figure of the driver," argues Seiler,

> embodied the ideological gulf separating the United States from its communist antagonists, and proved—to those antagonists, to allied nations, to those cultures the United States sought to annex ideologically, and, most important, to Americans themselves—the continuing vitality of the essential individual freedom enjoyed under liberalism and capitalism.⁴¹

Seiler's analysis helps to make sense of the charged meanings that infused the Ford Falcon as an artifact of the early Cold War era, when the messages conveyed in commercial advertising, government propaganda, and the middlebrow press all treated the private automobile as a totem to American exceptionalism: physical proof of the unique freedoms enjoyed by US citizens under capitalism.⁴²

The Ford Motor Company had placed itself at the center of that story in a 1953 film entitled *The American Road*, which was launched to mark the Model T's fiftieth anniversary.⁴³ It drew on the company's massive film archive to trace fifty years of American progress back to Henry Ford's invention of the world's first affordable car, with lavish production values that included an original score by renowned composer Alex North and narration by actor Raymond Massey. The opening scenes depict the hardships of American life before mass motorization, with shots of rural isolation and urban overcrowding. The film then reviews a series of Henry Ford's mechanical experiments, culminating in the development of the fully integrated assembly line at Ford Motors. Massey's voice-over spells out to viewers the practical benefits and sensory delights that the affordable Model T had brought to American society by the 1920s:

> Everywhere you looked, you saw the Model T. It became a part of the American scene. . . . Not only did it save time; it gave the average citizen a wonderful new way to spend the time he saved. Now for the first time Americans were able to travel inexpensively across their own country in their own cars and see the grandeur of their inheritance. . . . There was a new look in people's faces: a look of discovery, and wonderment, and pleasure. A whole new world had been opened up for them.

The American Road skims quickly over the 1930s without mentioning the bitter labor struggles that rocked Ford Motors and the other automakers, saying only that "even the grim Depression . . . could not stop the powerful forces that had been set in motion." It then attributes the US victory in World War II to the power of the assembly line and mass production. A brief, silent montage of war images ends with the dropping of the atomic bomb before the film cuts straight to a closeup shot of a spinning tire on a passenger car. "Nothing can stop us," declares Massey ominously. "We have kept on working, kept on building. . . . The whole nation has become swift and mobile, flowing along a great network of highways."

Six years later, Ford Motors drew on this same historical narrative to identify its new Falcon sedan with the historic Model T. It published a twenty-page advertising supplement in the Sunday *New York Times* in the fall of 1959 to spell out the modern social science research and engineering know-how that had gone into the Falcon. A commissioned article by *Harper's* magazine editor Russell Lynes chronicles the "painstaking, plodding, intensive" statistical analysis that underpinned the car's design.[44] A two-page photo spread displays the company's new research and engineering center in Dearborn, Michigan. Some seven thousand men dressed in matching white shirts and dark ties—roughly three quarters of Ford's engineering and research personnel—stand arrayed in troop formation in front of the parking lot, resembling an army of Robert McNamara look-alikes. A new Falcon is parked front and center, flanked by a Model A and a Model T.[45] The headline reads, "Today it takes ten thousand engineers to create something for everyone in automobiles." Another article by popular historian Roger Butterfield spells out how the new Falcon promises to deliver on Fordism's "three great revolutions" in transportation, production, and living standards. Butterfield quotes Henry Ford in describing the new sedan as a car "for the great multitude, . . . large enough for the family but small enough for the individual to run and care for."[46] Butterfield takes the rhetoric a notch higher when he observes that Henry Ford had "made a liar out of [Karl] Marx" by launching his automotive revolution, thereby pushing "enlightened American capitalism along the road it has been following ever since: the road toward high wages, higher profits, and a car (or two) in every garage." The humble little Falcon was thus cast as a champion in the Cold War battle for hearts and minds.

Ford's new compact sedan enjoyed immediate success, selling more than a million units in its first two years.[47] That turnaround brought Robert McNamara a promotion to the presidency of Ford Motors in November 1960, making him one of a handful of people from outside the family to hold that position.[48] Yet he left the company less than a month later to join President John F. Kennedy's administration as secretary of defense, where he applied his statistical control methods to Cold War policy overseas, most notoriously in the bombing campaigns of the Vietnam War. As a champion of efficiency, McNamara also went on to promote the US policy known as the National Security Doctrine in Latin America. It sought to protect the Americas against internal threats of communism and avoid the costs and risks of direct US intervention by funneling resources to the Latin American militaries, who were now charged with policing their own populations. Over the next three decades, this material and training support would undermine democratic institutions across the continent and have devastating consequences for civilian populations, who would suffer appalling human rights abuses at the hands of military and paramilitary forces.[49] Ironically, the Falcon sedan that had begun as McNamara's brainchild at Ford Motors later served as a key weapon and symbol of this military power and impunity in Argentina.

The Falcon's success helped Ford Motors assert itself as a revitalized and integrated multinational corporation; between 1955 and 1962 it invested nearly $670 million in overseas operations, including a new manufacturing facility in Argentina.[50] Ford also went back to producing flashier models as the American economy revived in the 1960s. The company's new rising star, Lee Iacocca, dressed the Falcon up in 1964 by offering a convertible model, a move that reportedly enraged McNamara.[51] He then launched the Mustang, a sportier two-door pony car that added stylish details like a longer hood and bucket seats to the Falcon's unified frame design. With luxury options and a more powerful engine, the Mustang made the practical, family-oriented Falcon look dowdy by comparison. Within a year it had eclipsed its predecessor and become Ford's best-selling car since the Model A. The company ended Falcon production in the United States in 1970.[52]

While the American love affair with the Falcon was short-lived, the car found more lasting success in smaller international markets with less buying power than the United States. First-generation Falcons were assembled briefly at plants in Australia, Canada, Mexico, Chile, and Argentina between 1959 and 1963. After that, full-scale Falcon manufacturing continued only in Australia and Argentina, two countries that shared certain broad characteristics. Both had large territories and relatively low population densities, especially in their vast interior regions. In both countries, governments were trying to overcome their historical dependence on agricultural exports by promoting industrial growth through policies that would encourage local car manufacturing.[53] The Falcon enjoyed its longest run in Australia, where Ford's subsidiary produced over three million vehicles under the Falcon brand until 2016, including not only sedans but wagons, utility vehicles ("utes"), and vans. Ford Australia also exported semi-assembled vehicles to South Africa, New Zealand, and Southeast Asia. Beginning in the 1970s, however, a series of style changes took the Australian models away from the original Falcon design, updating the car's lines as automotive trends evolved over the decades.[54]

In Argentina's more limited and volatile market, Ford manufactured just under half a million Falcons between 1963 and 1991.[55] It may have been a more modest achievement than in Australia, but those sales figures made the Falcon the best-selling car model in Argentina's manufacturing history. Ford's Argentine subsidiary also offered local variants of the Falcon Rural station wagon and Ranchero pickup truck, and it exported vehicles to other Latin American countries like Chile and Cuba. In contrast with Australia, however, it kept design modifications to the bare minimum to control manufacturing costs, much as Volkswagen retained the original Beetle design over several decades. Aside from cosmetic changes such as modified grilles, headlights, and trim, late-model Argentine Falcons looked much like Robert McNamara's original sedan.

AUTOMOBILITY

By locating the Falcon at the center of my analysis, I draw on a rich body of interdisciplinary research that takes the social and cultural lives of automobiles seriously.[56] Over the past three decades, scholars have moved beyond treating cars merely as utilitarian machines or units of industrial output, counting them instead among the most culturally significant objects of the twentieth century. They have dissected the unique experience of automobility, or self-propelled movement, which was made possible by the spread of passenger cars. Some have mapped out how mass motorization reshaped landscapes and accelerated the flow of goods in an increasingly globalized economy, while others have examined how race, gender, class, and other social determinants shaped people's access to the new experience of driving. Cultural analyses have examined the car's representations in art, film, and literature and studied how proponents of automotive transportation associated the act of driving with nation-building projects and potent values like freedom.

In an influential article from 2004, sociologist John Urry proposed that these different aspects of the car's history be understood as parts of an interconnected and dynamic system that he termed "automobility." That system contained several elements: the mass production techniques and marketing strategies that underpinned mass motorization and propelled the global spread of some of the twentieth century's most iconic corporations (such as Ford Motors and Volkswagen); the infrastructure of roadways, regulations, and governance created to facilitate the circulation of motor vehicles; the marshaling of vast natural resources including oil, rubber, and metals demanded by the automotive sector; the global consumer culture that expanded around cars and identified driving with positive values such as freedom and modernity; the primacy of automotive transportation over other forms of mobility (such as cycling or walking); and the spatial and ecological impacts of mass automobile use.[57] Urry makes a convincing case that the automobile deserves more attention as a constitutive technology of twentieth-century globalization, and his definition of automobility has the virtue of bringing together the diverse processes that made cars so ubiquitous around the world by the end of the twentieth century.

At the same time, Urry's definition of automobility as an autonomous and self-reproducing system could be considered deterministic and devoid of human agency. Political economist Matthew Paterson later amended it with a more historically grounded definition that leaves room for human action and keeps in sharper focus both the production and consumption sides of automobility.[58] Paterson argues that, just as passenger cars gave drivers new experiences of speed and autonomy, automobility brought about a "speed-up" of capitalist accumulation. It did so through revolutionary new methods of industrial manufacturing centered on the moving assembly line, its drive to expand consumption and consumer credit, and its circulation of people and commodities across new frontiers. Rather than a closed system, however, automobility was shaped by the actions of diverse social actors. These included corporate interests, autoworkers and their unions, engineers, urbanists, advertisers, policy makers, tourism promoters, consumers, drivers, retailers, and more. The entire regime also faced multiple forms of challenge and contestation at different points along the chain from production to consumption. Workers resisted the intense pace of automotive manufacturing with slowdowns or sit-down strikes, citizens fought to prevent freeway projects from cutting through their neighborhoods, cyclists and transit activists pushed back against the car's domination of city streets, and environmentalists denounced the destructive and polluting effects of the entire petroleum-driven system.

Empirical studies of automobility have also moved away from treating (white) US car culture, with its shopping malls and drive-in movie theaters, as the exemplar against which all other experiences of motorization should be measured. These include, for example, critical examinations of the risks of "driving while Black" in the United States, where racial segregation and violence have made driving a fraught experience for African Americans.[59] Beyond North America, studies have examined communist automobility in the Soviet Union and Eastern Europe, where governments promoted vehicle manufacturing while rejecting the car's associations with private property and consumerism.[60] Studies of early twentieth-century Africa examine the car alongside other technologies of empire like the railway or telegraph used by colonial officials, missionaries, and adventurers to lay claim to the continent. The smaller size and greater versatility of motorized vehicles meant that they could more easily be appropriated by colonized people to assert their own identities and values.[61] Australian historians Georgine Clarsen and Lorenzo Veracini have made a similar case for Australia as a model of "settler-colonial automobility," where white settlers used motorized vehicles and road-building projects to claim possession over the landscape, but where alternative aboriginal car cultures also flourished.[62]

The Falcon sedan was conceived during an era of infatuation with the private automobile that is hard to imagine from the perspective of the twenty-first century. In the postwar era, economic recovery in Europe and North America brought expanded consumerism and a proliferation of futuristic car designs that ignited popular imaginations. In 1955, French philosopher Roland Barthes even went so far as to declare modern automobiles to be "the exact equivalent of the great Gothic cathedrals," which had represented the pinnacle of architectural design in medieval Europe. Barthes was responding to the furor provoked by the launch of French automaker Citroën's new DS at the Paris Auto Salon that year. The DS, pronounced *déesse*, or "goddess" in French, sported curving lines and rounded windows that set it apart from all other cars on display, making it look to Barthes like an object "from another universe." Reflecting on the excitement it had provoked among the French public, he concluded that cars had become "the supreme creation of an era ... consumed in image if not in usage by a whole population which appropriates them as a purely magical object."[63]

The postwar years also saw governments around the world promote automotive manufacturing as the cornerstone to industrial modernization and economic development. Most countries trying to break into car production were forced to negotiate with multinational firms, just as Argentina's government would use economic policies to prod Ford Motors to invest in a manufacturing facility outside Buenos Aires. Even if their pedigree was not entirely local, the vehicles produced in those new factories could still come to symbolize national aspirations and pride. Certainly, automakers went out of their way to nationalize their vehicles. In the 1970s, for example, Ford Motors subsidiaries in Australia and Argentina marketed the Falcon as "the Great Australian Road Car" in one country and "an Argentine Classic" in the other. Ford was no doubt taking a cue from its rival Volkswagen, which had used clever advertising to rebrand Hitler's "Strength through Joy" car as the cute and harmless "Beetle" in the 1950s. As the German carmaker opened factories across the Americas, that same car morphed into a national icon in at least three different countries: the beloved "Bug" in the United States, the "Vocho" in Mexico, and the "Fusca" in Brazil.[64]

These transformations amounted to more than manipulation by advertising executives, however. Locals like Falcon taxi driver Alberto Lucas could also invest a vehicle of foreign provenance with their own meanings, appropriating it as an object of personal and social significance. Ethnographic studies have demonstrated how people from diverse cultures have anthropomorphized cars by decorating them, giving them names, and treating them as valued friends and family members.[65] Cumulatively, such individual actions have contributed to the automobile's cultural power and malleability across time and space. In one setting, like a white suburban neighborhood, a particular automobile like a high-end Cadillac might represent masculinity, ambition, and personal success. In another, like a remote aboriginal community in Australia, a car might function instead as a form of social property used collectively by community members to access sacred sites or hunting grounds.[66] These many forms of appropriation point to what anthropologist Daniel Miller calls the car's "humanity," referring to its embeddedness within human relationships of power and meaning. "The car today," he observes, "is associated with the aggregate of vast systems of transport and roadways that make the car's environment our environment, and yet at the same time there are the highly personal and intimate relationships which individuals have found through their possession and use of cars."[67]

That same intimacy can also make cars potent carriers of memory, both personal and collective. Material historian Leora Auslander has urged other historians to incorporate more physical objects into their research, arguing that objects communicate social and cultural meanings distinctly from written texts. As she puts it, "experiences come to be lodged in things," whether these are royal scepters or family heirlooms.[68] Auslander argues that certain kinds of objects, either handmade or mass produced, evoke such strong emotional and psychological responses that they provide insights into historical memory: the process by which people make meaning out of their past. Her own research focuses on personal possessions like furniture and clothing in moments of intense political violence, but her criteria apply just as well to automobiles. To function as memory cues, she observes, objects need to "engage all the senses, and especially the sense of touch." The most meaningful items are "three-dimensional objects with which people come into bodily contact" and that are designed with attention to style or aesthetics.[69] Midcentury passenger cars like the Falcon fit the bill perfectly. They were carefully designed by teams of engineers and stylists and promoted through marketing campaigns that charged them with meaning before they left the factory. They also fully enveloped their human users in sensory experiences including sounds, interior textures, views of the passing world, and the sensation of movement itself.[70] As will be detailed below, Falcon promotional materials celebrated such sensory experiences. More grimly, they also registered vividly in the memories of those who survived death squad abductions during the dictatorship years.

The current volume does not offer a comprehensive examination of Argentine automobility, though it does aim to inspire further studies in that direction. Instead, it draws on the concept of automobility to analyze the Falcon as a central artifact of Argentina's experiment with import substitution industrialization and the political struggles and violence that tore that project apart. Unlike other studies that have focused exclusively on the Falcon as a symbol of state terrorism in Argentina, it takes a broad perspective on the car's mutations from the 1960s onward. These include its early identification with Cold War values of technological modernization and prosperity, the labor struggles and political violence that took hold inside the factory where the Falcon was produced, and the car's redefinition as a tool of right-wing violence even before the military coup of 1976. In the post-dictatorship era, the Falcon emerged as a symbol of military impunity in artistic works that explored the legacies of military rule. Finally, the Ford survivors undertook extraordinary efforts to write themselves back into the Falcon's history by exposing Ford Argentina's complicity in their disappearances and reappropriating the car as a symbol of their own fight against impunity.

CHAPTER SUMMARIES

By focusing on Ford's manufacturing operations in Argentina, *Driving Terror* seeks to expand understandings of how grassroots labor organizers experienced, remembered, and sought redress for the violence unleashed against them by both state and nonstate actors. It also pays attention to the broader cultural evolution of the Falcon itself as an artifact of memory and contestation. The narrative unfolds across six chronological and thematic chapters. Chapter 1, "The Falcon Family," analyzes the Ford Motor Company's history in Argentina from the early twentieth century to the 1960s, when the company established its first full-scale manufacturing plant there. It locates that investment within the context of President Arturo Frondizi's "developmentalist" economic reform program and the Kennedy administration's Alliance for Progress. The Falcon project was launched amid ambitious claims about Fordism's promise for Argentina: that a heavy industrial economy based on car manufacturing would bring with it American technology, prosperity, and social stability. It reconstructs the "Falcon-mania" of the early 1960s, showing how this car came to be identified with the grand claims of progress characteristic of this period.

Chapter 2, "From Aristocracy to Insurgency," tracks the political expectations that accompanied the growth of Argentina's new automotive sector and related heavy industries in parts manufacturing and petrochemicals. Midcentury social scientists and policy makers predicted that workers in these new industries would pacify the broader Argentine working class because of the relatively high wages and benefits offered by multinationals like Ford. Aiming to calm the class divisions laid bare during the presidency of Juan Domingo Perón, President Frondizi and his advisers hoped the new autoworkers would form an "aristocracy of labor" that would turn Argentine workers away from class-based politics like Peronism and socialism. However, the expansion of heavy industry had unexpected political effects in Argentina, as it did elsewhere. Although workers at Ford Argentina's plant remained mostly unorganized in the 1960s, by the end of that decade, observers were shocked to see other "new" industrial workers, including autoworkers, involved in major general strikes and even insurrections.

Chapter 3, "'It Was Like a War,'" narrows its focus to the Ford factory in the province of Buenos Aires, describing union organizing efforts there from the late 1960s through the coup of 1976. The men who began to address concrete issues of safety and working conditions at the factory saw themselves as mainstream Peronist unionists functioning within a set of legally recognized labor institutions that dated back to the 1940s. However, they won their first victories in the early 1970s, a time of escalating polarization and political violence in Argentina, and a global crisis in the automotive sector. The chapter traces how these broader forces affected the Ford unionists and eventually culminated in the military occupation of the factory and the mass disappearance of its leading union activists.

Chapter 4, "Driving Terror," analyzes the Falcon's significance as an instrument of state terrorism during the dictatorship years. The junta's systematic use of extrajudicial kidnapping, or "disappearance," as a tool of repression has been well documented over the years. So has the national network of clandestine detention centers where those prisoners were detained and tortured.[71] Unmarked Ford Falcons were used in most of these kidnapping operations. Drawing on the automobility literature, this chapter investigates why cars were so important to the junta's strategy and why the same qualities that made the Falcon popular with Argentine consumers also made it an ideal tool of state terrorism.

Chapter 5, "Survivors and Citizens," returns to the story of the Ford workers abducted in 1976, following their efforts to rebuild their lives after their release from prison a year later. It also examines the steps they took to share their stories and seek justice after the military regime relinquished power to the civilian government of Raúl Alfonsín in late 1983. A small group of Ford survivors showed remarkable courage in testifying to Argentina's National Commission on the Disappearance of Persons and petitioning the courts for redress in the early democratic transition era, a time of great uncertainty and continued military threats. The chapter also spells out the longer-term legacies of the dictatorship's labor and economic policies, especially in the industrial neighborhoods that surrounded the capital.

Finally, chapter 6, "History, Justice, Memory," carries the Ford story into the twenty-first century. It traces the long evolution of the court case launched by the Ford survivors against military officials and executives at Ford Argentina, culminating in their historic legal victory in 2018. It moves between local and transnational contexts to show how grassroots activism and legal innovation made this case possible in the context of evolving human rights norms. It also examines how different actors within Argentine society contributed to the outcome of the Ford case by exposing and investigating Ford Argentina's ties to the military dictatorship as part of that country's rich process of memory work. These included artists and activists who deployed the Falcon's image as a symbol of impunity; progressive union activists who documented the junta's attacks on organized labor; journalists, academics, and archivists who methodically pieced together hidden stories of labor repression; and lawyers who developed new strategies to address human rights crimes committed by nonstate actors. At the center of that story stood the Ford survivors themselves and their families, who remained steadfast over more than four decades in their efforts to achieve justice and to write their experiences into the historical record.

The tragic irony of this story is that those same families had once been inspired by the grand promises associated with the Ford Motor Company's decision to manufacture vehicles in Argentina. They had sought work at Ford's Pacheco plant because of the brand's prestige, and because the relatively high wages and benefits offered them an avenue to domestic security through home ownership and a stable family income. In other words, they put their trust in the Fordist ideal that American opinion makers and propagandists identified with the "American dream" in the early Cold War era. Yet when they and other autoworkers organized to secure wages and working conditions comparable to those enjoyed in the United States, they attracted suspicion, surveillance, and ultimately, brutal violence. Like many people across Latin America in these years, their youthful aspirations for change made them prime targets of state repression, and they spent the rest of their lives trying to recover from that trauma and regain some of the rights they had once enjoyed. The Ford survivors and their family supporters eventually came to articulate their experiences as a profound betrayal: by the military authorities who oversaw their torture and detention, by their employers at Ford who blacklisted them, by their union bosses who failed to protect them, and by the judicial system that took so long to respond to their demands.

CHAPTER ONE

The Falcon Family

He doesn't sell cars. He sells ideas on wheels.

—JUAN JOSÉ SEBRELI, describing Ford dealer and
soccer promoter Alberto J. Armando (1964)

In May 2008, a young family from Argentina took employees by surprise at the headquarters of the Ford Motor Company in Dearborn, Michigan, when they drove up unannounced in their 1981 Ford Falcon Rural Deluxe station wagon. Diego Percivaldi had overhauled the car's engine and spent three years planning for this trip, fulfilling a dream long shared with his wife, Cecilia.[1] He had driven for more than six weeks through eleven countries—a total distance of nearly ten thousand miles—in his wine-colored Falcon to make the pilgrimage to Ford. Cecilia and their three-year-old son, Tomás, had joined him for the last push through Mexico. While the family's dedication puzzled Ford employees and local reporters in Michigan, it exemplified the kind of fanatical loyalty that the Falcon continued to inspire among its most committed fans in Argentina.[2]

Ford advertisers of an earlier generation would have celebrated the Percivaldi family's brand loyalty. When Ford Motors began manufacturing the Falcon in Argentina in the early 1960s, they crafted an identity for the car that resonated with the period's prevailing ideals of modernity, consumerism, and national economic development. Working with multinational advertising firm J. Walter Thompson (JWT), the corporation and its network of Argentine dealers used elaborate marketing strategies to cast the Falcon as the quintessential middle-class family sedan and the embodiment of national pride. Though designed as an economy compact for the US market, the Falcon was a large and expensive car by Argentine standards. With its spacious trunk and seating for six, it was big enough to introduce a new generation of respectable Argentine families to the pleasures of American-style car culture:

Sunday picnics, shopping trips, and driving holidays. Ford used full-page print advertisements and television ads to emphasize the car's rugged dependability and modern design. It even invested in a popular television series, *La familia Falcón* (The Falcon Family), which revolutionized Argentine television and demonstrated that the corporation was promoting an image of middle-class family life as much as it was selling a car.[3]

"LA FORD" IN ARGENTINA

Argentine consumers and racing enthusiasts already had a long-standing relationship with the Ford brand by the time of the Falcon's launch. Both the Ford Motor Company and its advertiser, JWT, had deep roots in the country that dated back to the era of the Model T. They counted among the first American corporations to set up shop in Argentina, introducing commercial innovations such as franchising, market surveys, promotional events, and consumer credit to the local market in the early decades of the twentieth century.[4] In doing so, they helped to shape Argentina's early car culture and raise ambitions that the country might even take its place alongside the United States as a modern and motorized nation. By the time Ford Motors started selling the Falcon in Argentina, local consumers were well placed to grasp the rhetoric that equated the car with the original Model T.

At the turn of the twentieth century, Argentina had been the first country in Latin America to rank among the world's fledgling motorized societies thanks to the enormous wealth generated by its export boom. A thinly populated frontier zone for most of the colonial period, the country built one of Latin America's most prosperous export economies in the late nineteenth century, after elites used military force to put down regional rebellions and seize control of the Pampas region from indigenous peoples. The rich, loamy soil of the Pampas made Argentina into one of the world's most fertile farming regions, and powerful families carved it into vast ranches (estancias) where they raised products for export: sheep for wool, and later wheat and beef cattle. The spread of steam shipping and then refrigeration transformed Argentina into Great Britain's breadbasket as it became feasible to transport bulky foodstuffs across the Atlantic. Over two million people, mainly southern Europeans, migrated to Argentina between 1890 and 1914 to seek their fortunes, while the country's landowning oligarchy entered the ranks of the global elite.[5]

The first cars in Argentina were fine European vehicles imported by those wealthy families. Early car owners here, as elsewhere, valued handcrafted automobiles as rarified luxury goods. For the Argentine oligarchs they also bore the "allure of the foreign," the special cultural prestige that Latin American elites of the era attached to imported luxury goods like finely crafted furniture and Parisian fashions.[6] By the 1910s, however, rapid commercial growth, immigration, and urbanization had given rise to a broader class of consumers such as retail merchants, bankers, doctors, and other professionals. American automakers soon came to dominate the local market, expanding access to car ownership with their more affordable models and consumer credit.[7] Cars like the Model T were not only cheaper but also better suited to the Argentine landscape than European vehicles designed for shorter distances and more urban environments.

The Argentine market looked promising enough that in early 1914, the Ford Motor Company hired Santiago Gregorio O'Farrell, a lawyer and businessman from one of Argentina's great landowning families, as its first sales agent in Buenos Aires.[8] O'Farrell put the Model T on display in a downtown showroom and quickly won enough sales to warrant importing knockdown units: semi-assembled cars that were cheaper to ship. In 1916, Ford rented a former cigar factory, where staff mounted tires and added finishing touches to the imported Model Ts. Demand soared as World War I blocked European imports, and in 1922 the company opened a custom-built assembly plant that occupied a full city block in the neighborhood of La Boca, adjacent to the city's port and railheads.[9] By the end of that decade, Ford boasted nearly three hundred dealerships around the country, and a popular slogan claimed that "eight out of every ten cars" circulating in Argentina was a Ford.[10]

As the first American advertiser to follow US corporations into foreign markets, the J. Walter Thompson Company opened its own Buenos Aires office in 1928. At the time, however, it provided services to Ford's main rival, General Motors. Since Ford sold only the Model T until 1928, it did not yet rely on sophisticated marketing. By contrast, under Alfred P. Sloan's leadership, General Motors was pitching a wide range of cars to different classes of buyers in the United States and around the world.[11] Two agents in Buenos Aires began importing unassembled Chevrolets from GM in 1922, and the corporation opened its own office three years later. It built an assembly plant in the neighborhood of Barracas and started offering models ranging from the modest Chevy all the way up to the Buick and Cadillac.[12]

Figure 1. Ford Motors assembly plant in La Boca, Buenos Aires (ca. 1925). Public domain.

Argentina's middle classes embraced the American automobile and its associations with freedom and modernity.[13] Between 1920 and 1930, the number of vehicles in the country jumped nearly one hundred times, from 4,800 to 435,000.[14] By the end of that decade, American cars accounted for well over 90 percent of the local market, and the two rival US carmakers became the first companies ever to operate nationwide retail services and advertising campaigns across Argentina.[15] In fact, at one point in the 1920s Argentina ranked fourth worldwide in per capita automobile consumption, ahead of Britain, France, and Denmark: a startling rate given the country's rudimentary road network and total dependence on imports.[16] As historian Ricardo Salvatore observes, even though carmakers targeted only the top quarter of the population, deemed wealthy enough to buy an automobile, the relatively high number of private vehicles put Argentina "a step ahead of the rest of Latin America on the road to mass-consumer modernity."[17] It also added to Argentines' sense of their own exceptionalism relative to their Latin American neighbors.

CRIOLLO CAR CULTURE

Through the first half of the twentieth century, a unique car culture evolved in Argentina that combined US precedents with local characteristics. The Argentine Automobile Club (ACA) served as the conduit linking local driving enthusiasts, foreign carmakers, and policy makers in the interwar period. Founded in 1904 as an elite social club, its membership exploded in the 1920s when local car sales were booming, and representatives of US automakers figured prominently in its leadership.[18] The ACA promoted automobility in Argentina as a broad social good by organizing car exhibits, publishing maps and tourist guides, and fostering motorsports as a form of mass entertainment, emulating the distinctive car culture that was then taking shape in the United States.[19] Car importers, oil companies, and driving clubs lobbied governments for investments in road and tourism infrastructure. "Our Republic needs three things," repeated the ACA leadership in print messages: "Roads, roads, and roads."[20] A Ford advertisement from 1925 invited potential buyers to experience the pleasures of car tourism: "There are so many beautiful places near the city that you and your family have not visited," it stated. "Buy a Ford and get to know all the city's neighborhoods and the picturesque locations on its outskirts."²¹ In fact, the ACA built campground facilities to introduce Argentine drivers to American-style nature holidays and promoted the idea of a Pan-American highway system that would tie the countries of the Americas closer together.²²

Such efforts amounted to more than the imposition of American values on passive Argentine consumers.²³ Companies like Ford Motors, General Motors, and Standard Oil actively promoted the idea of an authentic Argentine driving culture as they sought to identify their own brands with what they deemed to be local values.²⁴ American business interests were keenly aware that many Latin Americans feared and resented growing US power over the continent. Although Argentine intellectuals were generally confident that distance protected them from direct US imperialism, they denounced American interventions in the Caribbean and Central America. Employees at JWT discovered "an intense and widespread reaction against American foreign policies" and US oil interests in a 1929 survey of the local press.²⁵ They took pains to minimize the associations between their products and aggressive American imperialism by identifying US brands with what they deemed to be "authentic" Argentine culture. This strategy would be central to the Falcon's marketing decades later.

American advertisers tapped into a new rhetoric of Argentine nationalism in the early years of the twentieth century, a time of mounting anxiety about the pace of social and political change. As Buenos Aires became one of the world's largest and fastest-growing cities, writers and statesmen became nostalgic about criollo (creole), or rural, traditions rooted in the colonial and early independence eras. They turned to an idealized image of the countryside as home to the nation's "true" identity and to the rural gaucho, or cowboy, as the embodiment of Argentine virtues such as ruggedness and independence.²⁶ Like other nationalist ideals of the era, the *gauchesco* genre was full of irony and contradiction. Educated Argentines began to wax poetic about the gaucho lifestyle after the export boom had done away with it. The expansion of capitalist agriculture for export that underpinned the wealth of the national oligarchy had wiped out the original gaucho way of life and pushed the landless rural population into the status of dependent laborers. Nevertheless, the literary figure of the gaucho came to the fore just as American admen began looking for national symbols to attach to their products.²⁷ For example, JWT helped General Motors attract crowds to Buenos Aires's first-ever auto show by offering a Chevy Phaeton sedan as a door prize. Adman

Russell Pierce chose the traditional Spanish-style Teatro Cervantes as the venue for the event and draped the walls with paintings of what he deemed to be "typical" rural landscapes as backdrops for the Chevrolet vehicles on display.[28] Decades later, JWT would use similar strategies to market the locally manufactured Ford Falcon as an "Argentine classic," identifying it with iconic tourist landscapes and clichés of national culture.

Ford Motors and Chevrolet also invested in motorsports at a time when the Argentine state began promoting auto racing as a tool of national unification. Private car clubs had been running overland Gran Premio races since 1910, copying the long-distance "raids" that were popular in Europe. Torrential rains, impassable mud, and accidents transformed the first Gran Premio into "an odyssey that tested the durability of machines and drivers alike."[29] In this early era of racing, intrepid drivers and mechanics adapted their vehicles to build speed, adding extra fuel tanks and exhaust systems, tinkering with shock absorbers and brakes. Many of them lost their lives in ghastly accidents.[30] Thus emerged a kind of mythology of the criollo driver: the rugged, masculine traveler who, just like the gauchos of the past, relied on ingenuity and courage to survive in the punishing Argentine interior.

The Ford and Chevrolet teams came to dominate Argentine motorsports after the federal government began regulating overland racing in 1937 to promote its national road-building program and foster a greater sense of national unity. In the new sport of "road touring," or Turismo Carretera (TC), teams had to drive ordinary consumer vehicles and complete long overland routes in each of the nation's provinces while following everyday traffic rules and maintaining a maximum speed of seventy-five miles per hour. The government used the TC to promote long-distance driving as a key to national unification, staging events that were exciting enough to draw crowds but safe enough to reduce accidents. The highly publicized races allowed fans to travel vicariously across distant landscapes, from the mountains and foothills of the Andes to the tropical forests of the northeast and the windy, treeless expanses of Patagonia. They helped "machines, drivers, and the broader public" not only discover new regions of the country but "take possession of the national territory."[31] Ford and Chevrolet came to dominate Turismo Carretera as racing became more expensive and technically demanding, initiating a decades-long rivalry that attracted fan loyalties comparable to those of Argentina's great football clubs.[32] It was another way to foster enthusiasm about automobiles and identify their brands with local culture and aspirations. The Ford team dominated the TC through midcentury, and its two main drivers, brothers Oscar and Juan Gálvez, became national celebrities.[33]

By the 1930s, Argentina had developed most of the basic institutions associated with automobility: car clubs, a network of service stations and tourism facilities, an active racing circuit, and a federal road-building program modeled heavily on US precedents.[34] The state, media, and civil society groups all promoted driving as a positive good that served the national interest. While American automakers dominated the local market, they deferred to Argentine sensibilities by identifying their own progress with that of the nation. Yet the Depression and World War II exposed the weaknesses in Argentina's system of automobility, which was missing one crucial element: car manufacturing. The country remained dependent on imports of cars and fuel to sustain the infrastructure of a motorized society, and Argentine automobility suffered a serious shock when the Depression closed off access to foreign markets. In 1930, per capita vehicle ownership collapsed back to one-quarter of what it had been in the early 1920s and remained stagnant for the next three decades.[35] Ford Motors shut down its assembly plant in La Boca. The breakdown of international shipping and the American turn to military production during World War II further hampered imports of vehicles and parts, and severely limited access to petroleum. The pleasures associated with American-style car culture that had appeared so tangible in the 1920s receded beyond the reach of most Argentine consumers for years to come.

DREAMS OF AUTOMOTIVE DEVELOPMENT

Argentina's automotive ambitions revived in the middle of the twentieth century as part of the global economic recovery that followed World War II. In 1957, Ford Motors resumed assembling vehicles at its plant in La Boca. In the next five years it founded a new Argentine subsidiary, Ford Argentina SCA, and built its first full-scale manufacturing plant outside the capital city. In 1963, the new factory unveiled its first Falcon sedan: the first "Big Three" American car ever to be fully built in Argentina. Ford spared no expense in promoting the Falcon through special events, print ads, and television programming with the help of the J. Walter Thompson Company, which had taken charge of Ford's global advertising after the war. Before examining the branding strategies that defined the early Falcon for Argentine consumers,

Chapter One

however, it is worth taking stock of this midcentury moment from a southern perspective. Just as cars had become totems to American exceptionalism in the early Cold War era, automotive manufacturing had come to symbolize growing ambitions for economic development and prosperity in Argentina.

By midcentury, the cars driving on Argentina's roads were, on average, sixteen years old, and the country had lost its position of leadership as Latin America's most motorized society.[36] Neighboring Brazil had taken concrete steps to promote automobility under its modernizing president Getúlio Vargas (1930–1945, 1951–1954), who expanded the country's road network, instituted a national traffic code, and promoted local steel production. While Argentine neutrality had damaged the country's relations with the United States during World War II, Brazil's support for the US war effort had brought American investment and technological expertise that helped the country inaugurate Latin America's first modern steel mill at Volta Redonda in 1946. President Juscelino Kubitschek (1956–1961) later built on these precedents by using tariffs and incentives to entice multinational automakers to build factories in Brazil, making it the first Latin American country to manufacture its own cars.[37]

Argentine presidents Juan Domingo Perón (1945–1955) and Arturo Frondizi (1958–1962) followed Brazilian developments closely as they took their own steps to modernize the Argentine economy. The two leaders are often remembered as bitter rivals and political opposites: Perón, the military man and populist who built a political movement by mobilizing Argentine workers, versus Frondizi, the middle-class intellectual who championed foreign investment.[38] However, they shared similar ambitions to remake their country and coincided on certain broad economic priorities. Both sought to overcome Argentina's historical role as a producer of raw materials for the global market, though without dismantling the country's agricultural export sector or challenging the capitalist system.[39] Although the 1930s Depression had prompted politicians to offer more support to local industry with some tariffs and foreign exchange controls, Perón and Frondizi were also the first to break fully with earlier laissez-faire policies.[40] They saw industry as the solution to Argentina's economic and social woes. Like modernizing reformers in other parts of the postwar world, they championed automotive manufacturing for its symbolic value as "the sine qua non for advancement into the ranks of the developed nations."[41]

This shift was part of a global rethinking of economics in the aftermath of the "age of catastrophe," when two world wars and the Depression swept away the nineteenth-century economic order based on European dominance and unregulated free trade. New ideas emerged around the world at midcentury about the state's responsibility to promote citizens' well-being and protect both economic and social stability. In Europe, Keynesian economists brought in new market regulations and social welfare policies to safeguard their economies against the extreme crises that had fueled the rise of fascism and Nazism. In Africa and Asia, decolonization activists denounced colonial policies that had funneled their natural resources out to the industrialized nations; they promised that political independence would deliver a better standard of living to their people by orienting economies toward local priorities. In Latin America, the Economic Commission for Latin America and the Caribbean (Comisión Económica para América Latina y el Caribe), a United Nations office established in Santiago de Chile in 1948, became an incubator for debates about economic nationalism and industrial development. Through the midcentury years, governments across the continent experimented with solutions to endemic problems of inequality, economic backwardness, and instability. These ranged widely, including market-based efforts to attract foreign investment, social policies like the short-lived Guatemalan land reform, national populist programs of wealth redistribution, and full-scale revolution and socialism in the Cuban case.[42]

For reformers in Latin America, expanded US investment in the postwar years brought new opportunities for capital and technology transfer, but it also revived anxieties about US influence and power, fears that only deepened after the CIA-backed coup in Guatemala in 1954 and the Bay of Pigs invasion of Cuba in 1961. Latin American political leaders had to negotiate these new prospects and hazards as they promised their citizens economic growth and improved living standards. In Argentina, both Perón and Frondizi sought partnerships with foreign automakers and oil companies to increase their country's industrial capacity, and both faced criticism from political opponents who accused them of selling out the national interest. In fact, Frondizi boosted his own political career by denouncing Perón's contracts with US oil companies in the early 1950s.[43] Yet, once in the presidency, he deepened foreign investment and partnerships with multinational corporations, especially from the United States.

Consumer goods became highly politicized within this context as promises of economic reform raised broad expectations about what it meant to live a good life in a modern society.[44] This process began during the presidency of Juan Domingo Perón, the first modern head of state in Argentina to attack traditional symbols of privilege and champion working people as the backbone of the nation. Perón's government quickly delivered material benefits such as rent controls, wage hikes, and year-end bonuses that boosted the real incomes of urban workers after he took office, and his early economic policies favored local industries that provided the basic consumer comforts valued by the poor: affordable clothing, foodstuffs, and household appliances. These policies generated a new kind of Peronist material culture by imbuing commodities with special cultural and social meanings. As historian Eduardo Elena has observed, "everyday objects—from an imported Frigidaire to a child's Christmas toy, a humble hunk of cheese to a brand-name motor scooter—became freighted with significance as competing symbols of elite selfishness and social justice, populist excess and national progress."[45]

Private automobiles, traditionally identified with elite consumption, fit awkwardly within Peronist rhetoric. Early on, Perón promised that Argentine workers would no longer suffer while the old oligarchy maintained "their luxuries, their automobiles, and their excesses."[46] Yet as a master propagandist, he understood the popularity of motorsports and recognized that mass motorization was an internationally recognized marker of technological progress.[47] He quickly transformed the Argentine Automobile Club into an arm of the Peronist propaganda machine, using state funds to underwrite ambitious events like the 1948 Gran Premio de la América del Sur, which ran from Buenos Aires all the way to Caracas.[48] Perón saw the Gran Premio as an opportunity for Argentine drivers to show off their temerity in the monumental landscapes of Latin America, and he proclaimed that they would soon be driving cars manufactured at home. He even subsidized the two Ferraris used by Juan Manuel Fangio to win the Italian Grand Prix in 1949, transforming Fangio "the Maestro" into a symbol of Argentine ambitions to compete alongside the world's industrialized nations.[49]

Before his overthrow in a military coup in 1955, Perón also tried to jump-start local car manufacturing, declaring it a "national priority" in 1951. He first reached out to General Motors despite the anti-American rhetoric he used at home with his political base.[50] Rebuffed, he signed a truck manufacturing deal with Mercedes-Benz, a contract with Fiat to build heavy machinery, and a partnership with the small American company Kaiser Motors to build locally manufactured automobiles.[51] Industrialist Henry J. Kaiser had traveled to

Latin America looking to offload his machinery after failing to break into the US domestic auto market, and he won extremely favorable terms with Perón even though he was bringing outdated technology into the country.[52] Industrias Kaiser Argentina (IKA), a joint venture funded mainly with private and public money from Argentina, was founded in the months preceding Perón's ouster.

Perón also promoted motorization by founding Industrias Aeronauticas y Mecánicas del Estado (IAME; State Aeronautical and Mechanical Industries), a conglomerate of state-owned factories to produce aircraft, tractors, cars, and motorcycles. In April 1952 he unveiled the Justicialista, a small four-seater named for his own political party that would, he promised, bring the joys of driving to working-class families. It was clearly inspired by earlier "people's cars" like the Model T and the Nazi Volkswagen. Although Perón forecast annual sales of ten thousand vehicles, IAME struggled to produce half that, and the inefficiencies of its small-scale production priced the car well out of reach for working families.[53] Perón's critics denounced his motorsport ventures and industrialization schemes as frivolous and corrupt. However, scholars have argued more recently that his policies did lay the foundations for the automotive sector that took shape in the 1960s. Government loans helped expand the local auto parts sector and, in 1958, IKA, IAME, and other local producers manufactured nearly twenty-eight thousand vehicles.[54] It was a modest start, but it still marked the beginning of a new era of automobility in Argentina, where citizens might have the possibility of purchasing a car manufactured in a local factory.

Peronist-era manufactured goods even had the power to impress visitors from the industrial North. Just before the coup against Perón in September 1955, JWT adman Shirley Woodell sent a letter from Buenos Aires to his bosses in New York, observing that he had "expected to see empty shop windows and poverty" in the capital city. Instead, he was amazed to find "windows full of merchandise largely of local origin." Though he dismissed Perón's "unimpressive" Justicialista automobile, he conceded that "refrigerators, radio sets, TV chassis, stoves, kitchen ware and other household items made much more of an impression."[55] By the time of Woodell's visit, JWT had been running the Ford Motor Company's global advertising for eight years. They would soon help the company expand its business in Argentina with the launch of the Falcon.

MIDDLE-CLASS MODERNITY

The leaders of the military and civilian coalition that overthrew Perón in 1955 dubbed their actions a "liberating revolution" (Revolución Libertadora). They seized assets held by politicians and union leaders close to Perón, launched dozens of corruption investigations against the former government, and jailed roughly fifty thousand Peronist supporters between September 1955 and May 1958. The government of General Pedro Eugenio Aramburu banned the Justicialista Party and put the national Peronist unions into receivership. It even criminalized the mention of Perón's name in public or the production of any visual images that could be construed as Peronist propaganda. Meanwhile, inflation and antilabor policies cut deeply into the material gains won by Argentine workers over the previous decade. Working-class Argentines mourned Perón's overthrow in silence or joined the underground Peronist resistance, fighting the new regime with work slowdowns, pamphleteering, acts of sabotage, and bombings.[56]

In the brief period of military rule from 1955 to 1958 that preceded Ford's manufacturing investment in Argentina, anti-Peronists of all political stripes began to invoke the ideal of a noble "middle class" that was destined to restore balance to Argentine society and counter the excesses of the Peronist era.[57] In this new climate, even conservatives from some of the country's most aristocratic families extolled the virtues of white-collar employees and small businessmen as the true representatives of Argentina, countering Perón's rhetorical celebrations of the working class. For example, when Cambridge-educated economist Carlos Coll Benegas flew to New York City in 1956 to court US business investment, he offered assurances about the "moral fiber" of Argentina's "strong and capable middle class." Patrician businessman Álvaro Alsogaray, who held commerce and industry portfolios in the military government, also published a middlebrow tabloid entitled *Tribuna Cívica* that was aimed at housewives. In its editorials, the magazine described the "middle classes" as "the best people," the "guarantors of order and progress in all the civilized countries."[58]

Arturo Frondizi, Argentina's next civilian president, tapped into this language in his run for the presidency. Campaigning for the Radical Civic Union Party's Intransigent faction on a program of economic "developmentalism" (*desarrollismo*), Frondizi promised to heal the rift in Argentine society through rapid economic growth and technological modernization. Countering Perón's rhetoric of social justice, he declared that the "fundamental problem of Latin American countries is not distribution" but "production. . . . It is the need for technical-economic transformation."[59] Like his Brazilian contemporary Juscelino Kubitschek, Frondizi believed he could use policy measures to harness private capital to a project of national economic development that would, in turn, provide broad social benefits. A sense of urgency underpinned both men's efforts to remake their national economies around an American model of Fordist automobility. Upon taking office in January 1956, the Brazilian leader had made vehicle manufacturing the cornerstone of his goal to achieve "fifty years" of industrial progress "in five," using a mix of financial incentives and import restrictions to entice foreign automakers to build factories in Brazil. After 1960, cars containing less than 90 percent locally made parts would face heavy tariffs.[60]

Frondizi similarly aimed to attract an infusion of foreign investment and know-how—especially from the United States—to carry Argentina into a new industrial era focused on metalworking, automotive manufacturing, and petrochemicals. In economic terms, he believed that the boost to local industrial capacity would cut back on costly imports while meeting local needs. In social terms, local automotive manufacturing would boost working-class wages and middle-class consumption, fostering a class alliance that would benefit workers, industrialists, and white-collar professionals.[61] This optimistic vision of Argentina's future won over a significant segment of the Argentine public during the brief political honeymoon that carried Frondizi to the presidency. One commentator even dubbed him "the Perón of the middle classes."[62]

Frondizi shared in Kubitschek's optimism about technological progress, but in the more politically divided context of Argentina he also felt pressured to deliver on his campaign promises as quickly as possible. Indeed, he faced challenges on all sides. Undermined by cronyism and faction fighting, Argentina's federal bureaucracy lacked the professional expertise that Kubitschek relied on in Brazil. Workers remained loyal to Perón and the Justicialista Party, and they were prepared to resist economic policies that further undercut their standard of living. The military, meanwhile, distrusted Frondizi's conciliatory attitude toward the Peronists. The new president and his advisers calculated that they had just one or two years to push through their ambitious economic reforms before facing yet another military coup.[63] In December 1958, President Frondizi liberalized rules restricting foreign capital in a new Law on Foreign Investment, and one month later he signed off on his Regime for the Promotion of the Automotive Industry.[64] It offered corporations tax exemptions on imports of capital, machinery, parts, and other industrial inputs and gave the executive office control over manufacturing permits. As in Brazil, the policy (and its later amendments) imposed escalating requirements for local parts content. The Frondizi government approved every truck and car proposal it received, so that, on paper at least, some twenty-three vehicle manufacturers were operating in Argentina by the end of 1960. These ranged from IKA, which produced over seventy-five thousand trucks and cars that year, all the way down to tiny local producers like Panambí and Dinborg, whose production counted in the hundreds.[65]

Ford Motors and GM had been slow to invest in Brazil's automotive sector because they considered the country's internal market too limited. However, foreign automakers had no choice but to accommodate local aspirations for industrial growth once Argentina and Mexico followed Brazil's lead.[66] The American business and foreign-policy establishments were also jolted into a deeper reckoning with Latin American demands for change after the Cuban revolutionary victory on January 1, 1959. When Fidel Castro's armed guerrillas forced dictator Fulgencio Batista from office, they brought down a key US ally in the country with Latin America's most Americanized economy. Castro had built a following in Cuba by promising to overturn the island's economic order, which had long been dominated by US business, tourism, and organized crime. His victory convinced President Dwight D. Eisenhower that Latin America had become "a critical Cold War battleground" where unresolved popular frustrations threatened to overturn US hegemony. In fact, Eisenhower privately acknowledged the basis of Latin American frustration. Since 1945, the United States had invested heavily in the reconstruction of Europe while propping up dictators across the Americas. The president's advisers concluded that Latin America appeared to be on the brink of a new "age of revolution" that would demand more creative and generous responses from the United States.[67] Eisenhower embarked on a Latin American tour in February, visiting moderate reformers like Arturo Frondizi, Juscelino Kubitschek, and Chile's Jorge Alessandri to offset Castro's revolutionary example and signal American commitments to capitalist development.

BRANCH-PLANT AUTOMOBILITY

Henry Ford II beat the president to Buenos Aires. He left for Latin America before the end of January 1959, meeting with Frondizi, Kubitschek, and Mexican president Adolfo López Mateos. Ford Motors soon announced new sales and assembly operations in Venezuela and Colombia as well as major manufacturing investments in Mexico, Brazil, and Argentina, where it would replace its old assembly plants with modern automotive factories. By August of that year, the new subsidiary Ford Argentina had purchased a 250-acre property in General Pacheco, a growing suburb in the province of Buenos Aires roughly ten miles north of the capital. It began construction of a truck plant and announced plans to expand the facilities to produce locally manufactured Ford Falcon sedans.[68]

Other multinational firms followed suit, clustering their new car plants near the Argentine capital. The older factories founded during the Peronist years had mainly been located in Córdoba, Argentina's second-largest city, which was home to the state-run IAME factories, the plant built by IKA, and two heavy machinery factories built by Fiat's local manufacturing subsidiary, Concord.[69] Since Frondizi's policies focused on passenger cars more than industrial and farming machinery, automakers preferred to locate near Buenos Aires, where most potential car buyers lived. In 1959, General Motors refurbished a shuttered factory it owned in the municipality of Caseros, just west of the capital, and Fiat Concord built its first automotive factory nearby in 1960. French automaker Citroën purchased and retooled a factory in Barracas, an older working-class neighborhood in the city. A local company, Industriales Argentinos Fabricantes de Automotores (IAFA), signed a deal with Peugeot and began construction in 1961 of a manufacturing facility in Berazategui, between Buenos Aires and La Plata.[70] Argentine appliance producer SIAM also built a new car factory in Monte Chingolo, south of the capital, to build cars under a licensing agreement with the British Motors Corporation.

The Falcon stood out from the field of new cars produced in the early 1960s because of its relative size, power, and American styling, though it was not the only American model available. General Motors brought out the Chevrolet 400 in 1962 and the "Chevy" (a local version of the Nova) in 1969. Like the Falcon, these were considered compacts in the United States but were sold as large cars in Argentina. Neither model made much headway against the Falcon in local markets, however. Even the more successful Chevy sold fewer than seventy thousand units between 1969 and 1978, when GM shut down its Argentine car manufacturing operation altogether.[71] Industrias Kaiser Argentina had more success when it launched the Torino in 1966 as a direct competitor to the Falcon. Produced from 1967 to 1975 by the newly merged IKA-Renault and from 1975 to 1981 under the Renault brand, the Torino was built on the base of another American compact: the AMC Rambler Rogue. It was marketed as the first car designed specifically for the Argentine market, because IKA had hired the Italian design firm Pininfarina to restyle the Rogue. After disappointing sales in its launch year, IKA-Renault boosted the car's horsepower and promoted it as a world-class race car, running it in both the national and European circuits. The Torino came to rival the Falcon as a beloved Argentine muscle car and was similarly favored by taxi drivers and Argentine police forces because of its power and dependability. It reached its peak sales and racing achievements around 1970, even briefly outselling the Falcon as Argentina's favorite large car, but it gradually lost ground and was discontinued in 1981, a decade before the Falcon.[72]

Most cars manufactured in Argentina's new factories were smaller, rounded European compacts. These included the Renault Dauphine, which was also produced by IKA; the Riley 4/68, marketed by SIAM as the Di Tella 1500; and Citroën's tough little 2CV, which had been designed to help motorize the French countryside. The most successful small car was the Fiat 600, whose diminutive size earned it the nickname *Fitito* ("Little Fiat") among Argentine fans. Designed in Italy to compete with the Volkswagen Beetle, the 600 had a similar rounded shape, a tiny rear engine, and room for four tightly packed passengers. It was nearly four feet shorter than the Falcon and had one-third the horsepower. Still, its affordable price and fuel efficiency made it a hit with modest buyers in Argentina. Fiat sold some three hundred thousand Fititos between 1960 and 1982, along with small five-seat sedans like the 1100, the 1500, and the locally designed Vignale coupe.[73]

A VEHICLE FOR PROGRESS

Of all the multinational firms that responded to Argentina's new automotive policies, the Ford Motor Company loomed largest in President Frondizi's dreams of development. Frondizi visited the construction site in General Pacheco several times in 1959 and sought to align himself with the company's prestigious brand. As Chrysler, Mercedes-Benz, and Ford Motors were all preparing their first passenger car proposals in early 1961, Argentine officials secretly contacted Ford executives, offering the company special concessions to give it an advantage over its rivals. An internal Ford memo noted that president Frondizi considered that "a substantial share of credit for the success to date of the industrialization of Argentina is due to Mr. Henry Ford's 'vote of confidence'" in building the company's truck manufacturing plant.[74] On at least two occasions, he requested that Henry Ford II personally return to Argentina to announce the Falcon program as a public endorsement of his government's policies. Ford declined Frondizi's invitation and expressed some ambivalence about his company's Latin American investments when speaking to his peers in the United States. "Whether we like it or not," he declared to an audience in Dearborn in 1961,

> Africa, Asia, Latin America are going all-out into the industrial age. It does no good to tell them that this is all very unsound, that they ought not to try to do so much so fast. . . . If we want to share in these markets, rich and vast as they will someday surely be, . . . we are going to have to go in with our capital and tools and know-how and help them get the things they want.[75]

When addressing Argentine audiences, however, Ford executives repeatedly proclaimed their commitment to local dreams of industrial development and progress. At a 1959 banquet for Ford dealers and members of Argentina's business elite, outgoing Ford Argentina general manager Henry H. West spoke of his pride at having been present in the country during "one of its most glorious eras," referring to the country's transformation since Perón's overthrow. West celebrated Argentina as "a nation firmly committed to the culture and spirit of Western civilization."[76] Later, at the ceremony marking the inauguration of the Pacheco truck plant, Ford Argentina president D. B. Kitterman began his speech by noting that the factory was a noisy spot for a champagne dinner. "However," he added, "that background noise can only be interpreted as the sound of 'Argentina on the move!'"[77]

In January 1962, Ford Argentina unveiled its first locally assembled Falcon in a lavish ceremony at the Teatro Gran Rex in downtown Buenos Aires. Although Henry Ford II did not attend, Ford Motors vice president M. H. Willey traveled from Dearborn for the occasion. In his speech, he recalled the corporation's long history in Argentina, and he identified the Falcon with the original Model T: "If the epic Ford T opened up new roads in this vast land, the new FALCON will symbolize Argentina's commitment to a bright and secure future!"[78] Individual dealers also staged their own promotional events, which included fashion shows, cocktail parties, and celebrity appearances. In February, retired racing star Oscar Gálvez opened his own Ford dealership, showcasing the Falcon in a day-long event with festivities that included a formal blessing by a Catholic priest and a guest appearance by Formula 1 racing idol Juan Manuel Fangio.[79] These were the typical clichés and rituals of midcentury automotive promotion. The speeches and ceremonies identified the new Falcon with a cluster of values close to those espoused by Robert McNamara himself: technological progress, capitalist economic growth, and middle-class respectability. However, as observed earlier, such commercial messages could not be divorced from the broader political context of the early Cold War. They echoed the claims of American exceptionalism articulated in US government propaganda and middlebrow publishing, messages aimed at a variety of audiences including "those cultures the United States sought to annex ideologically," to recall the words of Cotten Seiler.[80] In Latin America, they dovetailed with the promises of President Kennedy's new Alliance for Progress, an ambitious program of investment and aid launched as a response to the Cuban Revolution.

The Latin American developmentalists had been pressuring the United States for this kind of economic assistance since at least 1958, when Juscelino Kubitschek had called for a summit to negotiate a Marshall Plan for Latin America, which he dubbed "Operation Pan America." At first, the US government was cool to Kubitschek's warning that democracy was "difficult to defend" in Latin America, "with misery weighing on so many lives."[81] Yet after the Cuban revolutionary victory, Eisenhower quickly approved $500 million in development assistance for the continent. Kennedy announced the Alliance for Progress as his own version of Operation Pan America in March 1961, just two months after he assumed the presidency and one month before the disastrous Bay of Pigs invasion. Like Eisenhower before him, Kennedy aimed to dampen the appeal of Castro's revolution by introducing more Latin Americans to the tangible benefits of American-style capitalist development. In his announcement speech, he promised that an influx of $20 billion in American investment, aid, and technical assistance would solve centuries-old problems of inequality, poverty, and economic backwardness.⁸² The 1960s would be the "decade of development" for Latin America.

Kennedy derived this confidence from his economic adviser Walt Whitman Rostow, whose influential 1960 work, *The Stages of Economic Growth: A Non-Communist Manifesto*, had offered a simple formula for economic "modernization" that could be applied to any country in the world. Rostow's modernization theory treated rapid economic growth as a straightforward process that would deliver social and political stability to "Third World" regions like Latin America. In retrospect, the whole program smacked of the same technocratic boosterism voiced by that other new Kennedy adviser, Robert McNamara. Yet it rang true to Argentine president Arturo Frondizi, who saw the Alliance for Progress as another high-profile endorsement of his own vision for Argentina.⁸³ He urged the Kennedy administration to provide meaningful economic and technical assistance rather than Band-Aid charity: "What is required," he warned the president, "is a basic attack on the conditions that produced Castro."⁸⁴

American corporations doing business in Latin America became unofficial ambassadors for Kennedy's project. A confidential State Department memorandum from August 1962 reported that US business representatives were taking part in a "wide variety of activities which, directly or indirectly, support the Alliance for Progress," whether through charitable donations, social projects, or regular business operations. Embassy staff across the continent worked to encourage and coordinate such collaborations, although in some countries like Venezuela, Honduras, and Costa Rica, American businesses found it politically imprudent to associate themselves so openly with US foreign policy. The Buenos Aires embassy reported, however, that local US business leaders were participating in monthly "off-the-record" meetings with the ambassador, the economic counselor, and the director of Kennedy's newly created US Agency for International Development (USAID). "The principal contribution of the [American business] community," read the report, "is made through normal business activity, by diffusing new technology, advanced managerial methods, and improved labor policy."⁸⁵

Another Alliance for Progress initiative, known as the American Institute for Free Labor Development (AIFLD), aimed to transfer US business unionism to Latin America as part of this broader package of direct investment. American social scientists trained in midcentury ideas of scientific management and industrial relations originally conceived of the AIFLD as an independent nonprofit training institute that would teach Latin American union organizers about the benefits of American-style collective bargaining. These academics reasoned that such training would support the broader process of industrial modernization by winning Latin American workers over to the idea that they could improve their lives through capitalism and bureaucratic unionism.[86] Although a few voices in the United States cautioned that any collaboration between US and Latin American labor would fuel anti-imperialist resentments across the continent, the AIFLD went ahead in 1961. It was soon absorbed into the State Department apparatus, receiving some $58 million in government funding between 1962 and 1974. Its training initiatives were taken over by fanatical anticommunists like George Meany at the head of the AFL-CIO, the largest labor federation in the United States.[87] As will be outlined in later chapters, the AIFLD's operations in Argentina would focus particularly on the national autoworkers' union, Sindicato de Mecánicos y Afines del Transporte (SMATA).

BRANDING "EL FALCON"

As the most important American corporation operating in Argentina in the early 1960s, Ford Motors aligned itself with the rhetoric of the Alliance for Progress in its full-scale branding campaign for the new Falcon, outspending all its rivals in the local automotive sector with its print and television promotions.[88] Falcon ads from the early 1960s were as didactic and wordy as the promotional materials that had accompanied the car's US launch. They spelled out for potential buyers the meanings embedded in the car's design, and they associated the Falcon with positive values such as modernity, upward social mobility, prestige, and progress. Advertisements also instructed potential buyers on how to interpret the sensory experiences of driving in a new Falcon sedan, emphasizing its distinctiveness when compared with the diminutive European models sold by Ford's competitors. In all these ways, the Ford Motor Company and its advertising agency, J. Walter Thompson, sought to define the early Falcon as a product that embodied the dominant values of the early 1960s and the respectable middle-class aspirations of Argentine consumers.

The first Falcon ads published in Argentina were straight translations from American copy, like the full-color spread titled "It Has to Be the Ford Falcon" ("Tiene que ser el Ford Falcon"), which shows a white family of four driving down a suburban American street lined with bungalows and white picket fences. While the father focuses on the road, the children and mother point excitedly toward a red Falcon coming in the other direction. The ad includes a full paragraph of explanatory text that details the car's many virtues: "its luxurious comfort for six adults, elegant interior, incredibly generous trunk space, and responsive motor that can handle all situations." The Falcon offered everything a purchaser could desire: smooth suspension, fuel economy, and "surprising" speed. Best of all, it offered a visceral experience of progress, "because its solid structure and graceful design belong to a new dimension: a future dimension that you can enjoy right now . . . in your own '62 Ford Falcon!"[89]

Another translated American advertisement from that same year features a large image of a Ford Falcon interior viewed through the windshield. Inside are six smiling and well-dressed passengers: two men in suits and ties, two women with Jackie Kennedy hairstyles and pearls, and two children. "The Ford Falcon offers real comfort for six people!" announces the title. The explanatory text brings the point home by implicitly contrasting the Falcon's straight lines and expansive windows with the curved and miniature design of its European competitors. "How pleasant it is to travel in the Ford Falcon! Its cozy and elegantly upholstered interior offers luxury comfort for six adults." After once again describing the car's ample trunk space and smooth ride, this ad emphasizes the large windows that "offer a new vision of the landscape!" and an opportunity to be seen by admiring viewers. "In the driver's seat," it assures potential buyers, "you will appreciate [the Falcon's] power, take advantage of its fuel economy, and advance confidently into the future."[90] Here, again, Falcon buyers were promised a visceral experience of modernity and progress.

Another early print advertisement was prepared specifically for Argentine readers, but it still stressed the Falcon's identity as an American car. It features side-by-side photos of identical Falcon sedans in different settings: one on the Avenida 9 de Julio in downtown Buenos Aires, the other on a street festooned with US flags. "Can you find any difference between these two FALCONS?" asks the title; "Of course not!" The small-print text vouches for the quality of the locally built Falcon by identifying it with the enduring prestige of the Ford brand, which was so familiar to Argentine readers. Its tone is reassuring, perhaps to allay doubts about whether Ford's fledgling Pacheco factory could meet the standards associated with the famous River Rouge complex back in the United States. "Both cars were manufactured using the same strict production norms. Their parts and components are of identical quality . . . [and] they were both designed and built by engineers, technicians, and specialists who share the same pride in their work."[91] A print ad from 1965 went further by announcing that Ford Motors had chosen to display an Argentine-built Falcon in its enormous pavilion at the New York World's Fair the previous year, where it was seen by millions of visitors. "The Falcon," it observed, "has thus served as an example of the high quality achieved by our country's automobile industry."[92]

Argentine advertisements also followed US precedents by associating the Falcon with Ford's Model T. By the late 1960s, ad copy regularly touted the Falcon as Ford's "Model T for the year 2000," recalling that car's long history in Argentina. Ads also illustrated the car's dependability by depicting it in iconic landscapes from the Argentine interior, like the dry and mountainous terrain of Córdoba. As noted earlier, Ford and other American brands like General Motors and Standard Oil had been employing this strategy for decades to associate their products with idealized images of the Argentine nation and to avoid stirring up anti-American anxieties. Print and television advertisements for the Falcon from 1963 show a team of Ford trucks and Falcons that had driven the full length of the country, from Ushuaia in the South to La Quiaca, at the border with Bolivia. Magazine photos show the car in an empty desertscape in La Rioja Province. The explanatory text underlines the ad's meaning and associates the Falcon with long-standing values of criollo automobility in Argentina: "By choosing the steepest and most rugged roads to cross the country, the Falcon showed off its robust frame, its practical road clearance, and the comfort it offers during long drives lasting many hours."[93] One advertisement shows a Falcon making its way on a treacherous mountain pass. "This is where you'll prove the value of your Ford," it reads. "You, your Ford, and a difficult road." It suggests that the ordinary Falcon owner would be able to repeat the heroic adventures of the early TC drivers, venturing out of the city to experience the freedoms associated with criollo driving culture.

Once the Falcon was established in the local market, advertisements began to identify it with local symbols of class privilege, refinement, and conservative values. A full-color magazine ad from 1963 offers up "the Sumptuous Interior of the New Ford Falcon . . . A Style of Living." It once again emphasizes the car's large windows, promising that they will offer passengers a new perspective on the world and a chance to take note of "the admiration" of onlookers.[94] An early television advertisement pitches the car to upper middle-class buyers by showing a Falcon driving from a home in the wealthy suburb of Vicente López to a private yacht club. A 1966 advertisement for the Falcon De Luxe includes an illustration of a father ushering two smartly dressed young children into the back seat of a Falcon as a priest looks on. The text assures potential buyers that this high-end Falcon offers "luxurious comfort for the whole family" and is recognized as a "prestige automobile."[95]

Playing again on this idea of the car as a symbol of social standing and technological modernity, another print ad from the same year encourages consumers to trade up to a Falcon. The upper left-hand corner of the page shows a line drawing of a typically rounded European compact car being pulled on a string like a toy. The heading reads: "At first, a small car is a good choice." To the right, a photo shows a Ford Falcon parked in front of the capital city's new Galileo Galilei Planetarium. The building, designed and lit to look like a spaceship, resembles the observatory that featured so prominently in the original American Falcon television promotion. It is situated in the Parque Tres de Febrero, the Buenos Aires equivalent of Central Park, in the fashionable neighborhood of Palermo. The ad's accompanying text urges car owners to trade in their small cars to upgrade to a Falcon: "A couple of years with a small car is good training," it reads, but "now, buy a FALCON . . . Because the FALCON isn't just a large car, it's a FORD."[96] These visual and textual details hammer home the car's associations with technological modernity and aspirations for social mobility.

Ford and JWT went so far as to invest in a long-running television series to showcase the Falcon to Argentine consumers, drawing on years of broadcasting experience in the United States. Ford Motors had sponsored *Wagon Train* and *The Lucy-Desi Comedy Hour*, and JWT had helped to create such iconic family sitcoms as *Father Knows Best* and *The Adventures of Ozzie and Harriet*: programs that became synonymous with dominant ideals of white, middle-class American family life in the 1950s. By the end of that decade, Ford executives considered television the ideal medium for promoting cars, and the marketing division carefully calculated investments based on ratings and exposure.[97] Although the company's international division was keen to develop programming in more markets around the world, licensing laws barred American firms from producing local content everywhere except Latin America, where television was still in its infancy.[98]

Ford and other US corporations heavily influenced Argentine television in the 1960s, when the medium first became a common feature in middle-class households.[99] In fact, television promotion was another modernizing goal shared by Presidents Perón and Frondizi. Juan Perón had launched Latin America's first rudimentary television broadcast in 1951, and Arturo Frondizi, in 1958, was the first Argentine president to broadcast his inauguration live. Between 1960 and 1973, Argentina's consumption of television sets expanded nearly tenfold, from 450,000 to roughly 4 million.[100] As media scholar Gonzalo Aguilar observes, the medium gradually colonized and transformed ideas about the home and family sphere. It also introduced Argentine families to new forms of advertising from corporate sponsors such as automaker Industrias Kaiser Argentina, General Electric, Palmolive, and Esso.[101]

Ford Argentina launched its own ambitious weekly program, *La familia Falcon* (The Falcon Family), in this context. The show began to air in 1962, although Argentine fans quickly hispanized the title to *La familia Falcón*, identifying the car's name with a common Spanish surname. Modeled on contemporary American successes like *The Dick Van Dyke Show*, which also aired in Argentina, *La familia Falcón* centered on the domestic life of a supposedly archetypal Argentine middle-class household: "a man, his wife, four children, and even a bachelor uncle," according to the theme song, which failed to mention the live-in maid who was the other regular character. High production costs for exterior filming meant that the program itself could not feature the Falcon sedan in motion. Instead, like other series of the period, the stories played out inside a stage set of the household. Opening and closing advertising sequences featured footage of the car itself, including shots of racing star Oscar Gálvez driving on the new test track at the Pacheco plant: the first of its kind in the continent.[102]

La familia Falcón presented a model of family harmony in which the benevolent and prudent parents (contrasted with the playboy uncle) transmitted simple life lessons to their children. It invited viewers to embrace the characters as "a family like any other, like yours, like anyone in your neighborhood who lives like other Buenos Aires families."[103] Written by

Hugo Moser, a conservative "with a tendency to make it very clear how he would like [the world] to be" in his scripts, the program hammered home the Falcon's associations with conservative middle-class values.[104] The father, who works in a management position, regularly harangues his dissolute brother about his libertine habits, urging him to follow his own example of hard work and family commitment. The mother, meanwhile, is depicted as the perfect housewife who puts up graciously with the foibles of her male family members and is adored by her obedient maid. The younger generation includes the eldest son, who is completing his mandatory military service, his wife, a (mildly) rebellious teenage son, and a young boy. Although some commentators objected that the stereotyped characters were "nothing like a typical Argentine family," the program was an undeniable hit.[105] It was reprised in a feature film of the same name in 1963 and remained on the air until 1969. Today it is considered an iconic example of the new commercial television revolution of the 1960s and the forerunner of a popular genre of family programming in Argentina, although later series would take on more complex and controversial social issues.[106]

Ford tried to shake off the "square" associations of *La familia Falcón* and update the Falcon's image in the early 1970s, as Argentina developed its own youth counterculture.[107] Since the country's tiny consumer market made it unfeasible to launch the Mustang locally, Ford relied on marketing to pitch the same Falcon sedan to different kinds of buyers. For example, one 1970 magazine ad showed a father and son facing off over the family Falcon, with the heading "The Falcon Closes the Generation Gap." The father, dressed in a dark suit, celebrates the car's durability and classic style, "superior to fickle changes of fashion." The son, with longer hair and a floral shirt, values it as a muscle car designed to attract girls. "Susi doesn't say anything, but I know she likes it when we leave all the other cars behind. What she doesn't like are all the looks I get from the other girls when they see me in my Falcon."[108] The most shocking ad in this vein—one that already makes a crass association between the car and violent machismo—shows a Falcon with a tagline in huge letters that dominates the page: "Punish me. Mistreat me. Starve me. Exploit me ... I'm all yours." One of the letters is replaced with what looks like a hand-drawn heart shape. Here, the car stands in for an abused wife or girlfriend, loyal to her man no matter what.[109]

CONCLUSION

By the time Ford Motors began manufacturing the Falcon sedan in Argentina, that country had developed an established car culture with some of its own unique inflection. Although influenced by American precedents, criollo driving culture also celebrated local mechanical ingenuity and endurance in the tough landscapes of the Argentine interior. National car enthusiasts took pride in their country's early embrace of the automobile and in their heroes' racing successes at home and abroad. They even projected confidence that Argentina might once again lead Latin America as a modern, motorized society comparable to the United States itself. After years of decline in automotive consumption during the 1930s and 1940s, these nationalist hopes were revived during Juan Perón's presidency as the government took steps to promote local car manufacturing and invested in motorsports both at home and abroad. Ford Motors and its advertiser, JWT, were well placed to wed the new Falcon sedan's identity to long-standing aspirations for modernization and economic development in Argentina. They had decades of experience in the country, and they had even helped to craft the values that underpinned the national model of automobility since the 1920s. By the late 1960s, Ford Argentina projected an image of itself as a "thriving and modern automotive company that is the pride of all Argentines."[110]

The original Falcon exemplified the values of the early Cold War at both ends of the Americas. It was a totem to a high modernist automobility founded on the unshakable belief that technocratic expertise wedded to modern technology could bring about rapid economic development and social progress. That ideal was shared by a generation of Ford executives, Argentine reformers, and American policy makers. For Ford Motors, the Falcon's record-breaking sales in 1961 and 1962 signaled that the corporation had successfully modernized and recovered from its near collapse at the end of World War II. For developmentalists like Arturo Frondizi, partnerships with multinationals like Ford Motors promised to transfer modern industrial technology to Argentina and restore the country's place as a "modern" motorized society. The Falcon itself would symbolize the ascendancy of the Argentine middle class, while automotive manufacturing would provide higher-paying jobs to win over the working class and mend the social rift opened by the Peronist years. Finally, for policy makers behind the Kennedy administration's Alliance for Progress, US business expansion in Latin

America would carry the benefits of American-style consumerism to counter the appeal of revolutionary communism after the 1959 Cuban Revolution.

However, the grand modernization projects of the early 1960s provoked unexpected and destabilizing effects in Argentina, as they did across Latin America.[111] President Frondizi's policies certainly bore fruit in economic terms by inaugurating a new era of automobility. Argentina became self-sufficient in oil production thanks to his controversial deals with American oil companies, and his government oversaw the creation of a national petrochemical industry. Local steel production expanded, and his government built some ten thousand kilometers of new roads. The new automotive sector stood as his major achievement, accounting for most of Argentina's economic growth in the 1960s.[112] Things went far less smoothly for Frondizi himself, however, as he struggled to manage the competing pressures of the early Cold War period. His single-minded focus on economic growth over democracy alienated workers and progressive sectors of the middle class, who denounced his top-down policy measures and close ties with American multinationals. Workers "[refused] to play the role of junior partners" in his development schemes, launching repeated strikes, especially in the older railway and meat-packing sectors.[113] Economic nationalists viewed him as a sell-out (*entreguista*) to foreign interests. The military also threatened Frondizi with multiple insurrections because they resented his outreach to the Peronists and inability to control the labor movement. Meanwhile, his efforts to maintain an independent foreign policy earned him the distrust of the US government, especially after he held a secret meeting with Argentine-born revolutionary Ernesto "Che" Guevara in August 1961. The Argentine armed forces ousted him in a coup on March 29, 1962, just a few weeks after the unveiling ceremony for that first locally assembled Falcon.

By then, the Kennedy administration was already prioritizing security over economic development in Latin America, and Defense Secretary Robert McNamara was reorganizing the US armed forces around the same principles of planning and efficiency he had brought to Ford Motors.[114] After Frondizi's overthrow, the US Army quickly invited an Argentine military delegation led by Brigadier General Carlos R. Moore to visit military bases and industrial facilities across the United States. During that visit, the Ford Motor Company treated the delegation to a tour of the River Rouge factory and a preview of the newest model Falcon.[115] As Kennedy's top military adviser, McNamara argued that it was politically and economically more cost effective for Latin

American security forces to police their own populations than for the United States to land boots on the ground to stamp out every uprising or communist threat. As he put it to the House Appropriations Committee in 1963, "Probably the greatest return on our military-assistance investment comes from the training of selected officers and key specialists at our military schools and training centers in the United States and overseas. These students . . . are the coming leaders, the men who will have the know-how and impart it to their forces. . . . It is beyond price for us to make friends of such men."[116] This strategy of empowering Latin American military leaders was to have devastating consequences for civilians in Argentina and throughout the continent in the years to come.

By 1964, Argentina's fledgling automotive sector had already added sixty thousand new industrial jobs to the country's economy and accounted for five of the country's ten largest corporations.[117] Growth continued through the 1960s. Yet, as will be explored more fully in chapters 2 and 3, the unintended consequence of this success was the revitalization of the country's labor movement. The young people who flooded into the new automotive, metalworking, and auto parts factories expanded union membership and pushed for greater union democracy. By decade's end, sectors of Argentina's expanded industrial working class were challenging the status quo on several fronts. Not only did they mobilize to demand improved working conditions from their employers but they also challenged the union bureaucrats who attempted to control and pacify their shop-floor mobilization. At key moments of protest, they joined forces across industrial sectors and seemed poised to threaten the entire social order.

Meanwhile, the middle class that Frondizi, Kennedy, and Henry Ford II had all proclaimed to be a force for stability in Argentina also fragmented politically in the 1960s. While some sectors embraced the authoritarian politics embodied in the 1966 coup led by General Juan Carlos Onganía, others built a New Left movement inspired by the Cuban Revolution that sought to radically reorder Argentine society.[118] Within a decade after the Falcon's Argentine launch, the optimism of the Frondizi years had evaporated, and new voices had emerged to denounce foreign multinationals like Ford as agents of imperialism.

CHAPTER TWO

From Aristocracy to Insurgency

Pedro Troiani was just seventeen years old in 1963 when he began working at Ford Argentina's manufacturing plant in General Pacheco: the modern factory celebrated by President Frondizi as the showcase for his developmentalist project. Like Frondizi, he was the son of Italian immigrants. He lived his entire life in the municipality of Beccar, a nineteenth-century railway town that had evolved into a middling suburb of the capital. A warm and funny family man with a slight, wiry build and restless energy, he was also known for his stubbornness and quick temper: qualities that served him well during his long years as a labor and human rights activist. Yet even after spending decades fighting to hold Ford Argentina accountable for substandard working conditions and human rights violations, Pedro Troiani could still evoke his youthful excitement at joining the Ford workforce back in 1963: "It was unbelievable, especially since my dad and I had always been huge Ford racing fans!" That emotion was echoed by Adolfo Sánchez, another Ford worker who entered the Pacheco plant in 1971. Sánchez described his own enthusiasm and wonder in similar terms: "I mean, to get hired at Ford! Ford was number one!" He threw himself into his factory job right away, taking overtime shifts and working weekends, accumulating savings for the first time in his life. "I worked twelve-hour days on the assembly line, and on Saturdays and Sundays I'd work like a maniac in the stamping plant," he told an interviewer many years later. "I was young, and I liked to work, and I liked the money."[1]

Some of the thrill shared by Troiani and Sánchez had to do with the prestige surrounding the Ford brand itself, which had dominated Argentine car culture since the 1920s. In the long-standing racing rivalry between Ford and General Motors, their families had cheered on the Ford team led by brothers Oscar and Juan Gálvez, who had been not only sports celebrities but public allies of Juan Perón and thus heroes of the Peronist working class.[2] Now, thousands of young people like Troiani and Sánchez sought the opportunity to work at Ford's new automotive plant and play a role in building the Falcon sedan. Arcelia Ortiz, whose husband and brother both worked at

Figure 2. Workers at the Ford Argentina factory, General Pacheco, Buenos Aires (1960s). Courtesy of Elisa Charlín.

Pacheco, recalled that "everyone tried to get hired at Ford. Young men would apply over and over again," attracted by the relatively high wages, the modern facilities, and the opportunity to be part of the beloved Ford brand.³ "You really felt privileged to get a job [at Ford]," Troiani observed. "There was lots of talk about the 'Ford family,' and they'd have a big Christmas party every year and raffle off a new Falcon."⁴

The Falcon's popularity in the 1960s and early 1970s also provided the men with steady work. Ford Argentina sold just over 5,000 Falcons in 1962, when they were still being manufactured in the United States and assembled locally. By 1966, annual sales of locally built Falcons had tripled to 15,709. They more than doubled again by 1973, when Ford produced 35,719 Falcons, including the basic and luxury models, Falcon taxis, and Rural station wagons. These numbers may have been modest by US standards, but they were high for Argentina, especially considering the Falcon was a relatively large and expensive car for local buyers. "The demand for the Falcon was incredible,"

Figure 3. Pedro Troiani at the Ford Argentina factory, General Pacheco, Buenos Aires (1960s). Courtesy of Elisa Charlín.

according to Troiani. "Taxi drivers fought to get one, and they would even line up at the factory gates. People were so desperate that some had to wait six or seven months to receive their car." With such high demand, Ford workers could earn extra money by taking on overtime shifts. Just four months after starting at Ford, Adolfo Sánchez was able to purchase his first car: a tiny Fiat 600. He also began buying construction materials to build his first home in the municipality of Tigre on a property shared with his in-laws.[5]

When Pedro Troiani married Elisa Charlín, a young woman from his neighborhood of Beccar, his wages and overtime benefits helped them pay for a honeymoon in Mar del Plata, the once-exclusive coastal resort that had become a beloved working-class holiday spot during Juan Perón's presidency. For Arcelia Ortiz, who had moved to Buenos Aires from rural Corrientes Province, her husband Ismael Portillo's job at Ford provided the security of a house with a garden and the possibility of leaving her own factory job to stay home with her children.[6] For Ford worker Carlos Alberto Propato, who

Figure 4. Pedro Troiani and Elisa Charlín on their honeymoon in Mar del Plata, Argentina. Courtesy of Elisa Charlín.

had grown up in poverty and precarious housing, it meant living in a solid structure with a door that locked.[7] Carlos Gareis, another Ford worker, saved up his earnings to buy a small plot of land near the Pacheco factory, hoping to move out of the crowded accommodations his young family shared with relatives far on the other side of Buenos Aires. His dream was to have more time with his children rather than spending hours commuting by public transit each day. These young families were proud of their association with Ford Argentina, believing that it would bring them lasting financial security to help them build their own version of the Fordist American dream: a living wage and a stable family home.

The honeymoon period at Ford Argentina turned out to be remarkably short-lived for all these men. By the early 1970s, most had become active in union organizing around issues of health, safety, and working conditions at the Ford plant. Troiani, Sánchez, and Propato were elected by their coworkers as delegates to the national autoworkers' union, Sindicato de Mecánicos y Afines del Transporte (SMATA), and as members of the factory's internal claims committee (*comisión interna de reclamos*), a shop-floor organizing body that mediated directly between workers and management.[8] They then found themselves under violent attack for their union activities after a military junta seized power on March 24, 1976, initiating Argentina's last and most brutal period of military rule. Within the first three weeks after the coup, at least twenty-four union activists at Ford were kidnapped, tortured, and held in secret detention for several weeks without contact with their families, before being transferred into regular prisons.[9] Several, including Troiani and Propato, were detained on the premises of the Pacheco factory itself. Inside the recreation facilities where they had formerly played soccer and enjoyed company picnics, they were beaten and accused of being "terrorists" and "subversives." "That was the worst moment," Troiani would testify decades later. "That was when we endured the worst torture. There we were made to feel like rats."[10]

How did the men's fortunes change so profoundly in such a short span of time? How did a group of autoworkers suddenly find themselves locked away without charges in crowded and filthy conditions, unable to contact their families? The next two chapters aim to make sense of the men's experience by situating it within deeper patterns of labor mobilization and political violence in Argentina leading up to the military coup of March 1976. In fact, although the men's story was terrifying and bewildering, it was by no means unique. In 1984, the *Nunca Más* report published by Argentina's National Commission on the Disappearance of Persons calculated that blue-collar workers accounted for 30.2 percent of the people disappeared by the military: kidnapped by unidentified assailants, held in clandestine detention centers, and usually murdered and disposed of in secret.[11] Over the years, Pedro and the other men from Ford who miraculously survived their detention learned about thousands of other shop-floor activists who had faced similar repression. The timing and ferocity of these attacks point to a concerted offensive against the grass roots of Argentina's historically powerful union movement, one orchestrated not only by the military but also by business interests and even some union bosses.[12]

Chapter Two

AUTOWORKER POLITICS

In the early 1960s, political and economic leaders at both ends of the Americas had promised that rapid economic development modeled on US industrial consumerism would bring a smooth transition toward prosperity and social harmony. They predicted that higher-paid workers in a modernized industrial economy would turn away from disruptive political movements and dedicate themselves to more private lives focused on family and consumption. Autoworkers were expected to be the key agents of this process, since the US model of efficient industrial production and relatively high wages had first been developed by Henry Ford in the mass production of the Model T. In fact, the Ford brand had been the face of American capitalism since the 1920s, when Italian Marxist philosopher Antonio Gramsci first coined the term "Fordism" to identify the unique capitalist regime being forged at the massive River Rouge auto plant Ford was building in Dearborn, Michigan.[13] By combining intensive production methods with comparatively high factory wages, Fordism sought to win workers over to a new regime of exploitation through the promise of consumerism.

Argentina was one of Latin America's principal testing grounds for such theories in the 1960s, attracting a huge influx of American investment that challenged the country's historical orientation toward Europe and profoundly restructured its industrial economy.[14] While they produced thousands of new jobs, these policies had unforeseen political effects. Workers pressured for more democratic participation and deeper social policy efforts to address the country's history of inequality and exploitation, and they fought against economic policies that undercut the gains they had achieved in the Peronist years. Meanwhile, Frondizi and his successors struggled to achieve lasting economic and political stability. Such conflicts were magnified by the broader Cold War context and by Argentina's powerful labor movement, energetic civil society, and recalcitrant armed forces. Through the 1960s and early 1970s, workers mobilized with ever greater force to defend labor gains and resist government attempts to impose austerity policies. Meanwhile, young people in universities and leftist organizations drew inspiration from the Cuban Revolution and the global surge of youth political activism to organize for revolutionary change. The armed forces also repeatedly intervened in politics, further eroding Argentina's weak democratic institutions, and right-wing paramilitary groups formed to target their leftist opponents. By the early

1970s, shop-floor union activists like Pedro Troiani and Adolfo Sánchez found themselves at the center of a perfect storm of political pressures and mounting violence.

Research on the broader history of autoworkers helps to explain how a factory like Ford Argentina's could become such a political pressure cooker by the 1970s. In a masterful survey of global labor activism across the twentieth century, historical sociologist Beverly Silver has demonstrated how the spread of automobile manufacturing provoked unexpected political effects in countries around the world.[15] Fordism's emphasis on unskilled and interchangeable workers organized around a moving assembly line posed an existential threat to skilled craft workers and their associations in countries like Great Britain and France, where they had a long history. However, it did not have the feared effect of destroying organized labor altogether. Rather, according to Silver, it paradoxically transformed autoworkers into a new kind of mass political force by concentrating them in large numbers and giving them unique strategic power within industrial economies. Fordism's intensely vertical integration—the interdependence of every part of the production process—made the system vulnerable to work stoppages that could shut down the whole assembly line and ripple out across an entire national economy.

As the first country to motorize on a mass scale, the United States saw the first big autoworker strikes in the 1930s, which eventually paved the way for stronger labor standards and higher wages in that country. Then, after World War II, countries like France, Italy, Brazil, Argentina, South Africa, and South Korea adopted American-style car manufacturing to modernize their own economies. Silver identifies strikingly similar patterns of labor unrest virtually everywhere that Fordism took hold. Whether in Dearborn, Michigan, in the 1930s, Paris in the 1960s, or São Paulo in the 1980s, autoworkers "burst on the scene with a suddenness and strength that was unexpected by contemporaries."[16] Even relatively small numbers of committed activists within a large automotive plant could paralyze production with strategic actions like slowdowns or sit-down strikes. Moreover, since the automotive sector had linkages to other sectors such as steel and oil production, transportation, and the service economy, autoworkers could, under the right circumstances, exercise strong political leverage to win concessions from employers.

In fact, Silver argues that this pattern of labor conflict was one of the factors motivating the automobile industry's global expansion. Faced with militant workers in one location, car manufacturers turned to mechanization and/or moved production altogether, preferably to countries with weak unions or authoritarian governments that promised labor peace. Yet as autoworkers in one country saw their gains undercut by these strategies, new working classes took shape wherever the carmakers established themselves, and similar patterns emerged.[17] The organizing confidence and experience developed by workers in the automotive sector could also translate to other forms of political activism. Some union activists became leaders of broader democratization movements that challenged authoritarian regimes in countries as far-flung as Spain, Brazil, South Africa, and South Korea; Brazil's president Luiz Inácio "Lula" da Silva is only the most famous such example. Silver thus argues that Fordism contributed in unforeseen and contradictory ways to the spread of democratic citizenship in the twentieth century.[18]

Silver does not discuss Argentina in detail, focusing instead on Brazil as her Latin American case study. However, labor mobilization in the Argentine automotive sector followed a similar pattern in the years preceding the last military coup of 1976. In the early 1960s, when Ford Motors and other multinational automakers were building their factories near the capital, policy makers and social scientists predicted that a new generation of autoworkers would emerge as an "aristocracy of labor" that would calm working-class political passions.[19] Instead, less than a decade later, the country's establishment was shocked to see autoworkers and other new industrial workers leading general strikes, plant takeovers, and mass marches. By the early 1970s, political activists and armed revolutionaries also came to view Argentina's industrial working class as a mass political force that could be steered toward revolution. Either way, people from across the political spectrum projected their own political expectations onto this new generation of industrial workers. As a result, grassroots labor activists like Pedro Troiani and Adolfo Sánchez found themselves caught up in an epic struggle of Cold War ideologies as they tried to organize for improved safety and working conditions at the Pacheco plant.

PACHECO AND THE ZONA NORTE

The executives who laid the cornerstone for the new "Ford Industrial Center" in January 1960 chose the location in General Pacheco for its strategic advantages.[20] The 250-acre property, situated roughly ten miles north of the perimeter of Buenos Aires, was oriented toward the industrial belt that stretched northwest through the steel towns of the Paraná River to the provincial cities of Rosario and Córdoba. The property also bordered on the new Pan-American Freeway (Autopista Panamericana) that was then under construction, connecting the capital city to its northern suburbs in the province of Buenos Aires. The pace of construction at Pacheco was "unprecedented" in Argentina.[21] Within sixteen months, Ford Argentina had built administrative offices, a motor manufacturing plant, quality-control laboratories, and a power station; it had also laid the first stretch of a vehicle testing ground that would be the largest in Latin America. At first, the Pacheco factory produced motors for the Ford trucks that were still being assembled at the old plant in La Boca and then for Falcon sedans that were also assembled with imported parts. Then, in January 1963, a few months after the military ousted President Frondizi, Henry Ford II finally returned to Argentina to see the Pacheco Industrial Center in full operation. The La Boca assembly plant closed later that year, and the first locally manufactured Falcon sedan rolled out of the Pacheco factory in August 1963.[22]

The Ford factory quickly became an anchor to the whole Zona Norte. Sparsely populated and semirural in the first half of the twentieth century, the suburbs around Buenos Aires were transformed by the industrialization policies introduced by Presidents Perón and Frondizi. In the mid-1960s, the outlying districts of the greater metropolitan area, known as Gran Buenos Aires, concentrated more than two-thirds of Argentina's industrial workforce in an area that accounted for less than 1 percent of the country's territory.[23] By 1974, roughly half a million people in Gran Buenos Aires worked for industries ranging from the large auto plants and shipyards to smaller workshops and parts suppliers.[24] This influx of industry and population introduced new contrasts to the Zona Norte. The districts along the riverfront closest to the capital city concentrated some of Argentina's most fashionable residential suburbs: Vicente López, San Isidro, and Olivos, which was home to the presidential residence. Wealthy *porteños* (residents of the capital) had built summer villas in these neighborhoods in the 1800s to escape the heat and disease of the growing city. With improved railway and then automotive access, they became year-round suburbs with their own commercial centers and private schools, as well as exclusive venues like yacht clubs and the San Isidro Racecourse (Hipódromo de San Isidro).[25]

Outlying areas of the Zona Norte, like the vast district of Tigre, home to the municipality of General Pacheco, took on a very different character as local officials openly courted American multinationals like Ford, Rockwell Standard, Union Carbide, Standard Electric, and Sylvania with offers of affordable land. A few European manufacturers also set up shop in the Zona Norte, and local companies opened smaller workshops and factories to supply parts to the bigger plants.[26] One of Argentina's oldest national manufacturers, food processor Terrabusi, inaugurated its Terrabusi Model Establishment right near the Ford plant in 1963.[27] Although they were keen to attract investment, local governments did not build sufficient infrastructure like water mains, gas lines, or public schools to support the Zona Norte's growing population, which gave the industrial districts a "pioneer" quality.[28] Most migrants to the area hailed from Argentina's interior provinces and neighboring countries like Bolivia, Chile, and Paraguay. The first arrivals were more likely to find better-paying factory work, and the lucky ones accumulated enough money to build their own small bungalows with materials purchased in small quantities. In fact, home building was such a high priority for working-class families that employees at Ford Argentina petitioned the company for permission to salvage lumber for their building projects from the huge shipping crates that carried imported parts and machinery to the Pacheco factory. As late as the mid-1970s, only about half of the plant's blue-collar workforce had achieved that dream of single-family home ownership.[29] Many lived in cramped rooming houses or shared accommodations with extended family to save money for a small plot of land.

Still, the Ford workers were privileged compared to most migrants to the Zona Norte, who found themselves in precarious and low-paying jobs in construction and domestic service, forced to live in growing shantytowns (*villas miserias*) that sprang up in the 1950s and 1960s.[30] In the villas, which took shape on the most marginal or abandoned lands, people built makeshift shelters with dirt floors out of whatever materials they could find: cardboard, metal sheeting, and the like. Basic diseases of poverty plagued families in these settlements, including respiratory complaints and waterborne illnesses associated with contaminated drinking water. The contrasts of the Zona Norte became impossible to ignore by the early 1970s, when just three miles separated the yacht clubs of San Isidro from La Cava, one of the largest villas in the entire province of Buenos Aires.[31]

The last major feature of the Zona Norte was the Campo de Mayo military base, one of the largest military installations in Latin America. It stretched across more than fifteen square miles along the district of Tigre's western

Buenos Aires and the *Zona Norte*

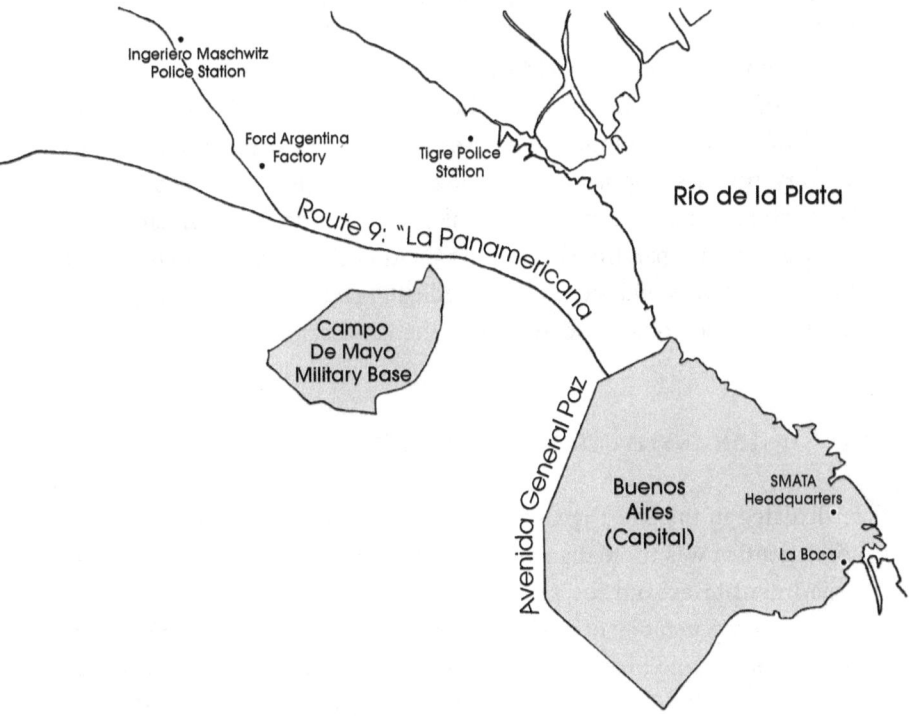

Figure 5. Map of the Zona Norte, showing the locations of the Ford factory, the Campo de Mayo military base, and the police stations in Tigre and Ingeniero Maschwitz. Prepared by the author.

flank. Founded in 1901 when the area was still dotted with cattle ranches and villages, by the 1960s Campo de Mayo was increasingly hemmed in by residential neighborhoods.[32] It operated as an army training site with facilities that included cavalry installations, an airfield, a military prison, and a hospital. The camp's barracks and facilities clustered along its western perimeter in the district of San Miguel, while the woods and fields that stretched into Tigre were used for training maneuvers. "Here soldiers practiced firing with artillery, mortars, and heavy machine-guns," reports one study of the base. "Observers could often witness warlike scenes as soldiers parachuted into the area used for paratrooper training."[33] After the coup of March 24, 1976, Campo de Mayo would become the coordinating hub for state terror operations throughout the Zona Norte, including the Ford factory.[34]

UNION INSTITUTIONS: 1940S TO 1970S

Articulated in the late 1950s, President Frondizi's developmentalist vision for Argentina was more than an economic policy; it was also a grand social experiment to expand the size of the country's industrial workforce and create a new generation of modern and productive factory workers.[35] In many ways, Frondizi and his closest advisers shared the same preoccupation with efficiency that Robert McNamara was bringing to the Ford Motor Company in these same years. Yet in attempting to restructure an entire economy as quickly as possible, the developmentalists needed more than just number crunching and rational planning; they needed to win the cooperation of the Argentine working class. Frondizi and his main policy adviser, Rogelio Frigerio, envisioned developmentalism as the integration of capital and labor in a common economic project to benefit the nation. In practice, however, they expected workers to accept a subordinate role in that project. "Workers ... must serve the interests of the whole country above their own immediate interests," declared Frigerio, "because if we succeed in liberating the Nation [from 'underdevelopment'], we will create the economic conditions to meet workers' rightful demands."[36]

Frondizi and Frigerio underestimated workers' organizing power, rooted in a long and vibrant history of labor activism that predated Perón's presidency. In the early twentieth century, anarchist, syndicalist, and socialist movements had all been active in Buenos Aires. Early labor organizers had experimented with forms of workplace democracy through the election of shop stewards, and in 1930 they founded the country's first national labor federation, the Confederación General de Trabajo (CGT). In these early years, however, workers faced intense repression from employers, right-wing vigilante groups, and the state.[37] When Juan Domingo Perón became head of the Ministry of Labor in the military government that took power in 1943, labor activists lobbied him for better protections; he, in turn, saw the potential to build a political base among Argentina's frustrated working class.[38]

Perón drafted a new law on professional associations (Law 23,852), which was adopted in 1945 by the military government headed by de facto president General Edelmiro Julián Farrell. It created a vertical system of labor institutions that addressed workers' demands while also tying the labor movement firmly to the state. The law established a system of centralized national-level unions representing all workers in a particular economic sector: all metalworkers, textile workers, bank employees, and so on. The federal government conferred legal recognition (*personería jurídica*) on a single national union for each sector, giving it sole authority to represent those workers across the country.[39] A voluminous literature has tracked how Argentina's CGT labor federation evolved into a virtual arm of the Peronist state between 1946 and 1955, with national-level union leaders boosting their own power through their alliance with Perón.[40] However, recent scholarship has also revealed the dynamics of shop-floor organizing at the base of those unions, where workers developed new confidence and organizing skills by participating in new structures of workplace representation.[41] The history of these shop-floor institutions provides context to better understand the challenges facing Frondizi's developmentalist project as well as the political pressures brought to bear against shop-floor labor organizers like Pedro Troiani and Adolfo Sánchez by the 1970s.

Perón's law on professional associations introduced language that recognized workers' rights to elect their own representatives, creating a legal space for more democratic practices of union representation at the grass roots. Soon, the government formalized these rights into a legally recognized system of representation whereby workers in any workplace with more than ten employees had the right to choose their own shop stewards or union delegates. In larger workplaces, a smaller group could form an internal claims committee, which mediated among workers, plant management, and the national union leadership. Members of this committee might be chosen

directly by the workers or appointed from among the elected shop stewards.⁴²
Perón expected these internal claims committees to accept a subordinate role,
relaying directives from above and maintaining union discipline at the grass
roots. Nonetheless, the institution of the *comisión interna*, which remained
in place from the mid-1940s until the mid-1970s, represented "one of the
most important achievements of the Argentine labor movement," according
to labor historian Victoria Basualdo.⁴³ It set the country apart from the rest of
Latin America, where workers never won such enduring legal protections for
grassroots representation. Shop stewards helped to defend new labor gains
by monitoring workplace conditions and reporting back to their union leadership.⁴⁴ Most significantly, the law protected them from wrongful dismissal
or retaliation by their employers.

The legal recognition of the comisión interna meant that management
was forced to negotiate directly with workers over the organization of
production, a concession deeply resented by business interests throughout
this period.⁴⁵ Employers began denouncing the comisiones internas while
Perón was still in government, complaining that they fostered "arrogance"
among workers and stymied management efforts to increase productivity.
Entrepreneur José Ber Gelbard founded the General Economic Confederation
(Confederación General Económica, or CGE) in 1954 to represent small and
medium-size businesses as a counterweight to the Peronist labor institutions.
He argued that the internal claims committees had boosted workers' sense
of autonomy to the point that they had forgotten that their "mission [was] to
complete an honest day's work for an honest day's pay." The CGE protested in
1954 that shop stewards "had arbitrarily assumed the right to accept or reject
management proposals to modify production methods, speed up machinery,
or eliminate unnecessary tasks."⁴⁶

Perón tried to appease business and reassert his control over labor by
inviting Gelbard into his cabinet and organizing a "Congress on Productivity"
in 1955, but he was overthrown that same year. The new government cracked
down on Perón's supporters and dismantled labor protections introduced in
1945, provoking underground resistance from loyal Peronists.⁴⁷ The Argentine
security services also developed new surveillance mechanisms to monitor
grassroots labor activists in the factories. In January 1956, just four months
after Perón's overthrow, the Buenos Aires provincial police inaugurated its first
intelligence service, the Dirección de Inteligencia de la Policía de la Provincia
de Buenos Aires (DIPPBA), which would continue to operate for more than

four decades. One of its first and most consistent mandates was to report on political and labor activism inside the province's industrial workplaces.[48]

Political instability defined the years of Perón's forced exile, from 1955 to 1973, as successive military and civilian governments struggled to undo his legacy. The armed forces took a particularly heavy hand by banning Perón's Justicialista Party from participating in elections and unseating any civilian government that tried to reverse this prohibition. Three civilian presidents and eleven different generals occupied the presidential office in the span of just eighteen years, the latter either as individuals or as members of a governing junta. Despite their many political and strategic differences, these leaders shared the goal of demobilizing and disciplining Argentine workers. Some, like President Frondizi, tried to do so by winning them over with promises of economic security and prosperity. Others, like General Juan Carlos Onganía, who seized power in the self-proclaimed Argentine Revolution of 1966, tried to force workers into submission while he accelerated Frondizi's developmentalist economic agenda.[49] Meanwhile, union bosses at the head of the CGT labor federation positioned themselves as political power brokers in Perón's absence. They negotiated with both civilian and military governments, promoting their own interests by alternately promising to keep Argentina's labor force passive and threatening to cripple the economy with general strikes. However, their own opportunism put them increasingly out of touch with their union members, who used the shop steward system and the internal claims committees to address their own priorities, and pressure from below for greater union democracy.[50]

Even the armed forces were divided over how to respond to the challenge of Peronism; their fears only deepened after the Cuban Revolution of 1959 and Cuba's subsequent alliance with the Soviet Union. Like other militaries in the continent, they allied ever more closely with the United States and the Cold War National Security Doctrine, which tasked them with policing their own populations to root out communism while the United States protected the Americas from external nuclear threats.[51] Yet Peronism did not fit neatly into Cold War binaries. Perón had appeared progressive in the late 1940s, when he drew on Argentina's buoyant postwar economy to underwrite new welfare policies, but his priorities were ultimately conservative, and he had used intimidation and repression to push aside socialist and communist activists in the union movement.[52] The most powerful Peronist union bosses of the 1960s, such as Augusto

Chapter Two

Vandor, head of the metalworkers' union, were also committed anticommunists. The Argentine military splintered into rival "Blue" and "Red" factions in the 1960s as they struggled to deal with these contradictions. While the Blues deplored Peronism's demagogy and excesses, they found merit in its nationalist values and perceived it as a bulwark against the far greater threat of communism. They were prepared to enlist the aid of Peronist union bosses to steer Argentine workers toward moderation and class compromise. The Reds, on the other hand, viewed Peronism as a destabilizing force just as dangerous as communism itself.

THE AUTO SECTOR TAKES SHAPE

This was the tumultuous political backdrop for the expansion of Argentina's automotive sector. By 1966, not only Ford Motors but Mercedes-Benz, Chrysler, Citroën, Peugeot, Fiat, and General Motors had all built factories near the capital in the province of Buenos Aires, and pent-up demand for vehicles brought booming sales. Already by 1966, one in nineteen Argentine jobs depended directly or indirectly on the automotive sector.[53] By then, most of the fledgling local carmakers like SIAM di Tella had either failed or been bought up, while five of the multinationals, including Ford Argentina, ranked among the country's ten largest corporations.[54] In that same year, the foreign automakers organized themselves into the Association of Automotive Factories (Asociación de Fabricantes de Automotores, or ADEFA). The organization's first annual report touted the local car manufacturing boom with a cover photo of streaming headlights on a busy highway and the title "1,000,000 Argentine Automobiles." Inside, the report began with the epigraph "The automobile is the decisive factor through which the individual is incorporated into the socioeconomic community of the modern world."[55] It was a declaration that Argentina was well on its way to fulfilling its dreams of automobility.

The new auto plants did indeed introduce modern innovations to the local economy as President Frondizi had hoped, including more complex machinery, new standards for training and quality control, and modern employee management techniques.[56] Workers who applied at the Pacheco plant had to undergo a physical examination as well as a battery of skills tests and interviews, whereas prospective hires at the older Kaiser factory in Córdoba did nothing but a simple aptitude test.[57] "Anyone who managed to get hired at Ford had to be in great shape," later recalled Arcelia Ortiz, wife of Ford worker Ismael Portillo, "because they tested everything!"[58] Roberto Cantello, another survivor of disappearance from Ford, was hired as a welder in 1970 after passing several soldering tests and two separate interviews, including one where he was asked his opinion about communism.[59] Ford managers took these measures because they were looking for workers who could, and would, adapt themselves to the intense pace of Fordist production methods. At Pacheco, their every movement was monitored as they performed tightly defined and repetitive tasks as efficiently as possible. They worked under the oversight of timekeepers and supervisors whose responsibility was to keep them focused and ensure that Ford met its daily production quotas. Workers were not allowed to talk to each other on the assembly line. They had to fill out a form for each bathroom break, recording the precise length of their absence, and carry an internal passport to keep them from wandering beyond their immediate work sector.[60]

By the time Cantello joined the workforce at Ford Argentina, the multinational had assembled a vertically integrated set of companies to support the operations of the Pacheco plant. These included parts manufacturer Transax SA in Córdoba, steel producer Metcon (Metalúrgica Constitución SA) in the province of Santa Fe, and small appliance maker Philco Argentina SA. Ford had also built up its financial assets with investments in the Boston Finance Corporation (Corporación Financiera Boston SA) and two new firms of its own: Finve SA and the Ford Financial Company (Compañía Financiera Ford SA).[61] Big changes had occurred on the Pacheco property as well. Ford Argentina had opened the Henry Ford Technical School, where students could get specialized training on the machinery before going on to practicums inside the factory and at Transax and Metcon.[62] The company had also hired an industrial psychologist and invested in facilities to build company loyalty among its workers. These included a large recreation center on the factory grounds complete with soccer fields, ping-pong tables, a running track, and basketball courts. They also built a pair of large, open-air dining areas (*quinchos*), where groups of over a hundred employees could share in that classic ritual of masculine sociability: the traditional Argentine barbecue, or asado. "Any occasion provides an excuse to throw a barbecue," declared an in-house publication in 1968, "whether it's a game between veterans of the plant . . .

or a sporting challenge between factory and office workers: it always ends up in the *quincho*."⁶³ Those quinchos later became key organizing spaces for labor activists at the factory. Then, after the coup of March 24, 1976, soldiers occupied the recreation grounds as a military encampment and transformed one of the quinchos into the makeshift detention center where Pedro Troiani and other workers were imprisoned and tortured.

LABOR AND THE LEFT

The year 1966, which saw the multinationals consolidate their control over the local automotive sector, also marked a turning point for labor organizing in the auto plants, although the impacts would not become apparent at Ford Argentina for a few more years. Autoworkers had remained largely aloof from broader labor conflicts in the first half of the decade, as they benefited from new jobs and relatively high wages in a dynamic new industry. Political leaders had intentionally kept them distanced from the strong Peronist unions. In 1955, after Perón's overthrow, General Pedro Eugenio Aramburu had assigned autoworkers at the Kaiser plant to the small and weak national union known as SMATA, which represented garage mechanics. He did so to keep them out of the powerful metalworkers' union, the Unión de Obreros Metalúrgicos (UOM), which was a pillar of the Peronist movement. President Frondizi continued this practice by giving SMATA sole legal authority to represent autoworkers across the country, thus protecting the new multinationals from having to negotiate with the UOM. He also allowed for factory-level negotiations in the auto plants, as opposed to the national-level collective agreements that had been the norm in other economic sectors since the 1940s. For a while at least, these measures had the desired effect of keeping the auto plants quiet. At Ford Argentina's Pacheco factory, hardly anyone even bothered to affiliate with SMATA until the late 1960s.⁶⁴

Frondizi's developmentalist agenda, which remained the guiding economic policy of subsequent governments up until the coup of 1976, introduced wrenching dislocations to other sectors of the economy. He brought "an almost personal obsession" to the goal of removing what he considered to be irrational obstacles to capitalist growth introduced during the Peronist years.⁶⁵ He moved aggressively to eliminate price and wage controls, cut back on government spending, and attract foreign investment.⁶⁶ Workers in older economic sectors like the railways and meat-packing plants fought hard to resist these policies, which drastically undercut their standard of living. They staged lockdowns and plant takeovers, and Frondizi responded by suspending civil liberties and mobilizing the armed forces to put down labor unrest in a secretive plan that some scholars have identified as a precursor to the repression of the latter 1970s.⁶⁷

Meanwhile, the new industrial sector faced daunting challenges to growth that would make it hard to deliver on the grand promises of the early 1960s. Desarrollismo was a policy of import substitution aimed at meeting the needs of Argentina's internal market, which was painfully small by international standards. The country's population stood at just over twenty-two million in 1966, and only the middle and upper classes could afford to purchase a new vehicle. Argentina had come to automotive manufacturing and its associated heavy industries so late in the century that it had little hope of breaking into international markets. Ford Argentina sold small numbers of vehicles to Chile and was pressured briefly by the Argentine state to export Falcons to Cuba in the early 1970s, but the numbers were negligible by global standards. By then, Brazil, with a much larger economy than Argentina's, had made its own transition to vehicle exports and was supplying cars to several South American countries.⁶⁸ This meant that after the first surge of local demand for vehicles was met, Ford and the other new automakers would be competing for a share of a very small Argentine pie.

Politics in the auto plants heated up after General Onganía seized power in late June 1966, declaring himself the leader of a new "Argentine Revolution." Onganía had more ambitious goals than other recent coup leaders in Argentina, who usually intervened in politics temporarily with the intention of returning power to civilian politicians. He admired the military government that had taken control of Brazil two years earlier and aimed to repeat their far-reaching program of social and economic restructuring. However, Onganía, like Frondizi before him, underestimated the historical memory and organizing capacity of the Argentine working class, who were deeply disillusioned by the losses they had suffered since Perón's overthrow. He thought the Argentine economy needed a period of shock to jump-start productivity and achieve the kind of sustained growth that the desarrollistas had originally promised, and his policies gave even more concessions to foreign investors and multinational corporations. Onganía reasoned that only an authoritarian government could overcome the labor resistance and social protest that such a shock would provoke, but the longer-term benefits of economic growth would make the short-term pain worthwhile. He froze wages and suspended the right to strike, while his finance minister, Adalbert Krieger Vasena, devalued the Argentine peso by 40 percent. These austerity policies hit the public-sector unions hardest, but they also had significant impacts in the automotive sector, especially the older factories of Córdoba. Onganía also clamped down on the universities, which he saw as breeding grounds for communist ideology and youth immorality. He cut funding for higher education and purged leftist faculty and students from campuses.

Onganía's "Argentine Revolution" alienated broad swaths of Argentine society and galvanized opposition among grassroots labor organizers, students, and leftist militants. At key moments these groups came together to denounce the dictatorship, particularly in interior cities like Córdoba, Rosario, and Tucumán that had been hit hard by austerity policies and benefited far less from new industrial investment than Gran Buenos Aires. Córdoba in particular, home to Argentina's older vehicle and parts manufacturers as well as the country's oldest university, came to be known as a hotbed of leftist revolt. There, a new generation of labor activists pressed local demands in defiance of employers, the military regime, and the big union bosses headquartered in Buenos Aires. The most famous among them, like Agustín Tosco and Raimundo Ongaro, became known as *clasistas* who articulated labor demands in Marxist terms, while even many loyal Peronists fought for local autonomy from the centralized CGT. The clasistas also attracted a following among student activists at the National University of Córdoba.[69]

By the late 1960s, a diverse and fractious New Left movement had taken shape in Argentina, as in many other countries around the world. Marxist economists debated the new critiques of capitalist development that were coming out of the Chilean headquarters of the United Nations Economic Commission for Latin America and the Caribbean (Comisión Económica para América Latina y el Caribe, or CEPAL). In 1966, Brazilian sociologist Fernando Henrique Cardoso and Chilean economist Enzo Faletto had synthesized these ideas in their hugely influential book *Dependency and Development in Latin America*. The emerging "dependency school" thinkers challenged the assumptions of universal progress and growth that underpinned desarrollismo.

They argued that historical and structural inequalities in the world economy kept the poorer "peripheral" countries of Latin America in a situation of dependency on the wealthier, more industrialized countries of the "center," like the United States. In this reading, the desarrollistas' partnerships with multinational corporations like Ford Motors might have succeeded in bringing new technologies and industrial methods to a country like Argentina, but the host country continued to depend on machinery, technology, and other inputs from the wealthier economy, which siphoned off most of the gains. Critical voices began to denounce the companies as agents of a new kind of imperialism, arguing that this "dependent development" would never overturn the deep inequalities that plagued Argentine society.[70]

As they debated more effective strategies to bring about change, leftist intellectuals and youth activists drew inspiration from the Cuban Revolution, Russian and Chinese communism, Trotskyism, and anticolonial struggles in Africa and Asia. Some were also politicized by the upsurge in youth activism in Europe and by progressive movements taking hold in the Catholic Church, including liberation theology and the Third World Priests' movement.[71] Young people debated the merits of armed struggle versus nonviolent political organizing, considered whether it was possible to re-create Che Guevara's *foco* method of rural insurgency in an urbanized country like Argentina, and looked to political movements in neighboring countries like Chile and Uruguay. In the former, socialist and communist parties were working through the mainstream political system, which was impossible in Onganía's Argentina. In Uruguay, however, students and professionals had founded the charismatic Tupamaro urban guerrilla movement in the early 1960s, launching Robin Hood–style bank robberies and kidnappings and then distributing stolen food and money to the poor.[72]

The guerrilla option held appeal for many young people on the Argentine Left who had lost all faith in the country's democratic institutions, which had suffered repeated military interventions and consistently barred Perón's Justicialista Party from running candidates. Some youth from the middle and upper classes pushed back against the staunch anti-Peronism of their parents' generation and found germs of progressive thought in Perón's language of "social justice." However, they rejected those who claimed to represent Perón's legacy within Argentina: Peronist labor bosses like Augusto Vandor, who controlled the CGT labor federation. Many young people also shared in the assumption that the relatively privileged new industrial workers in the automotive factories and metalworking plants constituted an "aristocracy of labor" that was, by definition, self-interested and politically apathetic. Instead of working within the Peronist union system, the new generation organized a left-wing Peronist movement that sought to bring Perón back from exile to lead the working class toward socialism. The armed wing of this movement would become known as the Montoneros, an urban guerrilla force that would borrow tactics from the Tupamaros and the Algerian independence forces fighting against French occupation. Perón, ever the opportunist, encouraged these young activists from exile, counting on them to help secure his return to power, while he secretly allied himself ever more closely with the right wing of Peronism.[73]

Those on Argentina's more traditional Marxist Left rejected the Peronist Left's position as naïve, but many became equally convinced that armed struggle was the only way to bring about fundamental change. They were part of a generation of Latin American youth inspired by figures like Argentine-born revolutionary Che Guevara, whose mystique only grew after Bolivian and American forces hunted him down and killed him in the mountains of Bolivia in 1967. For many living through this era of accelerating political change, Che's model of heroic self-sacrifice held more appeal than the slower, traditional work of nonviolent political organizing. For example, when Trotskyist militant Nahuel Moreno proposed in 1968 that his organization, the Revolutionary Workers' Party (Partido Revolucionario de los Trabajadores, or PRT), dedicate their energies to organizing workers in the automotive factories of Gran Buenos Aires and Córdoba, the party split. Most members opted instead to retreat to the province of Tucumán and take up arms in a rural guerrilla movement that eventually came to be known as the People's Revolutionary Army (Partido Revolucionario de los Trabajadores–Ejército Revolucionario del Pueblo, or PRT-ERP). By the early 1970s, the ERP would become one of the largest rural insurgencies in Latin America. Moreno's small cadre of student activists settled instead in the Zona Norte of the province of Buenos Aires, where they sought work in the larger automotive and parts factories. Their goal was to get to know the workers and steer them toward socialism by winning leadership positions as shop stewards and members of the comisiones internas.[74]

INSURRECTION

Within a year of that split, a huge urban insurrection in Córdoba shocked Argentine society and caused many on the left to rethink their views about workers in Argentina's newer industrial sectors, including the automotive factories. Although the events that came to be known as the Cordobazo took place over four hundred miles from Ford Argentina's factory in General Pacheco, they marked a watershed in Argentine politics that had profound implications for subsequent labor and political organizing in the Zona Norte.[75] On May 28, 1969, labor leaders representing Córdoba's automotive, transportation, and utility workers called a general strike for the following day. They were protesting recent decrees imposed by the Onganía regime that simultaneously increased their weekly work hours and cut back their salaries. The older automotive and parts plants in Córdoba were struggling to compete with the newer factories located in Gran Buenos Aires, and workers were already on edge because of repeated layoffs and some bankruptcies. Local grievances stemmed not only from deteriorating working conditions but also from the oppressive political climate. In fact, the planned strike and accompanying march came after several weeks of mobilizations against the Onganía regime, which had brought together students and labor activists of diverse union and political affiliations. The plan was for strikers and students to march peacefully together into downtown Córdoba in two separate columns, one led by autoworkers from the IKA-Renault plant south of the city and the other by workers in the Light and Power union. They were to converge in the city center for a rally in front of the local headquarters of the CGT labor federation.

Events began as planned on the morning of May 29, although the march quickly took on a momentum beyond anything the organizers had foreseen. Workers at IKA-Renault filed out of the factory, many of them carrying metal bars and tools in anticipation of the repression they would encounter from security forces. As they passed through industrial and residential neighborhoods on their way into the city, thousands of students, residents, and workers joined them, including many members of unions that were normally passive. When word spread about a huge blockade of mounted police and attack dogs arrayed to stop the marchers from reaching the CGT headquarters, city residents "rushed out to give the protesters brooms, bottles, anything they thought could be used as a defence."[76] Events spiraled from there. Police on the blockade panicked and opened fire when they saw the size of the marching crowd, killing one worker and injuring many others. The terrified police then fled the scene altogether and organizers lost control of the march, which turned into a mass popular insurrection. Although labor leaders like Agustín Tosco who were popular with both workers and students tried to restore some discipline to the protest, they could not keep up with events on the ground. Rebellion spread spontaneously across the city until protesters had seized control of some 150 blocks, erecting barricades and setting bonfires. By evening, many workers had retreated to their homes, but as many as fifty thousand students and residents remained in the streets. Soldiers and police began to retake the city by the evening of May 29, and by the next morning, Córdoba was "an occupied city."[77] Waves of arrests brought an end to the insurrection by the evening of May 30.

Looting and violence were relatively rare during the Cordobazo, although protesters did choose a few key political symbols to attack. Tellingly, these were mainly offices and storefronts of foreign corporations like Xerox and Citroën: brands that had come to be associated with the new imperialism of multinational capital.[78] Although protesters in earlier decades had targeted symbols of elite privilege like private clubs, such anticorporate attacks would become more common after the Cordobazo and would soon touch Ford Argentina directly. In fact, according to historian James P. Brennan, the insurrection itself was significant mainly in symbolic terms because of how it was interpreted by political observers at the time. Brennan argues that the uprising was more than a workers' revolt. It mobilized workers from across the political spectrum of union activism, but also thousands of students and ordinary residents who joined in spontaneously. Witnesses described a climate of euphoria and many surprising instances of cross-class solidarity, with middle-class families sheltering students from security forces and poor construction laborers and domestic servants coming to the aid of unionized workers.[79]

The Cordobazo was immediately transformed into myth in the heady political atmosphere of the late 1960s, coming on the heels of the famous May 1968 uprisings in France, where Renault autoworkers had also protested alongside university students. That myth would, in turn, inspire a surge of political and labor activism across the country that would end only with the coup of March 1976. In fact, the Cordobazo was only the most spectacular in a series of urban uprisings that shook cities in Argentina's interior provinces between 1969 and 1972. These revolts, which took place at a distance from the centralized power of the capital, included other examples of solidarity between radicalized students and workers. For example, university students in the city of Rosario protested against Onganía with support from the local CGT union offices roughly two weeks before the march in Córdoba; in Tucumán, students came out to show solidarity with sugar workers fighting to defend their jobs as numerous sugar refineries closed their operations.[80]

In Córdoba itself, the insurrection of May 1969 ignited months of intense labor mobilization at the city's two Fiat factories, where workers fought back against their own complacent union bosses and launched experiments in shop-floor union democracy. At the height of these conflicts, in March 1971, Fiat workers launched takeovers of their respective plants, inspiring workers at IKA-Renault to do the same. The latter even took hostages, including many French supervisors sent to Argentina by Renault.[81] The sudden politicization at Fiat was especially shocking to observers, since the Italian automaker had always exercised tight control over its workforce and Fiat workers had not even participated in the Cordobazo protests.[82] All these conflicts put an end to General Onganía's leadership; factions within the armed forces demanded that he resign, and a junta overthrew him in June 1970 when he refused.

Observers on the right and the left immediately projected their own hopes and fears onto these events as they struggled to comprehend them. General Onganía's own minister of finance, Krieger Vasena, was dumbfounded by the Cordobazo: How could it be that some of the highest-paid workers in the country had revolted against his economic policies?[83] Meanwhile, as Brennan demonstrates, the different underground parties and militant organizations on the left interpreted the insurrection according to their own political ideologies. Maoists read it as a vindication of their strategy of achieving socialism through a revolutionary general strike and popular insurrection; Trotskyists and Guevaristas argued that it confirmed their focus on armed struggle to confront state repression; and those on the left wing of Peronism concluded that it proved the revolutionary potential of the Peronist working class.[84] The Cordobazo also galvanized leftist intellectuals in Argentina and abroad, who sought to fit the insurrection into their evolving theories of social and political change. The young Ernesto Laclau, who went on to become one of the most important political philosophers of his generation, had just moved from Argentina to Britain to study under the great Marxist historian Eric Hobsbawm. Laclau published an essay in the *New Left Review* that declared the May crisis in Córdoba to be "the first act in the emergence of a pole of mass attraction to unite future struggles in Argentina." He continued in a tone that was typical of the era: "An alliance between the working class and the petty bourgeoisie, with all its explosive potential, was established on the barricades of Córdoba, Tucumán and Rosario," he announced. "It is now an irreversible historical fact."[85]

EARLY UNIONIZATION AT FORD

Autoworkers at Ford Argentina, who counted among the highest-paid workers in the country, were relative latecomers to organizing as the labor aristocracy theorists had predicted, and even those who spearheaded unionization efforts in the late 1960s looked to mainstream union institutions rather than leftist parties. As noted earlier, President Frondizi had provided a concession to the multinational carmakers by giving workers in the automotive sector the right to form plant-level unions rather than be forced to affiliate with a national union like SMATA. This policy was meant to keep autoworkers fragmented, and it helped Ford management to successfully block the first efforts to create a company-based union at Pacheco in the 1960s. Organizers like Pedro Troiani then decided to back a new group vying for the SMATA leadership in the national union elections of 1968. The so-called Green List candidates were by no means leftists; in fact, they weren't even assembly-line workers. Dirck Kloosterman, who was running for the position of SMATA secretary-general, was a timekeeper at Peugeot, one of the employees paid to track the pace of the assembly line. His running mate, José Rodríguez, who was vying for SMATA leadership in the province of Buenos Aires, worked in accounting at German tractor maker Deutz.[86] Nonetheless, fledgling organizers at Ford, who needed support beyond Pacheco, decided to give them a chance. "We decided, OK, let's see what's going on with these people," Troiani later recalled.[87]

The Green List won a landslide victory, and workers at Pacheco started a union membership drive. By 1973, nearly three-quarters of the factory's five-thousand-strong workforce had affiliated with SMATA's Green List and elected roughly one hundred shop stewards to address their concerns. Troiani and other early organizers at Ford saw Kloosterman as an honest leader who was winning significant material gains for union members, including wage parity across the country and expanded social and recreational benefits. "We could see how the union was progressing," he later recalled, noting that SMATA union headquarters had "started out as a dump" compared with the head offices of stronger and wealthier unions like the UOM. Under Kloosterman's leadership, SMATA members gained access to a new medical and dental clinic, a campground, and two hotels in different parts of the province of Buenos Aires. The union also bought a large building for its headquarters in downtown Buenos Aires, near the main offices of the CGT labor federation, signaling that SMATA was asserting its place alongside the great Peronist unions.[88]

CONCLUSION

By the time autoworkers at Ford's Pacheco factory got serious about unionization at the end of the 1960s, Argentina's political landscape was becoming more complex and dangerous than ever. The Cordobazo and other revolts between 1969 and 1972 swept away the confident claims of the desarrollistas, who had promised that modernization would deliver social peace and stability to Argentina. Workers, no matter their political or union affiliation, had instead demonstrated their capacity to organize and defend their interests, and some young people from the middle classes had at least temporarily made common cause with them. Most surprisingly, even relatively privileged workers like those at the Renault and Fiat plants in Córdoba had suddenly "exploded onto the [political] scene," to recall the words of labor sociologist Beverly Silver, who mapped out similar patterns of mobilization in automotive plants around the world. Argentina's armed forces split over how to respond to these protests, and the diverse leftist parties and armed movements that had been working clandestinely under the repressive Onganía regime came out into the open.[89]

These events challenged the sunny, optimistic rhetoric that had ushered in Argentina's Cold War automobility project. They also shaped the context for labor organizing at Ford Argentina in the early 1970s, when workers like Pedro Troiani and Adolfo Sánchez put their names forward in shop-floor elections as delegates to the national SMATA union. The men also won election to the factory's internal claims committee, that uniquely Argentine labor institution that had the potential to foster labor democracy but that had also attracted resentment from managers and employers since midcentury. As we will see in the coming chapter, those early activists at Ford quickly built their confidence and organizing skills, winning significant concessions from their employer. They pressured for health and safety measures, expanded union membership beyond the factory floor, and even demanded a say in the pace of the assembly line, all while continuing to identify themselves as mainstream Peronists. However, they faced extraordinary risks as politics in Argentina became ever more polarized and violent, and as the country's conservative military and civilian institutions mounted a backlash to stamp out grassroots dissent for once and for all.

CHAPTER THREE

"It Was Like a War"

When the first generation of shop-floor activists at Ford Argentina began organizing for improved safety and working conditions in the early 1970s, they became participants in a massive surge of labor mobilization that gripped Argentina's entire industrial sector in the years spanning from the Cordobazo insurrection of 1969 to the coup of March 1976.[1] Men like Pedro Troiani, Adolfo Sánchez, and the other members of the factory's internal claims committee sought to address concrete workplace issues at the Pacheco plant.[2] However, their work became highly politicized in the aftermath of the Cordobazo, which some observers had interpreted as the harbinger of a coming revolution that would unite industrial workers and student activists. Whether they welcomed or dreaded such an outcome, people from diverse backgrounds—leftist militants, union bosses, business leaders, politicians, right-wing paramilitaries, and government security forces—all sought to control the political dynamics inside Argentina's large factories. Pressures mounted in the industrial suburbs of Gran Buenos Aires, where the bulk of Argentina's newer industries were concentrated.

The violence unleashed by the coup of 1976 later demonstrated just how important the factories were to those who sought to end Argentina's long history of working-class dissent once and for all.[3] As the flagship industrial facility for the entire Zona Norte and the local embodiment of one of America's most iconic brands, the Ford factory could not help but be drawn into these political struggles. The new SMATA delegates quickly found themselves navigating immense risks as Argentina's political climate became ever more polarized and violent in the early 1970s, one of the most complex periods in Argentine history.[4] The purpose of this chapter is to describe the Ford union organizers' strategies and victories while also capturing that atmosphere of urgency and danger, which culminated in the military occupation of the Pacheco factory and the mass disappearance of the plant's leading labor activists in 1976.

In an essay on the violence of the Cold War era in Latin America, historian Greg Grandin has described this sense of accelerating change and violence as the experience of "living in revolutionary time." In these years, he observes, "terror expanded into an almost inconceivable scale, confirming for 'ordinary' Latin Americans that the terms of history had changed." Adapting historian Arno Mayer's insights regarding the violence of the French and Russian Revolutions, Grandin goes on: "The speeding up of felt time corresponded to, and was driven by, an acceleration of the state's capacity to repress. For untold numbers of Latin Americans, living through revolutionary times meant living part of a life in which political violence and terror were the stuff of everyday existence."[5] Grandin's examples include the devastating massacres suffered by villagers in Central America and the shock experienced by Cuban peasants who awoke to find Soviet missiles in their fields in 1962.[6] At the other end of the continent, the labor activists at Ford Argentina experienced that same fear and bewilderment in the 1970s, as political militants and undercover security agents infiltrated the Pacheco factory and as military personnel began patrolling the facilities well before the coup of March 1976.

This chapter begins with early organizing efforts at Pacheco and the issues that first motivated men like Pedro Troiani and Adolfo Sánchez to put their names forward as shop stewards. It highlights their early victories, sense of common purpose, and growing confidence in their abilities to address workplace priorities. These men saw themselves as mainstream Peronist union organizers working within a system of legal labor institutions that had been in place since the 1940s. However, their organizing efforts could not be divorced from broader economic forces and political struggles that extended well beyond the confines of the Pacheco factory, and even beyond the borders of Argentina itself. Their assertion of shop-floor priorities around safety and working conditions paralleled the struggles of autoworkers in the United States, France, and Italy in these same years, which marked the twilight of the era of Fordist mass production.

The chapter goes on to detail how the Cold War context in Argentina magnified the political implications of these labor conflicts. As Latin American nationalists denounced American corporations as agents of imperialism, US-trained union leaders and local anticommunists sought to suppress the unrest in Argentina's automotive plants. Meanwhile, leftist youth militants infiltrated workplaces, and armed guerrilla groups targeted corporations in Argentina with bombings and kidnappings. It is no wonder, then, that the members of Ford's internal claims committee later recalled the early 1970s as a period not of triumph but of fear and uncertainty.[7] Despite their organizing victories, they found themselves living in "revolutionary time," when history seemed to be speeding up around them. The chapter ends with a detailed accounting of the deepening military presence at the Pacheco factory and the wave of detentions that swept away the plant's leading union activists beginning on the day of the coup.

HEALTH AND SAFETY

Safety was one of the top issues motivating organizers at the Pacheco factory. Automotive plants were notoriously dangerous workplaces, and as much as the men enjoyed the relatively high wages and overtime benefits at Ford, they also suffered the stresses and risks of working on a fast-paced assembly line. Adolfo Sánchez first put his name forward in a plant-level union election in 1971 after witnessing several grisly accidents. On two different occasions he saw coworkers lose arms in the heavy machinery. The first lost his footing and got caught in the metal stamping press: "It crushed his arm . . . I mean, it just destroyed it," Sánchez later recalled. "I saw the desperation on [his] face." The second man returned to work after his accident with a metal hook in place of his hand, an image that still haunted Sánchez decades later: "It was just awful, just weird, to see that worker with a normal hand one day and then see him with that hook." Sánchez himself was almost crushed while assembling a Falcon, and he was on his shift when another worker died, "cut in half" by the machinery.[8]

Welder Roberto Cantello was similarly motivated by workplace safety concerns. Nicknamed "the priest" by his coworkers because of his years in the seminary, Cantello already had extensive welding experience when he started working at Ford in 1970. In fact, at his job interview, he had questioned the quality of the safety aprons provided to welders at the Pacheco plant.[9] The welding medium used at Pacheco contained a mixture of lead and tin, and lead dust filled the air and coated the floor in the stamping plant. In 1974, Cantello was elected shop steward, and he joined the internal claims committee as secretary because he knew how to type. He dedicated himself to safety issues related to lead poisoning and noise violations, tracking reports published by the Ministry of Health regarding specific workplace risks.[10] Cantello was certain that the welders at Ford faced risks of lead poisoning, but when the internal claims committee asked Ford management to address the issue, neither the company nor the national SMATA union leadership took them seriously. The committee then approached researchers at the University of Buenos Aires Faculty of Medicine and asked them to run independent tests, which confirmed Cantello's suspicions. The men won their first significant victory when Ford finally agreed to shorten the shift time for welders and introduced longer breaks to limit their lead exposure.[11] Unfortunately, it was too late for Roberto Cantello, who suffered for the rest of his life from fevers, insomnia, and neurological symptoms caused by lead poisoning.[12]

The members of Ford's *comisión interna* "moved like a group," according to Cantello.[13] They met weekly in a small office that Ford management provided to them as required by law, and they built strong relationships with each other and with workers on the shop floor. While ordinary assembly line workers were not allowed to leave their immediate zones without permission, the members of the internal claims committee were free to move throughout the Pacheco facility.[14] Adolfo Sánchez's work as leader of the factory's union delegates put him in touch with people from across the Pacheco Industrial Center, which employed some 5,000 factory workers and another 2,500 white-collar employees by 1976: "I was in contact with all the other shop stewards and with coworkers in the assembly and motor sections," he later explained. "We got together whenever there was an issue in the union or in the company."[15]

The men's other early organizing victories related to workplace benefits. Sánchez recalled with pride years later that he had led a drive in the early 1970s to win special vacation bonuses equivalent to one hundred working hours, which were paid out on top of workers' regular vacation pay. "In other words, you already had your two weeks or four weeks of paid vacation time, and then you got paid for another hundred hours on top of that." The organizers also pressured Ford Argentina to build a new dining hall in the stamping plant, because workers there had no time to get to the cafeteria at the other end of the Pacheco facility during their meal breaks. "It was the most expensive dining facility in any auto plant," Sánchez noted with pride years later.[16] These cafeterias, which could seat hundreds of workers at a time, not only provided affordable meals; they also became crucial organizing spaces within the factory.

As Beverly Silver observes in her global analysis of autoworker labor activism, even a small group of effective organizers could paralyze a highly integrated automotive plant like the Pacheco Industrial Center, where management set the pace of production through the rhythm of the assembly line. Since the factory's different work areas were interdependent, a stoppage or slowdown in just one sector could affect the entire production line. The indoor meal halls and the open-air barbecue areas (*quinchos*) in the plant's recreation facilities were the only large spaces where workers could interact freely without interference from supervisors and timekeepers. Troiani recalled that the earliest organizing efforts at Ford took shape in these spaces. In the 1960s, "small groups started to gather in the corners of the meal hall, and gradually others started to join in." Later, as the labor force at Ford became more mobilized, workers used the cafeterias and quinchos to stage large-scale workers' assemblies. One early organizer even earned the nickname "Ambulance" because of his ability to command attention across the entire meal hall.[17]

THE TWILIGHT OF FORDISM

The early organizing achievements of Ford's internal claims committee coincided with Fordism's global "twilight," a time of retrenchment in the automotive sector that put workers on the defensive around the world.[18] By the late 1960s, the Fordist model of mass automotive production had become ascendant worldwide, and US and European automakers had built branch plants like Ford's Pacheco Industrial Center on every continent. However, those companies now found themselves competing over shrinking markets, because the world's buyers could purchase only so many cars, which still ranked as the century's most expensive consumer goods. Faced with dwindling returns, the automakers sought to boost productivity to gain an advantage over their rivals, and their strategies directly threatened the working conditions and earnings of workers on the shop floor. The companies sought to speed up assembly lines or cut labor costs by either laying off workers periodically when markets were slow or replacing them altogether with machines. Autoworkers now found themselves forced to work harder to earn the same pay or face the threat of job loss.

Not surprisingly, these pressures translated into pitched labor conflicts and deepening violence in auto plants around the world in the late 1960s and early 1970s. In France, workers at Renault and other metalworking factories linked to the automotive sector launched the largest strike wave in the country's history in May 1968, while the French state was preoccupied with mass student protests.[19] In that same month, African American workers at Chrysler's Dodge assembly plant in Detroit founded the Dodge Revolutionary Union Movement (DRUM). Politicized in the Black Power movement, they not only demanded improved working conditions from Chrysler but also defied the moderate leadership of the United Auto Workers and called for a radical transformation of American social and economic structures. Argentina's Cordobazo insurrection, which was sparked partly by a labor conflict at Renault, took place in May 1969, and Fiat workers in Córdoba erupted in revolt later that year. By then, however, the Italian automaker was facing far greater challenges at home. A wave of wildcat strikes by workers at the company's massive Mirafiori industrial complex in Turin marked the high point of a "hot autumn" of labor conflicts in 1969 that "profoundly altered Italian industrial relations and national politics," according to historian Nicola Pizzolato.[20]

Like Beverly Silver, Pizzolato argues that these clashes should be understood not as isolated events but as manifestations of pressures that affected workers across the global economy, particularly in its most dynamic and strategic industrial sectors. One could also interpret them as challenges to the Fordist model of automobility, which had become ascendant in the postwar era. Autoworkers around the world had been promised high wages and benefits in the new automotive plants, and they expected to achieve an enduring improvement in their standard of living. Instead, once the global economy faltered, they faced ever more pressure on the assembly line and uncertainty over their future. Although overshadowed in popular memory and in the academic literature by the middle-class student protests of the "global 1960s," the conflicts that erupted in the world's motor cities challenged the foundations of the Fordist system—especially its "wage-productivity nexus."[21] As Pizzolato demonstrates in his close analysis of the Detroit and Turin conflicts, labor demands "rarely focused on wage increases only, but tended rather to involve changes in the organization of work or in the balance of authority at the point of production, and safety issues raised by the production process." Ordinary workers challenged not only their foremen and managers but also national union leaders who failed to address their concerns. "[When] the workforce mobilized, decision-making shifted away from union and corporate boardrooms onto the shop floor," observes Pizzolato.[22] By the early 1970s, these same dynamics were also evident in the newer industrial plants of Gran Buenos Aires, including the Pacheco complex.

These industrial conflicts also intersected in complex ways with other youth-driven New Left movements of the era: the Black Power movement, the student movement, and overtly anticapitalist movements like Italy's Lotta Continua and Potere Operaio. "Workers hardly needed to be convinced by students of the desirability of resisting the exhausting demands of the assembly line," notes Pizzolato, but their experiments in democratic unionism shared some common features with other forms of grassroots organizing.[23] Even spontaneous collaborations with radical youth movements could magnify the impact of shop-floor struggles, as noted earlier in the case of the Cordobazo protest. Both Silver and Pizzolato contend that these pitched struggles over authority in the world's automotive plants contributed to Fordism's collapse as the dominant system of industrial production in the 1970s. Automakers faced with stocks of unsold vehicles and militant workforces now sought more "flexible" models of production. They imposed mass layoffs, moved their production facilities to new locations where unionization was weak, and invested heavily in robotization to undercut the strategic power of labor.[24] The postwar Fordist boom ended in 1973 as the global economy slid into a severe recession, made worse by the surge in oil prices that followed the OPEC oil embargo in October of that year.

COLD WAR CONTEXTS

In 1970s Argentina, the labor conflicts typical of Fordism's twilight years took a more deadly turn, intensified by the deep polarization of Argentine politics, the contradictory legacies of Peronism, and the country's long history of political violence. They were also magnified by the Cold War context, which put multinational corporations like Ford Argentina at the center of political battles over US imperialism in Latin America. As noted in chapter 1, American companies operating in Argentina had taken pains to avoid being identified with US foreign policy as far back as the 1920s by aligning themselves with local identities and priorities in their advertising campaigns. Yet as the century wore on and US corporations became directly embroiled in Cold War conflicts across the continent, such associations became unavoidable. In the 1950s, the United Fruit Company played a central role in US aggression against the democratically elected government of Jacobo Árbenz in Guatemala, which culminated in a US-backed coup in 1954.[25]

American conflicts with Cuba after the revolution of 1959 also centered on business interests when Fidel Castro's government nationalized dozens of US companies including oil refineries, utilities, and banks. Castro did not merely seize control of prominent US businesses in Cuba. He made a public spectacle out of the expropriations, proclaiming a Week of Popular Jubilation in August 1960. Crowds celebrated as signs for United Fruit and Esso were removed from buildings in downtown Havana, and events culminated in a raucous public "funeral" in which coffins bearing the names of prominent American corporations were thrown into the ocean.[26]

Deeply alarmed, US foreign policy agencies took new steps to protect American corporations in Latin America, working behind the scenes to avoid further enflaming public anger. One key institution in this effort was the American Institute for Free Labor Development (AIFLD), the labor training organization founded as part of President Kennedy's Alliance for Progress.[27] Originally conceived as an independent agency to be run by academic experts, the AIFLD quickly became "a de facto subsidiary of the U.S. government, directly managed by the upper echelons of organized labor, and firmly allied with U.S. capital," according to historian Jeff Schuhrke.[28] By the end of the 1960s, it had trained well over one hundred thousand Latin American workers in "free" trade unionism and anticommunist organizing. That training included workshops on collective bargaining, union finances, and communications, but notably not on strike organizing.[29]

Argentina became a high priority for the AIFLD in the 1960s as US corporations like Ford Motors invested heavily in the country. At first, the institute's leaders distrusted the Peronist union movement and sought to foster relationships with non-Peronist unions. In the mid-1960s, though, they shifted tactics and allied with right-wing Peronist union bosses at the head of the CGT labor federation.[30] Their goal was to undermine the different leftist or clasista currents present in the Argentine labor movement, which they inaccurately lumped together as "communist." They did so by courting friendly union leaders with training, salaries, and benefits, and they offered local unions funding for affordable housing projects. The application process to obtain this housing assistance was really a front for intelligence gathering. Any union that sought funding had to submit detailed questionnaires with information about its leaders and members, supplying personal data such as names, home addresses, photographs, and personal incomes. The questionnaires also asked about the union's sources of "political support" and about any "internal friction" among its leaders and members. Once it had collected this information, the AIFLD was notoriously slow about following through on its promises, delivering very few homes that ordinary workers could afford.[31]

Soon after his SMATA election victory in 1968, Dirck Kloosterman traveled to Washington, DC, to take part in an advanced training program at the AIFLD headquarters. The institute soon sent more trainers to Argentina to work with SMATA, counting Kloosterman's running mate, José Rodríguez, as another key ally.[32] By then, the organization had been denounced as a front for US foreign policy and intelligence work. For example, AIFLD graduates had played a key role in the US-backed military coup in Brazil in 1964.[33] Brazilian unionists trained in Washington had assisted the military by stopping the Radio, Telegraph, and Telephone Workers' Union from blocking communications. The new military regime also appointed four AIFLD graduates to take control of unions that were deemed communist.[34] Trainees in Washington were taught to stifle dissenting voices within their unions and identify those who criticized American power as "Red infiltrators." At a 1966 session, for example, participants rehearsed an imaginary meeting of Argentine autoworkers. The student playing the union leader practiced shouting down hecklers who called him "a puppet of Yankee imperialists trained in Washington!" He retorted: "American workers are the highest paid in the world under the free enterprise system of class cooperation . . . And what did you communists learn in Cuba? How to reduce living standards by 15 percent in five years? Is that how you plan to 'emancipate the working class'?"[35]

Early union organizers at Ford Argentina like Pedro Troiani had no idea about the SMATA leadership's ties to the AIFLD. Yet as they were beginning to organize themselves in the late 1960s and early 1970s, Kloosterman and Rodríguez were working to transform SMATA into an efficient and "responsible" business union by stamping out internal dissent.[36] Compared with Argentina's mighty metalworkers' and textile unions, though, SMATA still lacked the resources to control its rank and file through patronage and intimidation. It also had a unique federated structure, which meant that shop-floor delegates and regional branches had more autonomy and control over their own finances.[37] Together, these factors created space for greater workplace democracy and challenges to top-down control in the automotive sector. This was especially true in the interior city of Córdoba, where even moderate workers resented meddling by the Buenos Aires union bosses.[38] There, organizers at IKA-Renault played a central role in organizing the general strike that spun out into the Cordobazo insurrection of May 1969.[39]

Kloosterman and Rodríguez continued to face dissent from Córdoba into the early 1970s, despite intense government repression against the city's labor activists. For example, a diverse group of organizers from several Córdoba factories, including Ford Argentina's parts subsidiary Transax, built a coalition movement in 1971 that they called the Movement for Union Recovery (Movimiento de Recuperación Sindical, or MRS) to assert greater shop-floor autonomy and challenge the top-down leadership of SMATA.[40] Some were affiliated with leftist and left-Peronist political parties like Vanguardia Comunista and Peronismo de Base, but others were independents who simply wanted more honest and responsive union leadership. The MRS even put together an alternative slate of candidates to challenge Kloosterman's "Green List" in the national SMATA elections the following year. Kloosterman and Rodríguez fought back with a smear campaign that painted the MRS activists as terrorists. "Violence no, justice yes!" they announced in their national publicity campaign, suggesting that the MRS was tied to an armed "subversive" Left that threatened Argentine institutions, including the unions. This tactic of equating grassroots union activism with left-wing guerrilla violence became ever more common in the years leading up to the coup of 1976, heightening the risks faced by plant-level union activists like the men who made up the *comisión interna* at Ford Argentina.[41]

Shop-floor challenges then emerged in the auto plants in and around Buenos Aires, where labor relations had for the most part remained calm through the 1960s. Six months after the Cordobazo, workers at General Motors' old assembly plant in the neighborhood of Barracas and, to a lesser degree, at its newer factory in Gran Buenos Aires launched a series of slowdowns and work-to-rule actions to resist layoffs and efforts to speed up production.[42] When Kloosterman met with some 1,200 GM workers and asked them to comply with government orders to end the strike, he faced exactly the kind of heckling that had been rehearsed in the AIFLD training sessions in Washington. "Workers at Citroën, Deca, Mercedes-Benz, and Chrysler accepted conciliation," called out a GM worker from the floor. "And what happened? They lost their jobs. At Peugeot, they didn't back down. They formed a strike fund, got organized, and looked for support in other factories. What happened? They won. So why do you want to sell us out now?"⁴³ This assertion of shop-floor independence was typical of the era of late Fordism, when autoworkers in many parts of the world were fighting against deteriorating labor conditions and challenging union leaders who did not back up their demands. Until this moment, however, such dissent had been absent in the newer factories of Gran Buenos Aires.

REVOLUTION IN THE FACTORIES

The Argentine Left's discovery of industrial workers after the Cordobazo insurrection added yet another level of complexity to union organizing at the factory level.⁴⁴ By the early 1970s, several left-wing parties had sent young militants into factories throughout the industrial belt that extended from Córdoba southward along the Paraná River through Rosario and across the suburbs of Gran Buenos Aires.⁴⁵ There, they tried to win workers away from Peronist union structures. Some were aligned with nonviolent political movements, while others were part of the new guerrilla forces that emerged in these years.⁴⁶ In early 1975, clasista activists from the Communist Party, the Revolutionary Workers' Party (PRT), the Socialist Workers' Party, and the Peronist Youth Workers movement formed their own grievance committee at the Pacheco plant to challenge the SMATA union delegates.⁴⁷ Adolfo Sánchez later described how "everything got polarized ... and politicized" by the presence of these left-wing militants.⁴⁸ Security forces also infiltrated the plant in these years. Declassified records from the Intelligence Bureau of the Buenos Aires Provincial Police (Dirección de Inteligencia de la Policía de la Provincia de Buenos Aires, or DIPPBA) later confirmed that undercover police agents had been employed at Ford to monitor politics inside the plant.⁴⁹ "You never knew who you were talking to," stated union delegate Carlos Alberto Propato in a 2006 interview.⁵⁰

To further complicate matters for bread-and-butter union organizers, the first half of the 1970s also saw an explosion of urban guerrilla warfare in Argentina, including attacks on major corporations and executives.⁵¹ By then, leaders from across the political spectrum had infused political discourse with violence. These included, among others, General Juan Carlos Onganía, who used heated rhetoric to justify his ferocious attacks on workers and student activists, and Juan Perón, who sent secret messages from Spain encouraging Peronist youth to take up arms. However, even those who committed themselves to armed struggle differed on matters of strategy. While the People's

Revolutionary Army embraced the rural foco strategy of the Cuban Revolution, the left-Peronist Montoneros and other smaller guerrilla forces focused on Argentina's cities. Some three hundred urban guerrilla attacks took place in 1970 alone, several of them in the Zona Norte. For example, a group called the Peronist Armed Forces (Fuerzas Armadas Peronistas, or FAP) launched several sensational operations, including an incursion into the Campo de Mayo military base to steal weapons, the takeover of a radio station near the Pacheco plant, and a raid on the homes of US military personnel employed at the American embassy.[52]

Guerrilla groups staged such bold actions to win over public sympathies, especially among the poor and working class, whom they generally claimed to represent as a form of revolutionary vanguard. Sometimes they also staged "Robin Hood" attacks in which they stole trucks carrying food, which they redistributed in poor neighborhoods. Finally, the guerrillas enacted what they termed "revolutionary justice" by executing public figures they deemed to be enemies of the people.[53] In June 1969, a small commando of left-wing Peronists gunned down Peronist union boss Augusto Vandor inside the headquarters of the National Metalworkers' Union.[54] In 1970, the Montoneros burst onto the public scene by kidnapping and murdering General Pedro Eugenio Aramburu, who had overseen the anti-Peronist repression of the late 1950s.[55] The armed Left also kidnapped corporate executives in the early 1970s. Although framed in the same political terms as operations in a revolutionary war, ransom payments also provided financing to guerrilla organizations. In a study of sixty-five such kidnappings between 1970 and 1977, historian Vera Carnovale notes that fifty operations targeted businessmen or their family members.[56] Between them, the two main guerrilla forces (the PRT-ERP and the Montoneros) claimed responsibility for thirty-six of these operations, while the rest were undertaken by at least six other armed factions. Victims worked for national firms like Acindar and Bunge & Born, as well as multinationals such as Coca-Cola, Kodak, Firestone, and the Bank of London. Automakers Peugeot, Mercedes-Benz, and Fiat all suffered attacks on executives, as did Ford Argentina and its parts subsidiary Transax. While guerrilla organizations often claimed to be acting in solidarity with workers organizing in the factories, they did not necessarily consult with plant-level activists, and they mainly kept the ransom payments for themselves. Their success encouraged similar kidnappings by common criminals, adding to the general lawlessness and insecurity of the early 1970s.

POLITICAL WHIPLASH

The year 1973 marked another watershed in Argentina's accelerating political polarization. As the global financial downturn hit and the military government led by General Alejandro Lanusse struggled to manage the deepening political crisis, the armed forces decided to call elections and allow Juan Perón back from exile after eighteen years. The Peronist Left rejoiced at first, while other leftist organizations continued to reject any electoral strategy for change. For their part, US business interests were deeply alarmed by the prospect of a new Peronist government, particularly one that might be aligned with the left wing of Peronism. US corporations in the region were already on the defensive because of the 1970 election of socialist Salvador Allende in neighboring Chile. One of Allende's first actions had been to nationalize the American Kennecott and Anaconda mines that controlled Chile's vast copper resources, which he referred to as "Chile's wages" (*el sueldo de Chile*). This action enjoyed broad support among Chileans, who had come to resent the historical American monopoly on copper.[57]

Employees at the J. Walter Thompson advertising office in Buenos Aires expressed concern about the implications of Argentina's political opening in 1973. A report from April of that year observed: "Big business is usually the target of socialist or labor governments. Our large clients are big businesses in this country. Government problems with Ford—Lever—Pan Am—S. C. Johnson, etc., will reflect immediately on us."[58] Despite these fears, Juan Perón aligned himself with the hard right wing of his movement when he returned to Argentina in June 1973. In his first public appearance, on June 21, 1973, he openly denounced the Peronist left in inflammatory terms, referring to them as "covert, cloaked, and disguised enemies" of the people and warning that they would be "put in their place" if they did not give up their efforts to push Peronism toward the left.[59] The Montonero guerrillas then vowed to keep fighting against their former hero. On October 12, 1973, Perón began a brief final term as president of Argentina, during which he passed a series of laws including a "social pact" that strengthened the power of employers and union leaders over shop-floor workers. He died on July 1, 1974, leaving the government in the hands of his widow and vice president, María Estela (Isabel) Martínez de Perón.

By then, right-wing forces had taken control in neighboring Uruguay and Chile. In February 1973, Uruguay's civilian president, Juan María Bordaberry, launched a self-coup under pressure from the armed forces. While he remained as nominal head of state, true governing power was transferred to a new National Security Council that dismissed Uruguay's elected general assembly in June of that year. Then, on September 11, a military coup led by General Augusto Pinochet overthrew the Allende government in Chile. Although internal social conflicts contributed decisively to that outcome, declassified records have proven that US president Richard Nixon and his foreign policy adviser, Henry Kissinger, had been plotting against Allende since his inauguration. Their goal, according to political analyst Peter Kornbluh, was to bring Allende down "so that he could not establish a successful, and attractive, model for structural change that other countries might emulate."[60]

A darkly comical memo from the JWT advertising office in Buenos Aires captured the sense of chaos and political whiplash that engulfed the Southern Cone between 1970 and 1974. Executive J. G. O. Webster reported to his head office in New York about the booming business enjoyed by client Pan American Airlines:

> Pan Am is doing well as usual. After all, when you consider the last few years, it looks something like this:
>
> 1971: Anticommunist Chileans leaving Chile. Many going to Australia—via Pan Am.
> 1972: Right-wing Uruguayans leaving Uruguay to go to Australia—via Pan Am.
> 1973: Antiperonists leaving Argentina for everywhere, but mostly for Brazil and the U.S.
> Right-wing Uruguayans coming back to Uruguay.
> Left-wing Uruguayans leaving Uruguay, mostly to socialistic countries, Argentina, and Australia.
> Anticommunist Chileans returning to Chile. Mostly from Argentina and Australia.
> Communist Chileans leaving for anywhere that will take them but mostly to Mexico.
> 1974: Uruguayans of all colors leaving Uruguay (no work) for anywhere, but mostly Australia.[61]

THE COLD WAR COMES TO PACHECO

Battles between the left and right wings of the Peronist movement reached workers at the Pacheco factory in May 1973, after the Montonero guerrillas published a picture of a target on the back cover of their publication *El Descamisado* with a photograph of SMATA secretary-general Dirck Kloosterman at its center. The accompanying article denounced Kloosterman as a puppet of the US State Department based on his close relationship with the AIFLD and his nomination to the US-controlled International Metalworkers' Federation. It claimed that federal police intelligence agents had a permanent office at their disposal in the SMATA headquarters, and that Kloosterman had been complicit in the dismissals of union activists from General Motors, Mercedes-Benz, Peugeot, Citroën, and Chrysler.[62] Kloosterman was gunned down outside his house that same month, with the Peronist Armed Forces claiming responsibility.[63] José Rodríguez took over as secretary-general of SMATA.

Guerrilla forces attacked Ford Argentina just days after Kloosterman's murder. Two Ford management employees, cost accountant Luis V. Giovanelli and personnel employee Noemí Barry de la Rin, were shot in a botched kidnapping attempt by the "August 22 Command," a branch of the People's Revolutionary Army, as they left the administrative offices on the Pacheco grounds.[64] Giovanelli died a month later from his machine-gun wounds.[65] The guerrillas extorted $1 million from Ford Argentina to be distributed to hospitals, schools, and villas miserias in exchange for protection from further attacks. Despite objections from the Argentine and US governments, Ford began making payments almost immediately. Just six days after the shooting, the company issued a check to the Children's Hospital of Buenos Aires for the equivalent of US$400,000, and the Pacheco factory began building twenty-two ambulances, which were to be distributed to each of the Argentine provinces. Ford began sending cash donations to shantytowns across the greater Buenos Aires area.[66]

Six months after Ford Argentina's payout to the ERP guerrillas, the Peronist Armed Forces gunned down John Swint, president of Ford Argentina's parts subsidiary Transax in the city of Córdoba. In their communiqué, they threatened to murder more American-born Ford executives and their Argentine "lackeys."[67] They also denounced Ford as "one of the huge multinational companies responsible for the pillaging of our country from 1922 onward by the super-exploitation of the workers," describing the attack as an advance in a "popular war" that would unite "the working class and the Peronist people" to bring about socialism. The FAP threatened to keep attacking US-born executives unless Ford paid it $4 million in protection money. Within a week, the company had evacuated twenty-two American employees and their families.[68] Ford then demanded that the government guarantee security at the Pacheco factory, threatening to shut down its Argentine manufacturing operations altogether. Juan Perón assigned forces from the National Gendarmerie (Gendarmería Nacional) and the Naval Command (Prefectura) to the Ford factory, where they patrolled the perimeter of the grounds. In early 1976, this security presence would be supplemented by a larger contingent of soldiers from the Campo de Mayo military base.

In early August 1974, a month after Perón's death and his widow's assumption of power, JWT ad executive Webster reported to his New York office about the situation facing foreign business interests in Buenos Aires. "There are practically no American businessmen left in the Argentine," he observed.[69] Kidnappings by armed guerrilla groups and ordinary criminals remained common, although Webster noted that many went unreported due to a lack of faith in the police. Ford Motors executive Mike Collins was now using the JWT offices as a base of operations during his visits to Buenos Aires to avoid going to the Pacheco Industrial Center. By the end of August, Collins was reassigned, along with three other executives who had been running Ford Argentina's operations out of Rio de Janeiro for the previous nine months. Faced with political upheaval across the Southern Cone, Ford Motors had decided to relocate its Latin American headquarters to Mexico City.[70] Ford Argentina was to be left in the hands of local management, with Chilean-born Ford executive Juan Courard appointed as its president.

ORGANIZING IN REVOLUTIONARY TIME

These acts of violence did nothing to help workers at the Pacheco plant, who later reported that dealings with the national SMATA leadership deteriorated after José Rodríguez took over as secretary-general following Kloosterman's murder. Under Rodríguez, workers noticed that the SMATA bosses began driving fancy cars and eating at expensive restaurants. When the internal claims committee at Pacheco petitioned them for help resolving workplace issues, the union heads "showed up at the factory when they felt like it and made deals directly with the company," according to Pedro Troiani.[71] Like many grassroots SMATA activists, the men were also horrified by the guerrilla attacks. After Ford management employee Luis Giovanelli's death, workers at Pacheco collected money for his widow, and a small group ventured onto the overpass near the plant to remove the PRT-ERP banner that had been left by the guerrillas, though they were terrified that this would make them targets as well.[72] When asked years later to choose one word to describe what it felt like to lead organizing efforts at Pacheco in these years, Troiani and Carlos Alberto Propato responded without hesitation: fear.[73]

Even more militant clasista organizers opposed the guerrilla operations, understanding that right-wing forces could use this violence to justify attacks on nonviolent organizers inside workplaces.[74] The leaders at SMATA Córdoba, for instance, denounced Kloosterman's assassination, which they feared would be used against them. They published a statement to that effect in May 1974, clarifying that while they considered Kloosterman and Rodríguez "accomplices" to corporate and imperialist interests, their own objective was to defeat them through "the permanent mobilization of workers and the deepening of labor struggles," not through armed struggle.[75] Workers at Córdoba's Fiat plants, who had been among the first autoworkers in the country to use confrontational methods such as plant occupations, also protested against the assassination of a Fiat executive.[76] Argentina's guerrilla movements thus became ever more isolated from the working people they claimed to represent as they focused on military strategy at the expense of grassroots organizing.[77]

Forces on the Argentine right did use leftist violence to justify attacks on workers, as the clasista activists had feared. In 1974, a fascist paramilitary organization called the Triple A (Argentine Anticommunist Alliance) began to assassinate prominent figures on the left, including labor activists. Although the group's operations were clandestine, research has indicated that its forces included union thugs from the National Metalworkers' Union (UOM) under the leadership of Lorenzo Miguel, who took over after Vandor's assassination.[78] SMATA leaders tried to pressure the members of Ford's internal claims committee to take up arms as well. "One time," Pedro Troiani reported to a researcher years later, "José Rodríguez called us to the union headquarters. He told us, 'Leftist groups are trying to take over the union, and we aren't going to allow it . . . Who's got the balls to defend the union?'" Rodríguez took the men down to the basement and showed them a stockpile of weapons.

Though bewildered at the time, Troiani later concluded that SMATA was also collaborating with the Triple A paramilitaries.[79]

Labor mobilization in the Zona Norte reached its zenith in mid-1975 when workers across the capital's northern suburbs exploded in protest. In early June of that year, President Isabel Perón's finance minister, Celestino Rodrigo, announced a slate of aggressive austerity measures. These included a currency devaluation, a 100 percent increase in utility and transportation fees, a 180 percent increase in the price of fuel, and only a 45 percent wage increase.[80] Opponents dubbed the plan the "Rodrigazo," characterizing it as an assault on wage workers. Sensing the outrage of their union members, leaders at the CGT labor federation even took the unprecedented step of calling a two-day general strike against a Peronist government.[81] Yet political activists inside the factories of the Zona Norte challenged the old union structures and encouraged workers to voice their outrage through tactics of direct action. They formed "interfactory coordinating committees" (*coordinadoras interfabriles*) that aimed to mobilize workers across multiple industrial sectors, regardless of their union affiliation.[82] At Ford, workers allied with the Revolutionary Workers' Party, the political wing of the ERP guerrillas, called a general assembly in early June to strategize about how to respond to Rodrigo's announcements. They rejoiced at the strong turnout and the workers' enthusiastic endorsement of direct protest measures, despite the objections raised by "most of the union delegates." When SMATA headquarters sent a top union representative named Mercado to the Pacheco plant to try to gain control of the situation, he was driven out by the workers.[83]

By mid-June, activists in the Zona Norte had rallied workers behind plans for a massive march to demand that the government repeal its austerity policies. The strategy was to unite employees from multiple factories, among them Ford's Pacheco plant, the nearby Terrabusi food processing plant, and the Tigre and San Fernando shipyards. Together they would form a huge column and march some twenty miles down the Pan-American Freeway into the capital, continuing until they reached the CGT headquarters building in downtown Buenos Aires.[84] This route, which would require several hours to complete on foot, would take them from the outlying industrial suburbs through some of Argentina's most exclusive residential neighborhoods, and into the heart of the capital. The action would carry immense political symbolism, recalling both the union marches that had set off the Cordobazo insurrection of 1969 and the massive working-class mobilization of 1945 that had carried Juan Perón to the presidency.[85]

Workers at the Pacheco plant voted to join the march in an assembly held on June 16, although the members of the internal claims committee thought the action was too risky. "We had a meeting," Pedro Troiani recalled later, "and we tried to convince people not to head out into the streets. We told them the army was circulating nearby."[86] A few union delegates went to the SMATA offices to pressure the union leadership to demonstrate support for shop-floor workers by demanding a wage increase of 100 percent to offset inflation. Then, on the scheduled day of the march, June 18, workers at Pacheco debated whether to participate. According to a declassified police report, some four thousand workers assembled in midafternoon as the morning shift was ending and the evening shift was due to begin. Some voted to march downtown, while "others just wanted to go home."[87] After debating strategy for nearly two hours, roughly two thousand Ford workers decided to remain at Pacheco, where they voted in favor of a sit-down strike and a plant occupation. They held the factory and paralyzed production for five days.[88]

The other half of the workforce left the plant to join the march. "Workers just poured out of the factory," later recalled shop steward Carlos Garey.[89] While some SMATA delegates stayed behind, others decided to join the marchers out of a sense of responsibility. Troiani and Propato went along, though they were nervous. They later reported that some of the PRT-ERP activists were carrying weapons, and Ford workers with no previous organizing experience were getting caught up in the euphoria of the moment.[90] One, for instance, took a spot at the head of the huge column of marchers and waved a large flag. Meanwhile, military helicopters flew overhead, and police took photographs of the marching workers from the overpasses that spanned the highway. The column grew to some five thousand marchers as residents and workers from other factories joined them. They walked for six hours down the freeway until they reached Avenida General Paz, the ring road that delineates the border between the capital city and its surrounding suburbs. There, they encountered a massive police and military force that blocked them from entering the city and dispersed the crowd.[91] Still, this exercise in mass direct action did bear fruit when Finance Minister Rodrigo resigned and the federal government abandoned its austerity plans.

Chapter Three

The members of Ford's internal claims committee kept up their organizing efforts amid this chaos and mounting violence. They met weekly with management representatives to discuss concrete workplace issues, demanding adequate safety equipment and pressuring for mandated pay increases when workers were assigned to new tasks above their pay grade. Perhaps the most remarkable point of negotiation, however, was the pace of the assembly line itself. Shop stewards learned to calculate the speed of the machinery by counting the links of chain as they passed. In Troiani's words, they "monitored the production lines so they functioned as they were supposed to, since the supervisors would accelerate the lines to increase the number of units produced."[92] Whenever the men detected a speed-up, they requested that workers be added to the line to absorb the increased workload. Thus, even though they never identified themselves with the clasista movements, they invoked a sense of moral economy to challenge the "wage-productivity nexus" at the heart of the Fordist production regime, refusing to treat the speed-up as a normal feature of assembly-line work.[93] By asserting that the production line was "supposed to" operate at a certain pace, they defied management efforts to deepen their exploitation. Like workers in Detroit, Paris, and Turin, they fought to defend their share of the benefits associated with automobility.

The SMATA delegates also fought with José Rodríguez for the right to negotiate the preliminary terms of their contract directly with Ford management, even though Argentine labor law dictated that national union bodies were responsible for setting the terms of collective agreements.[94] Like autoworkers in Europe and the United States, they were trying to pull the center of negotiating power from the boardroom down to the shop floor. Both Ford executives and SMATA union bosses resented these efforts. Shop steward Luis María Degiusti later described the contempt they felt from their superiors at the Pacheco facility: "At Ford, they viewed us like today you might view a rapist. It was like we were throwing bombs, like we were against work, against everything."[95] Nonetheless, when faced with all-out rebellion from the shop floor in 1975, Ford management agreed to negotiate terms with the internal claims committee.

The men later recalled the remarkable gains they achieved in those discussions. One involved the SMATA affiliation of the cafeteria workers and some white-collar employees from Ford's Department of Inventory and Material Cost Analysis (Departamento de Análisis de Costos de Material e Inventorios). Kitchen staff moved to SMATA from the much weaker food workers' union

"It Was Like a War"

(Unión de Trabajadores Gastronómicos de la República Argentina), winning significant wage increases, safety improvements, and benefits. These included proper boots, gloves, and jackets to work in the industrial freezers and waste repositories. Female workers also won the right to the *día femenino*, a paid day off each month during their menstruation, and Ford agreed to subsidize the workplace day care.[96] The unionization of administrative employees signified a new challenge to management control, because they could pass sensitive information to the union in future negotiations. Moreover, work disruption in the offices could affect not just manufacturing but all of Ford's commercial operations.

Management and state security forces appear to have well understood the strategic significance of these union gains. As will be detailed below, the three new delegates representing the cafeteria workers and white-collar employees counted among the first workers kidnapped from Ford. The SMATA leadership also rejected the contract because it cut them out of the negotiations and failed to reward them as brokers positioned between management and the labor force.[97] "In 1975 we won the best collective agreement," later reported one of the shop stewards, "but the union wasn't prepared to accept it. It was a fight with José Rodríguez. One time we were there arguing until midnight."[98] The men were so frustrated by the lack of support from SMATA headquarters that they announced at a plant assembly that they would renounce their positions on the internal claims committee. José Rodríguez rejected their resignation, but communication virtually ended between the Ford SMATA delegates and the union leadership.[99]

BACKLASH

In 1975, SMATA leaders asserted their power by negotiating a new national contract for autoworkers across Argentina, rejecting the past practice of negotiating company by company. That collective agreement, ratified by President Isabel Perón in early July, included significant payouts to the national union organization. Outraged workers at Pacheco responded by taking over the plant for thirty-six hours and holding mass assemblies to debate their next steps. Faced with continued shop-floor militancy, Ford Argentina president Juan Courard held a meeting with José Rodríguez and police chief Héctor "the Jackal" García Rey, who would later be identified as a member of the Triple

A death squad. The men agreed to declare the Ford strike illegal, fire some three hundred workers they identified with the anti-SMATA Left, and impose greater police control and surveillance inside the plant.[100] By mid-July, Ford had fired 446 workers without paying them their legally mandated severance packages, without any opposition from SMATA.

Public figures began to raise the specter of "industrial guerrilla forces" (*guerrilla fabril*) operating in Argentina's industrial workplaces in 1975. This new phrase was used by conservative church leaders, politicians opposed to the government of Isabel Perón, and "orthodox" union bosses like Lorenzo Miguel and SMATA's own José Rodríguez. Conservative dailies such as *La Razón* and *La Opinión* published editorials in 1975 reassuring readers that business and military leaders were meeting to determine how to confront the new dangers associated with "industrial guerrillas," an intentionally vague term that elided elected union delegates with armed terrorists.[101] Even US embassy staff under conservative ambassador Robert Hill commented on the slipperiness of the expression. A memo from December 2, 1975, reported on "the war being waged by industrial guerrillas" in Argentine workplaces, but also conceded that the fears expressed by military, political, and union leaders were "not completely based on an objective analysis, since many of them equate any form of labor organizing with 'subversion.'" It went on to observe that, while there were no concrete plans yet in place to "counter industrial subversion," a military plan was likely imminent.[102]

In December 1975, Ford Argentina tried to clear activists from the Pacheco plant by offering them a voluntary severance package. They called the members of the internal claims committee to an office where a table was covered in bundles of cash.[103] Adolfo Sánchez later remarked that they offered him enough money "to buy several cars."[104] Sánchez, Pedro Troiani, and others turned down the money, though they noted that several youth militants from left-wing parties left the factory at this time.[105] Roberto Cantello, who had spearheaded safety investigations during his brief time as union steward for the welders at Pacheco, was relieved to take the payout. He was already showing signs of lead poisoning and had abandoned his union activism in frustration; he turned in his work tools and employee identification card and bought himself a welding kit with part of the money. Cantello found a job at American soap maker Lever Atkinson, where he kept his distance from union politics.[106] After the coup, however, he still found himself swept up in the repression against the Ford union activists.

The military presence at Ford deepened in the weeks leading up to coup. Although personnel from the gendarmerie and naval command had been a regular presence on the factory grounds since 1974, this occupation was different. Now the focus of surveillance was not on the perimeter of the factory but on the workers themselves. In February 1976, military vehicles began moving through the grounds, and the cafeteria staff started serving food to soldiers from the Campo de Mayo military base. Former Ford worker Ricardo Avalos testified years later that plastic guard huts appeared on the roof of the stamping plant at least a month before the coup, and soldiers watched the workers as they came and went. Army personnel also took over the recreation area, including the quinchos where the workers had held union meetings. They occupied the changing rooms and checked people's identification papers as they entered and exited the factory.[107]

In early March 1976, roughly two weeks before the military takeover, SMATA secretary-general José Rodríguez informed Pedro Troiani and other shop stewards from Ford that a coup was imminent. The men had gone to union headquarters in downtown Buenos Aires for help with a workplace problem, but Rodríguez told them they might as well let it go, under the circumstances. As Troiani later testified, "He told us, 'You can't do anything about it because the coup is coming.'" Rodríguez added a cryptic warning: "Take care of yourselves, because tough times are on the way and . . . the middle ranks of the union are going to end up in prison."[108] The men were shocked and confused: as members of the factory's internal claims committee, they obviously counted among those "middle ranks." However, they were elected union stewards and members of their workplace internal claims committee, an institution that had been protected by law since the 1940s. On what grounds could they be arrested? Moreover, with families to feed, what option did they have but to continue working?

"IT WAS LIKE A WAR"

Troops took up positions surrounding Argentina's most important factories and union headquarters during the night of March 23, 1976, in preparation for the coup announcement that came early on the morning of March 24.[109] Before dawn, military forces took over the National Congress and the presidential palace, known as the Casa Rosada, in downtown Buenos Aires. They then seized control of television and radio stations and announced that a military junta representing the three branches of the armed forces had overthrown President Isabel Perón. According to witness testimony, the Ford factory came "under siege" that day as military trucks, armored vehicles, and helicopters descended on the grounds. "It was like a war," recalled Troiani years later, "and all of that [military equipment] was aimed at us, the workers!"[110] Armed soldiers "invaded the factory and filled the walkways between the assembly lines," later recalled another worker present in the factory that day.[111]

On March 25, the new governing junta announced the suspension of union activities across the country. Ford's industrial relations manager, Guillermo Galarraga, called a meeting that day with the internal claims committee. He was joined by Ford labor relations manager Luis Pérez and the general manager of the stamping plant, named Marcos, who had a reputation among the workers as a bully.[112] Nine union delegates attended the brief meeting, which left them bewildered at the time but which remained engraved in their memories. Juan Carlos Amoroso testified in 1984 to Argentina's National Commission on the Disappearance of Persons that Galarraga told the men to "get to work and forget about any [union] demands because all the problems [at Ford] were over."[113] Galarraga used a mocking and aggressive tone as he announced that Ford managers no longer recognized the men's authority as elected union delegates. "Drop your rackets," he told them, "the ball is in our court now!"[114] When one of the delegates asked why Ford management was severing relations with them, Galarraga responded that the Pacheco facility was "to become a military objective and priority."[115]

The most confusing moment came at the end of the meeting, when Galarraga told Amoroso: "Give my regards to Camps," which provoked a burst of laughter from Marcos. The workers were confused, since they did not recognize the name. Adolfo Sánchez later recalled that he thought it might have been a reference to an Argentine athlete who had been in the news, though he could not understand the relevance.[116] When Amoroso asked Galarraga to clarify the identity of this "Camps," the manager replied, "You'll find out soon enough."[117] This cryptic statement did, indeed, soon become clear to the men, and it eventually served as damning evidence that Ford managers had advance knowledge of the violence that was to be unleashed against them. On March 25, 1976, Ramón Camps was still an obscure army colonel unknown to the broader Argentine public, but he was about to be appointed by the junta as director of the Buenos Aires provincial police. In that role, he oversaw a network of clandestine detention centers and prisons that became known as the "Camps circuit." He later boasted publicly about his involvement in more than fifteen thousand cases of forced disappearance, and after the return to democracy he was sentenced to twenty-five years in prison for human rights crimes.[118]

THE CAMPS CIRCUIT

The Ford union stewards spent most of the following year detained inside facilities that were part of that "Camps circuit." For many of them, the first stop in that horrifying journey was the quincho on the grounds of the Pacheco factory where they had once enjoyed company barbecues and more recently participated in union assemblies. No one knows precisely how many people employed at Ford's Pacheco Industrial Center were "disappeared" during the last dictatorship—detained by unidentified armed men and transported to secret detention centers. The best documented stories relate to the twenty-four men who ultimately survived their detentions and went on to pursue legal redress for their ordeal.[119] These cases share certain common features. The detainees had a history of union organizing or disputes with management; at the time of their abductions, most either were or had been elected shop stewards, and several had also served on the factory's *comisión interna*. Others had participated in workers' assemblies or mass mobilizations or been identified as "troublemakers."

Twenty-two of these abductions occurred within the first month of military rule, suggesting that the labor organizers at Ford counted among the military's top priorities. Seventeen of the men were detained in the factory, while the others were seized from their homes or other locations by assailants who carried photographs drawn from their Ford personnel files. The workers abducted from the factory were detained at the No. 1 Police Station in the municipality of Tigre, east of the Ford plant, while those seized outside the Ford premises were first held at the police station in the nearby town of Ingeniero Maschwitz and later moved to Tigre. All of them suffered hunger, beatings, death threats, and filthy and cramped conditions. Several were tortured, subjected to mock executions, or both. It is worthwhile enumerating the individual cases one by one to capture the bewildering pace

Chapter Three

of the disappearances from Ford, and to recognize how dramatically power relations shifted inside the plant on March 24, 1976.

The disappearances began the day of the coup. Cafeteria delegate Luis Degiusti decided to stay on after the end of his shift to reassure people. Around dusk someone approached him and another cafeteria delegate, Jorge Enrique Constanzo, to say that a group of men were looking for them. Degiusti and Constanzo were detained by several men in civilian clothes as well as two heavily armed men in fatigues who identified themselves only as part of the "security forces." A coworker was so alarmed that she called the Ford security office and the personnel manager, Guillermo Galarraga. The assailants took Constanzo and Degiusti to one of the quinchos in the factory's recreation area, where the open walls had been wrapped in canvas to create a makeshift cell. There, they tied the men's hands with wire, hooded them with their own shirts, and beat them savagely. After holding them there for several hours, they loaded them into a Ford Falcon and drove them to an empty lot near the Ford factory, where they subjected them to mock executions. They then transported them to the police station in Tigre, where they locked them up in a closet under a staircase.

Around midnight that same night, uniformed men were checking workers' identity papers at the factory exit. They seized Marcelino Victor Repossi and used a Falcon to drive him back to the quincho, where they beat him and demanded to know "how many soldiers he had killed." Repossi also suffered mock executions and found himself locked up alone in another cramped closet at the Tigre police station. All three men remained in those dark, cramped spaces for between five days and a week without food or water, forced to drink their own urine. They all endured torture sessions with electric shock and heard the screams of women being tortured during the night. Seven more union delegates were abducted two days later, this time mainly outside the workplace. Francisco Guillermo Perrotta, an employee in Ford's department of inventory, was a newer union delegate representing white-collar workers who had recently won affiliation with SMATA. Two men in plain clothes called out his name as he was crossing the parking lot to head home, telling him that some soldiers were looking for him. They pushed him into a light blue Falcon and pulled his sweater over his head. According to sworn testimony presented in federal court years later, they showed Perrotta the photo taken from his Ford personnel file and said that personnel employees had described what he was wearing that day to make it easier to identify him. When they stopped to switch vehicles, he heard them tell someone they had "picked up the package from Ford." Perrotta endured at least three torture sessions with electric shock at the Tigre police station. In his 1984 statement to the Commission on the Disappearance of Persons, he observed that the nature of the interrogation suggested that a Ford employee was in the room: "Only someone from Ford could address such specific details about the company, considering that some 5,000 workers and 2,500 administrative employees worked there."

The other six men, all current or former union delegates at Ford, were abducted from their homes. A group of between six and eight armed men in civilian clothes seized machinist Adolfo Sánchez while he was playing with his children. They did not identify themselves, but they did show his father-in-law the photograph from Sánchez's personnel file at Ford. They then picked up Pastor José Murúa, identifying themselves as army personnel.[120] Three men in civilian clothes driving a Ford Rural station wagon arrived at the home of Roberto Cantello around 11:00 p.m. and identified themselves as members of the federal police. Cantello had taken the buyout from Ford management just before the coup, having worked there for five years and serving briefly as union delegate. Yet even though he had left the company, he was still abducted along with the other Ford union delegates. The same assailants then drove to the home of Rubén Ernesto Manzano, SMATA delegate for the metal stamping section, and loaded him into the vehicle with Cantello. Finally, two unidentified armed men in civilian clothes seized Carlos Enrique Chitarroni, shop steward in the bodywork section at Ford, as he was arriving home in Tigre with his wife. They then drove to Juan Carlos Amoroso's home, smashed in the door, and demanded to know if he was a Ford union steward. They loaded him on top of Chitarroni and hooded him with his sweater. These victims were all transported to the Ingeniero Maschwitz police station and held together in a cell for several days without food or water before being transferred to the Tigre police station, where they encountered their fellow shop stewards.

As word spread about the detentions, even more experienced union activists struggled to comprehend what was happening. They had never heard of mainstream union delegates being targeted like this: detained without charge and held in secret, unable to communicate with their families. Troiani's wife, Elisa Charlín, asked him to stay home from work when she got word of the first detentions, but Pedro assured her that as an elected shop steward affiliated with SMATA he was legally protected and had nothing to worry about. By now, however, more than one hundred soldiers from the Campo de Mayo base had taken over the recreational grounds at the back of the factory, transforming it into an encampment. Armed soldiers patrolled inside the workplace and verified the identity papers of all workers entering or leaving the plant. They took over the changing rooms and watched over the workers at gunpoint as they changed clothes after their shifts. Former overseer Ángel Migliaccio testified years later that "everyone knew" that the soldiers "had been given" control over the quinchos adjacent to the sports fields.

Meanwhile, the disappearances continued. Juan Carlos Ballesteros was not home on the evening of March 28 when four unidentified armed men showed up looking for him, but he presented himself the following day at the regional police unit in Tigre to ask if there was an arrest warrant in his name. The police detained him on the spot and transferred him to the Tigre police station, where he was held with the other Ford workers.[121] The next wave of disappearances took place back at the Ford factory roughly two weeks later. On April 12, Hugo Adolfo Núñez and Carlos Rosendo Gareis were detained at gunpoint by four soldiers and taken to the quincho in the recreation area. Núñez later testified under oath that the army officer who was in charge had spoken by radio with his superior, Lieutenant Colonel Antonio Francisco Molinari, to report that they "had numbers two and four." Groups of soldiers stationed inside the plant rounded up four more men from their places on the assembly line the next morning: Pedro Troiani, Juan Carlos Conti, Vicente Ismael Portillo, and Carlos Alberto Propato. Both Portillo and Troiani later testified that the soldiers paraded them down the assembly line in front of their coworkers as if to show off their fate. One of Propato's assailants checked his name against a list after the foreman pointed him out. All five men were taken back to the quincho, where the soldiers tied their hands, hooded them, and beat them severely, threatening to kill them for being "fucking guerrillas, without God or homeland." After keeping them there all day without food or water, the soldiers transported the men to the Tigre police station around dusk.

Luciano Bocco and Fernando Groisman were detained a week later, and then Héctor Zubarán and Ricardo Avalos on April 21, all of them from the factory. Although Zubarán had failed to win election as a union delegate, he had been an active organizer inside the plant. Avalos had been less of a leader, though he had participated in several workers' assemblies. As he testified in court years later, he had been on sick leave from the factory for a week. When he returned to work, his foreman, nicknamed "the Turk," told him he should leave because some men were looking for him with the photo from his Ford personnel file. Avalos ignored him, and around 2:00 p.m. "the Turk" returned in tears, saying, "I told you to get lost and now I have to hand you over!" Both Bocco and Groisman ended up in the quincho, where they were tied and beaten as well. The last two disappearances occurred months later, on August 20, 1976, when Eduardo Norberto Pulega and Raimundo Cayetano Robledo were accused of sabotaging cars that had come off the assembly line. According to sworn testimony, Pulega's overseer sent him to the Ford personnel office, where the head of plant security, Héctor Francisco Jesús Sibilla, witnessed as two armed men in civilian clothes handcuffed him, taped over his eyes, beat him, and threatened to kill him.

CONCLUSION

In the early 1970s, the dynamics of shop-floor organizing at Ford and at Argentina's other automotive factories resembled struggles taking place thousands of miles away in Detroit, Turin, and Paris. Autoworkers asserted their rights to address concrete priorities relating to safety, working conditions, and management control over the production process as the global Fordist experiment went into crisis. Put another way, they fought to defend their interests within the dominant regime of automobility, which had taken shape in the postwar period, by organizing collectively rather than accepting speed-ups and wage cuts. Their position at the heart of their respective national economies gave them great bargaining power, because a disciplined work stoppage or sit-down strike in a single automotive factory could cripple production and ripple out across other economic sectors. For this reason, battles over working conditions in the auto plants took on greater political resonance and often intersected with other mass political movements of that era, including the Civil Rights Movement in the United States and anticapitalist youth movements in Europe.

Fordism's history was especially compressed in Argentina, which came relatively late to automotive manufacturing. Just fifteen years separated the inauguration of Ford's Pacheco Industrial Center and the military occupation that descended on the plant in March 1976. Through the early part of that short period, Ford workers had seemed to fulfill the "aristocracy of labor" ideal envisioned by developmentalist policy makers. They had remained outside the labor conflicts of the early 1960s as they benefited from relatively high wages and the booming demand for Ford vehicles. Many of them felt intense pride to be working for Ford, and the company used the latest management techniques to encourage that loyalty. However, workers at Pacheco demonstrated their capacity to assert their own interests in the late 1960s when they began to organize around crucial safety issues like lead poisoning. As the global economic crisis deepened in the early 1970s, they developed greater confidence and organizing capacity to resist management speed-ups and defend rights enshrined in Argentine labor law. In doing so, they drew on institutions of shop-floor representation like the internal claims committee, which dated back to the 1940s and made Argentina's labor movement one of the strongest in Latin America.

While organizers like Pedro Troiani and Adolfo Sánchez were focused on the dynamics playing out on the factory floor at Pacheco, they found themselves caught up in much larger and more dangerous power struggles that were typical of Latin America's Cold War era. Those shadowy forces contributed to the sense of "revolutionary time" that closed in on the men and culminated in their abductions in 1976. The autoworkers' union, SMATA, was being shaped from behind the scenes by the American AIFLD, which sought to strengthen right-wing forces against the left wing of Argentina's labor movement. Former president Juan Perón, who was a hero to the Ford organizers and to most Argentine workers, also secretly allied himself with the hard right wing of Peronism from exile in Spain, even while he courted left-wing Peronist youth activists in the hopes that their militancy would win his return to Argentina. When he succeeded, he denounced those youth activists and strengthened the power of employers and union bosses like José Rodríguez to suppress grassroots labor organizing. Meanwhile, left-wing militants and clandestine security forces infiltrated the Pacheco plant, deepening the organizers' sense of insecurity. Yet even cryptic warnings and threats from their union and workplace superiors did not prepare the men for the violence coming their way, because they viewed themselves as mainstream union representatives operating within the bounds of the law, and they assumed that those laws would continue to protect them. Like most Argentine citizens, they could not imagine the scale of repression that was to be unleashed on March 24, 1976.

CHAPTER FOUR

Driving Terror

As repression deepened inside the Ford factory, the Falcon sedans built inside that facility came to be identified with a new regime of terror unleashed across Argentina. One family's story powerfully captures this transformation. Jorge Ademar Falcone and his wife, Nelva Alicia Méndez de Falcone, were among Argentina's first generation of enthusiastic Ford Falcon owners. In the 1960s, they and their two children, Jorge and María Claudia, seemed like the perfect "Falcon family" drawn straight from a Ford advertisement. Jorge Senior, a family physician and former provincial politician during the Peronist years, and Nelva, a teacher, traded in their Falcon for a new model every two or three years. The family took full advantage of the car's comforts and dependability, going on picnics and holidays together from their home in La Plata, the capital of Buenos Aires Province.[1] By the mid-1970s, however, the political polarization in Argentina had radically transformed their lives. Their children had joined the left-wing Peronist youth movement. Jorge was active in the Peronist University Youth organization (JUP) and María Claudia in the Union of Secondary School Students (UES), though she was secretly affiliated with the armed Montonero movement. In 1975, at age fifteen, María Claudia helped organize a successful campaign of petitions and protests that won transit subsidies for high school students in the city.[2]

After the coup of March 1976, María Claudia moved in with a great aunt to avoid surveillance and Nelva and Jorge Senior found themselves using the family's Falcon for strange new purposes: driving their children and their children's friends to safe houses and helping them empty their apartments of incriminating documents. Six months after the coup, María Claudia was disappeared during the infamous Night of the Pencils (*noche de los lápices*), a death squad operation organized by the junta's crack counterinsurgency squad, the 601st Battalion, against the teenage activists who had organized the transit campaign the year before. In January 1978, Jorge Junior asked his parents to remove politically sensitive documents from his home as he went into exile. The couple were picked up by one of the dictatorship's "task groups" while driving in their Falcon. Inside the clandestine detention center known as "the Bank" (El Banco), Jorge, who suffered from a heart condition, was forced to watch as they tortured Nelva with a cattle prod. The two were released without explanation after two agonizing months; bizarrely, their car eventually turned up in an abandoned lot and was returned to them by the police. Traumatized and weakened by this ordeal, Jorge died soon after.

By the time Argentina's generals relinquished power in 1983, Nelva Méndez had been fighting for years to find her daughter as an activist with the human rights organization known as the Mothers of the Plaza de Mayo, which had become famous around the world for its early defiance of the military junta. The Mothers had pooled information about their abducted children and reached out to foreign diplomats and journalists; they had also staged symbolic protests in the central Plaza de Mayo that faced Argentina's presidential palace.[3] In the early democratic transition era, Méndez also collaborated with director Héctor Olivera on a feature film about the *noche de los lápices* that was released in 1986, going so far as to lend her own Falcon sedan to the production to help re-create her daughter's kidnapping.[4] It was yet another bizarre and heartbreaking twist in the story of that car, which had once embodied family comfort and intimacy and which now served to represent the death squad attacks that had torn her family apart.

Though extreme, the chilling story of Nelva's Falcon is by no means unique. The violence unleashed against the labor activists at Ford and the Falcone family formed part of an ambitious "Process of National Reorganization" (Proceso de Reorganización Nacional) imposed by the military dictatorship that aimed to crush all forms of dissent and dismantle labor protections that had been in place for three decades. The armed forces used surveillance, terror, and their unchecked power to rewrite the law to sweep away the promises that had underpinned the import substitution industrialization model since the 1940s and impose a neofascist nationalist project in its place. Executives at Ford Argentina aligned themselves publicly with the ruling juntas through advertising and speeches, and they petitioned the generals behind the scenes for help in clearing the Pacheco factory of undesirable workers. After 1976, the Pacheco plant even operated as a de facto military base, providing logistical support for counterinsurgency operations in the surrounding neighborhoods.

These political events permanently transformed the Ford Falcon's social meaning within Argentine popular culture. As discussed in previous chapters, the branding campaigns of the 1960s had identified the Falcon with ideals of national economic development, middle-class prosperity, and social stability. Most famously, the *Familia Falcón* television series had infused the car with sanitized clichés of domesticity and family unity. Locally manufactured Falcons had also been a source of pride for workers at Ford and for racing fans who could now celebrate a national incarnation of the prestigious Ford brand. By the 1970s, the Falcon was also being touted as Argentina's own muscle car to compete with the IKA-Renault Torino. Ads called it "tough, strong, tireless: a titan."[5]

Ordinary passenger cars took on new, more ominous functions through the mid-1970s as Argentine politics polarized and the country's far right rallied itself to annihilate the revolutionary and Peronist left.[6] This rightwing backlash introduced a new kind of totalitarian automobility, where cars served as tools of state terror and surveillance. In the years leading up to the coup of 1976, security forces and paramilitary death squads began to experiment with extrajudicial kidnappings against so-called subversives. One specific model—the dull-green, unmarked Falcon sedan—became their vehicle of choice. The military expanded and systematized the practice of disappearance after it seized power in March 1976, and Ford continued to supply unmarked green Falcons to the Argentine security forces long after the car had become notoriously associated with human rights violations. The *Falcon verde* quickly became infused with new cultural meanings as an object of state and military power.[7]

Modeled on American and European precedents, Argentina's car culture had long celebrated the speed, power, and anonymity associated with driving. The privately owned automobile conferred on its owner/driver both freedom of movement and the comforts of a sheltered and quasi-private space.[8] Those very same qualities made the automobile a key technology within the apparatus of state terror under military rule. In the hands of the military junta's "task groups" or death squads, speeding cars "sucked" victims out of their lives and into the terrifying parallel world of the concentration camp system, where they were moved through secret detention centers and torture facilities before being killed.[9] Survivors' testimonies make it possible to reconstruct the rituals that surrounded the automobile as a weapon of state terror. For victims of disappearance, the claustrophobic space of the car marked their first encounter with systematic dehumanization and torture. For bystanders who witnessed the loud and violent abductions, the Falcon came to function as a sentinel, a constant reminder of the military's ubiquitous power.

Writer Graciela B. Gutiérrez traces the car's abrupt transformation within her own lifetime. In her early childhood, the Falcon had existed merely as part of a television show with a cheery jingle about a happy suburban family, but a very different identification was seared into her memory during her adolescence in the 1970s. Walking down a residential street in her middle-class neighborhood of Flores during the dictatorship, she witnessed a speeding procession of white Ford Falcons bearing men with heavy mustaches and dark glasses brandishing "ostentatious machine guns" out the windows. Looking back thirty years after the coup, she reflected on how the Falcon had become indelibly associated with state terrorism in Argentines' collective memory: "When a story contains any mention of a *Falcon verde*," she observed, "our memory immediately associates it with thirty thousand voyages toward torture and death."[10]

CARS AND COLD WAR VIOLENCE

The Ford Falcon is, of course, by no means the first car in history to be associated with violence or raw power. Historian Kurt Möser has argued that the earliest years of elite driving culture in Europe fostered a taste for aggression that primed Europeans for World War I. Avant-garde artists like the Italian futurists celebrated the early automobile's speed and brutality, and proponents of social Darwinism interpreted car-related deaths in heroic terms. The sensationalized media surrounding international racing events drew huge crowds and fostered aggressive national rivalries.[11] The great dictators of the interwar era—Benito Mussolini, Adolf Hitler, and Joseph Stalin—also promoted mass vehicle production to prepare their countries for war and projected their personal power by appearing in public in large, luxurious cars.[12] In early twentieth-century Africa, colonial missionaries and officials relied on cars not only for practical reasons of mobility and comfort but as technologies of power that were meant to provoke awe and fear in subject peoples.[13]

As historian Mike Davis has demonstrated, the Cold War era linked automobiles to new kinds of political violence in the form of car bombings. By the 1960s and 1970s, the global expansion of automobility had made passenger cars ubiquitous in cities around the world. Unmarked cars provided an easy cover of secrecy; they were affordable, mobile, and easy to hide in plain sight.

Once-marginal political groups like the Basque separatist group Euskadi ta Askatasuna (ETA), the Irish Republican Army, and the neofascist Organisation de l'Armée Secrète (OAS) in Algeria adopted them as effective bomb delivery systems. Davis describes these car bombs as a form of sensational "political propaganda" that catapulted once-unknown political organizations onto the world stage and contributed to the twentieth century's blurring of the lines between military and civilian targets.[14]

Those same properties of speed and anonymity also made unmarked cars efficient tools of state surveillance and terror in the Cold War years, no matter how quaint they might now appear when compared to digital technologies of cyber surveillance, facial recognition, and drone warfare. In Latin America, paramilitary forces began using them to kidnap, torture, and murder activists, often with training and support from the United States. These operations began on a small scale in Guatemala and Venezuela in the 1960s and expanded to the Southern Cone countries by the early 1970s. When combined with other technologies such as tape recorders, electric cattle prods, and modern filing systems, unmarked cars helped security forces efficiently track and terrorize those people they considered to be enemies of the state.[15] Just like the car bombings taking place in Europe and North Africa, the Latin American death squads' noisy, spectacular raids against so-called subversives operated as a kind of political theater that proclaimed the beginning of a new era.

A COVERT TURN

In Argentina, the first abductions using unmarked Ford Falcons occurred at least two years before the coup. During Juan Perón's final presidential term, the paramilitary death squad known as the Argentine Anticommunist Alliance (Alianza Anticomunista Argentina, or Triple A) launched a campaign of terrorist violence against leftist intellectuals, politicians, and cultural figures. It was a direct precursor to the task groups that carried out the mass disappearances of the dictatorship years, founded in late 1973 by Perón's social welfare minister, José "the Sorcerer" López Rega, and Alberto Villar, a Nazi sympathizer and graduate of the US training facility known as the School of the Americas.[16] The Triple A brought together right-wing Peronists from the police, labor unions, and youth organizations who shared the common goal of wiping out the Peronist Left. Its operatives executed some nine hundred people in the three years leading up to the coup: politicians, progressive church leaders, union representatives, intellectuals, and leftist militants. The organization made no effort to hide its relationship with the Peronist government, going so far as to print death threats and hit lists in its publication *El Caudillo*, which was sold in regular newsstands carrying advertisements from the Ministry of Welfare.[17]

The men who carried out the Triple A attacks drove unmarked cars, provoking outrage from the few public figures who dared to challenge the organization in print. Ford Argentina had been selling Falcon patrol cars to local police since the 1960s, as they had in the United States. These vehicles bore standardized police colors, identifying symbols, and official license plates to identify them with their respective police forces. By contrast, the cars used in the Triple A attacks were usually a dull military green with no markings that could associate them with police or military institutions. British-born journalist Robert Cox, editor of the English-language *Buenos Aires Herald*, was one of the only media figures to denounce these shadowy attacks and accuse official security forces of being behind them. When celebrated illustrator Menchi Sabat was abducted in October 1975, Cox wrote: "Is there any possible situation that would justify the use by police of unmarked cars without number plates?"[18] A few days later, eleven heavily armed men, including one uniformed officer, raided the *Herald*'s offices to arrest journalist Andrew Graham-Yooll on charges of terrorism. Cox likely saved Graham-Yooll's life by accompanying him to the station; they were driven there in a caravan of unmarked Falcons.[19]

By 1975, unmarked cars were being used more openly as tools of military impunity under the nominally democratic government of Juan Perón's widow, Isabel Perón. The armed forces began strengthening their counterinsurgency capacities against left-wing guerrilla movements during Perón's puppet government. General Acdel Vilas, who commanded an assault on guerrilla forces in the province of Tucumán known as Operation Independence (Operación Independencia), described the effectiveness of unmarked cars in an internal military report:

> If the detentions had been carried out by my men dressed in army uniform, we would have been forced to hand prisoners over to the justice system, which would have released them within

hours. But things changed completely once I realized how the "justice" system and party politics really work, and I ordered the operations to be performed by men dressed in civilian clothes and driving unmarked vehicles.[20]

In March 1975, a full year before the coup, unmarked Ford Falcons were also used on an exemplary scale in one of the decade's most brutal attacks on organized labor: a full-scale assault on the steel town of Villa Constitución, in the province of Santa Fe. The town was home to the Acindar steelworks, where labor activists had organized effective sit-down strikes and plant occupations. Some four thousand uniformed and paramilitary forces descended upon the city in a caravan of vehicles more than half a mile long, among them many Ford Falcons. They detained roughly three hundred workers, including the members of Acindar's internal claims committee, who were subjected to abuses and mock executions. Security forces also used company offices at Acindar to operate a surveillance headquarters and clandestine detention center, a formula that would be repeated at Ford's Pacheco plant after the coup of March 1976.[21]

A new Defense Council founded in 1975 laid the groundwork for the coming repression. Its mandate was to "execute the military and security operations necessary to annihilate the actions of the subversive elements throughout the country's territory."[22] The council divided Argentina's national territory into five command zones through which they organized counterinsurgency operations, coordinating the actions of police, armed forces, and prison personnel. It also created a parallel command structure of loosely organized "task forces" and subordinate "task groups" (*grupos de tarea*) to carry out a sweeping campaign of covert repression. These small, fluid, and relatively autonomous groups mirrored the structure of the guerrilla cells that were purportedly their main targets, though most of their victims were not armed militants but shop-floor labor activists, peasant leaders, student organizers, and political militants.[23]

The geography of this command structure demonstrates how prominently the industrial districts of Gran Buenos Aires figured among the military's security concerns. While most zones covered entire provinces or regions of the interior, Zone 4 encompassed a much smaller territory containing just the Zona Norte and Zona Oeste in Gran Buenos Aires: home to the Ford factory; the Astarsa shipyard, where sixty union activists were kidnapped in the early weeks after the coup; and the Campo de Mayo military base, which came to house four separate clandestine detention centers that left almost no survivors.[24] Security forces assigned to the area were given different responsibilities. Police were charged with surveilling working-class neighborhoods and workplaces for signs of revolutionary politics, while thousands of career soldiers and conscripts were assigned to infrastructural support and combat against armed guerrilla forces from the Montoneros and the ERP. The task groups, meanwhile, handled extrajudicial kidnappings and torture operations against labor and neighborhood activists, intellectuals, artists, and political organizers. These "gangs" (*patotas*) absorbed members of the Triple A into the parallel command structure.[25]

MASS DISAPPEARANCE

The Argentine dictatorship that took power in March 1976 was the first authoritarian regime in Latin America to adopt disappearance as its principal strategy of state power.[26] While neighboring military governments used methods such as widespread torture, mass imprisonment, and even public executions, they did not employ the tactic of secretive kidnappings and clandestine detention on anything like the scale of Argentina's military juntas.[27] The 1984 report of the country's National Commission on the Disappearance of Persons (Comisión Nacional Sobre la Desaparición de Personas, or CONADEP) documented 8,960 cases of disappearance between 1976 and 1983, and evidence uncovered later pushed that number far higher.[28] A Chilean intelligence report came to light in 2002 that calculated, based on Argentine military sources, that some 22,000 people had been killed or disappeared by security forces between 1975 and 1978. Human rights organizations have generally estimated the total number of victims at 30,000, though of course the secretive nature of the disappearances makes a precise calculation impossible.[29]

The turn to mass disappearance stemmed from both ideological and pragmatic motives. The most extreme elements within the security forces developed an increasingly apocalyptic vision of their society in the years spanning from the Cordobazo riots of 1969 to the coup of 1976, as they rallied themselves to launch a war of extermination against those they identified as "subversives." Although their ideology had roots in Argentina's own traditions of Catholic neofascism, they gained new capacities to operationalize those theories thanks to training and material assistance from US and French counterinsurgency experts.[30] Inside Argentina, they collaborated with an eclectic mix of social actors—business elites, members of the Catholic hierarchy, politicians, and union bosses—who shared their desire to impose order and stamp out not only Argentina's armed guerrilla movements but also the radical ideas and organizing strategies that had taken hold of the country's factories and workplaces, schools and universities, urban squatter settlements, and peasant cooperatives.[31]

In unleashing the task groups against Argentina's civilian population, the generals behind the coup made the chilling calculation that mass disappearance offered the most efficient means to purge Argentina of its internal enemies. First, it would shield the ruling juntas from international criticism. "You can't just shoot seven thousand people," remarked General Ramón Díaz Bessone in a particularly candid interview with French journalist Marie-Monique Robin in 2003. "Look at all the fuss the pope made when [Spanish dictator Francisco] Franco killed just three people. The whole world would have come down on us."[32] Second, the swift and unpredictable kidnapping operations would disorient and fragment a populace that had proven its capacity for collective resistance. General Jorge Videla considered it the only way to neutralize Argentina's highly organized civil society, which "would not have stood for so many shootings: yesterday two in Buenos Aires, today six in Córdoba, tomorrow four in Rosario, and so on ... There was no other way to do it. We all agreed on that."[33] To the generals' surprise, these efficient counterinsurgency methods received behind-the-scenes endorsement from key officials in the US government. When Admiral César Guzzetti, the junta's first foreign minister, visited Washington in October 1976, he expected to receive stern warnings about human rights violations. Instead, he was warmly received by both Vice President Nelson Rockefeller and Secretary of State Henry Kissinger. Kissinger passed on a message urging the junta to "get the terrorist problem under control as quickly as possible," ideally before January 1977, when incoming president Jimmy Carter was to take office.[34]

That same sense of urgency underpinned the junta's efforts to accommodate the thousands of victims rounded up after March 24, 1976. Both military and civilian governments had been expanding Argentina's prison infrastructure since the late 1960s to house growing numbers of political prisoners. In 1970, following the Cordobazo insurrection, the civilian Federal Penitentiary Service had been transferred to military control and integrated into the state security apparatus. Officials had built additions onto some penitentiaries where political prisoners were segregated from common criminals.[35] However, even this enlarged penal system could not accommodate the numbers of new prisoners detained after the coup, nor did it provide the secrecy that would allow military interrogators full impunity in their actions. The junta scrambled to organize a network of clandestine detention centers scattered across the country, "black sites" where thousands of kidnapping victims would be detained, tortured, and, in most cases, murdered in secret. More than 600 were in operation after the coup, though that number stabilized by the end of 1976 to roughly 360.[36] In and around the capital, some detention centers operated in large military facilities like the Escuela Superior de Mecánica de la Armada (ESMA) or Campo de Mayo. Others were improvised and precarious like the quincho at Ford, where soldiers had wrapped the open-air structure in canvas, creating a makeshift cell where they beat and terrorized workers who were seized off the assembly line.

Many detention centers were embedded in densely populated urban neighborhoods, like the "Azopardo Garage," which operated in a building in downtown Buenos Aires that was later repurposed as a motor vehicle registration office. "Automotores Orletti," a rudimentary jail housed in an auto repair shop, stood sandwiched between a family home and a school in the heart of Floresta, a residential neighborhood on Buenos Aires's west side.[37] Nearby, the center known to the task groups as "Olympus" (El Olimpo) occupied a full city block in a converted tramway station. Prisoners could hear traffic and easily make out the voice of a newspaper delivery man who passed each day. Presumably neighbors also detected what was going on inside, since occupants of the two-story home right across the street bricked up their upstairs balcony, which overlooked the site.[38] Such was the intimacy of the terror system, at least in urban areas, where the realms of normality and fascist horror coexisted in tight quarters.

AUTHORITARIAN AUTOMOBILITY

The ruling junta moved quickly to impose order over the cityscape of Buenos Aires.[39] Authorities first seized control of the city's streets and plazas by imposing curfews and bans on public gatherings, putting an end to the mass mobilizations of the early 1970s. They appointed air force brigadier Osvaldo

Cacciatore as mayor of Buenos Aires, giving him free rein to reorganize the city around values of hygiene, order, and social hierarchy. Their overall plans were detailed in a new Urban Planning Code in 1977 that prioritized efficient traffic circulation, new construction, and improvements to green spaces in anticipation of Argentina's hosting of the World Cup in 1978, an event the junta saw as an opportunity to showcase the achievements of the "new" Argentina. What followed was a draconian exercise in urban renewal that favored cars over people, property owners over tenants, and large-scale building projects over neighborhood priorities. Brigadier Cacciatore silenced opposition by firing thousands of municipal employees and doing away with established practices of consultation for major public works projects. The government also expelled thousands of poor residents from the capital by lifting rent controls and forcibly clearing several villas miserias that existed within the city limits.[40]

Cacciatore named lawyer and highway promoter Guillermo Laura as the city's new public works secretary, putting him in charge of the most ambitious project of all: a US$500 million plan to cut nine new freeways through the capital. Although Laura had no training as a civil engineer, in 1970 he had outlined his vision of a new highway plan for Buenos Aires in a self-published book entitled *The Arterial City* (*La ciudad arterial*). In it, he celebrated American-style freeway building as a technocratic exercise in modernization, and he proposed Los Angeles as the model to be emulated in Argentina's capital.[41] An admirer of urbanists such as Le Corbusier and Robert Moses, Laura promoted a similar top-down model of urban design that prioritized the smooth and swift circulation of automobiles as a universal good. He called for rapid expropriations of private property in the service of road widening and highway building, and he disregarded the rights of tenants who might be affected by his proposals. Indeed, if fully realized, Laura's plan would have razed entire neighborhoods across Buenos Aires and displaced another 150,000 residents.[42] In the end, military authorities managed to complete only one of his proposed arteries before losing power in 1983. They cut the 25 de Mayo Freeway from downtown Buenos Aires to the city's southwest, where it connected to the new Perito Moreno Highway. Yet even that limited project had a major impact on the city by fragmenting older neighborhoods and cutting through popular green spaces.

As these policies reshaped the cityscape of Buenos Aires, the junta imposed an authoritarian model of automobility that saw ordinary passenger

Chapter Four

cars deployed as tools of state surveillance, propaganda, and terror. The dictatorship's task groups used unmarked passenger cars in their kidnapping operations, and the Ford Falcon quickly became recognized as their vehicle of choice. Ford Argentina was not the only automaker to provide vehicles to the security services.[43] In fact, a growing body of research has illuminated the close ties between the junta and Argentina's business community, including both national and multinational corporations.[44] Insider sources and investigative reports have accused other automakers of collaborating with the security forces by supplying vehicles and other resources used in the repression. Víctor Ibáñez, a former army sergeant stationed in the clandestine detention center known as El Campito, claimed that Peugeot had donated new cars to military officers and commandos.[45] German journalist Gaby Weber's documentary *There Are No Miracles* (*Milagros no hay*) documents the disappearance of fifteen workers and union activists from the Mercedes-Benz factory in the province of Buenos Aires. In researching the collusion between Mercedes-Benz executives and the autoworkers' union leadership in these disappearances, Weber uncovered evidence that the corporation had donated a neonatal unit to the Campo de Mayo military base—a seemingly irrelevant detail, except for the fact that this facility was used by authorities to detain pregnant political prisoners until they gave birth, later removing their babies and placing them with families of officers and collaborators.[46]

The task groups also relied on stolen vehicles, as observed in the opening story of the Falcone family. Omar Torres served in the Gendarmería Nacional during most of the dictatorship years and testified later about the security forces' practice of stealing and disposing of cars. He observed that the vehicles driven by officers and some noncommissioned officers of the "gangs" (or death squads) were generally stolen right off the street. Some were appropriated for private use; others were used in subsequent terror operations; and the remainder were stripped down for parts, discarded in abandoned lots, and burned.[47] When asked how he knew these vehicles were stolen, he answered, "Because they talked about it openly. They'd say 'It's time to go get some vehicles' and they'd decide whose turn it was to go out, and twenty or thirty minutes later they'd be back with practically new cars. Then they would take off the license plates, strip off serial numbers, and sometimes repaint them." General Guillermo Suárez Mason reportedly put a stop to these anarchic robberies, disciplining some of the men and ordering that any future vehicle thefts would occur only under his orders. However, naval officer Adolfo Scilingo, one of a handful of "dirty warriors" who have described the inner workings of the repression, later claimed that the navy ran its own office inside the ESMA detention center where lawyers falsified documents to disguise the vehicles stolen from political prisoners.[48]

Although the task groups sometimes used other vehicles, accounts by survivors and witnesses demonstrate how closely the Ford Falcon came to be identified with their attacks. The car figured prominently in *Buenos Aires Herald* editor Robert Cox's denunciations of the military's tactics after the coup: "Imagine for a moment what would happen if those Ford Falcons without number plates suddenly disappeared," he asked in one editorial. "And imagine what would happen if there were no more arbitrary arrests? Would it make a great deal of difference if those people suspected of being involved with terrorist organizations were arrested by uniformed policemen, identifying themselves, showing arrest warrants and informing relatives where they intended to take their prisoners?"[49] Cox and his family suffered repeated death threats and endured several of their own traumatic Falcon encounters before they finally left Argentina in late 1979. A Falcon nearly ran down Cox's wife, Maud Daverio Cox, on one occasion; on another, a group of men leaped from a Falcon and approached her threateningly, as if to take her away.[50]

Some military figures also denounced the Falcon as symbol of a new kind of military impunity. Retired brigadier general Manuel Alberto Laprida, who hailed from an earlier generation less steeped in neofascist ideology, later testified under oath that he had personally confronted the military's minister of the interior, General Albano Harguindeguy, about the death squad attacks. Harguindeguy had worked under Laprida in the 1960s, and the elder officer visited him soon after the coup to tell him to call off the paramilitary operations: "I used a common expression," he later recalled. "I told him it was time to put an end to the Falcons that were driving around Buenos Aires with [Ithaca machine guns] out the windows."[51] Believing that the task groups were operating outside the chain of command, Laprida expressed concern about a breakdown of military discipline: "The monopoly of force must remain in the hands of the armed forces; decision making must remain at the highest level of command and with the law in hand." Laprida's interpretation was half right. The overlapping allegiances of security personnel to formal institutions and ultra-right-wing groups like the Triple A had in fact fostered a lawless culture within the armed forces.[52] However, the junta leaders had deliberately fostered that lawlessness. As US diplomat Maxwell Chaplin reported to Washington in July 1976, "In our opinion, the only 'right-wing assassins' operating in Argentina at this point . . . are members of the government security forces."[53]

Even ordinary people far from the workings of power quickly came to identify the Ford Falcon with the new regime of terror unleashed in March 1976. The loud and violent abductions enacted by the grupos de tarea demonstrated to anyone watching that the junta's new terror apparatus could irrupt into ordinary daily life without warning.[54] "Elena," a convenience store owner in the city of Córdoba, recalled that her first experience of the coup came early on the morning of March 24, 1976. She awoke to loud noises at 5:00 a.m. and, peeking furtively through her bedroom blinds, witnessed the abduction of a neighbor across the street, a young man she knew only as an autoworker at Fiat or Renault. The operation unfolded in a fashion that would soon become routine: three men in plain clothes pulled up in a Ford Falcon, shouted that they were from the police, and forced their way into the home when no one opened the door for them. They dragged the young man out, spitting at him and hitting him, and then pushed him into the back of the Falcon and drove away. When she later turned on the radio, she heard the announcement that the military had taken power: a common occurrence in her lifetime. Still, she later told an interviewer that the kidnapping scene filled her with a new kind of dread.[55] Within just a few weeks, this kind of attack became so routine that a death threat issued to former university rector Emilio Mignone stated simply: "The unmarked Falcons will be there soon."[56]

These and other pieces of evidence suggest that executives at Ford Argentina must have known that the cars they were supplying to the Argentine military were being used in counterinsurgency operations. As noted earlier, Ford had been selling Falcon patrol cars to police and military services since the 1960s, and these vehicles normally bore official insignia and government license places. A rare set of surviving documents from General Harguindeguy's own secret archive at the Ministry of the Interior includes purchase orders to Ford Argentina for ninety unmarked Falcons. Dated October 1977, they specified that the vehicles in question should bear no markings that could link them back to the state, adding that an earlier shipment of 179 cars had "performed with excellent results." Although government vehicle purchases would normally have required a public tender, the junta's own accounting law allowed it to sidestep tendering in circumstances requiring secrecy.[57] Why would the purchase of a car fleet constitute a state secret, unless those vehicles were to be used in covert and illegal operations?

The cars driven by the dictatorship's task groups projected the power of state terrorism throughout the streets of the capital and beyond. First, they sowed confusion by blurring the identity of the men who carried out the kidnapping operations. Attackers moved quickly, leaving detainees little time to react or cry for help. For example, sixteen-year-old Ana María Careaga was kidnapped from a busy street corner in Buenos Aires in broad daylight as she stood waiting for her parents to pick her up. "I was startled when a car pulled up right in front of me," she later recalled when testifying about her ordeal. "A person got out and started walking toward me. I stood there, thinking he was heading into a store, but he quickly grabbed me by the arm. Another man came and grabbed the other and they immediately pushed me into a car. I tried to scream but it all happened in seconds, and I had no time to react."[58] More seasoned political activists quickly developed protocols and defense mechanisms to respond to such attacks, though there was nothing they could do to prevent their own kidnappings. Graciela Irma Trotta, who was a few years older than Careaga, had a bit more time and presence of mind when she was kidnapped from a corner café in Buenos Aires. Two cars pulled up and a group of men grabbed her, handcuffed her, and pushed her into a Falcon. As they forced her across the sidewalk, she screamed out her name and announced that she was being kidnapped; her assailants assured onlookers that she was on drugs.[59]

Cars also functioned as a key surveillance technology in this era before cell phones and digital communications. The task forces used unmarked vehicles to stake out suspects and follow their movements. They also sought to control other networks of circulating cars by intervening in the national taxi drivers' association, imposing a new director who was later denounced by critics as a "commissar of the repression."[60] The military even used privately owned cars as propaganda devices. In 1979, on the eve of a visit by a delegation from the Inter-American Commission on Human Rights, the junta contracted US public relations firm Burson-Marsteller to help them counter international criticism of attacks on civilians. The company came up with the slogan "We Argentines are righteous and human" ("Los argentinos somos derechos y humanos"), an awkward reworking of the phrase "human rights." General Harguindeguy, serving as interior minister, ordered a quarter million decals bearing the catchphrase, which were meant to be displayed in car windows to show off public support for the regime. While some were distributed as inserts in popular magazines that catered to conservative readers, thousands were given to security forces manning checkpoints around the city. After they stopped drivers to review their identification papers or examine their trunks, soldiers affixed the decals to their windshields before allowing them to leave.[61] In this way, the junta projected an image of consensus or at least conformity through the traffic that circulated in and around the capital.

DRIVING THE DISAPPEARED

The stories told by survivors of disappearance speak eloquently to the significance of the death squad vehicles that roamed across the Argentine landscape with their masked identities. In fact, the vast majority of evidence about the repression in Argentina comes from such stories, because the military's "terror archives" have never come to light as they have in Guatemala and Brazil.[62] Although documents discovered in Paraguay have illuminated the Argentine junta's role in Operation Condor—the secret network through which several South American dictatorships coordinated their intelligence-gathering and terror operations—most records of the junta's operations within Argentina have either been destroyed or remain hidden.[63] In their absence, civil society has spent decades building its own archives of the dictatorship years by accumulating thousands of pieces of testimony from survivors, activists, and family members of the disappeared. A small number of individuals who served inside the terror apparatus, either as career soldiers or as conscripts, have also shared their stories.[64] The earliest survivors' testimonies provide especially vivid insights into the sensory experience of disappearance and the significance of unmarked cars as instruments of state terror. Collected in the 1980s when individuals did not yet have a collective narrative through which to frame their individual stories, these early accounts convey the immediacy of the experience and the efforts undertaken by survivors to make sense of what had happened to them.

Common patterns emerge across these stories. Most immediately, the speeding vehicles used by the grupos de tarea gave victims a visceral experience of state terrorism as the sensory experiences normally associated with driving became distorted and magnified. Here, the Falcon's relatively large interior and ample trunk space made it an ideal tool of disappearance, especially when multiple people were rounded up at once, as occurred with several of the Ford workers. Assailants worked to annihilate any markers of time or place that might help prisoners identify their surroundings. They blindfolded or hooded them, forced them onto the floor or into the trunk, and drove in circles playing loud music to muffle sounds from outside. In their later testimonials, survivors reconstructed their mental efforts to use their senses and remain connected to that outside world.

For example, the unidentified men who kidnapped Adriana Elba Arce off the street in the provincial city of Rosario removed her watch and blindfolded her right after pushing her into a Falcon. Testifying seven years later, she clearly remembered the steps she had taken to orient herself as the car moved through the city: "At that time they were doing a lot of repairs in the city because of the World Cup. . . . After taking a bunch of turns we headed along Ovido Lagos Street, which was under construction. Even with the blindfold it was easy for me to recognize because of the construction, because it was right near where I lived."[65] In a particularly moving account, Guillermo Puerta, a doctor kidnapped from his apartment in Córdoba in October 1976, recalled the liminal sensation of traveling, bound and hooded, in the truck that took him away: "We drove along for a while, though I couldn't tell you exactly how long. During those moments, contradictory thoughts were passing through my mind. I was thinking that I should be trying to keep track of where they were taking me, but on the other hand I was saying goodbye to my life."[66]

Survivors' accounts also emphasized the jarring noises that accompanied the death squad operations: shouts, screams, screeching tires, slamming doors. These intense auditory memories stemmed partly from the theatrical qualities of the attacks themselves. Carlos Rafael López Echague remembered that several cars had been involved in his abduction, and that the members of the task group that kidnapped him had shouted openly in the street. They forced López Echague out of his apartment in the central neighborhood of Barrio Norte and onto the floor of one vehicle. He then heard several other vehicle engines roar to life at the same time, as men shouted to each other to coordinate their next actions: "This was right in the middle of Paraguay Street," he later testified. Like the loud attack that awoke shopkeeper "Elena" on the morning of the coup, the clamorous noises of López Echague's disappearance were clearly intended to provoke awe among onlookers.

Sounds and physical sensations were also intensified because victims spent most of their time hooded or blindfolded—"walled up," according to the junta's twisted lexicon.[67] Adriana Calvo de Laborde, abducted by the task group known as "the gang" in 1977, recalled hearing nothing but the constant sound of cars as she sat on the floor blindfolded during her first day in the Arana detention center: "This all started around 10:00 a.m. All day pretty much the only sounds were of cars coming and going as they added more people to the group of prisoners."[68] Carmen Floriani, a survivor featured in the documentary *Mansión Seré*, reflects on camera about the experience of driving with her captor while blindfolded. Traveling by car with the camera crew across the public park that today occupies the grounds of the former detention center, she observes: "Notice every movement we can feel now in the car. At that moment, with the blindfold on, it all felt so much bigger, every bump we're feeling now. We took so many turns, I didn't know if we were way out in the countryside. . . . Closing my eyes, . . . I can remember the magnitude of it all."[69]

Prisoners often moved through several clandestine centers before their murder or release, partly because the security forces struggled to oversee such a broad network of sites. Many of the earliest and most rudimentary centers were abandoned in 1977 and 1978, their prisoners transferred to more permanent locations.[70] Some were moved from the clandestine realm into the regular prison system, but "transfers" were usually more deadly. Jorge Federico Watts, survivor of the Vesubio detention center, observed that "this idea of the transfer was often synonymous with death. . . . Most of the transfers that happened . . . no one came out alive. They came to get them, driving Falcon automobiles. Sometimes they put them into the trunk, and they took them to the Palomar Air Base and threw them into the river."[71] Calvo de Laborde, who later helped establish the Association of Former Detained and Disappeared Persons (Asociación de Ex Detenidos Desaparecidos), suffered through several car voyages while in detention. Her experiences graphically illustrate how those experiences of car travel intertwined the realms of freedom and disappearance; they also attest to the special horrors faced by pregnant detainees.

In her 1985 testimony at the Trial of the Military Juntas, Calvo de Laborde described the circumstances of her kidnapping in February 1977 from her home in La Plata. A physicist and union activist, the pregnant Laborde was at home with her young son when a group of roughly ten armed men in plain clothes burst into her home.[72] They gave her time to change clothes and grab a pack of cigarettes, and they left the crying boy with neighbors. At first, they told her she would be home in no time. Yet once the car turned the corner, they hooded her with a sweater and pushed her to the floor, holding her down with their feet and threatening to kill her.[73]

Laborde remained disappeared through the rest of her pregnancy, transferred through three detention sites. When she went into labor and asked to be taken to hospital, she was bound and blindfolded and placed in the back seat of a car with another prisoner. As the car sped along, she screamed that was about to give birth, but her assailants refused to help her, saying they were only planning to kill her and the baby anyway. Somehow, she managed to wriggle out of her undergarments and gave birth to her daughter, Teresa, right there. At one point, the driver even got lost and had to stop to ask for directions, with Laborde lying half-naked and the newborn crying on the dirty floor of the back seat.[74] When the car finally stopped, Laborde found herself not at a hospital but at the Banfield Pit (Pozo de Banfield), a secret detention center in the suburbs south of Buenos Aires, where several pregnant prisoners were held and where their babies were taken away and given to military collaborators. Miraculously, she and her daughter remained together and were liberated on April 28, 1977.

Car rides marked the transition back out of the concentration camp system for those who survived. Yet the task groups used the voyage to remind prisoners of the constant surveillance and threats that would continue to haunt them outside. They dragged out the time in the car, driving in circles to re-create the disorientation of the original abduction, and they often followed prisoners for a distance as they traveled back into their ordinary lives. Rubén Fernando Schell recalled just such an experience in his testimony to the Trial of the Military Juntas in 1985.[75] He was imprisoned for four months in the detention center known as the Quilmes Pit (Pozo de Quilmes) in the suburbs south of Buenos Aires. On February 21, 1978, he was strip-searched and blindfolded, then thrown into the back of a car that had music playing. Eventually the car stopped, and the men left Schell face down on the ground, telling him: "You stay like that for half an hour, or we'll blow you away. We've already killed so many people, one more makes no difference to us. Then get up and go home." Schell lost track of time as he lay in the ditch, certain the men were going to shoot him. Eventually he loosened the cloth bindings around his hands and removed his blindfold. "I lay there looking at the stars for a long time," he remembered, and he soon realized he was under the overpass of a busy highway. Twice he passed an orange Ford Falcon parked across the street with two men inside as he searched for a bus stop. Both times the men stared him down and opened the car door so that Schell could see their weapons. Hearing the same music that had been playing during the car ride, Schell "played dumb and just kept walking."

By no means had all members of Argentine society lived the repression to the same degree or in the same ways. Millions of people went about their lives without a direct experience of the unbridled fascism that reigned inside the concentration camps, and large numbers of them either actively or passively supported the military regime.[76] Yet even casual brushes with the Ford Falcon could instantly transform an otherwise normal social situation, indicating that there was widespread, if unspoken, understanding of the car's significance to the broader terror apparatus. Historian David Sheinin describes one such encounter involving boxer Juan Martín "the Whip" Coggi:

> Coggi was fighting in the street in the working-class town of Brandsen for cash before an audience of about three hundred when somebody shouted that a Ford Falcon was coming. Everyone scattered. When I asked him why, Coggi answered that "some assholes went by in a Ford Falcon." Everybody knew that Falcons were what military task force units drove. What happened after that? "Nothing," Coggi replied. "We came back and started the fight again."[77]

FEAR AND LOATHING IN FORD ADVERTISING

Thousands of such direct and indirect encounters contributed to the Falcon's resignification in the late 1970s as an object of state and military power, and Ford's own publicity campaigns reinforced this identity by playing up the brand's close ties to the military and identifying the car with the aggressive nationalist values promoted by the junta. In fact, executives at Ford Argentina showed a surprising lack of discretion in their public embrace of South America's most murderous dictatorship. Juan Courard, the Chilean-born manager who took over as president when US executives were evacuated in 1973, was particularly brazen in this regard. He may have felt emboldened by the strength of the Pinochet dictatorship in his home country, or he may have wanted to exact revenge after suffering guerrilla attacks on his home before the coup. Whatever the specific reason, Courard's words and actions suggest that he shared the junta's triumphalism and belief that state terrorism had successfully brought about an "end of history" that would keep the military in power indefinitely.[78] This was certainly the message of a full-page Ford ad published in *Clarín*, Argentina's biggest daily newspaper, in January 1977. It read: "1976. Argentina finds its way once again. 1977. A new year of trust and hope for all Argentines of good will. Ford Argentina and its personnel commit themselves to the effort to bring about the Nation's great destiny. Once again, Ford gives you more."[79]

When General Motors announced its plans to withdraw from Argentina in August 1977, Courard reasserted his company's commitment to doing business with the junta. In fact, he went out of his way to praise the military leadership for doing away with the government of Isabel Perón two years earlier, recalling the challenges Ford Argentina had faced in the years preceding the coup. Following a well-established pattern, Courard elided the violence of armed guerrilla movements with the legal organizing work of recognized union representatives. "Our own employees suffered persecution at the hands of guerrilla subversives, as did soldiers, union leaders, judges, etc. . . . We stood by as helpless victims in the face of union excesses." He then thanked the military for addressing these problems: "Thanks to the Process of National Reorganization, created to correct the problems that affected our national production and economy, today we live in a state of order and improved discipline."[80] With these public declarations, Courard endorsed the legitimacy of the ruling junta and aligned the Ford brand with the military regime.

Two days later, Courard announced a major expansion plan that would soon double the size of the Pacheco plant. The project was to include a new assembly line and expanded warehousing capacity, as well as the introduction of upgraded machinery. If completed, Courard promised that the new facility would expand Ford's workforce from nine thousand to some fourteen thousand workers, including new hiring in its subsidiaries Transax and Metalúrgica Constitución. He ended his remarks by reasserting the Ford Motor Company's firm commitment to doing business with the junta despite US president Jimmy Carter's recent statements of concern about the local human rights situation: "The company's intention to remain in the country and expand demonstrates that the decisions of the American automobile industry have no connection to Washington's human rights policies."[81]

Ford Argentina's endorsement of the dictatorship continued into the next decade. In 1981, President Courard hosted a groundbreaking ceremony for the promised truck plant at Ford's property in General Pacheco. Guests of honor included Finance Minister José Alfredo Martínez de Hoz, Secretary of Industrial Development Alberto Luis Grimoldi, and Generals Juan Bautista Sasiaiñ and Cristino Nicolaides. General Nicolaides was one of the military's most fervent anticommunists, and General Sasiaiñ had recently been named chief of the federal police. He had just spent three years overseeing clandestine detention centers in the province of Córdoba, including the infamous center known as La Perla, estimated to have held some three thousand prisoners.[82] In his speech, Courard underscored Ford Argentina's active support for the junta:

> Ford Argentina agreed that change was needed. And when those changes touched it directly, the company adapted and got right to work to take full advantage of the new situation. Ford Argentina believed in the Process of National Reorganization because the company saw it as the means to put the country back on the right track. The changes underway at that time demanded first and foremost that we do our own work better and better. That we give more of ourselves, so that our products could offer more. To compete with a head start, not only to be part of the struggle, but to win.[83]

Here was the typical obfuscating language of the dictatorship: a blend of threat and platitude that aligned Ford Argentina's priorities with the military's Process of National Reorganization.[84]

Advertisements for the Falcon sedan more subtly echoed the values espoused by the junta. Argentine popular culture had been glamorizing violence for several years, reflecting what historian Sebastián Carassai has described as "an increasing subconscious acceptance of violence shared by broad sectors of Argentine society" regardless of political affiliation.[85] In the late 1960s and early 1970s, images of firearms and sensational car accidents were used to market products as banal as pantyhose and toothpaste.[86] In fact, in a bizarre prefiguring of later events, Ford Argentina even ran a television ad in the 1960s featuring a fake news story about the inexplicable disappearance of a number of high-level executives—all of them well-to-do owners of Falcon's high-end Futura model. It eventually became clear that each of these supposed "victims" had simply escaped from their families to enjoy the solitary freedoms of the open road.

After the coup, advertisements deepened the Falcon's associations with the conservative nationalism promoted by the junta. Ford launched its most famous advertising campaign in late May 1978, on the eve of the World Cup, coining a new slogan that identified the Falcon as "an Argentine Classic."[87] Here, the company once again aligned itself with official discourse. The junta used Argentina's hosting of the World Cup to whip up nationalist sentiments, denouncing international outcry over human rights violations as "anti-Argentine." That language became more intense after Argentina's national team defeated the Netherlands in the finals. Throughout that year, Ford Argentina and the J. Walter Thompson advertising agency drew on well-established methods to identify the Falcon with the nationalist values espoused by the ruling junta. Print ads depicted the car in a series of iconic tourist landscapes, recalling visual tropes of Argentine identity that dated back to the early twentieth century.[88] No people appeared in these photos. Instead, the Falcon stood alone, as if it were having its picture taken while on vacation. One advertisement showed a Falcon at the waterfront in Mar del Plata, the country's most popular beach resort. Another located the car in the northern village of Purmamarca, whose colonial-style architecture was artfully decorated with a poncho hanging in a doorway: the classic symbol of criollo identity.

Television ads from 1978 identified the Falcon with a host of nationalist clichés: tango, gauchos, football, and horses. One, set on a ranch or estancia, opens with a shot of the estanciero buying a horse from a man dressed in typical gaucho clothing.[89] As he leans on the hood of his Falcon Ranchero station wagon to write a check, strains of tango play in the background. A male narrator provides a running commentary of platitudes in a deep, growling voice: "Each day is a blank page that we go out and write on with everything we've got." The camera then cuts to a ranch hand loading boxes into the back of the car while a young woman looks on, nuzzling a baby chick. "There's so much to do," proclaims the narrator, "and the Ford Falcon is the car we choose to write the story of each day." The next frames show a Falcon driving through a muddy field, a dirt road where a Falcon overtakes an old Model T, a scene of children heading into a rural school, an older couple coming out of a small-town general store, and a Falcon overtaking a pair of racing horses. "Because it's solid, dependable, durable, *gaucho* . . . because it does whatever it takes to defend what we have invested in it. Ford Falcon: it's with us all."[90] The threatening tone was unmistakable, particularly in the context of 1978: a year of aggressive nationalist rhetoric and continuing operations by the grupos de tarea.

Chapter Four

AFTERSHOCKS

For survivors of repression, the Falcon threat remained a palpable sense memory well past the years of the dictatorship. Metalworker and union activist Arnaldo "Lalo" Piñón was secretly detained for a month in the Vesubio detention center with his wife, Cristina, in late 1978. They were then transferred to a regular prison in La Plata, where they remained until May 1979. Years later, Lalo recalled the difficult transition after their release. Even the ordinary colors and movements of daily life could be overwhelming after months in close captivity, including long periods blindfolded. Automotive sounds particularly distressed Cristina, who was suffering deep psychological trauma. "We were both still really on edge," he recalled. "We couldn't handle the sounds of cars braking suddenly, car doors slamming, [sounds that produced] that awful sensation that someone was coming, that they were going to grab you and take you away again. It was a feeling of total uncertainty."[91] The sensory overload so central to the tactic of disappearance resonated for years to come.

In fact, Ford Falcons continued to be used after the end of the dictatorship in all kinds of anonymous intimidation operations because of their clear identification with paramilitary violence and impunity. Such threats were particularly menacing during the tentative early years of democracy under President Raúl Alfonsín, when survivors and family members were being called upon to testify about their experiences while the armed forces repeatedly threatened a new coup. Omar Torres, a former gendarmerie agent, suffered threats after testifying to the CONADEP about his experiences inside the repressive apparatus. Some men began looking for him in his hometown about a month after his testimony. They asked neighbors about his whereabouts when they couldn't locate him. Each day they returned with a different story: they had money to deliver, they needed to reach him about a real estate matter, and so on. Torres later testified at the Trial of the Military Juntas that "on the third day there were three of them, and this time they showed up in a Ford Falcon," adding, "since I knew about the operations followed by the task forces [and] the procedures that they tended to follow, I never went back."[92]

CONCLUSION

From the early 1970s through the early 1980s, the Argentine far right shifted tactics in its fight against those it deemed "subversives." Although the country had a long tradition of authoritarian violence, this period witnessed a decisive turn from methods of overt repression toward covert terror. Working first through paramilitary organizations like the Triple A and then through the dictatorship's task groups, Argentine neofascists sought to annihilate not only the country's leftist insurgents but any individuals who were broadly sympathetic toward Peronism or the Marxist Left. Extrajudicial kidnapping became their primary tactic because it offered the possibility of wiping out an entire generation of activists without provoking a backlash at home and abroad. This method became the cornerstone of a militarized system of automobility that saw passenger cars appropriated to a project of state power. As military authorities promoted more efficient traffic circulation in the capital through their road-building schemes, they enlisted ordinary automobiles as tools of surveillance, propaganda, and state terrorism.

Although they were not the only vehicles used in the disappearances, the unmarked Falcon sedans sold to Argentine security forces became indelibly associated with the work of the task groups. In pragmatic terms, they helped move thousands of political prisoners into the underground realm of the clandestine detention centers, where victims found themselves literally "arrested": trapped, immobilized, cut off from the flow of life. The cars also took on new symbolic meanings as they became associated with the ritualistic and spectacular attacks by the grupos de tarea. They blended in seamlessly with the thousands of other Falcons already on the road, contributing to the overall climate of fear. Philosopher and author José Pablo Feinmann has written eloquently about this uncanny juxtaposition of horror and normality that prevailed during the years of military rule:

> One was aware of the permanent state of horror. Yet the most horrifying thing about heading out into the street was to witness the normal unfolding of daily life. People went to work, they

traveled on buses and taxis; they took the trains, crossed streets, and walked along sidewalks. The sun came out and it was bright, and some autumn days were even warm. . . . I want to underscore this subtle and terrible experience of horror: ordinary daily life concealing the dormant presence of death.[93]

The thousands of death squad operations that occurred between 1974 and 1983 layered new sensory memories and associations onto the Falcon, a car that already had a powerful symbolic place in Argentine culture. Fifteen years of promotional campaigns had identified the car with national ambitions for modernization, progress, and prosperity. Ford had played up the Falcon's unique design qualities compared to most cars in Argentina: its relatively large size, expansive windows, and ample storage space. Both advertisements and the *Familia Falcón* television program had also associated the car with the respectable middle-class values of dependability, family loyalty, and security. Now, however, thousands of Argentine victims and innumerable witnesses had experienced the Falcon in a whole new way: as a tool of state terrorism. Their intense sensory experiences and emotional responses imbued the car with new meanings in the post-dictatorship era, transforming it into an enduring symbol of military impunity and the struggle for justice.

CHAPTER FIVE

Survivors and Citizens

> Why would the army detain a worker . . . or *many* workers? Why would it get involved in these kidnappings and detentions? Someone had to give me an answer, and it had to be credible.
>
> —ARCELIA ORTIZ DE PORTILLO, wife of Ismael Portillo, Ford worker disappeared in April 1976

In mid-April 1976, the wives and mothers of the disappeared Ford union delegates converged on a nondescript police station in the district of Tigre, in the Zona Norte. The mother of Francisco Perrotta, detained on March 26, had received word that the men were being held there, although officials continued to deny it over the next several weeks. The women showed up daily with food and clothing, demanding their family members' release, and gradually they were joined by wives and mothers of workers from other factories in the Zona Norte.[1] Arcelia Ortiz, whose husband, Ismael, had been kidnapped from the Pacheco factory, described the circumstances years later: "We'd go to the police station in a group, and we'd start asking 'Where is your family member from?' At first it was all 'Ford,' 'Ford,' 'Ford,' and then 'Astilleros,' [and then processed-food manufacturer] 'Terrabusi.'" The women were dumbfounded. "Caramba! What is going on?" Arcelia recalled thinking. "What *exactly* is going on?"

Although she was then a young mother barely out of her teens, Arcelia went on to become a fierce and articulate activist in the cause of the Ford workers. She was determined to understand why her husband, a soft-spoken man who worked at the Pacheco factory to support his family but who dreamed of a career as a professional singer, would be targeted so brutally. The questions she wanted answered would take decades to unravel: Why were shop-floor union activists from Argentina's biggest industrial facilities being spirited away by security forces? If these men were legally recognized union stewards, what crime had they committed to warrant such a response from the state? Why were they being kidnapped in secret and not arrested? Finally, what role were the companies playing in this wave of repression and what was their relationship to the military junta? In their long search for answers, Ortiz and the other Ford activists confronted some of Argentina's most powerful and patriarchal institutions: the armed forces and police, the union bureaucracy, the judiciary, and the Ford Motor Company itself.

Other women in the circle of the Ford activists showed similar resolve. Pedro Troiani's wife, Elisa Charlín, went to the Tigre Regional Police Unit (Unidad Regional de Tigre) within days of his disappearance to demand a meeting with Army Lieutenant Colonel Antonio Francisco Molinari, chief of military operations for the area. That encounter, which she described in interviews and judicial testimony years later, gave her some insight into the relationship between Ford management and the security forces: "When I asked him to explain why my husband had been detained, he replied that it was for a routine background check." Molinari's hand was resting on a piece of paper with Ford letterhead that contained a typed list of names. "This is the list they gave me," he told her.[2]

When family members went to the Pacheco industrial facility for answers, Ford management personnel claimed to know nothing about the detained workers, even though roughly half the men had been abducted in front of their supervisors, and the quincho where they were tortured stood in full view of a Ford security post. An employee flanked by armed guards met Eduardo Norberto Pulega's family at the factory fence and told them the company "could not give them any information about what had happened."[3] Instead of assistance, Ford sent telegrams to the men's homes warning that they would lose their jobs if they did not return to work. Charlín sent her own curt message back, stating that Pedro had been "detained inside the factory," but Ford returned it on the grounds that it was "inappropriate."[4] When the women went to SMATA headquarters to ask the union for help, they faced threats and sexual harassment. "The union never gave my wife so much as five cents to buy milk for my kids," Adolfo Sánchez recalled bitterly years later.[5]

The Ford workers had viewed both their employer and the SMATA union as sources of security. They had sought employment at the Pacheco plant because of its promise of high working standards, wages, and benefits that would help them sustain their families, and they had joined the union to help them hold their employer to those standards. Some had taken a leading role in unionization by winning positions on the internal claims committee and negotiating directly with Ford management and their union bosses. Now, however, the men were gone, and their families had lost their sole source of income. When young women like Elisa Charlín and Arcelia Ortiz reached out for help to feed their children and win their husbands' release, powerful men—union bosses, company executives, and military officers—all closed ranks against them. Ortiz could still be moved to tears decades later as she recalled those dark days, beginning with the phone call that informed her of her husband's abduction from the assembly line at Ford: "From that moment on," she told a television crew in 2022, "my life changed forever."[6]

The twenty-four Ford workers who later took Ford to court survived their detention, though they never recovered the security they had once enjoyed as members of Argentina's aristocracy of labor. Instead, their ordeal at the Pacheco plant continued to haunt them as they found themselves blacklisted from other unionized workplaces, abandoned by their union, and subjected to continuing police harassment. Some remained too traumatized to talk about their time in detention, even with close family members. Yet a core group among the men and their relatives reemerged as activists as soon as the military retreated from power in 1983. Over the long years of Argentina's post-transition era, they took advantage of every opportunity to share their stories and fight for justice against the military authorities and corporate executives who had delivered them into the horrific underworld of the terror apparatus.

In their doggedness and creativity, the Ford survivors and their family members also emerged as crucial witnesses to the broader attacks on shop-floor labor organizers that had claimed thousands of working-class lives during the years of military rule. Those experiences did not resonate fully within the dominant human rights discourse of 1980s Argentina, for reasons that will be analyzed below. In fact, it took decades to piece together answers to the tough questions articulated by Arcelia Ortiz in 1976 about the motives behind her husband's disappearance and the identity of those responsible for his detention and torture. That long, arduous effort involved the work of countless allies, near and far: artists who kept up pressure on the Ford brand by repeatedly reminding audiences of the Falcon's dark associations; activists and archivists who painstakingly collected documents and firsthand accounts; lawyers and judges who experimented with new applications of human rights law; and researchers who reconstructed the social, political, and economic structures that underpinned the dictatorship.

Still, a full thirty-five years passed between the return to democracy in 1983 and the historic legal decision in 2018 that found two Ford Argentina executives and one military commander criminally responsible for the Ford workers' disappearances and torture. While that decision marked an important watershed for human rights law in Argentina and abroad, it came tragically late for many of the plaintiffs, who died without seeing the case's resolution. The repeated delays and setbacks along the way attest to the David and Goliath dimension of this struggle that pitted a group of autoworkers and their families against one of the most powerful and iconic corporations of the twentieth century. They also illuminated the broader power structures that shaped Argentine society in the Cold War and post–Cold War eras. As we will see, it was ultimately far easier to convict the generals who had overseen the system of state terrorism than to prove that corporate executives had colluded in attacks on their own workers.

PEN PRISONERS

The Ford workers spent several weeks in secret detention in the Maschwitz and Tigre police precincts before being officially recognized as political prisoners and moved into regular prison facilities in May 1976.[7] Their legal status remained extremely precarious, however. On the day of the coup, the junta had declared a state of siege and suspended individual liberties, assuming the authority to detain citizens indefinitely and without formal charge under the system of executive order, known in Spanish by the acronym PEN (Poder Ejecutivo Nacional).[8] The Ford detainees counted among 3,485 political prisoners detained under the PEN in the first nine months of military rule. For the junta, the PEN provided a veneer of legality to the secretive system of mass disappearance; when pressed by foreign diplomats regarding the human rights situation, they could point to their release of political prisoners as a sign of improvement.[9] In reality, however, PEN prisoners occupied a kind of legal limbo that was not far removed from the conditions of the disappeared. Since they faced no formal charges, they never knew why they had been detained and could do nothing to plead their cases.[10] Many PEN prisoners, including the Ford workers, were moved between secret and official detention facilities.

As reported later in Argentina's *Nunca Más* report, a detainee's official designation as political prisoner often came days or even weeks after their initial detention. In the intervening period, they, like the men from Ford, remained "disappeared" inside secret detention facilities, and authorities made no effort to account for these discrepancies.[11] Even more ominously, some prisoners suffered the opposite trajectory: after a period of official detention under the PEN, they were released from prison in the middle of the night only to be murdered or kidnapped on the outside.[12]

Although the Ford workers could receive visitors under the PEN system, prison conditions were appalling and family members were subjected to humiliating physical and sexual abuse.[13] Inside, the men were grouped with workers from other industrial plants, suggesting that they were categorized at a similar risk level, though they received no official explanation of why they were being detained or when they might be released. The only clue came when Pedro Troiani heard there might be an opportunity to go into exile. When he communicated his wish to apply for exile to Italy, the warden at the La Plata prison scoffed and told him he didn't need to leave the country because he "wasn't dangerous" and would be free within a year. "Not dangerous?!" Pedro remembered thinking. "Then what the hell am I doing in here suffering like this?"[14] Though the warden refused to say more, his prediction turned out to be true. Like roughly four thousand other PEN prisoners detained between 1976 and 1983, the twenty-four shop stewards who would go on to challenge Ford Argentina in court were released within a year of their abductions.[15]

As typical for prisoners held under the PEN system, the Ford workers never received any explanation for their detentions or for the timing or reasons behind their release. However, a major investigation in 2015 into workplace repression during military rule posited that the timing had to do with legal changes to the labor code that made it easier for employers to rid themselves of unwanted workers.[16] Declassified police intelligence records reveal that Ford Argentina's management repeatedly lobbied the junta for changes to the labor code along these lines. Two weeks after the coup, Ford executives urged the generals to overturn the existing Labor Contract Law and implement "measures and/or legislation to help management get rid of personnel whose attitude or conduct was deemed harmful."[17] Three days later, another police report communicated that Ford was looking for "a vote of confidence" from the military authorities "to help employers carry out whatever dismissals they deem necessary."[18]

A report from early May 1976 noted that some four hundred workers had been fired from the Pacheco plant, including "not only activists and labor agitators . . . but also those who demonstrated a poor work ethic or took advantage of medical leaves."[19] It added that the company had followed prevailing labor laws in these dismissals, which were deemed a success: production rates had already shown some improvement and absenteeism had dropped. In mid-May, Ford laid off more than four thousand workers for two weeks because of a collapse in vehicle sales. The company also obtained special permission from the junta to break normal contract conditions regarding vacation time so that they could order the whole workforce to take their annual four weeks of vacation simultaneously. This measure allowed them to shut down the factory until late June to ride out the economic crisis without imposing long-term layoffs that could provoke workplace unrest.

Ford management kept pressuring the military authorities to dismantle long-standing labor protections, particularly pertaining to job security and severance pay. The Argentine labor movement had fought hard over the decades to defend workers from arbitrary dismissal; even the big union bosses had staked their leadership on their ability to protect their members' jobs. Such protections had been strengthened by legislation passed during Juan Perón's last brief presidential term in the early 1970s, which prevented Ford Argentina from imposing a mass layoff during the downturn of 1975 because of the high cost of severance payouts required under Argentine law.[20] These stringent job security protections undercut the main strategy used by automakers to weather fluctuations in demand for their vehicles: mass temporary layoffs, which were common in auto plants around the world. Argentina's strong labor laws also weakened management's power to rid themselves of workers they deemed "troublemakers."

In September 1976, the junta imposed a new "industrial security" code, which included a provision governing workers held as political prisoners under executive order. It allowed businesses to suspend the contracts of workers detained under the PEN. Employers would be required to keep those jobs open for three months, after which time the positions could be terminated, with the affected workers losing all rights to severance pay.[21] In November 1976, the junta finally completed its rewriting of Argentina's labor laws, replacing the old Law of Professional Associations with a new union law that, in the words of historian Victoria Basualdo, "undercut the institutional and economic foundations of the labor movement."[22] Then, in the middle of December, precisely three months after the passing of the junta's industrial security law, Ford management sent out final dismissal telegrams to the homes of the union delegates who were still imprisoned under the PEN system. They announced that the men's contracts had been terminated and that, according to law, they had no right to severance compensation. In other words, Ford applied the terms of the industrial security law retroactively, since the men's detentions had occurred months before the law's implementation.[23]

LIVING IN LIMBO

In early 1977, the Ford workers began to emerge from prison. Adolfo Sánchez later observed that he was afraid to leave because he was certain he would be murdered on the outside, but he was among the first men discharged in January 1977, along with Pastor José Murúa and Juan Carlos Ballesteros.[24] They were released from the La Plata prison in the evening, left to make their way back to Buenos Aires by train. Soldiers stopped them at the Retiro railway station in the capital and almost detained them again because they had no identification documents, and Sánchez was so terrified that he stayed hidden inside his house for a week.[25] In the following months, more Ford workers were turned out of prison individually or in small groups without explanation or notification to their families. By April 1977, only two of the men remained behind bars: Carlos Propato and Ismael Portillo.

It was in this context that Portillo's wife, Arcelia Ortiz, saw the same Ford blacklist that Elisa Charlín had glimpsed at her meeting with Lieutenant Colonel Molinari in April 1976. Ortiz had become Molinari's "shadow" that year, visiting him repeatedly inside the Campo de Mayo military base. Little did she know at the time that the massive complex housed four separate clandestine detention centers and a secret maternity ward where pregnant detainees delivered their babies, only to have them taken away.[26] As Ortiz later recounted in press interviews and judicial testimony, Molinari tried to defend his honor at this last meeting. He pulled the same list of names on Ford letterhead out of a drawer, saying, "Do you think I went and picked up your husband because of his pretty face, his name, or his good looks? No. The list was given to me by the company."[27] The names of all the released Ford detainees had been crossed off, with only Portillo's and Propato's remaining. Thankfully, Portillo made it home soon afterward, although his unannounced arrival in the middle of the night terrified Ortiz, since she believed that assailants had come to take her away as well.[28]

When the Ford union delegates finally left prison in 1977, they emerged into an utterly changed economy. In the year since their detention, the ruling junta had moved quickly to dismantle three decades of government supports for industrial development and impose a new economic model based on financial deregulation and sharp cuts to public spending. Like General Augusto Pinochet in neighboring Chile, they had used violent repression, censorship, and a ban on unions and political parties to enforce economic policies that would have been hotly contested by civil society under normal circumstances.[29] Those measures produced a "phenomenal" upward transfer of wealth, gaping social inequality, and the quadrupling of Argentina's external debt by 1983.[30]

The man appointed to oversee these economic shock policies was José Alfredo Martínez de Hoz, CEO of the Acindar steelworks, where security forces had launched a massive assault against grassroots labor activists a year before the military coup. An Oxford graduate with strong ties to international banks and friendships with David Rockefeller and Margaret Thatcher, Martínez de Hoz wielded enormous power over economic policy in Argentina for the next five years. He moved swiftly to dismantle the developmentalist project that had been the mainstay of economic policy since Arturo Frondizi's presidency in the late 1950s.[31] Developmentalism had been founded upon the ideal that workers and industrialists could collaborate in the forging of a modern industrial consumer economy under the guidance of enlightened policy makers. The junta's new finance minister aimed instead to remove state interference and "liberate" the economy's "productive forces."[32] International lending agencies and private banks rewarded this policy shift with massive loans, beginning with an International Monetary Fund award of special drawing rights to Argentina worth over $100 million: the biggest loan the institution had ever made to a Latin American country.[33] Private banks such as Lloyds, Citibank, Chase Manhattan, and the Bank of Montreal also rushed to do business with the military regime, even after US president Jimmy Carter and some European governments withheld loans to pressure the junta to improve the human rights situation.[34]

The new free-market policies drove thousands of smaller industrial firms into bankruptcy and cut deeply into the incomes of those who depended on wage work. Martínez de Hoz froze salaries in 1976 when inflation was running at an annual rate of 1,000 percent, causing a 40 percent collapse in real wages during the military's first year in power.[35] In 1978, he removed tariff barriers that had protected local industries, opening the country up to cheaper imports. As thousands of smaller companies went bankrupt, industrial employment fell steadily between 1976 and 1982, with the economy shedding more than a third of its factory jobs.[36] Eduardo Basualdo, one of Argentina's most respected economists, has characterized these policies as an exercise in "class retaliation" that wiped out the gains made by organized labor over several decades and led to an "unprecedented" and enduring pattern of wealth inequality.[37]

Left-wing journalist Rodolfo Walsh was one of the first people to articulate the links between the junta's physical and economic violence, though his words did not find a broad audience in Argentina until many years later. A seasoned investigative reporter who had joined the Montonero guerrilla movement in the early 1970s, Walsh went underground after the coup. He operated a volunteer-run clandestine news agency, Agencia de Noticias Clandestinas (ANCLA), which pieced together stories of the miseries faced by ordinary people under military rule, circulating them to embassies and foreign journalists.[38] Walsh's years of experience writing about Argentine labor and politics, his underground connections, and his internal exile out in the suburbs of Gran Buenos Aires gave him a unique perspective on the changes wrought by the dictatorship.[39]

On March 24, 1977, the first anniversary of the coup, Walsh penned his "Letter from a Writer to the Military Junta," which condemned the suffering inflicted on Argentina's civilian population during the first year of military rule. After enumerating the scale of the disappearances and denouncing the task groups' torture methods, Walsh turned his fury to the junta's economic restructuring. "You only have to walk around greater Buenos Aires for a few hours," he noted, "to check the speed with which such a policy transforms the city into a 'shantytown' of ten million people."[40] Walsh's blistering words showed a keen understanding of what was happening to workers in the industrial belt surrounding the capital:

> Freezing wages with rifle butts while prices rise at bayonet point, abolishing all forms of collective bargaining, prohibiting assemblies and internal commissions, extending working days, raising unemployment to a record 9 percent, promising greater heights with 300,000 layoffs, have taken the relations of production

back to the beginning of the industrial era; and when workers complain they are branded "subversives," with entire union delegations kidnapped, some of whom reappear as corpses, the others disappeared.[41]

Walsh was gunned down the following day when he traveled into the capital to post multiple copies of his letter.[42] His wife, Lilia, escaped to Mexico in July 1978, where a version of the letter was published in a magazine run by the Montonero leadership in exile. Significantly, though, the publication edited out Walsh's economic analysis, featuring only his denunciation of attacks on guerrilla forces.[43] As we shall see, this erasure of the political economy of state terrorism and, by extension, of the specific working-class experience of the dictatorship era, would be repeated for years to come. The Ford survivors and activists eventually helped to bring those experiences into public consciousness.

At the time of their release in 1977, though, the men found themselves utterly isolated: blacklisted from their old jobs, abandoned by their union, and shunned by acquaintances who were terrified to associate with them or suspicious that they had collaborated with security forces to win their release.[44] They also suffered police harassment and surveillance through the end of military rule. Because they were officially under probationary release, they had to check in at the local police station once a month and request permission if they wanted to leave the city for any reason.[45] Police fueled suspicions among their acquaintances by showing up at their homes periodically and questioning their neighbors about their activities. Many of the men lost touch with one another as they struggled to support their families and manage their emotional trauma and fear. One Ford worker, Carlos Gareis, kept silent about his ordeal in detention for thirty-five years, even with his wife and children. He never found solid unionized employment again; at his lowest point, he was reduced to peddling socks on the street.[46]

The men who had been expelled so violently from the Pacheco factory faced multiple challenges in the new economy. Not only were wages low and industrial jobs scarcer than before but security forces monitored workplaces to keep out anyone with a history of labor activism. For example, when Pedro Troiani went to look for a job at the Mercedes-Benz factory after his release, he quickly realized he was on a no-hire list. He eventually found employment in a large body shop, where he worked hard and avoided trouble.

Eight months later, though, his foreman announced that he had been tipped off about Troiani's union activism and imprisonment, warning him to stay away from the other workers. Troiani quit ten days later.[47] "You can imagine what it meant to finally collect a paycheck every two weeks," he later told an interviewer, "but I was just too anxious. It just messed with my head too much."[48] Similarly, Adolfo Sánchez could only find work as an apprentice bricklayer after his release. After doing overtime shifts at Ford to save up for a car and materials to build a family home, he spent three years doing this precarious work normally associated with residents of the Zona Norte's villas miserias. Sánchez later described this period as "three more years of the same torture" he had experienced in detention. "It was like we had a red cross on our backs," he later recalled. "When you went to ask about a job, as soon as you said you had worked at Ford, no one called you back."[49]

PEACE, BREAD, AND WORK

The military's grip on power began showing signs of stress in 1981 as the new economic system unraveled. Along with his rollback of union rights and working-class wages, Martínez de Hoz had ushered in drastic financial deregulation and artificially raised interest rates to attract foreign investment. The overvalued peso had introduced an era of easy money (*plata dulce*), when well-to-do consumers could afford to travel abroad on shopping sprees and major investors could earn fabulous returns through financial speculation. Argentina's leading corporations—both national conglomerates and multinational firms like Ford—earned huge profits during the military years by borrowing large sums from foreign banks at low interest rates and then buying up local bonds and securities. Rather than reinvest in machinery or production innovations, they simply pocketed the difference between local and international interest rates.[50] They then took advantage of the new financial deregulation to funnel 90 percent of those profits back out of the country to more secure banks in North America and Europe.

The recession of 1981 forced Martínez de Hoz and his main military ally, General Jorge Videla, to resign, with General Roberto Viola taking over as head of state. Its most severe impacts were felt in the industrial zones around the capital, where massive job losses pushed families into poverty and food insecurity. Gran Buenos Aires had already taken the brunt of the repression between 1976 and 1979; now the population suffered the devastating impacts of unemployment and hunger.[51] A wave of grassroots antipoverty organizing and popular unrest through the latter part of 1981 and 1982 challenged the military's hold on power. Priests set up soup kitchens (*ollas populares*), unemployed workers held rallies and marches, union activists revived their organizations, and poor people seized land collectively to demand decent housing.[52] On March 30, 1982, progressive union activists called a general strike, inviting both workers and the unemployed to amass in the Plaza de Mayo in front of the presidential palace under the banner Peace, Bread, and Work. When columns of protesters flooded into downtown Buenos Aires chanting slogans against the regime, they found the plaza blockaded by patrol cars, armored vehicles, water cannons, and mounted police. The resulting pandemonium ended with over three thousand arrests.[53]

Faced with such opposition, Argentina's armed forces tried to rally the nation behind a patriotic cause by launching a reckless invasion of the British-controlled Falkland Islands, known as the Islas Malvinas in Argentina. Instead, within just a few weeks they suffered a humiliating defeat by the British navy, and the armed forces' image was further tarnished when conscripts returned to the mainland with stories of abuse suffered at the hands of their own commanding officers. Civil society groups seized on this moment of weakness to pressure the generals to call elections and step aside, which created a unique political opening in Argentina. In every other Latin American country that emerged from military rule in the 1980s and 1990s, exiting military officials were able to manage a "pacted" transition that protected them from prosecution.[54] In Argentina, however, the discredited military forces soon faced a reconstituted civil society that demanded human rights investigations and trials.

The last ruling junta did take steps to protect themselves and their closest allies as they saw that they were losing power. One of their most controversial moves directly enriched the country's largest corporations, including Ford Argentina, and hobbled the new democratic government's ability to address the population's economic and social needs. On November 17, 1982, the military government passed a decree that absorbed over US$14.5 billion of corporate debt into the state, passing the burden of repayment on to Argentine citizens. As noted above, most of that money had been gambled in the currency exchange market, with profits spirited out of the country. By the time the generals relinquished power, major corporations had been absolved of their obligations, and the newly democratic Argentine state found itself owing an unprecedented $45 billion to creditors.[55]

The junta leaders also tried to shield themselves from future prosecution by destroying evidence. On April 28, 1983, General Reynaldo Bignone ordered the destruction of all documents relating to political prisoners who had been detained under the PEN system.[56] The military thus erased an archive that might have clarified the urgent questions plaguing the Ford union activists about why they had been targeted and who had ordered their release. Finally, on September 23, just a month before the scheduled democratic elections, the generals passed a self-amnesty law, called the Law of National Pacification, which justified the military takeover and declared the actions taken during the "counter-subversive struggle" to be immune from legal prosecution.[57]

THE FALCON REIMAGINED

In October 1983, Argentines voted in national elections for the first time in a decade, giving a strong mandate to lawyer and Radical Party politician Raúl Alfonsín. Alfonsín ran an optimistic campaign that promised to address demands for human rights investigations, democratic reform, and improved social welfare. He even won over many traditional Peronist supporters in Gran Buenos Aires with his talk of pensions, food relief, and full employment: measures to restore the economic security that had been decimated during the dictatorship.[58] It was a time of great uncertainty because the entire security apparatus remained intact, including the fearsome Buenos Aires provincial police, who had done much of the junta's dirty work in Gran Buenos Aires. Still, popular expectations ran high as censorship was lifted, exiles began returning to the country, and people of many different backgrounds—human rights activists, lawyers, artists, grassroots organizers, and ordinary citizens—all articulated their vision of a more just society. This sense of possibility brought an explosion of creative expression in the early 1980s as artists working in a variety of media sought to represent the recent trauma of state terrorism and the hopes of a new generation.[59] The Ford Falcon quickly emerged as a common trope within this protest art, since its identification with the dictatorship's task group operations made it an instantly recognizable metonym for the entire state terror apparatus. It continued to be reimagined and reinvented by artists over the years as Argentine society grappled with the long-term legacies of military rule.

The first artist to feature the Falcon was a young singer named Pipo Cipolatti, who was part of a new wave of *rock argentino* that emerged in the last years of military rule. Influenced by ska, punk, and rockabilly sounds from abroad, the young musicians who started jamming in the early 1980s rejected the Latin American political music of the pre-dictatorship era, with its folk stylings and earnest lyrics. Instead, they produced upbeat tunes that used satire to address the social and political issues of their day. They also became experts at dodging arrest when they performed in underground clubs and public spaces. Cipolatti, son of a clerk in the federal police, even carried around a copy of the police training manual as a prop to fend off harassment.[60] His 1982 song "Pensé que se trataba de cieguitos" ("I Thought They Were Blind Guys"), composed when the military was still in power, audaciously satirized this climate of police intimidation. Opening with a driving snare beat and the sound of a siren, it describes an encounter with a group of six men wearing dark glasses who "invite" the singer to get into a green Falcon. They then "politely" ask him to stay with them for several days after a "brief interrogation" that lasts more than four hours. In the last verse they release him, but not before assuring him repeatedly that they will see him again. The disjuncture between this horrifying scenario and the catchy, danceable music struck a chord with young audiences. It became a huge hit for Cipolatti's rockabilly band, Los Twist, and one of the most influential recordings of the early democratic era.

Another early work that shaped the Falcon's post-dictatorship identity was a short film entitled *Ford Falcon, buen estado* (*Ford Falcon in Good Shape*) by director José González Asturias. Screened in 1985 at the General San Martín Cultural Center, one of the capital's most dynamic cultural spaces, the nineteen-minute film made a deep impression on the audience by presenting a condensed version of the car's recent transformation from coveted consumer good to terrifying tool of repression.[61] The film also circulated widely to new audiences over the years, first as part of playwright Néstor Sabatini's stage production *De esto ni una palabra a nadie* (*Not a Word about This to Anyone*) and later as a regular screening on public television to mark commemorative dates such as the anniversary of the 1976 military coup.[62] Like Cipolatti's enduring hit, the film thus served to keep alive a public consciousness of the Falcon's close associations with the dictatorship era's death squad attacks.

The film opens with a dark parody of the middlebrow desires that underpinned Argentina's car culture. Its protagonist fits an archetype well known to Argentine audiences and regularly caricatured in the works of celebrated cartoonist Quino: the modestly paid "everyman" who works in a nondescript office and lives out a dull and anonymous existence in the big city. In the opening scene, he discovers a classified ad for a Falcon sedan "in good shape" at a price that is too good to be true. Thrilled by the possibility of owning such a coveted car, the man sets up a meeting with the seller. The model for sale turns out to be a dull-green Falcon bearing one of the dictatorship's propaganda stickers reading "Los argentinos somos derechos y humanos": a quintessential death squad vehicle. The nervous seller is clearly anxious to seal the transaction, and the buyer soon drives away happily.

The new Falcon owner heads home to take his family on their first driving picnic. They marvel at the car's size and comfort, filling the spacious trunk with toys and baskets of food, just like in the early Falcon ads of the 1960s. At the park, however, the car begins to behave strangely: the trunk nearly snaps shut on the young daughter's hand, and later the vehicle lurches at her for no apparent reason. At first the family shrug off these incidents, thrilled to enjoy the comforts associated with car ownership. The next morning, however, the father finds his new Falcon parked about a hundred feet from where he had left it the night before. He becomes increasingly obsessed as he finds it farther from his front door each morning. His family relationships soon deteriorate, and his wife becomes alarmed by other strange occurrences, such as the unexplained disappearance of two young neighbors from across the street.

The protagonist asks a friend to help him stake out his vehicle at night, assuming that joy riders have been using the car. Instead, the two men are shocked to see the Falcon roar to life of its own accord and pull away driverless. They follow it for a long way, heading off the road and into a deserted area, where the Falcon's doors suddenly fly open. The trunk rises, and sounds of shouting and gunfire ring out even though no one can be seen: "Come on, hurry up! Grab him! Get the machine gun. Come on, you son of a bitch. Blow him away!" The invisible victim cries out but is quickly silenced by multiple gunshots. The car's trunk closes, the doors shut calmly, and the Falcon pulls away again into the shadows. When the men find it parked once again near the protagonist's home, they decide not to tell anyone what they have witnessed. The film's closing scene shows the shaken Falcon owner at the newspaper office, putting in his own classified ad for a "Ford Falcon in good shape."[63]

Chapter Five

Ford Falcon, buen estado compresses the Falcon's recent history into just a few minutes with its simple yet powerful premise. It juxtaposes the light fantasy of middle-class car ownership presented in *La familia Falcón* with the car's more recent incarnation as an instrument of state violence. González Asturias's film did not shock its audience with information they did not already possess. Rather, it drew on raw sensory details, condensing the sounds of car doors, screeching tires, and gunfire into an archetypal horror story. In the space of the cinema, audiences could share in the reenactment of a situation many of them had read about, privately witnessed, or even experienced directly. The entire film is infused with an atmosphere of the uncanny, just like an episode from *The Twilight Zone*, which was popular in Argentina. Like the American series, it intertwines light and dark, illuminating how an undercurrent of Cold War violence and fear could suddenly cut through the banal routines of middle-class life.[64]

SURVIVORS AND CITIZENS

While the Falcon could be deployed by artists in the early 1980s because of its broad recognition as a symbol of state terrorism, the Argentine public still knew virtually nothing about the attacks on shop-floor workers like the men at Ford's Pacheco plant. In fact, even human rights activists in downtown Buenos Aires were still largely unaware of the dictatorship's assaults against industrial sites and working-class neighborhoods in Gran Buenos Aires. Yet as soon as the political system showed signs of opening, a small group among the Ford survivors used every means at their disposal to share their stories with authorities and petition for justice. In doing so, they became participants in a remarkable wave of grassroots activism that human rights scholar Kathryn Sikkink has dubbed "the discovery of law": a process by which ordinary Argentines came to view the legal system as a forum where they might "hold the most powerful former leaders of their country accountable for past violations."[65] This "discovery" was by no means straightforward for the Ford survivors, however, who struggled against a recalcitrant judicial system and numerous obstacles in their search for justice.

Argentina's historic advances in human rights prosecutions have been well documented by Sikkink and others.[66] As soon as he took office in December 1983, President Alfonsín founded the world's first truth commission:

the National Commission on the Disappearance of Persons (CONADEP). The commission's final report, entitled *Nunca Más* (Never Again), became an instant bestseller, and its revelations of extrajudicial kidnappings and torture stoked public demands for criminal prosecutions.[67] Then, in 1985, Argentina became one of the first countries in history to use its own domestic laws to prosecute military leaders for human rights crimes.[68] The televised "Trial of the Military Juntas" ran for several months that year, culminating in the December 1985 conviction of former junta leaders Generals Jorge Videla, Roberto Viola, and Orlando Agosti, and Admirals Emilio Massera and Armando Lambuschini for crimes against humanity. It was an extraordinary assertion of the rule of law, coming just two years after the armed forces had relinquished power. For now, however, these historic investigations touched only the military chain of command and not the civilian actors—politicians, church and union leaders, or business elites—who might have collaborated in the repression. The issue of civilian complicity did not reach the courts for another two decades, leaving survivors of workplace repression like the men from Ford with many unanswered questions.

Still, the Ford workers lost no time in their search for justice, and in the process, they articulated their own sense of their rights as workers and citizens in the new democratic era. They first reached out directly to president-elect Alfonsín. Just days after the election in October 1983, Juan Carlos Amoroso, a former tool and die maker at Ford, contacted his old friend Pedro Troiani to tell him that Alfonsín was staying in a house nearby. Amoroso had been forced to work as an independent artisan after his release from prison, selling bronze equestrian fittings to wealthy clients including some in the exclusive neighborhood of La Horqueta, not far from Troiani's home. One of those clients had lent Alfonsín his home as a base of operations to prepare for his assumption of power. Amoroso proposed to Troiani that they write to the incoming president to ask him for help on behalf of the Ford survivors.[69]

With this gesture, the two men joined thousands of other ordinary Argentines who wrote to Alfonsín during his term in office. Historian Jennifer Adair, who has analyzed this correspondence, defines this spontaneous form of citizen expression as a "political act" through which ordinary people articulated an "evolving moral economy of democracy, which positioned individuals as both participants in and architects of constitutional return."[70] Troiani and Amoroso must have counted among the first to write. In their letter, they took pains to identify themselves as regular union organizers who had never been mixed up in "politics," by which they meant armed revolutionary movements. They asked the president to investigate the violence they had endured and to help them recover the economic security they had lost when they were dismissed from Ford without compensation. The men even delivered the letter personally with the help of neighbors who let them into a backyard adjoining the property where Alfonsín was staying. Although Troiani and Amoroso alarmed the bodyguards when they called out to Alfonsín over the fence, they were eventually allowed to pass on their missive.

When the new government took office in December, Troiani, Adolfo Sánchez, and Carlos Alberto Propato visited the Interior Ministry offices in downtown Buenos Aires to request information relating to their arrests. The files showed that they had been identified as "presumed" members of the "Montonero paramilitary organization."[71] This tactic of painting regular union activists as armed militants had been so common that one former political prisoner claimed that the military had even coined the verb *"montonerizar"*: to transform a workplace organizer into a Montonero guerrilla fighter in order to facilitate their disappearance.[72] While this information gave the Ford workers some clues about how the security forces had justified their detentions, it did not tell them who had branded them as terrorists or why their lives had ultimately been spared. Since the final junta had destroyed the archives relating to PEN detentions, no available records could answer those disturbing questions.

President Alfonsín moved quickly after taking office on December 10 to overturn the military's self-amnesty law and respond to public demands for investigations. After much internal party debate, and despite criticism from leading human rights organizations, the president decided against launching a congressional investigation into the junta's crimes. Instead, he appointed a group of respected public figures to the newly formed CONADEP, which would operate at arm's length from the state. The commission's mandate was almost impossibly restricted, however. It was to investigate only cases of disappearance, leaving aside other forms of military abuse, and it was given only six months to develop a research methodology, collect evidence, and prepare a final report.[73]

When the CONADEP called on Argentine citizens to come forward with their stories in January 1984, Troiani and his wife, Elisa Charlín, combed through the phone book to track down other Ford survivors and convince them to testify.[74] In the end, four men—Adolfo Sánchez, Pastor

José Murúa, Francisco Perrotta, and Juan Carlos Amoroso—accompanied Troiani to the commission offices, which occupied the upper floors of the General San Martín Cultural Center in downtown Buenos Aires. The small group counted among the roughly 1,200 survivors of disappearance who broke their isolation to testify to the CONADEP that year, coming forward to share stories of torture and abuse that they had been holding onto for several years. Prior to this moment, human rights groups had collected only seventy such testimonials.[75] Those who had passed through the detention system existed in a delicate limbo in these early years, when human rights activism was focused on recovering prisoners who remained disappeared. No organization yet existed to represent survivors, and some who had shared their stories of detention publicly had even faced attacks and suspicion as possible military collaborators.[76]

Understandably, then, Troiani and the other men were uneasy about the risks they were taking. A climate of fear surrounded the commission's work, and both members and witnesses received anonymous threats.[77] The men stood in the lobby of the Cultural Center debating whether to take the elevator upstairs. "We didn't know if we'd come out again once we went inside," Troiani explained years later.[78] Then, by chance, commission president Ernesto Sábato, one of Argentina's most respected intellectuals, approached them on his way upstairs. The men stood nervously in silence until Sábato asked them about themselves and offered to accompany them upstairs to the offices where they could give their testimony. Without that chance encounter, Troiani and the others might have turned around and gone home.

That meeting with the Ford workers likely made an impression on Sábato as well, because he later remarked on his surprise at discovering the scale of attacks on shop-floor union activists through his work with the commission. In a 1985 interview, Sábato observed that he and the other commission members, who all hailed from the educated middle classes, had expected most victims of disappearance to be student activists. Instead, after analyzing more than fifty-two thousand pages of evidence, they concluded that "the highest percentage of disappeared were workers. Union activists."[79] In fact, CONADEP members chose to highlight the Ford disappearances in their final report, describing events at the Pacheco plant as "one of the emblematic cases" of attacks against union delegates, who accounted for 30.2 percent of the 8,961 cases of detention and disappearance they had documented.[80] They noted that the timing of such attacks during the first weeks of military rule demonstrated that organized labor had ranked among the military's top priorities, citing the junta's stated mission to "neutralize situations of workplace conflict, whether provoked or exploited by subversive forces, to prevent mass agitation and insurrection and contribute to the efficient functioning" of the economy.[81] They also argued that military officials had deliberately used a vague definition of workplace "subversives" to give themselves license to target "any group or individual."[82]

The section dedicated to the events at Ford quoted extensively from the men's testimony, beginning with Adolfo Sánchez's description of the meeting when Ford labor relations manager Guillermo Galarraga had threatened the members of the internal claims committee with a cryptic reference to "his friend Camps."[83] Sánchez had explained to interviewers that he "did not understand who [Galarraga] was talking about until the day of his detention." The report then cited corroborating testimony from Pastor José Murúa and Juan Carlos Amoroso, quoting the latter at length: "[At] that meeting," Amoroso had testified, "Mr. Galarraga read from a paper that he said had been passed on by a colonel, though he wouldn't give his name. It exhorted the workers to get back to their jobs and forget about any [union] demands, because the problems were now over." Amoroso went on to explain how Galarraga had suddenly called an end to the meeting and "extended his hand to me, saying 'Amoroso, pass on my regards to Camps,' which made Mr. Marcos [the stamping plant manager] burst out laughing." When asked for clarification about the identity of Camps, "[Galarraga] had responded 'You'll find out soon enough,' and walked away laughing with Marcos." Amoroso also described how a "Mr. Herrero," from Ford Argentina's labor relations office, used the same mocking tone as he shouted after the members of the internal claims committee: "The ball is in our court now!"[84] Quotations drawn from Pedro Troiani's testimony provided more evidence that Ford managers had been directly involved in the disappearances: "We became aware of the first detentions from the plant the day after the coup. When we inquired about the abuse of authority being committed against those workers, the plant manager [Pedro Müller] told us to stay calm because they were prepared to take anybody away." Troiani also described how a Mr. Fernandez, who had worked in the plant's labor relations office and who was by then deceased, had confirmed privately to his wife, Elisa Charlín, "that the company had been a direct participant" in the detentions.[85]

Ernesto Sábato presented the *Nunca Más* report to President Alfonsín on September 20, 1984, and its first published run of forty thousand copies sold out in just two days in November of that year.[86] By all accounts, it marked a historic achievement for a fledgling democratic government in the immediate aftermath of such a brutal period of military rule. The commission's methodical approach to data collection and dispassionate tone cut through the lies propagated by the junta leaders: claims that the so-called disappeared had left the country or abandoned their families, or that abuses had been committed only by rogue soldiers. By juxtaposing so many individual stories and meticulously cataloguing the military's network of clandestine detention centers, *Nunca Más* made it clear that the disappearances had been part of a comprehensive plan organized through the chain of command. In fact, the Ford survivors cited the CONADEP report in later years to back up their stories and underscore the military's widespread attacks on organized labor. *Nunca Más* gave them a public voice for the first time by quoting their words verbatim, and its enormous success in publishing terms meant that those words would be read by thousands of people around the world.[87]

At the same time, though, the CONADEP report paradoxically closed off discussion of the questions that most haunted the Ford men and their families: questions about who was behind their detentions and why they had been abducted in the first place. One reason had to do with the intense political and time pressures surrounding the commission's work. With their tight six-month deadline, commissioners adopted the interviewing and cataloguing methodology employed by one of Argentina's first human rights groups, the Permanent Assembly for Human Rights (APDH). The APDH had, in turn, modeled its work on methods developed by international human rights organizations like the Inter-American Commission on Human Rights, the United Nations, and Amnesty International, which had all been undertaking on-site human rights investigations since the early 1970s.[88]

In defending individual human rights, these international institutions had chosen to promote an apolitical humanitarian discourse that sidestepped the Cold War era's polarizing binaries. For instance, Amnesty International adopted an individualistic approach to the problem of political violence by focusing on the basic humanity of victims it defined as "prisoners of conscience" rather than denouncing underlying political causes. Although this approach won the release of many prisoners, it also had political costs, since Amnesty's systems of documentation and reporting extracted those individuals from the political and historical circumstances that had led to their persecution in the first place. In following Amnesty's methods, the CONADEP also chose to identify individual victims using "neutral" categories such as age, occupation, address, and family ties, deliberately leaving out their affiliations with political movements or labor unions. Witnesses like the men from Ford were urged to stick to *"objective facts"* in their interviews regarding their kidnappings and detention and to "avoid personal or subjective interpretations" of the circumstances surrounding their detentions.[89]

This approach kept the CONADEP's focus squarely on the workings of the terror apparatus, which proved to be extremely effective for the immediate moral and legal battle that civil society groups waged against the junta. However, it provided little space for witnesses to contextualize their experiences. It was particularly limiting for working-class survivors like the men from Ford, who sought to understand what role their own union leaders and bosses had played in their abductions. Indeed, the focus on individual victims obscured the collective experiences of political violence that had affected many residents of Gran Buenos Aires. An example from the district of La Matanza, located in the province of Buenos Aires just west of the capital, illustrates this point. In March 1978, physician and community activist Norberto Liwski was caught up in a police raid on a solidarity mass held to honor a neighborhood organizer who had been detained. After his release, he went to the offices of the APDH in downtown Buenos Aires to report on the attack, which had resulted in some forty detentions. In a 1990 interview, Liwski noted that the APDH interviewers had struggled to understand his story, which was rooted in the realities of Gran Buenos Aires:

> It was very difficult to transmit in the context of the formal organizations what was happening [in La Matanza]. There was another dynamic in the human rights organizations which persisted in all the years that followed, which was a more individual perception of human rights violations: to the right to life, kidnapping, disappearance, and so on. This also created a certain difficulty in understanding that [in outlying neighborhoods] we were up against something gigantic.[90]

LAW AND PRECEDENT

Pedro Troiani and others among the Ford survivors wanted to do more than just share their stories in the early democratic era; they also sought to assert the rights they had once enjoyed as unionized workers and fight to recover the economic security they had lost. Few options were available to them at this early date, however, because no legal precedent yet existed in Argentina, or virtually anywhere in the world, for pursuing a human rights complaint against a private corporation in criminal court. It would take another decade for European and American courts to start ruling on matters of corporate human rights complicity, a topic that will be explored in the following chapter. For now, this lack of precedent meant that the Ford workers had no channel through which to accuse their former bosses at Ford Argentina of blacklisting them to the security forces. Their only recourse within the Argentine judicial system was to launch a wrongful dismissal case against Ford for firing them without compensation while they were imprisoned under the PEN.

Pedro Troiani was so desperate after suffering economic hardship since 1977 that he was even prepared to fight for his old job at the Pacheco plant. Yet when he approached the SMATA leadership for help, Secretary-General José Rodríguez responded with language that he interpreted as a threat: "Are you sure you want to go back there after everything you've been through?"[91] Undeterred, Troiani decided to press the issue on his own by filing a wrongful dismissal claim through the Ministry of Labor with the hope of at least recovering the severance pay owed to him. The problem was that under normal circumstances, the paperwork should have been filed within three months of the dismissal. In his claim, Troiani argued that Law 21.400, decreed by the junta in September 1976 to help employers fire workers detained under the PEN system, was unconstitutional. He appealed instead to Article 3980 of Argentina's civil code, which recognized that extenuating circumstances could prevent someone from meeting the three-month time limit prescribed by law.[92] Troiani argued that a "logical fear of reprisal" had deterred him from filing his wrongful dismissal claim before 1983 due to the "fundamental fact that the country was not being governed by a constitutional democracy" at the time.[93]

Other Ford survivors Juan Carlos Amoroso, Guillermo Perrotta, and Juan Carlos Conti launched their own wrongful dismissal complaints soon after, but Ford Argentina rejected all these demands on the grounds that the three-month statute of limitation had passed.[94] The Labor Ministry sided with the company, ignoring the context of military rule. When the men hired a lawyer to take their case to labor court in late July 1984, they lost again because of the three-month statute of limitations. This time, however, the presiding judge calculated that period from the date of President Alfonsín's assumption of office, arguing that the men should have filed their complaint with the court by March 10, 1984.[95] This ruling at least acknowledged that the years of military rule had marked a break with the normal functioning of legal institutions, as Troiani had argued in his original claim. However, the strict application of the three-month time frame did not make allowance for the continuing uncertainties of the early period of democratic transition.

The men pursued their cases with the Labor Appeals Court in 1986, but only one of them was successful: Juan Carlos Conti, who had been kidnapped the same day and under the same circumstances as Pedro Troiani. Conti's was the first appeal heard, and in his case, the judges found Law 14.200 unconstitutional.[96] They argued that the simple fact of being detained without charge by the military regime did not prove that a worker had committed a labor-related offense against their employer serious enough to warrant a dismissal without severance compensation. Tellingly, however, the court did an about-face when ruling on the other men's complaints, which came forward in the following weeks.[97] In those rulings, the judges reiterated the earlier statute of limitations argument, declaring that "the mere existence of a de facto [military] regime" did not excuse the delay. They also rejected the notion that Ford Argentina would have any interest in retaliating against workers for lodging a wrongful dismissal complaint during military rule.[98] One judge dissented, citing the CONADEP report's findings about the climate of fear that reigned at Ford Argentina, but the majority decision held sway.[99]

The Supreme Court also rejected Pedro Troiani's appeal in August 1988 in a decision of three to two. The ruling justices argued once again that "general considerations" relating to "the application of a regime of State terrorism" were insufficient to overrule the three-month statute of limitations required by law; such an exception would require new federal legislation. They also found that Troiani had presented insufficient evidence of "malicious maneuvers" by Ford Argentina. With these decisions, the courts placed an enormous burden on Troiani to prove the circumstances of his disappearance, detention, and continued harassment after his release, including spelling out the relationship between his former employer and military authorities. These were questions that he desperately wanted answered, but that no institution had even tried to investigate up to this point. Moreover, since the PEN records had been destroyed, the only repository that might have held documentation to support Troiani's argument was the corporate archive at Ford Argentina. There was no way to access these private records, especially since the company had already refused to cooperate with the CONADEP investigators in 1984.

While these fine details of legal argumentation may appear merely technical, they were vital to the Ford survivors, who saw their hopes for economic compensation dashed after having struggled for years to support their families. Moreover, official institutions had once again refused to acknowledge the political context of their ordeal. In 1984, the CONADEP interviewers had urged them to stick to just "the facts" of their disappearances without venturing into interpretation about the motivations behind them. Now the labor courts declared the context of state terrorism irrelevant to the men's delay in making their claim against Ford Argentina, even though they had been seized from their workplace, tortured on the factory grounds, banned from other industrial jobs, and harassed by police through the end of military rule. As we will see, the Inter-American Commission on Human Rights eventually sided with Troiani's claim against the Argentine government over its obstruction in the 1980s civil case, but that decision came decades later.

In parallel to the civil claim pursued in labor court, the Ford survivors also tried to include themselves as plaintiffs in criminal investigations launched against the military chain of command. The 1984 CONADEP report had fueled public demand for accountability, leading to the 1985 Trial of the Military Juntas. Although President Alfonsín hoped that the conviction of the junta leaders would satisfy public demand for human rights justice, Argentine citizens pushed the judicial process further by flooding the courts with more claims against lower-level officers and torturers. Once again, a core group among the Ford survivors seized on this opportunity to petition the democratic state for redress. They asked the SMATA leadership to provide them with a criminal lawyer when they learned that plaintiffs in the province of Buenos Aires had launched a criminal case against General Santiago Omar Riveros, the military commander who had overseen the repression in the Zona Norte from the Campo de Mayo base. When José Rodríguez refused to help them yet again, the men pooled their funds and hired the union's lawyer privately, adding their names to the case against Riveros.[100]

Unfortunately, that case also fell apart when President Alfonsín put an end to the human rights investigations. On Christmas Eve, 1986, Alfonsín passed the Full Stop law (*Ley de punto final*), which set a sixty-day time limit beyond which the courts would no longer accept new human rights cases. Argentine citizens responded by filing even more claims, initiating some three hundred new investigations. Then, in April 1987, officers at the Campo de Mayo base mutinied in a revolt they called Operation Dignity. Appearing with their faces painted for combat, the so-called *carapintadas* demanded that the government bring an end to the prosecutions. Thousands of ordinary citizens flooded Campo de Mayo to denounce the mutiny, and thousands more participated in a huge march to the Plaza de Mayo. Behind the scenes, however, the government negotiated with the armed forces. In early June, Congress passed the Due Obedience law (*Ley de obediencia debida*), which exempted all security forces below the junta from prosecution on the grounds that they had been following orders.[101] This law shut down the case against General Riveros, closing off the final avenue of justice pursued by Troiani and the other men from Ford in this early transition era.

A CORPORATE COUP

In the end, the Alfonsín government was brought down not by camouflaged mutineers but by powerful business and banking interests who crippled his government's ability to deliver on its reform promises and fueled a crushing hyperinflation crisis in 1989.[102] That denouement to the first hopeful phase of democratic transition underscored the lasting social and economic legacies of military rule, which had led to a massive concentration of capital. While thousands of small businesses and industries had gone bankrupt during the Martínez de Hoz years, a few major corporations, including Ford Argentina, had profited from lucrative government contracts and opportunities for financial speculation. In fact, Ford was one of only four automakers to survive the aggressive free-market policies imposed by Martínez de Hoz, which included an end to the import tariffs on automobiles that had protected the local automotive sector from international competition. Deprived of such preferential policies and facing a shrinking car market because of the junta's regressive economic policies, most carmakers had cut their Argentine investments after the coup.[103] Italian carmaker Fiat had chosen Argentina as its first overseas base of operations in the 1950s, and it had dominated the local car market with its tiny, affordable models. By the end of 1976, however, Fiat shifted most of its production to Brazil, which had handily outstripped Argentina in automotive production.[104] General Motors abandoned Argentina altogether in 1978 after more than half a century assembling and manufacturing cars in the country. As the world's largest corporation, GM could easily afford to walk away from Argentina's turbulent economy and politics. Its local subsidiary produced the same number of vehicles in a year that GM's American factories churned out in a single day.[105] Chrysler, Citroën, and Peugeot closed their own Argentine plants soon afterward.

Ford had weathered the economic storm that hit Argentina's automotive sector by aggressively rationalizing production at the Pacheco plant, selling off appliance maker Philco Argentina and telecom company Coradel SA and founding two new financial firms: Invercred SA and Plan Ovalo SA.[106] In fact, as the rest of the industrial sector went into free fall, Ford Argentina saw remarkable success, briefly taking its place as the country's second-highest performing corporation in 1979 and 1980.[107] The company found more customers looking for midrange to large cars after GM's departure, and, like Mercedes-Benz, it benefited from its vehicle contracts with the military government.[108] However, it mainly took advantage of new financial deregulations introduced in 1977 that removed controls on capital flows and artificially raised interest rates on the peso to attract foreign investment.

Ford Argentina was by no means the only major corporation to play this game. A few dozen firms had consolidated their power over the Argentine economy during the dictatorship years, the largest among them local holding companies like Techint, Macri, Pérez Companc, and Socma.[109] Critics referred to them as *la patria contratista* (contractor nation), pointing to their lucrative contracts with the military juntas. These corporations expanded their holdings under military rule and emerged as large conglomerates (*grupos económicos*) in control of entire sectors of Argentina's economy: agribusiness, steel, oil, banking, and so on. They and the multinationals like Ford that remained in Argentina enjoyed strong ties to international markets and lobbied the government on matters of shared concern through a handful of powerful business associations.[110]

President Alfonsín's fledgling democratic government thus found itself trying to implement economic reforms within an oligopoly: a highly concentrated economy where powerful business interests could choose to work together when it served their interests. It also faced a historic debt burden that had enriched those same corporations through the junta's laundering of dubious corporate loans.[111] Alfonsín had promised Argentine voters in 1983 that he would investigate the junta's borrowing and pay back only those loans deemed legitimate. However, he faced intense pressure from the International Monetary Fund (IMF) and the US Federal Reserve to prioritize repayment to international creditors.[112] Argentina was forced to turn to the IMF repeatedly in the 1980s for bridging loans to avoid default, which in turn gave that agency greater power to dictate economic policy. By 1989, the year of new elections to choose Alfonsín's successor, the country's foreign debt had ballooned to US$65 billion.[113] As dollar reserves flowed out of the Central Bank, inflation mounted, and the government introduced policies to stabilize prices. However, it faced resistance from Argentina's largest corporations and private banks, which had access to the foreign exchange so desperately needed by the government to pay its international creditors. By the middle of the year, inflation had reached 100 percent, and food prices had spiraled out of reach for many consumers.[114] People in the deindustrialized suburbs of Rosario, Córdoba, and Gran Buenos Aires began stealing food from supermarkets, sometimes quietly in small groups of women and children, sometimes more violently. By the end of May, those neighborhoods were rocked by unprecedented food riots. Alfonsín first declared a state of siege and then ceded power six months early to his successor, Carlos Menem, who had won the May elections.

Both domestic and international business leaders threw their support behind the new president as he quickly doubled down on the neoliberal economic policies introduced during the dictatorship. President Menem accelerated the privatization of state assets that Alfonsín had initiated to pay off Argentina's debt, and he imposed drastic cuts to public spending. Though elected as leader of the Peronist (Justicialista) Party, Menem had worked to sideline candidates with roots in the CGT labor federation. He transformed Peronism into a political machine that won votes in poor neighborhoods through direct patronage, not through the unions, which had also lost membership because of deindustrialization and unemployment.[115] On the human rights front, President Menem issued a series of blanket pardons in 1989 that saw the convicted junta leaders released from prison just a few years after their convictions. Those pardons also closed off prosecutions relating to the carapintada mutinies and abuses committed during the Malvinas/Falklands

War. Menem also extended amnesty to members of Argentina's armed guerrilla movements and to key military allies, including former finance minister José Alfredo Martínez de Hoz and Buenos Aires provincial police chief General Ramón Camps, who had overseen the detention centers across Gran Buenos Aires.[116] These far-reaching measures appeared to permanently close off all possibilities of justice.

CONCLUSION

Contradictory forces had defined these first years of democratic transition. On the one hand, a remobilized civil society had shown remarkable courage and creativity in confronting the security forces who had terrorized sectors of Argentina's civilian population under military rule. All kinds of people had contributed to this collective wave of defiance: musicians and artists, lawyers and politicians, human rights activists, and survivors. Ordinary citizens had written letters to the new president to voice their hopes and demands, while victims of horrible crimes had broken their silence to testify at the CONADEP hearings and the Trial of the Military Juntas. Thousands of people had put pressure on Argentina's judicial system by demanding investigations into allegations of torture and disappearance, and artists had used their work to hold up a mirror to the collective experience of state terrorism. On the other hand, military and political pressures had slowed and then reversed many of these early gains by the end of the decade.

The Ford workers and their family members had played their own role in these events, beginning with the wives who had bravely confronted military officials and Ford executives at the time of their husbands' abductions. Although the families suffered terrible economic loss and isolation while the military remained in power, a few survivors bravely came forward during the early democratic opening. They asserted themselves as citizens by pressing institutions and leaders to respond to their demands for justice and fair compensation. They wrote to President Alfonsín and made a lasting impression on the CONADEP commissioners, who featured their stories in the *Nunca Más* report. They also tried to recover their lost labor rights by petitioning the courts to acknowledge the exceptional circumstances surrounding their dismissals from Ford Argentina. Yet powerful institutions blocked their efforts in this early period. The men's former union leaders at

Chapter Five

SMATA refused every request for assistance, and Ford Argentina rejected their demands for compensation. The courts also proved unwilling to overturn laws that had been imposed during military rule, thus upholding the junta's stripping away of labor rights.

The hyperinflation of 1989 demonstrated that the dictatorship's economic policies had left their own deep scars, particularly in the industrial regions that had benefited most during the years of desarrollismo. Even workers who had avoided kidnapping and detention endured a collapse in their earning power after the coup, and thousands lost their jobs altogether in the wave of plant closures provoked by the Martínez de Hoz reforms. The impacts were especially stark in the neighborhoods of Gran Buenos Aires. In the year before the military coup, workers from factories across the Zona Norte had paraded defiantly down the Pan-American Freeway to demand an end to government austerity measures. By 1982, masses of unemployed people instead marched into the capital to appeal for their lost jobs, and by the end of the decade, residents of those same neighborhoods resorted to stealing food out of supermarkets to feed themselves and their families.

CHAPTER SIX

History, Justice, Memory

We're part of the Falcon, too.

—CARLOS ALBERTO PROPATO, Ford union activist and
survivor of disappearance

The early 1990s marked a low point for Argentina's progressive movements. The amnesty laws passed by Presidents Alfonsín and Menem had closed off judicial investigations into the abuses of the dictatorship era, and the devastating hyperinflation crisis of 1989 had left citizens further traumatized.[1] A climate of impunity reigned through much of the decade, as Argentine society turned away from the grand ideals of the early democratic years to focus on economic survival, and another wave of exiles left the country, now for economic rather than political reasons.[2] The generals convicted in the 1985 Trial of the Military Juntas resumed their private lives after their release from prison, and the unreformed judiciary and police institutions continued to operate with many of the same personnel in place since the dictatorship years. Police brutality remained rampant, especially against youth living in the poorer neighborhoods of Gran Buenos Aires.[3] Yet the mainstream press largely ignored such issues in the early 1990s, and much smaller groups turned out for annual human rights marches that had attracted tens of thousands a decade earlier.[4]

Despite this stifling atmosphere, committed activists, survivors, and lawyers continued to work behind the scenes, looking for mechanisms to challenge the amnesty laws and revive the aborted investigations of the previous decade.[5] They eventually found support beyond Argentina's borders from legal experts who were experimenting with the concept of "universal jurisdiction," whereby one country's justice system could be used to investigate crimes against humanity committed in another.[6] They also drew inspiration from new international initiatives to address civil complicity in human rights violations, including the actions of business elites and corporations that had collaborated with authoritarian governments. By the early 2000s, these efforts bore fruit in the overturning of Argentina's amnesty laws and the reopening of human rights investigations. What differentiated these new investigations from the trials of the 1980s was that they addressed crimes committed not only by members of the state security forces but also by civilian actors accused of collaborating in the repression, including priests, politicians, and business leaders.

The Ford survivors and their supporters played a crucial role in this renewed judicial inquiry into the dictatorship era. As Argentina's political and legal landscape shifted through the turn of the twenty-first century, they regrouped and revived their case against Ford Argentina, testing multiple avenues of justice with the help of a committed team of lawyers and researchers. The nature of their legal demands also evolved as new international precedents raised the possibility of charging their former bosses at Ford not just with wrongful dismissal but with direct participation in their abductions and torture. It would be an uphill battle, because the global framework for corporate human rights law was still new and evolving, and such a case had never been heard in Argentine courts. This kind of "transitional justice from below," pitting a group of aging South American autoworkers against one of the world's most powerful multinational corporations, was virtually untested anywhere in the world.[7] Success would depend on a delicate balance of political and judicial forces as well as painstaking research, innovative legal strategy, and tenacity.

In fighting to win official acknowledgment and justice for the ordeal they had suffered, the men also wrote themselves back into the history of Ford Argentina. They had been violently erased from that history in 1976: blacklisted and disappeared for their union work, tortured, and terrorized into silence. Although many witnesses had seen men like Pedro Troiani and Carlos Alberto Propato kidnapped right off the assembly line, Ford managers had feigned ignorance about their disappearance, claiming that the men had abandoned their workplace responsibilities. Even after their release from prison, the Ford survivors had found themselves cut off from unionized work, denied the economic security and collective supports they had once enjoyed. The betrayals had continued after the return to democracy when Ford Argentina refused to cooperate with the CONADEP investigations and blocked the men's labor court demands. The Ford workers' former union bosses at SMATA had also rejected all their appeals for help. In the early 2000s, however, the Ford survivors and their families gradually built new networks of support. Working both inside and outside the judicial arena, they took advantage of every opportunity to share their stories and expose the reality of the repression at Ford's Pacheco plant. Although their legal case faced repeated delays and setbacks, they pressed on with questions that had been left unanswered during the first round of human rights investigations in the 1980s, seeking to understand the role their bosses at Ford Argentina had played in their disappearance. In doing so, they helped uncover new evidence about Ford's actions during the dictatorship years, and they pushed Argentina's humanitarian discourse of human rights toward a deeper reckoning with civil complicity in the terror regime and with the political economy of military rule.

The slow evolution of the Ford case intersected with broader debates over memory and justice that animated Argentine society in the decades spanning the turn of the century. Memory work related to the dictatorship era both expanded and fragmented after the Argentine government led by President Menem abandoned the human rights agenda at the end of the 1980s.[8] Here, "memory work" refers to a broad variety of collective efforts to shape public understandings of the recent past undertaken by civil society actors like human rights organizations, unions, neighborhood associations, journalists, artists, and academics. In Argentina, these initiatives included commemorative rituals and public demonstrations, the dedication of monuments and markers on the landscape, and the recovery and protection of former clandestine detention centers as material evidence of the terror apparatus. Issues of memory and justice continued to inspire artists working in a wide range of media, and the Ford Falcon resurfaced repeatedly as a common trope within these works, though its meaning shifted over time. Finally, civil society groups promoted archival projects to preserve documents and collect interviews about the dictatorship era: now not only for judicial purposes but as a public record of Argentina's recent past.

These initiatives gradually generated more complex perspectives on the dictatorship and pre-coup eras, which challenged the dominant memory regimes of the 1980s. During those early transition years, the Argentine state, led by President Alfonsín, had taken the lead in framing debates over memory and justice, first through the creation of the National Commission on the Disappearance of Persons and then through the 1985 Trial of the Military

Juntas. While those developments quickly made Argentina a global leader in the realm of human rights law, they were also tightly managed by the state and harnessed to the project of consolidating liberal democratic institutions. As Greg Grandin has observed, such early experiments in post-transitional justice betrayed an ambivalence about history. While they documented the horrors of the recent past, they also sought to contain and ritualize that truth-telling exercise in service to the national democratic project.[9]

Two dominant discourses fed into what historian Emilio Crenzel has defined as the "emblematic memory regime" of the 1980s.[10] One was the humanitarian framework articulated by Argentina's leading human rights organizations like the Mothers of the Plaza de Mayo and the Permanent Assembly for Human Rights, of which President Alfonsín was a member. As noted earlier, these respected civil society groups had strong ties to international organizations like Amnesty International and the Inter-American Commission on Human Rights, and they took a leading role in pressuring the new democratic government to bring the generals to justice. They intentionally adopted Amnesty's depoliticized and humanitarian language to elicit sympathy for their disappeared loved ones and to counter the demonizing language that had been used by the military juntas to justify widespread repression against so-called subversives. Amnesty's methodology also influenced the procedures of the CONADEP, which used standardized forms to collect information from survivors about their experiences of arbitrary detention and torture and kept them focused on just "the facts" of their incarceration in their testimonials.[11] Similarly, prosecutors made sure that witnesses at the 1985 Trial of the Military Juntas reported on their firsthand experiences of the repression without delving into questions about the social and historical circumstances that had made them targets in the first place.

The Alfonsín government and its closest allies advanced another discourse about Argentina's recent past that came to be known as the "theory of two demons." It greatly oversimplified the country's experience of political violence by laying equivalent blame on the guerrilla movements of the 1970s and the armed forces, casting the rest of Argentina society as passive victims. This framing ironically reproduced the generals' own claims that they had resorted to extreme measures because they had found themselves fighting a "dirty war" against ruthless terrorists.[12] It erased the complex social and political mobilizations of the pre-coup era, once again eliding nonviolent organizers with armed insurgents. Finally, it closed off analysis of the socioeconomic factors that had led to the coup and absolved all other sectors of Argentine society of responsibility. This *teoría de los dos demonios* had its fullest expression in the 1984 prologue to the CONADEP's *Nunca Más* report, written by commission director Ernesto Sábato, the respected intellectual who had helped Pedro Troiani and other Ford survivors overcome their fears about testifying. The men's accounts, like other evidence cited in the body of the report, contradicted the simplified "two demons" framework, but Sábato's prologue nonetheless reproduced the Alfonsín regime's official narrative of events.[13]

That dissonance communicated a deep ambivalence toward history that was typical of the early post-transition period. To quote Greg Grandin:

> Truth commissions . . . had to deal with history, but . . . they were concerned that too close an attention to realms of human activity comfortably associated with historical inquiry—an examination, say, of economic interests and collective movements, or the unequal distribution of power in society—might grant moral pardons or inflame political passions.[14]

Over the decades that followed, different groups within Argentine society engaged more deeply with the complexities of Argentina's recent past. Pedro Troiani, the other survivors from Ford, and victims of labor repression more broadly helped shape these more historically grounded understandings by continuing to tell their stories and ask their difficult questions. This process could be fraught and bitter, as different groups within Argentine society competed for authority and advanced distinct historical narratives. It also provoked strong resistance from conservative forces. Ultimately, though, by subjecting that past to scrutiny, ordinary citizens like the Ford survivors confronted the disinformation that had underpinned military power. They also helped to set new precedents in human rights prosecutions, particularly in the realm of civil complicity. The pages that follow trace this story from the aftermath of the pardons decreed by President Menem to the 2018 convictions of retired Ford Argentina executives Pedro Müller and Héctor Sibilla, as well as of General Santiago Riveros, for the crimes against humanity committed against the former union stewards at the Pacheco plant.

Chapter Six

1990s: IMPUNITY

Ford Argentina finally ceased production of its Falcon sedan in 1991, after nearly thirty years of continuous manufacturing. The company had merged its Argentine and Brazilian operations with Volkswagen's four years earlier in a joint venture called Autolatina to weather Latin America's severe economic downturn of the 1980s. Autolatina decided to abandon Falcon manufacturing as part of that restructuring, though not without a proper ceremony to mark the occasion. In early September, the Pacheco Industrial Center hosted an elaborate, week-long send-off for its last Falcon sedan. The company organized daily photo ops where workers, white-collar employees, and executives gathered at different sites across the factory to toast the car as it inched its way through the assembly process.[15] Recalling the paternalistic practices of the 1960s, managers decided not to sell the last Falcon but to raffle it off among the six thousand employees at Autolatina's factories and parts plants across Argentina. The winner, Emilio Félix Poligiotto, was a thirty-year-old father of three who had been working for just a year at the Transax transmission factory in Córdoba. Tellingly, however, years of inflation and aggressive cuts to industrial wages meant that Poligiotto was unable to make use of his new Falcon because his monthly wages of just US$600 could not cover the cost of gasoline. Like most factory workers, he kept riding his bicycle to the Transax plant. The contrast with the early years of Falcon-mania was unmistakable. Grand promises of high employment, social mobility, and "PROGRESS" had accompanied the Falcon's launch in the early 1960s. Despite the fanfare organized by Autolatina executives, this last Falcon rolled out of the factory three decades later into an atmosphere of austerity and insecurity.

Argentina's middle classes were also struggling by the early 1990s, hit hard by inflation and job losses. While a small fraction of middle-class professionals had enriched themselves in the financial sector since the 1980s, a much larger segment had fallen into a category that academics referred to as the "new poor": people with university educations who had been pushed out of once-secure jobs and now scrambled to make ends meet.[16] The fragmentation and deepening insecurities of middle-class life fostered a culture of nostalgia for the 1960s, which was remembered as an era of relative peace, prosperity, and hope for the future.[17] For some, the retro Ford Falcon stood as an emblem of those happier days. New Falcon fan clubs proliferated across Argentina after the car went out of production, and many have remained

Figure 6. Ford Falcon in Bariloche, Argentina (2018), showing the mix of 1960s and 1980s design elements. Courtesy of Will Byers.

active ever since. These groups resemble vintage car clubs in other parts of the world, organizing monthly "meets" in parking lots, where club members and curious visitors mingle alongside rows of polished Falcons parked with their hoods raised to show off their engines.[18]

The fact that Ford Argentina had made limited changes to the car's design over three decades only heightened the nostalgic effect. Late-model Falcons contained many new parts and bore details such as headlights or grills that nodded to 1980s design, but the car's boxy profile remained firmly rooted in the Kennedy era.[19] That continuity contributed to the Falcon's timelessness and made it easier for fans to celebrate its more wholesome pre-dictatorship identity as a symbol of national manufacturing pride and middle-class family life, sidestepping the car's more sinister associations. Falcon fans associated the car with rich personal memories of family vacations, trips to the racetrack, and time spent tinkering. The car's legendary durability also stood for an era

Chapter Six

when Argentina was producing top-quality industrial goods that signaled the country's ambitions for the future. Ford Argentina encouraged such associations over the years, inviting members of the Buenos Aires Friends of the Falcon Club to annual barbecues and tours at the Pacheco plant.[20] Ford's racing team also kept the Falcon in circulation in the TC stock-car circuit long after the end of Falcon manufacturing.

Not everyone viewed the Falcon so wistfully in the 1990s, however. Activists and artists countered these sentimental memories with Falcon representations that instead communicated outrage over continued military and police impunity. One was a stencil that began to appear on the walls of Buenos Aires as part of a new graffiti scene that emerged in that decade.[21] Youth artists and activists were using graffiti, music, and street performances to draw attention to the issues that most affected them. Police reform ranked high on their priorities, since they were the most likely victims of ongoing police brutality.[22] This stencil image shows two Falcon sedans side by side, each with a male driver and a single male passenger in the front seat. The silhouette on the left shows the men wearing civilian clothes and dark sunglasses. The car's license plate reads "1976": a clear reference to the plainclothes members of the dictatorship's "task groups." On the right, the two men wear police uniforms, and the license plate shows the year the stencil was made. It is a chilling message about the continuities between the military and democratic eras, particularly in reference to the police agencies that had never been purged of their torturers.[23] This image resurfaced in subsequent years during protests over police violence and on key commemorative dates such as anniversaries of the military coup.[24]

Photographer Fernando Gutiérrez also employed the Ford Falcon as a trope for impunity in a series of images he captured through the 1990s and early 2000s. While working as a news photographer covering daily events, Gutiérrez dedicated himself to more subjective representations of trauma and memory in his artistic works. His photo essay *Treintamil*, whose title referred to the thirty thousand victims of disappearance cited by Argentine human rights organizations, was one of the first works of art photography to evoke issues of memory relating to Argentina's recent past.[25] It won Cuba's prestigious Casa de las Américas prize, one of the top arts awards in Latin America, in 1997. In *Treintamil*, Gutiérrez presents a collection of desolate black-and-white images not as documentary proof of specific events but as suggestive "traces" of the past to be interpreted by the viewer. The photos, unaccompanied by titles or explanatory captions, all make visual reference to the "machinery of terror": the technologies used by the Argentine security forces to isolate and eliminate their victims. In one, a prop plane with a windshield covering resembling a blindfold evokes the aircraft used in the "death flights" that sent drugged political prisoners into the waters of the South Atlantic.[26] Strings of barbed wire and bricked-up windows call to mind the clandestine detention centers where victims were interrogated and tortured, and several images conjure up the car voyages that carried those victims into that underworld. In contrast to the happy family road trips presented in car ads and tourist brochures, these blurred images taken through rain-soaked car windows suggest deep isolation and disorientation.

The one photo in the exhibit accompanied by explanatory text presents the crumpled shell of an abandoned car overgrown with weeds. Here, Gutiérrez shares a personal memory from his own childhood during the dictatorship.

> Santi was Batman, Beto was Robin, and the rest of us were attacking the Batmobile, an abandoned car on the banks of the Reconquista River. I took the wheel and when I looked back, I saw a patrol car coming toward us through the trees. The first impulse was to escape: a hundred-meter race run in ten seconds, cut short by the dry sounds of gunfire. Hands up.
> They forced us to go back. Standing next to each other nervously against some bushes, we heard: "If you don't tell us who it was, we'll rip you apart and throw you in the river. López, go get the machine gun." I kept my eyes on him.
> He went to the car and came right back. I couldn't stop staring at the barrel of the gun pointing at us. More questions, more shouting, and Santi became desperate, kneeling on the ground crying and begging them not to kill us because we didn't know anything. They let us go; this time we didn't run. It was the summer of 1980 and we were twelve years old.

This foundational and traumatic experience attuned Gutiérrez to the power of material objects—including automobiles—as carriers of memory. In his next award-winning photo essay, he focused his camera on the Ford Falcon, the car that carried the greatest symbolic weight in Argentine culture. *Secuela* (Aftermath) presents sixteen portraits of old Ford Falcons parked in

Figure 7. Detail from *Secuela*, a photo essay by Fernando Gutiérrez H. Courtesy of the artist.

shadowy streetscapes. Most are in black and white, with a few in subdued tones of blue. Each vehicle was shot from a direct side view, recalling the classic print advertisements that showed off the Falcon's clear lines and ample size for potential Argentine buyers. Yet these cars are neither shiny new Falcons for sale nor the lovingly restored Falcons shown off in the Falcon Club car meets. Instead, they are the old, durable Falcons that could still be found across Argentina, especially in small towns and modest neighborhoods outside the capital city. Gutiérrez's choice of moody lighting and deep contrasts accentuates their rust patches, crumpled fenders, and scratched paint. His framing of each car in the shadows of an uninhabited street gives the images a sinister quality that recalls the terrifying Falcon portrayed in the film *Ford Falcon, buen estado*. Taken during the years of impunity that followed the pardons of 1989, these bleak portraits speak to the lingering presence of the perpetrators who lived freely in Argentine society.

Artistic representations like these are not merely incidental sidenotes to the story of the Ford survivors. As scholars of memory in Argentina have noted, the judicial and symbolic realms of the human rights struggle have always been intertwined.[27] The Mothers of the Plaza de Mayo were the first activists to attract international attention and mobilize public outrage against the dictatorship by marching silently around the capital city's main plaza. They wore white headscarves and carried poster-size photographs enlarged from their missing children's national identity cards: official images that proved the Argentine state had once acknowledged their existence as citizens.[28] Mass street-art actions like the famous silhouette protest of 1983 had pressured incoming president Raúl Alfonsín to make good on his campaign promises to investigate human rights crimes. On this occasion, activists spent the night painting thirty thousand life-size human silhouettes on brown kraft paper. They hung them on the walls surrounding the Plaza de Mayo, symbolically making the disappeared visible in the center of political power.[29] In the same vein, songs, graffiti, and works of art featuring the Ford Falcon helped to keep public memories alive and provoke ongoing questions about Ford Argentina's relationship to the military regime. Recognition by arts awards committees and institutions also gave legitimacy to these representations, incorporating them into a shared public narrative about the past. For now, the story of the Ford workers themselves did not surface in these artworks, but as will be detailed below, the men and their supporters later created their own symbolic representations that connected their struggles to the broader trajectory of Argentina's human rights movement.

CONNECTIONS

In the meantime, Pedro Troiani remained determined to win some kind of compensation from Ford Argentina for the wrongful dismissal that had followed his detention in 1976. Working as an independent mechanic from his home in Beccar in the early 1990s, he refused to accept the legal decisions that had blocked his labor court demand against Ford. He shared his frustrations one day with a client: a labor lawyer named Rodolfo María Ojea Quintana, who had brought his car in for repairs. Since the Argentine courts had closed off Troiani's labor appeals, Ojea Quintana put him in touch with his son Tomás, a young lawyer with an interest in international human rights law, in the hope that he might find an outlet for Troiani's claim. Tomás Ojea Quintana's own tragic experiences during the years of military rule helped him connect deeply with the Troiani family. His parents had been detained as political prisoners for six years during his childhood, and two of his uncles had been disappeared.[30] He also shared Troiani's stubbornness and optimism that some kind of justice must be possible in the longer term, even if the immediate prospects in Argentina seemed bleak. The two men forged a strong bond of friendship, which lasted until Troiani's death in 2021. They worked together on the Ford case for nearly three decades, testing multiple legal strategies and gradually assembling a broad network of support that included other Ford survivors and their family members as well as legal professionals, human rights and labor activists, academic researchers, archivists, journalists, and educators.

Tomás Ojea Quintana was part of a generation of legal professionals who looked beyond Argentina's borders for legal precedents and innovations that might be brought to bear on the problem of impunity.[31] A group of such progressive jurists took steps to strengthen the application of international human rights standards in national courts when President Menem established a Constitutional Assembly in 1994. Menem's reformist ambitions were extremely limited; he merely wanted to change the law on presidential term limits so he could run for a third term in office. Once the assembly opened the constitution to debate, however, some delegates managed to push through an article requiring that Argentina's domestic laws conform to all international treaties that the country had ratified. At the time, these included both the Universal Declaration of Human Rights and the American Declaration of the Rights and Duties of Man as well as treaties on genocide and torture. With the ratification of this constitutional reform, all legal decisions in Argentina going forward would have to meet the standards spelled out in those international treaties.[32]

The reform also prompted a round of new training in international human rights law for Argentine lawyers, prosecutors, and judges, who needed to fully understand these treaties and their implications for local courts. Tomás Ojea Quintana, who was teaching as well as practicing law in Buenos Aires, played a key role in this effort. In 1999, he coauthored a six-hundred-page report for the Inter-American Development Bank entitled *La dimensión internacional de los derechos humanos* (The International Dimension of Human Rights). Designed for use in legal training, it brought together excerpts of international reports, opinions, and sentencing arguments pertaining to human rights and demonstrated how these precedents might be applied to a wide variety of Latin American concerns, ranging from freedom of expression to labor and indigenous rights.[33] The new ideas introduced by publications like this one inspired innovative legal strategies in Argentina that eventually helped overturn the country's amnesty laws in 2005.

CORPORATE ACCOUNTABILITY

Just as Argentine jurists were deepening their engagement with international law, new precedents were being set overseas that began to apply human rights standards to nonstate actors including business leaders and private corporations. These developments later had a direct impact on the Ford survivors by providing mechanisms to pursue a much more ambitious case against military authorities and corporate executives at Ford Argentina for their role in the men's disappearances. Economic globalization had become the new framework for understanding global affairs since the fall of the Soviet Union and the end of the Cold War. Activists around the world voiced concerns about the unbridled power of multinational corporations as the former Eastern Bloc nations rushed to implement free-market reforms, and Britain and the United States contended with the impacts of the Thatcher and Reagan years. Protesters in the antiglobalization movement denounced financial institutions like the World Bank and the International Monetary Fund for imposing austerity policies on the countries of Latin America and Africa. Corporations also came under fire for contributing to human suffering on a global scale. For example, activists denounced working conditions in shoemaker Nike's overseas factories and criticized Shell Oil for its close relationship with the Nigerian dictatorship after environmental activist Ken Saro-Wiwa was murdered in 1995.[34] Yet no binding international legal framework existed to hold corporations accountable for their actions in relation to human rights violations.

In Germany, the 1990s brought the first sustained demands for such accountability in relation to corporations that had collaborated with the Nazi regime a half-century earlier.³⁵ Although some three hundred German business figures had been tried for crimes against humanity in the immediate aftermath of World War II, those convictions had not translated into a prolonged legal engagement with the issue of corporate complicity.³⁶ Instead, most German corporations continued their operations without scrutiny until the late 1960s, when student activists started to raise difficult questions about their wartime activities. It took until the 1990s for survivors and their descendants to press for legal redress. Such investigations finally became possible with the end of the Cold War, the reunification of Germany, and the declassification of records in Germany, the United States, and the former Soviet Union. Holocaust survivors and victims of slave labor launched court cases against the Swiss banks that had profited from the dispossession of European Jews and the industrial firms that had supported the Nazi war machine or used the forced labor of Nazi prisoners.³⁷

In response to public pressure, several large corporations felt obliged to open their archives and commission independent researchers to investigate the accusations. These included not only German firms but also some American multinationals like the Ford Motor Company, General Motors, and IBM. The automakers stood accused of profiting from slave labor at their German factories, which had continued operating through the Nazi era. Worse yet, IBM was denounced for supplying the Nazis with tabulating machines that had facilitated the identification and deportation of European Jews to the death camps. As historians dug into the archives to develop a better understanding of the relationships between business interests and the Nazi state, a consensus emerged that not only states but private corporations could be held both morally and legally responsible for human rights crimes.³⁸

Lawyers in the United States had also begun experimenting with new legal mechanisms to hold corporations accountable for human rights violations, even in cases where those crimes were committed overseas. They sought to expand on a legal precedent set in 1980 in a famous case known as *Filártiga v. Peña-Irala*, in which prosecutors had successfully applied an obscure eighteenth-century law known as the Alien Tort Statute (ATS) to a contemporary human rights case. The ATS, also known as the Alien Tort Claims Act (ATCA), had been drafted in 1789 to give noncitizens the right to make a civil claim in US federal district courts for a wrong committed "in violation of the law of nations." It then sat largely dormant until lawyers representing a Paraguayan couple resuscitated it to prosecute a civil case against a former member of the Paraguayan security services for the kidnapping, torture, and murder of their family member in Paraguay. The lawyers advanced their claim in US courts on the grounds that the accused was living in the United States, even though his crimes had been committed abroad.[39] Their first claim was rejected based on the principle that modern human rights law did not exist at the time the ATS was drafted. In 1980, however, the US Court of Appeals for the Second Circuit supported the plaintiffs' argument, ruling that the courts must "interpret international law . . . as it has evolved and exists among the nations of the world today," particularly in the realm of human rights.[40] This was a groundbreaking decision that prompted a flurry of new ATS-related cases.

In the 1990s, American lawyers began testing the ATS's application to the overseas actions of American multinationals, since corporations had enjoyed the status of legal "personhood" in American law since the late nineteenth century.[41] They reasoned that if an American corporation could enjoy the same protections as an American citizen, it could also be held to the same standards of legal responsibility, including responsibility for harms committed outside US territory. In 1997, for instance, a legal team accused the US energy firm Unocal of complicity in "gross human rights abuses, including forced labor, rape, and other torture" committed by the Burmese military to protect its pipeline interests in southern Burma. Unocal decided to settle the case out of court, and its 2003 financial settlement with Burmese villagers marked the first time a US multinational corporation was forced to compensate victims for its role in human rights abuses. That case inspired other lawsuits against corporations such as ExxonMobil and Talisman Energy in the late 1990s and early 2000s, which marked the high point of Alien Tort Statute advances in the United States.[42]

The Ford Motor Company faced its own ATS challenge in October 1999 when a Russian-born Belgian citizen named Elsa Iwanowa filed a class action suit in US District Court on behalf of former slave laborers at Ford's German subsidiary, Ford Werke AG. Iwanowa had been kidnapped as a teenager by Nazi soldiers and transported to Germany, where she worked without pay under harsh conditions at the Ford Werke plant in Cologne from 1942 to the war's end in 1945. She sought compensation from both Ford Motors and Ford

Werke for "the reasonable value of her services, restitution of unjust enrichment flowing to [Ford Motors], as a consequence of her labor, and damages for the pain and suffering that [the] imposition of inhuman working conditions caused her."[43] Ford countered that it could not be held responsible for these abuses because its factory had been under Nazi control from 1940 through 1945. The question of the Alien Tort Statute's applicability was just one among many thorny issues in this immensely complex case, which also included the application of the statute of limitations, the interpretation of German law and international treaties between the United States and Germany, and more. Ultimately, the district judge ruled against Iwanowa based on considerations relating to post–World War II treaties, but he accepted the Alien Tort Statute's applicability to the case on the grounds that enslavement and deportation constituted crimes against humanity that fell within the scope of the ATS.[44] Although the Ford Motor Company continued to maintain its innocence, in March 2000 Ford Werke AG announced that it would contribute roughly US$13 million to a restitution fund established by the German government to compensate some 1.2 million survivors of Nazi slave labor.[45]

Argentine lawyer Tomás Ojea Quintana looked to such rulings and decided that the Alien Tort Statute might offer a mechanism for the Ford workers to achieve justice against their former employer. In 2003 he reached out to Los Angeles–based attorney Paul Hoffman, who was then part of the legal team representing Burmese villagers against Unocal. Hoffman and his partner Benjamin Schonbrun found the evidence in the Ford case compelling enough that they agreed to file an ATS lawsuit against the Ford Motor Company in US courts. They collected testimony from sixteen of the Ford survivors and filed their claim in the US District Court for the Central District of California on January 22, 2004. It accused the Ford Motor Company of being a coconspirator in "egregious human rights violations" committed against the men by the Argentine military in 1976.[46]

Unfortunately, US corporate and national security interests had already mounted a major challenge to the ATS by the time Hoffman and Schonbrun filed the Ford case, using a variety of veto tactics to block the law's application to corporate human rights violations.[47] Washington lobby groups had begun petitioning congressional representatives to weaken or repeal the law in 2002 on the grounds that it had harmed their corporate clients.[48] In 2004, the main business organizations representing US multinationals, including the National Foreign Trade Council (NFTC), the US Chamber of Commerce, the US Council for International Business, and the US Business Roundtable, filed an amicus curiae brief to the Supreme Court in its first consideration of the ATS. The case before the court, *Sosa v. Álvarez-Machaín*, had nothing to do with corporate human rights violations. It concerned the abduction of a Mexican citizen, Dr. Humberto Álvarez-Machaín, by another Mexican national, Francisco Sosa, who had been hired by the US Drug Enforcement Agency to bring the physician over the border to face trial for his involvement in the torture and murder of a DEA agent in Mexico. Although the case involved individuals and not corporations, it was the court's first opportunity to rule on the Alien Tort Statute's applicability to international human rights violations. The NFTC brief urged the court to nullify the Alien Tort Statute because its application to US-based multinationals "placed them at a competitive disadvantage in the global economy."[49] Corporations represented by the NFTC included several that had recently faced ATS challenges, including Unocal, Exxon, and the Ford Motor Company.

Those tasked with monitoring national security interests also raised alarms about the ATS, which they characterized as an "emerging threat to national security" in the post-9/11 era.[50] The government of President George W. Bush was relying heavily on private defense contractors to fight its wars in Afghanistan and Iraq, with hundreds of companies filling military and logistics roles that had been outsourced from the Department of Defense.[51] It was also experimenting with secret detention and torture (referred to euphemistically as "enhanced interrogation") in its global war on terror.[52] The Department of Justice filed several amicus curiae briefs urging the courts to annul the Alien Tort Statute, and it petitioned the Supreme Court directly in *Sosa v. Álvarez-Machaín*.[53] Although the DOJ failed to achieve its goal of eliminating the ATS, the court's June 2004 ruling did significantly narrow the scope of the law's application. In a 6–3 decision, it ruled that the Alien Tort Statute gave US courts jurisdiction only over the traditional torts—or damages—conceived at the time the law was written in the late 1700s. These included "violations over safe conduct, infringement of the rights of ambassadors, and piracy," but not crimes like the contracted abduction of a Mexican citizen.[54] That decision convinced attorneys Hoffman and Schonbrun that the Ford case had no hope for success in the American judicial system, and they withdrew their claim against the Ford Motor Company.[55]

Chapter Six

TRUTH TELLING

In the long run, business and government opposition in the United States stymied the Alien Tort Statute's potential as a corporate accountability tool for international human rights justice. Still, the cases brought forward during the law's heyday introduced innovative legal strategies and advanced the principle that corporations could and should be held accountable for complicity in crimes against humanity. Argentine lawyers like Tomás Ojea Quintana who were attentive to legal developments overseas applied similarly innovative strategies back in Argentina. Rather than give up hope when they found US legal channels blocked, Ojea Quintana and the Ford survivors looked for ways to advance their case at home. Thankfully, the domestic human rights landscape was rapidly evolving through the early 2000s, and a convergence of civil society activism, legal innovation, and political change all contributed to a more propitious environment for the renewed pursuit of human rights justice. New opportunities arose for the Ford survivors to share their stories and connect with other activists and researchers who were investigating working-class experiences of the dictatorship era, particularly as they related to attacks on organized labor.

One such forum was a uniquely Argentine legal experiment known as the *juicio por la verdad* (truth trial): a hybrid form of hearing that combined elements of a criminal trial and a truth commission.[56] This innovative institution was founded in response to demands from family members of the disappeared for *habeus data*: the right to information about the fate of their loved ones. Their immediate goal was to pressure the military to share records relating to political prisoners, even in the absence of prosecutorial power due to the amnesty laws. The longer-term hope was that the collective weight of this testimony might help overturn those laws. The Federal Appeals Court of La Plata, capital of the province of Buenos Aires, launched the first truth trials in April 1998. It had jurisdiction over the entire province, including the working-class neighborhoods of Gran Buenos Aires, and it had the power to conduct site inspections and seize government records of relevance to its investigations. During weekly hearings that continued for nearly ten years, the La Plata truth trials collected more than 1,800 testimonials, including many accounts of attacks against shop-floor union activists that echoed the experiences of the Ford survivors.

All in all, these hearings collected a far greater body of working-class testimony than had ever come to light since Argentina's democratic transition.[57] Until the launch of the La Plata truth trials, the only people concerned with documenting the dictatorship's attacks on organized labor were a group of activists in the fledgling Argentine Workers' Congress (Congreso de Trabajadores de la Argentina, or CTA). Founded in 1992 as an alternative to the Peronist CGT labor federation, the CTA's objective was to foster a more politically independent and democratic labor movement. Its founding members were themselves survivors of anti-union attacks and imprisonment during the dictatorship era.[58] In the mid-1990s, the CTA's human rights committee compiled a five-thousand-page report on labor repression under military rule that drew on judicial testimony, interviews with workers, investigative journalism, and academic research. It documented attacks on more than nine thousand Argentine workers who had been targeted for their labor activism, including the men from Ford's Pacheco factory. The report also addressed the social and economic causes of the repression, arguing that in 1976 Argentina's leading corporations and security forces had executed a "concerted plan . . . to implement state terrorism and genocide with the goal of imposing social discipline on the working class."[59] It was an innovative piece of research, but under the heavy weight of impunity during the 1990s, the group had no audience or outlet for their claims in Argentina.[60]

Once the La Plata truth trials began in 1998, however, more working-class witnesses were willing to share their experiences. They were likely reassured by the passage of time, since Argentina's democratic institutions had proven to be resilient, and the armed forces had lost much of their power over civil society.[61] The hearings themselves also offered a much more supportive setting than a typical adversarial courtroom.[62] Since the court had no power to prosecute, witnesses did not have to worry about confronting intimidating defendants. Instead, they occupied the center of the courtroom and spoke directly to a tribunal of judges, their words unmediated by lawyers. Those judges sometimes acted like counselors, offering comfort to witnesses and calling recesses when they became emotionally overwhelmed. The hearings were also open to the public, which meant that family and community members could be present to support those who testified. These procedures stood in sharp contrast to the operations of the CONADEP and the Trial of the Military Juntas in the 1980s, where interviewers and prosecutors had tightly managed the proceedings and scope of testimony. At the truth trials, witnesses were invited to tell their own stories as they saw fit, and to elaborate on the political and historical circumstances that had led to their encounters with the state terror apparatus.

Pedro Troiani was called to offer precisely this kind of contextual information when he was subpoenaed by the La Plata truth trials in September 2002 as part of an investigation into labor repression at Mercedes-Benz. In the mid-1970s, union activism at the Mercedes factory in the Buenos Aires suburb of González Catán had been even more militant than at Ford's Pacheco plant. In October 1975, the four thousand workers there broke completely with the national SMATA leadership and elected a more radicalized internal plant commission. The company responded quickly by firing more than one hundred labor activists with the support of SMATA secretary-general José Rodríguez, who was keen to reassert his power over the workforce. Then, while those who remained on the shop floor pressured management to reinstate their coworkers, Montonero guerrillas took matters into their own hands and kidnapped the factory's production manager, Heinrich Metz. They demanded that Mercedes-Benz pay a hefty ransom (to them, not the factory workers) and hire back those who had been laid off. Although the company acceded in the short term, a Mercedes-Benz executive contacted the federal police to pass on the names and home addresses of "troublemakers" among the plant activists. After the coup, sixteen of those men were disappeared, and only two survived their detention.[63]

The La Plata truth trials began investigating the Mercedes-Benz disappearances in 2001 after German-born journalist Gaby Weber published a book about the events that drew on firsthand testimonies as well as evidence uncovered in Germany.[64] The dearth of survivors prompted the court to call on Pedro Troiani to share his own observations about attacks on shop stewards in the automotive sector, and especially about the actions of union and business leaders.[65] Judge Leopoldo Schiffrin opened the proceedings by inviting Troiani to take the floor and tell his story in his own words, promising that the judges would intervene only to ask follow-up questions. This was Troiani's first opportunity to speak freely and publicly about what had happened to him in 1976, and it was taking place in an official court setting and recorded for posterity. He began by providing a timeline of his working years at Ford and the beginnings of his union activism. He then recounted key episodes from the lead-up to the coup, including Ford management's offers of a buy-out to the Pacheco union activists and the meeting where José Rodríguez had warned the Ford delegates about imminent attacks on the "middle ranks" of the autoworkers' union.

Judge Schiffrin, one of Argentina's preeminent jurists and promoters of human rights, offered gentle encouragement as Troiani continued his story.[66] When Troiani mentioned the growing presence of soldiers at Pacheco in the lead-up to the coup, the judge asked, "So they were visible inside the factory?" which prompted Troiani to elaborate: "Yes, completely visible, and they moved around in trucks that were supplied by the company, because we knew those trucks. The company gave them the space to move about freely through the factory, to go anywhere they wanted and pick up anyone they wanted." Looking back, Troiani remarked on his "utter naïveté" at the time, explaining that he and a group of union delegates had approached Lieutenant Colonel Antonio Francisco Molinari, commander of military operations at the plant, to complain about the attacks suffered by some other shop stewards: "We asked him what was going on, that some men had suffered raids on their houses, [and] that . . . their families had gone through a really tough time. And he told us not to worry because if we were on some kind of detention list, they would just let us know that we needed to present ourselves." Then he repeated: "See? We were totally naïve."

Troiani went on to describe the circumstances of his own detention roughly two weeks later, explaining that both his foreman and plant manager Pedro Müller had approached him soon after he clocked in to tell him not to move from his spot on the assembly line. "So then I realized it was my turn," he commented. "At about ten o'clock in the morning, a group of uniformed men drove into the plant in trucks, like they were ready for war." He described his temporary detention and beating in the quincho along with four other workers, and their transfer to the Tigre police precinct. Troiani estimated that he had spent fifty days in secret detention before being legally recognized as a political prisoner and moved to the Devoto prison. Judge Schiffrin then interrupted to say that the court had seized archives relating to political prisoners who had been held in provincial jails and that they would try to locate the relevant documentation. Human rights lawyer Marta Vedio, representing the Permanent Assembly for Human Rights at the proceedings, spoke up to say that she had a copy of the record attesting to

Pedro Troiani's imprisonment. Judge Schiffrin paused so that Troiani could look at the document, commenting that it was "a small act of justice for you to be able to see it."

Throughout the hearing, these kinds of dialogues validated Troiani's sense of injustice and provided him with the space to put his personal experiences into broader context. Asked about the union activists disappeared from Mercedes-Benz in 1977, he testified that he did not know any of the men personally, though they may have attended SMATA events at the same time. Judge Schiffrin then made an observation about the timing of the assaults on the two factories, noting that "it was like a kind of lightning strike at Ford, because . . . at Mercedes-Benz the events occurred in 1977, but at Ford they started from the day of the coup, and the clean-up was over within a month." This prompted a longer reflection from Troiani about the events at Pacheco on March 24, 1976, and the reasons for the ferocity of the attack:

> That same day [the security forces] launched an operation that looked like . . . I mean, there were even tanks and helicopters. To me, they did it to frighten everyone, because our group of shop stewards really had people's support. Because we fought hard to support people. For example, that was a time when production and sales were high and there was a lot of focus on production. Because they [management] wanted to get production up to 300 units, for example, and there were enough workers to get to 250 units. So we had to be tracking the pace of the assembly lines, and that really bothered Ford. They just wanted productivity and they didn't care how they got it; generally speaking, they got it by pushing people. And we were always on top of that, and people [in the factory] knew that. And I think that whole operation was to pacify and frighten people into thinking that what was happening to us could happen to any of them.

Later in the hearing, Troiani hypothesized about why he and his fellow detainees had been targeted for disappearance. Marta Vedio asked him how many elected shop stewards there were at the Pacheco factory, and he estimated that they numbered around fifty, of whom twenty-four had been detained. When Vedio asked him to account for the difference, Troiani responded: "What I have decided, after spending a long time trying to analyze these things, is that the delegates who got taken away were the ones who were in closest contact with people [on the shop floor]. . . . I had been a union steward for six years and I knew people from across the factory, because there were three separate plants, and I knew people in all of them." In the unique setting of the truth trial, the judges simply listened and recorded Troiani's observations. No one cross-examined him or told him to stick to "just the facts."

Asked about his views of SMATA secretary-general José Rodríguez, Troiani stressed that the Pacheco factory delegates had never broken with the SMATA leadership in the lead-up to their detentions, despite their differences. He also stated, however, that Rodríguez had done nothing to help them after their release from prison in 1977. He told the story of what happened when he and other former detainees went to SMATA to ask Rodríguez for help finding work. "Since SMATA is a union that also represents workers at independent garages and dealers, we thought we could get work in some small workshop." Instead, Rodríguez sent them to the Mercedes-Benz factory just when union activists there were under attack, with tacit support from the SMATA leadership. Troiani explained that the personnel manager at Mercedes "treated us like the worst kinds of delinquents." He also told the judges that Rodríguez had refused to help the men with their labor court claim against Ford Argentina, telling them that no lawyer would accept their case. Judge Schiffrin asked for clarification: "So how did that claim turn out? Because you were fired for absenteeism, but that wasn't right." Troiani explained that he and a small group had pursued their cases privately, but that only Juan Carlos Conti had won any indemnity from Ford. Schiffrin commiserated, assuring Troiani that there should be some kind of legal remedy for that injustice.

ARCHIVAL INITIATIVES

These early years of the century brought other opportunities for Troiani and some of his coplaintiffs to tell their stories and try to make sense of their experiences. One was an oral history initiative undertaken by Memoria Abierta (Open Memory), an independent human rights archive founded by several of Argentina's principle human rights organizations in March 2000.[67] Their goal was to pool their records, amounting to some twenty-seven thousand documents, and collaborate in research and education projects about Argentina's recent past. The Oral Archive project collected more than seven hundred interviews with activists, survivors, and family members of the military's victims.⁶⁸ Like the jurists who led the truth trials, the coordinators of this project wanted to move beyond the constrained memory regime of the 1980s and explore more complex questions surrounding the antecedents of state terrorism. Interviewers used the latest oral history methods, inviting their subjects to construct a meaningful life story out of their memories that stretched back to the early 1960s. The impulse behind this archive was to make state terrorism "intelligible" by "delving into the political, ideological, and cultural conflicts that [had] preceded and sustained it."⁶⁹ Ford survivors Pedro Troiani, Adolfo Sánchez, Carlos Propato, Luis Degiusti, and Ismael Portillo all provided interviews. So did José Paladino, an activist who joined the Ford workforce after the disappearances and described the repressive atmosphere inside the Pacheco plant. Portillo's wife, Arcelia Ortiz, who had badgered Lieutenant Colonel Molinari throughout the year of her husband's detention, added her voice to the archive, as did lawyer Tomás Ojea Quintana.⁷⁰

Such grassroots archival initiatives were crucial to Argentina's human rights movement, because the ruling juntas had wielded their power through the tight control of information. They had used censorship, lies, and euphemisms to obscure the identities of those who made up the dictatorship's "task groups," the fate of their victims, and the network of clandestine detention centers where detainees were held and tortured.⁷¹ The generals had also taken pains to purge incriminating internal documents like the records relating to the PEN detention system, as well as the personal papers of their victims. One great loss to the working-class history of the dictatorship era, for example, was the personal archive of underground journalist and Montonero militant Rodolfo Walsh, who had carefully tracked the impacts of the junta's policies in the neighborhoods of Gran Buenos Aires before his murder in March 1977.⁷²

For victims of workplace repression like the men from Ford, other valuable sources of documentation also remained out of reach. Officials at the SMATA union headquarters claimed that their records had been mysteriously destroyed by fire in the 1990s, conveniently erasing all evidence of the union leadership's activities in the pre- and postcoup eras. Indeed, few Argentine unions maintained consistent archives.⁷³ Worse still, the corporate records of industrial employers were considered private property under law and beyond the reach of ordinary citizens. Ford Argentina had refused to collaborate with the official CONADEP investigation in the early 1980s, denying investigators access to the Pacheco facility and to the company's files. In the case of multinational corporations like Ford and Mercedes-Benz, crucial records might even be housed thousands of miles away in overseas head offices, well beyond the reach of local survivors or lawyers. Up against these monumental obstacles, human rights activists and researchers came to view the realm of memory as "a battlefield" to be fought over through analysis and investigation, and they undertook to build their own archives of the dictatorship era.[74] Their efforts to locate and declassify records proved decisive in the renewed human rights investigations of the 2000s, especially in the complex and innovative field of corporate responsibility for human rights crimes.

Two major declassification projects from these years provided crucial evidence to the Ford case. The first was the recovery of intelligence records belonging to the Buenos Aires provincial police, which had been surveilling industrial workplaces and neighborhoods in Gran Buenos Aires for decades.[75] Citizen pressures for police reform had finally achieved a victory in 1999 when the province of Buenos Aires agreed to decommission the Buenos Aires Provincial Police Intelligence Bureau (Dirección de Inteligencia de la Policía de la Provincia de Buenos Aires, or DIPPBA), which had been operating out of a headquarters in La Plata since 1956. By then, the La Plata truth trials were already underway, and the Federal Appeals Court of La Plata seized and protected the DIPPBA records because of their historical and judicial significance. In a remarkable turn of events, the entire DIPPBA headquarters and its contents were transferred to an independent organization, the Provincial Memory Commission (Comisión Provincial por la Memoria). The commission, run by a board of human rights and labor activists, lawyers, and academics, was charged with preserving the police records and making them available to victims, researchers, educators, and the courts.[76] Since the surveillance of organized labor had been one of the bureau's key mandates dating back to its founding, the DIPPBA archive contained extensive records relating to industrial workplaces and union activities in the province. Records relating to Ford's Pacheco factory, which have been cited in earlier chapters, served as key evidence in the Ford case.

Another cache of declassified documents came to light in 2002, when US president Bill Clinton approved the release of more than 4,600 State Department records relating to human rights violations in Argentina between 1976 and 1983. Clinton was responding to dozens of petitions filed by Argentine victims, relatives, and lawyers since the beginning of the truth trials.[77] The new revelations that came out of those hearings left many

Argentines frustrated at the courts' inability to lay criminal charges, and human rights organizations and lawyers doubled down on their efforts to overturn the amnesty laws. One strategy was to seek documentation beyond Argentina's borders, especially relating to crimes that had not been covered by the amnesty laws, such as the abduction of minors.

Although the topic of labor repression was not a priority in this declassification project, the US embassy memos released by the Clinton government validated the stories of attacks on shop-floor union activists that had been compiled by researchers at the CTA labor federation. For instance, an August 1977 memo entitled "Argentina: Prison Population Profile" estimated that between 750 and 1,000 trade union activists were then detained, both in official jails and secret detention facilities, and that another 500 were presumed killed. It identified those prisoners as "factory or shop delegates, members of the 'Comisiones Internas,' or 'Coordinadoras sindicales,' trade union officials being held for union-related activities which were legal until the enactment of legislation after 3/25/76, without any associations with the subversive groups."[78] In April 1978, US embassy staff reported that "most of the union leaders and members currently under official detention were picked up in the months immediately following the coup in an effort to clean out the factories of suspected subversives."[79] One month later, Ambassador Raúl Castro described a report he had received from the French embassy that listed the names of "1142 workers detained or disappeared as of March 15, 1978," adding that "most appear to be simple rank-and-file workers."[80]

These documents, combined with the DIPPBA records, the CTA report, and the rich working-class testimonies being collected in the La Plata truth trials, now made it possible to reconstruct the dynamics of labor organizing and repression in the industrial districts of Gran Buenos Aires with greater attention to the circumstances leading up to the coup. Aside from their judicial application, these new sources also fostered a revival of interest in labor history, which had fallen out of academic favor in Argentina, as it had elsewhere after the end of the Cold War.[81] Newer studies moved away from an older top-down focus on union leaders and institutions toward a more bottom-up approach focused on specific workplaces or neighborhoods. They also drew on oral history interviews as well as documentary sources.[82]

Taken together, this body of literature shed new light on the dynamics of shop-floor organizing, political mobilization, and the activities of the internal claims committees (comisiones internas), producing a more nuanced and heterogeneous picture of working-class politics. It also complicated older assumptions about workers' political affiliations by blurring the distinction between Peronists and clasistas, whose organizing strategies were found to be broadly similar. Workplace studies demonstrated that even committed Marxists had sought to win over their peers through honest and effective leadership, not through ideological speeches.[83] Similarly, supposedly loyal Peronists like the members of the comisión interna at Ford's Pacheco plant were willing to copy strategies used by clasistas if they seemed effective. Either way, workers of all political stripes had effectively challenged management control over production as labor mobilization in Gran Buenos Aires hit its peak in 1975. This growing scholarship enriched legal investigations into attacks on labor activists after the coup and underpinned the strategy used by the lawyers representing the Ford survivors.

CRISIS AND REORIENTATION

As academics, jurists, and archivists were wrestling with the past at the turn of the new century, Argentina suffered through yet another financial crisis: the worst in the country's history. A renewed surge of citizen engagement in the wake of that shattering event forced a redirection of national priorities and a new reckoning with the economic and social legacies of the dictatorship era. In 2001, President Fernando de la Rúa was struggling to contain a new wave of capital flight that was facilitated by Argentina's still unregulated financial markets. On a single day, November 30, the country's largest corporations and private banks gutted the National Bank's foreign exchange reserves, loading US$1.3 billion in shrink-wrapped packages of bills onto airplanes that literally flew them out of the country.[84] De la Rúa tried to protect the banking system from total collapse by freezing personal bank accounts and limiting cash withdrawals to $250 per week, a drastic measure that hit middling households hardest, since Argentina's wealthiest citizens and corporations already kept most of their wealth outside the country. As the money supply dried up, the misery spread to the masses of poor people, who depended on the informal cash economy to survive through begging, street peddling, and day labor.

Protesters flooded the streets of Buenos Aires, banging pots and pans and demanding that the government step down. De la Rúa resigned on December 20, and four would-be presidential successors were ousted over the next two weeks. Argentines vented their rage in the capital city's financial district, protesting outside the private banks that had bankrupted the country. The crisis of 2001 focused greater scrutiny on the corporations that had profited from government ties since the coup of 1976. For roughly two decades, economists had been tracking how a few corporate conglomerates had profited from lucrative contracts with the military juntas and maintained their power over Argentina's economy in the democratic era.[85] Those same business elites and associations had resisted President Alfonsín's efforts to rebuild Argentina's welfare state and contributed to the hyperinflation of 1989. After 2001, years of corruption scandals and another devastating banking crisis shifted some sectors of public opinion toward the idea of holding private corporations accountable for their actions dating all the way back to the 1970s. Journalist Sergio Ciancaglini caught this mood when he observed: "Once upon a time there was a country called Argentina where many people disappeared and where, years later, the money disappeared, too. One thing is related to the other."[86]

CHALLENGING IMPUNITY

All of these overlapping political, economic, and social processes contributed to the dismantling of Argentina's amnesty laws in the early 2000s and the renewal of human rights investigations. In March 2001, federal criminal judge Gabriel Cavallo presented the first legal challenge in a 150-page decision that drew on both national and international precedents.[87] Tomás Ojea Quintana took advantage of this opening to try to move the Ford case ahead. In October 2002, he convinced federal prosecutor Federico Delgado to file a criminal complaint against executives at Ford Argentina for their role in the workers' abduction and torture. A month later, Judge Daniel Rafecas of the Third Federal Court agreed to open an investigation.[88] Meanwhile, decisions in other cases continued to chip away at the amnesty laws until May 2005, when the Argentine Supreme Court finally declared President Alfonsín's Full Stop and Due Obedience laws and President Menem's pardons unconstitutional.[89]

The 2003 election of Néstor Kirchner to the presidency also signaled an official reorientation of economic and human rights policy.[90] Kirchner, a relatively obscure provincial governor before the economic crisis of 2001, won the election by promising to address the suffering of those who had been impoverished by years of neoliberal economic reforms and shut out of the legal system by the amnesty laws. He had come of age as a university student in La Plata during the political turmoil of the early 1970s and had been moderately active in the left-wing Peronist Youth movement before moving back to his hometown of Río Gallegos to practice law in 1976. In his inauguration speech, he identified himself as "part of a decimated generation haunted by painful absences," and he celebrated the activists who were fighting to reopen human rights investigations.[91]

In his first year as president, Kirchner made Argentina a signatory to the United Nations Convention on the Non-Applicability of Statutory Limitations to War Crimes and Crimes against Humanity, a standard that was later crucial to the success of the Ford workers' case.[92] He also created a new National Archive of Memory to house and protect the records of the CONADEP, the Trial of the Military Juntas, and other official documents that had come to light since the 1980s.[93] The following year, Kirchner cemented his alliance with Argentina's human rights organizations by taking over the naval training school and former detention center known as the Escuela de Mecánica de la Armada (ESMA) and declaring that it would be rededicated as the Space of Memory and Human Rights. Finally, in a 2006 speech to cadets at the National Military College (Colegio Militar de la Nación), the president stated that the armed forces did not bear sole responsibility for Argentina's long and painful history of military coups: "Sectors of society, of the press, the church, the political class, and some citizens also played their part each time the constitutional order was subverted."[94] With this statement, the Kirchner government endorsed an expanded view of human rights culpability that extended to civilian actors.

By that time, Tomás Ojea Quintana and the Ford plaintiffs had compiled nearly a thousand pages of evidence to support their human rights claim, including personal testimonies, documents, and academic research.[95] They presented their files in a petition to public prosecutor Federico Delgado and Judge Daniel Rafecas, who had done little to advance their investigations since 2002. The claim asserted that Ford Argentina had "executed a precise and concrete plan" to crush union organizing at the Pacheco plant with the goal of creating "a form of Corporate Terrorism [*Terrorismo de Empresa*]." It argued that Ford Argentina had promoted that culture of fear to accelerate production by eliminating jobs quickly and cheaply, speeding up the assembly line, and ignoring unsafe working conditions at the Pacheco plant. The petition also argued that the corporation had not only "taken advantage of" the state terror apparatus installed after the coup but had actively participated in the repression of workers at Pacheco "by taking the unprecedented measure of supplying its own facilities for the operation of a Clandestine Detention Center and for the maintenance of military and security personnel."[96]

Since corporate entities could not face criminal charges in Argentina, Ojea Quintana asked the court to subpoena five individuals identified as criminally responsible for the abuses suffered by the Ford union activists. The first was Lieutenant Colonel Antonio Francisco Molinari, deputy director of the School of Engineers in 1976 and the officer who had overseen military operations at the Pacheco plant. It was Molinari who had shown Arcelia Ortiz the blacklist on Ford letterhead when she confronted him in 1977. Also named were four retired Ford Argentina executives: former president Nicolás Enrique Julian (Juan) Courard, industrial relations manager Guillermo Galarraga, plant manager Pedro Müller, and chief of security Héctor Sibilla. As noted earlier, Courard had publicly aligned Ford Argentina with the military juntas through speeches and published advertisements. Galarraga had been named in testimony by several Ford survivors because of his cryptic reference to Ramón Camps at the final meeting with the internal claims committee, suggesting that he had advance knowledge of the ordeal that awaited them. Müller oversaw the factory's operations and made daily visits to the shop floor, and Sibilla, a former army officer, oversaw all aspects of security at Pacheco.

On March 24, 2006, a small group representing the Ford workers participated for the first time in the annual human rights demonstration that commemorated the military takeover in 1976. The crowds were massive that year, which marked the thirtieth anniversary of the coup and the reopening of human rights trials. Pedro Troiani, Carlos Alberto Propato, Luis Degiusti, and Tomás Ojea Quintana paraded together carrying a sign that read "Survivors of the Ford Factory. The workers cry out 'Never Again!'"[97] Their slogan announced their collective identity, named their former employer, and identified their legal battle with the broader human rights struggle. Troiani and Propato, by then the unofficial spokespersons for the Ford plaintiffs, were invited to appear on Argentine television and radio programs marking the commemorative events. It was their first opportunity to share their stories on national media, and they contributed their own perspectives on the dictatorship era and its legacies by spelling out their accusations against their former bosses at Ford. One of their former union comrades at Ford, Carlos Gareis, heard them on the radio and broke his own silence with his family after thirty years. He came out of his isolation and traveled to downtown Buenos Aires to the national radio station to ask for contact details to reach Troiani and Propato. He and his family rebuilt their relationships with the surviving union activists from Ford.

Conservative elements in Argentine society did not remain passive in the face of such renewed human rights mobilization. The La Plata truth trials had sparked alarm beginning in the late 1990s because the judges had subpoenaed civil actors including politicians, government officials, and union leaders to testify about their actions. These witnesses were often at a loss to respond to questioning, since they had never been called to account for their dealings with the military regime.[98] Some denied any knowledge of the repression while others fought back against the entire process, denouncing the trials in the media as an exercise not in judicial investigation but in political vengeance. Current and former members of the security forces also took a defiant attitude when forced to testify, and some were jailed for contempt of court.[99] Several witnesses received anonymous threats, which one scholar attributes to "the existence of an entire network of social and political interests" who felt threatened by the proceedings. Indeed, beyond the province of Buenos Aires, conservative forces succeeded in shutting down virtually all the truth trials.[100]

The 2006 disappearance of retired bricklayer Jorge Julio López attested to the lingering dangers of challenging the forces of impunity.[101] Like the Ford workers, López had first been disappeared in 1976 and then detained in a regular prison under the PEN system before his release in 1979. He had maintained silence about his ordeal until 1999, when he came forward to testify at the La Plata truth trials. López then agreed to serve as a key witness in the 2006 criminal trial of former police official Miguel Osvaldo Etchecolatz, who had worked closely with Ramón Camps in coordinating the operations of the clandestine detention centers that made up the "Camps circuit" in the province of Buenos Aires. On September 18, López disappeared without a trace, just one day before Etchecolatz was sentenced to life in prison for crimes against humanity. His body was never discovered.

Chapter Six

DISMANTLING THE FALCON

These years also brought to light new artistic interpretations of the Falcon that celebrated the revival of human rights investigations and invited reflections on issues of civilian and corporate complicity. In 2004, sculptor José Ambrosio Rossanigo, who was based in Tandil, a small city in the heart of the wealthy Pampas region, drew inspiration from the mounting challenges to the amnesty laws. Though he normally produced abstract works in metal and stone, on this occasion he decided to craft an installation piece with a more recognizable message. Rossanigo designed the work, entitled *El broche* (The Clothespin), as an homage to the Grandmothers of the Plaza de Mayo, the women who had kept up their fight since the 1970s to recover their grandchildren who had been abducted or born in captivity under military rule.[102]

The artist purchased a vintage green Falcon in mint condition and deformed it in his workshop, leaving it compacted through the passenger compartment as if it had been mangled by a car crusher in a scrapyard. He then fashioned a mammoth clothespin out of metal and attached it to the car like a pair of massive pincers. The result was a striking visual metaphor: the simple domestic technology of the clothespin crushing the ominous and hypermasculine Falcon. Aside from the design's gender implications, Rossanigo also chose the metaphor and corresponding title to recall the colloquial expression *ponerle un broche*: literally to "put a clothespin on it," to bring an issue to its final resolution.[103] Finally, he deliberately left the car untreated with protective coating so that it would gradually rust and decay, once again emphasizing the way time could erode the power of once-invincible forces of terror.

Rossanigo had intended to donate his sculpture to a public commemorative space in the capital, where it would be widely seen. He loaded *El broche* onto a flatbed truck and drove it to Buenos Aires to participate in the annual march to commemorate the anniversary of the military coup on March 24, 2004, hoping to leave it at the former ESMA. However, he had underestimated the bureaucratic and political struggles involved in defining the new Space of Memory and Human Rights, which did not officially open for three more years.[104] Disappointed, he drove his sculpture back to Tandil, where it was briefly installed in the central Plaza de la Independencia. There, however, *El broche* suffered an unintended kind of damage. As evidence of the still contested memories surrounding the dictatorship era, particularly in

Figure 8. *El Broche*, sculpture by José Ambrosio Rossanigo, Plaza de la Independencia, Tandil, Buenos Aires. Courtesy of José Rossanigo.

Chapter Six

a region as conservative as Tandil, the work was repeatedly vandalized with spray paint. Rossanigo was eventually forced to relocate it to the campus of the University of Tandil, where it was safer from harm, though even further from the public eye.[105]

Another sculptural piece featuring the Falcon reached broader audiences in the capital and was eventually enshrined in the former ESMA. Entitled *Autores ideológicos* (Ideological Perpetrators), this large installation was featured in a 2006 commemorative arts exhibit at the Recoleta Cultural Center. A collective of six sculptors had begun collaborating on *Autores ideológicos* in 2003 when they discovered a newspaper advertisement announcing a sale of Ford Falcon sedans that had been used by the Buenos Aires provincial police during the years of military rule.[106] They purchased a green 1978 model and rented a workshop outside the city where they could work on it together. First, they observed the car closely, considering its past, and worked to overcome their instinctive sense of horror in its presence. They then dismantled it piece by piece, stripping it to its bare components and painting each part white.[107] They cut the entire chassis in half lengthwise and mounted the pieces on metal stands that raised them off the ground, closer to eye level.

Visitors to the exhibit were able to walk right through the middle of the Falcon and inspect each piece of its clinically white skeleton, which had been stripped of its power to provoke terror.[108] The overall visual effect of *Autores ideológicos* is of a collection of butterflies impaled on pins, helplessly exposed to minute, scientific scrutiny. The artists also displayed old Falcon ads and Ford publicity statements, including the incriminating full-page newspaper advertisement that Ford Argentina had published in January 1977 to celebrate the coup with the words "1976: Argentina Finds Its Way Once Again." This work offered another positive message about civil society's power to challenge totalitarian methods of shock and awe. Its title also spoke to the questions that were being raised about the broader economic and social power structures that had underwritten the military repression. After the Recoleta exhibition ended, *Autores ideológicos* was temporarily displayed behind glass in a Buenos Aires subway station. Eventually it made its way to the former ESMA detention facility, now renamed the ESMA Museum and Site of Memory. It still occupies a prominent space as part of the permanent collection at the Haroldo Conti Cultural Center.

INDICTMENT AND RESOLUTION

The Ford case languished in the Argentine judicial system with little momentum from 2006 until 2012, when it was finally transferred to Judge Alicia Vence of the Federal Criminal Court of San Martín (Tribunal Federal de San Martín). Acting on a long-standing request from the Ford survivors, Judge Vence arranged for the men to join her for a judicial inspection of the Pacheco factory—the men's first return to their former workplace since their detentions in 1976. Together they toured the facility and visited the quincho where several of them had been detained and tortured decades earlier. The inspection convinced Vence that Ford Argentina had collaborated with the military to repress labor activists at the plant out of a shared interest: "In this case," she wrote in a 2013 indictment, "the automaker wanted to increase productivity at a low cost; on the other hand, the military needed an internal 'enemy' to justify the establishment of its illegal regime."[109] The judge lamented in the same document that Argentine law provided no avenue to hold the corporation itself criminally responsible, leaving her with no choice but to indict three retired Ford Argentina executives: plant manager Pedro Müller, security chief Héctor Sibilla, and industrial relations manager Guillermo Galarraga. Former Ford Argentina president Juan Courard had died years earlier.

That same year saw the Ford survivors take another new step to write themselves back into the history of the Pacheco factory. In 2012, they created their own physical monument to draw attention to Ford Argentina's ties to the dictatorship. Drawing inspiration from the commemorative plaques, sculptures, and street markers that had become common features of the landscape, the men pooled their own funds and negotiated directly with the private company that maintained the Pan-American Freeway. In March 2012, they mounted a large metal sign on the traffic circle next to the Pacheco factory, where commuters would see it every day. It was headed by a prominent Ford logo surrounded by barbed wire. The sign read: "Kidnappings and torture occurred on this site, inside the quincho at Ford Argentina, during the civic-military dictatorship. Commission of Former Delegates and Workers at Ford 1976." Two years later, under pressure from the men and their supporters, the federal and provincial human rights secretariats raised an official human rights marker nearby.[110]

Chapter Six

The Ford trial was postponed two more times, beginning only in December 2017 and continuing through the following year. By then, two other lawyers had joined Ojea Quintana on the case: feminist human rights lawyer Elizabeth Gómez Alcorta and Ciro Annichiarico, who represented the federal government's Human Rights Secretariat. The legal team faced new challenges as the hearings finally began, since two more of the elderly defendants had died during the years of delay: Lieutenant Colonel Molinari and Ford's industrial relations manager, Guillermo Galarraga, who had taunted the members of the internal claims committee in 1976. The military side of the case would be relatively straightforward. In Molinari's absence, military responsibility passed to his superior, General Santiago Omar Riveros, who had overseen repressive operations throughout the Zona Norte as director of the Institutos Militares at the Campo de Mayo military base. Riveros had already been convicted in several other cases relating to the Zona Norte, and his position within the military chain of command was well documented.

The case against the remaining Ford executives would be more challenging, however, because the most damning evidence related to Ford Argentina president Courard and industrial relations manager Galarraga—both now deceased. Prosecutors would have to reconstruct a structure of authority within the Pacheco factory—a kind of management "chain of command"—to demonstrate that Müller and Sibilla had sufficient knowledge and authority to be implicated in the crimes. They also had to prove that the attacks on the Ford union delegates qualified as crimes against humanity and not common crimes, which would be exempt from prosecution due to the statute of limitations. This meant proving a high level of intent and coordination between the corporate executives and military authorities.

One important innovation used by the lawyers for the Ford plaintiffs was the appeal to social science research, which was key to establishing that the violence committed against the Ford workers qualified as crimes against humanity. Ojea Quintana and key plaintiffs like Pedro Troiani and Carlos Propato had spent years working with academic researchers, who had helped them put the events at the Pacheco plant into historical context. In the final hearings, the prosecution team called on several of these social scientists as expert witnesses. Senior economist Eduardo Basualdo drew on his years of published research to explain how Ford Argentina had benefited from the military's economic policies and deregulation of financial markets.[111] His daughter, historian Victoria Basualdo, testified about the military's widespread attacks on shop-floor union activists, and especially members of workplace internal claims committees, like the victims at Ford. She had collaborated on several major research projects about corporate involvement in human rights crimes committed during military rule, including a two-volume, 1,200-page report published in 2015 by the federal Ministry of Justice and Human Rights.[112] Sociologist Federico Vocos, who had been part of a research team that investigated production methods at Ford Argentina in the 1990s, gave the court a lesson on Fordism, explaining how that system's high levels of management control meant that managers like Müller and Sibilla must have been fully informed about events occurring on the shop floor.[113] Finally, archivist Claudia Bellingeri from the Provincial Memory Commission (Comisión Provincial por la Memoria) spoke to the significance of the declassified police intelligence records presented as evidence by the workers' legal team.

The lawyers representing defendants Müller and Sibilla were completely unprepared to counter this evidence, because their sole legal strategy was to have the case dismissed based on two premises: that the kidnappings in 1976 should be considered common crimes, and that the Ford managers could not be held responsible because they had lost control of the Pacheco factory once it came under military occupation. Ford Motors had used similar arguments in earlier investigations into the company's use of slave labor in Nazi Germany.[114] In Argentina, however, the lawyers representing Müller and Sibilla had underestimated the Ford workers and their supporters. Faced with a meticulously documented argument compiled over sixteen years, the defense team tried repeatedly to expunge prosecution evidence. They petitioned the judges to strike out sworn testimony provided by Ford workers who had died during the years of delays; they accused Bellingeri of providing false testimony about the DIPPBA police archive; and they suggested that Vocos had invented the term "Fordism."[115] During a recess from the court proceedings, Victoria Basualdo overheard one of the defense lawyers exclaim in frustration, "Who *is* this Victoria Basualdo?!?"[116]

The Ford plaintiffs and their family members sat together through the hearings displaying their own versions of the white handkerchiefs that had symbolized the Argentine human rights movement since the early days of the Mothers of the Plaza de Mayo. These handkerchiefs bore unique markings: an image of a Ford Falcon surrounded by a red circle bearing the years 1976 and 2018. Inside the circle were the words "Justicia y Castigo"

Figure 9. Ford plaintiffs displaying handkerchiefs in the courtroom in San Martín, Buenos Aires (2018). In the foreground: Pedro Troiani and Elisa Charlín. Getty Images.

(Justice and Punishment), the slogan voiced by early human rights activists in the 1980s to demand judicial investigations of military crimes. It was a symbolic reappropriation of the Falcon and another gesture that wedded the men's struggle to long-term efforts toward transitional justice. Although Argentina's commercial media mainly ignored the hearings, the courtroom in the provincial municipality of San Martín was consistently filled with family members and friends, as well as human rights activists, independent journalists, artists, and student observers. Video crews from the National Archive of Memory recorded the proceedings and the site visits made to the Ford factory and the Tigre and Ingeniero Maschwitz police precincts, creating a historical record that would be preserved by the state.[117] The federal Human

Rights Secretariat as well as universities, human rights organizations, and investigative journalists provided regular online coverage.[118]

On December 11, 2018, the three judges presiding over the Ford case, Osvaldo Alberto Facciano, Mario Jorge Gambacorta, and Eugenio J. Martínez Ferrero, delivered their unanimous ruling.[119] They rejected defense efforts to have the Ford case dismissed, ruling that the crimes committed against the union delegates from the Pacheco plant qualified as crimes against humanity. They convicted military commander Santiago Omar Riveros, who was already under house arrest for other human rights convictions, as criminally responsible for five counts of illegal raids, twenty-four counts of illegal detention aggravated by violence and threats, and twenty-four counts of aggravated torture of political prisoners. The judges sentenced Riveros to fifteen more years of imprisonment. They convicted Müller and Sibilla as accessories to these same crimes, sentencing the former to ten years in prison and the latter to twelve because of his close ties to police and military forces. Although the judges ordered that the sentences be served in federal prison facilities, for the time being Riveros was to remain under house arrest and Müller and Sibilla were to remain free but with probationary conditions preventing them from leaving the country and requiring them to check in monthly with authorities.[120]

Presiding judge Facciano drafted the 380-page legal decision that explained the reasoning behind these convictions.[121] He carefully summarized and cross-referenced the Ford survivors' accounts of their ordeal and explained why the judges had rejected the defense lawyers' multiple attempts to have the case dismissed. He cited the breadth of evidence presented: testimony from the Ford survivors, their family members, other former Ford employees, and soldiers who had served at the Pacheco factory in the 1970s, as well as declassified records from the DIPPBA archives and the US State Department, official military directives, and some management records from Ford Argentina. The judges agreed that the crimes committed at Ford qualified as crimes against humanity because they fit within a coordinated offensive against those who stood in the way of the military's project of "national reorganization." They concurred that shop-floor organizers like the members of Ford's internal claims committee had been targeted because they threatened the military's goal of restructuring Argentina's economy.

CONCLUSION

The hearings took an enormous toll on the Ford union delegates and their family members, who had to relive the horrors of the 1970s while defense lawyers cross-examined them and attacked their credibility. Carlos Alberto Propato, who had been an outspoken critic of Ford Argentina's role in the repression, suffered from inexplicable physical pain throughout 2018 that left him confined to a wheelchair by the time of the verdict. The workers' wives and children had testified in court for the first time, sharing their perspectives on the men's detention, the economic impact of their job loss, and the long-term trauma that had haunted their families. Yet despite their pain, several prosecution witnesses observed that the hearings had finally broken their silence and isolation. For the first time in decades, they felt part of a community that believed and supported them. On the day the decision was announced, crowds of human rights activists, political figures, family, and friends filled the court and spilled out into the street.[122] The judges' verdict also meant that the Argentine state, represented by its judiciary, had finally validated the Ford survivors' memories and responded to their long-standing demands for justice.

The resolution of the Ford case also signified a historic achievement for Argentina's progressive movements, especially given the stature of the Ford Motor Company. It marked the first human rights convictions in Argentine courts of executives representing a major multinational corporation. Furthermore, the verdict had come at a time when the political pendulum in Argentina had once again swung against support for human rights prosecutions. Since the election of conservative president Mauricio Macri in December 2015, the federal government had stopped collaborating in declassification initiatives and had cut funding to human rights institutions. Several other corporate complicity investigations had collapsed, further underlining the significance of the Ford workers' victory.[123] Longtime labor and human rights activist Victorio Paulón, then serving as human rights secretary of the CTA labor federation, declared the verdict "one of the most powerful rulings" in the history of Argentina's human rights prosecutions dating back to the 1980s.[124] Two years earlier, Paulón, a former steelworker, shop-floor organizer, and political prisoner, had offered a lucid analysis of the immense power structures arrayed against investigations into corporate complicity. His observations merit quoting at length:

I think justice is kind of moving forward on two timelines. In the case of the direct perpetrators, I think the process has proven to be very effective. With nearly a thousand perpetrators indicted in ordinary courts with due process, with the presentation of evidence, with acquittals in cases of insufficient evidence or lack of merit, I think this shows a healthy judicial process. But when it comes to the economic power of corporate groups, justice stutters. In general, the justice system goes backward before it goes forward. Cases are delayed or weakened; there are motions for acquittal with no explanation, without logic or rationale.

To me, this points to two things. First, economic leaders used the armed forces for their own purposes and then they discarded them like garbage. That was already clear in the Trial of the Military Juntas. So long as those proceedings did not touch civilian or economic actors, they just washed their hands. Second, those who committed human rights violations are old men: sixty-five, seventy years old or older. They're decrepit old men. Who is going to stand up for them? Maybe some family member? But the structures of economic power are alive and well, and fully active. They have set the conditions for successive governments, and they continue to govern the country today. . . . I think there will never be a definitive *Nunca Más* [Never Again] until this issue has been tackled in the courts, until it is opened to public scrutiny and definitively healed.[125]

Ultimately, the Ford case illustrates both the power and the limitations of the judicial sphere as a space for righting the wrongs of history. On one hand, the impetus to press the case forward in the courts brought to light documentary and testimonial evidence that might never have been collected otherwise. That evidence illuminated the social and economic forces that underpinned the dictatorship and answered questions that had plagued the Ford survivors for decades. The enormous effort of collecting it also connected the Ford workers and their families to new networks of support. On the other hand, the massive delays in the case undercut this victory, since thirteen of the original plaintiffs had died without seeing justice. Juan Courard, Guillermo Galarraga, Lieutenant Colonel Molinari, and SMATA secretary-general José Rodríguez had also died without facing prosecution. Finally, the limited scope of criminal law meant that a handful of old men were convicted, but Ford Argentina and the Ford Motor Company themselves had avoided answering for the events at the Pacheco plant.

Still, in their doggedness, the Ford survivors and activists never limited their efforts to the court case. They and their family members used every means available to expand debate about the dictatorship era in Argentina, to raise vexing questions about civil complicity in the repression, and to draw attention to the scale of attacks against working people. As this narrative has demonstrated, mainstream observers repeatedly missed, undervalued, or ignored that story of labor repression. Yet the Ford workers kept it alive over several decades by sharing their experiences with reporters, researchers, human rights investigators, and oral history interviewers. They participated in marches and spoke in public forums, and they used their own money to raise a monument outside the Pacheco factory to inform ordinary Argentines about the detention center that operated on the grounds in 1976. Their struggle was always for truth and memory as well as for justice.[126]

CONCLUSION

Endurance

In 2023, the association governing Argentina's popular Turismo Carretera motorsport circuit announced a modernization plan that would see older stock-car models gradually phased out of competition. As part of that plan, the Ford Falcon was to be retired by 2024, fully sixty years after its racing debut. The Falcon had been the Ford team's top performer over those six decades, delivering well over three hundred victories and twenty national championships, the last of them in 2015.[1] In the years before the TC moved to closed racetracks, it had proven itself in the long overland races through the Argentine interior, from tropical Misiones in the Northeast to snowy Patagonia in the South.[2] Its longevity and high performance in the TC attested to the legendary durability that had inspired such loyalty among the car's Argentine fans. Like its famous ancestor, the Model T, it had been designed to exacting standards of efficiency and reliability and built for the rugged landscapes of the Americas.

The Falcon's long racing career corresponds almost perfectly with the time span of the story presented here, which is fitting because it has served as a potent metonym for the political, economic, and symbolic struggles of Argentina's Cold War and post–Cold War eras. It has shifted identities and meanings repeatedly since the early 1960s while retaining a special cultural significance that far exceeds its utilitarian function as a piece of transportation machinery. Although the Falcon's stature in modern Argentine culture might seem quixotic to outside observers, it makes sense within the theoretical framework of automobility and the context of its historical era. The model was launched by Ford Motors in 1959, at the midpoint of Fordist automobility's golden age, which spanned from the end of World War II to the global recession and oil crisis of the early 1970s. The American system of mass automobile production spread to every continent during those three decades, and millions of people around the world achieved car ownership for the first time. The private automobile became a totem to the era's ideals

Conclusion

of technological modernity, economic growth, and consumerism: a "magical object," to recall the words of French philosopher Roland Barthes.[3]

Theories of automobility help to explain why certain cars like the VW Beetle, the Citroën DS, and the Falcon inspired such high cultural expectations in these years. In the 1960s, a private passenger car built in a modern automotive plant like the Pacheco Industrial Center stood as a signifier of a vast interconnected system of Fordist automobility. That regime comprised the global power and supply chains of multinational corporations like Ford, General Motors, Fiat, and Volkswagen; the mass production methods that had been honed over several decades since the era of the Model T; and the expanding road and highway networks being built to accommodate those cars. It also included sophisticated marketing techniques that infused the automobile with cultural power and identified the act of driving itself as an embodied experience of individual freedom. In countries like Argentina that were trying to jump-start their industrial modernization through policies to promote local automotive manufacturing, that car could also stand in for broad expectations around economic "development." Cars were also culturally malleable objects, and the Falcon was not the only automobile to morph along with changing political circumstances. The East German Trabant, or "Trabi," went through its own transformations in the same years. In the late Cold War era, it attracted ridicule as an example of the Eastern Bloc's shoddy manufacturing and substandard consumer goods. After the reunification of Germany in the early 1990s, however, it became an emblem of *Ostalgie* or nostalgia for the communist past.[4]

Automotive advertising emphasized just the final product: the gleaming automobile that appeared in full-color magazine spreads or in the television ads that were beamed into ever more households during these years. Behind the glossy images, however, stood a messy web of human connections that had brought that car into being. Like all complex human systems, it contained points of tension where people's competing interests and expectations could come into conflict. In the system of Fordist automobility, one of the most vulnerable points was the factory floor, where workers and corporate managers negotiated over the "wage-productivity nexus": the organization and pace of work, and the safety issues that arose when management sought to extract as much profit as possible from the manufacturing process. Workers like the activists on the shop-floor commission at Ford's Pacheco plant wanted a share of the prosperity associated with the Fordist project, and they fought against management changes that cut into their livelihoods by stopping work or holding workers' assemblies in the factory cafeterias. Military officials who cracked down on industrial union activism and used cars for surveillance, kidnapping operations, and propaganda purposes also sought to shape automobility according to their own priorities of control and discipline.

The Ford Falcon embodied its own set of meanings for the young people who sought employment at the Pacheco facility in the 1960s and early 1970s. It was an object of pride for men like Pedro Troiani and Adolfo Sánchez: an Argentine incarnation of the Ford brand, a hugely popular car with local buyers, and a champion on the racetrack. They and thousands of other young workers like them were thrilled to join Ford and ready to work hard for their own version of the postwar American dream: a tract house built in a new subdivision with a Falcon (or two) in the driveway. Young Ford wives like Arcelia Ortiz and Elisa Charlín were equally happy to be able to leave their own factory jobs and raise their children at home. In Argentina, however, that suburban dream was more modest in scale than in North America. Even for Ford workers, who enjoyed some of the highest industrial wages and benefits in the country, it involved saving up gradually to buy a small plot of land and escape overcrowded rooming houses or shared accommodations with extended family. Rather than buy a prefabricated bungalow, even the successful Ford line worker was more likely to build his own house with materials accumulated over time, including wood salvaged from the shipping crates unloaded at the factory. His family would not have the purchasing power to buy a Falcon, which was sold to the Argentine upper middle class, though with enough overtime hours he might get a second-hand car or a tiny Fiat like the one purchased by Adolfo Sánchez. He was more likely to take public transportation or cycle to work.

The Ford workers may have counted themselves lucky to work at the Pacheco plant, but they were still prepared to organize and defend their livelihoods and their personal safety. Like other autoworkers in the late 1960s and early 1970s, they got into power struggles with management over the pace of the assembly line, relative wages, and safety concerns. They also fought for greater union democracy, taking matters into their own hands at the shop-floor level when the national leaders of the SMATA union did not defend their interests. They organized plant-level assemblies, consulted with outside experts over safety concerns, and joined with workers from other factories in the Zona Norte to repudiate austerity measures in mid-1975. The political context in Argentina made those efforts difficult and dangerous, as both armed leftists and military forces infiltrated the factory to try to control the political direction of Argentina's industrial working class.

The paradox of the private automobile is that even while it stands in for complex political, social, and economic relationships, it can also embody very personal qualities for its human users. A car might support someone's livelihood, whether that person is a taxi driver who has relied on his trusty vehicle for his entire working life or an autoworker putting in extra time on the assembly line to support his family. For the person who finally achieves their dream of car ownership, like the protagonist in the film *Ford Falcon, buen estado*, that vehicle might instead serve as a tangible representation of success or social mobility. In specific political circumstances, a passenger car might operate as a bomb delivery system, a tool of surveillance, or a mechanism of disappearance.

Regardless of the situation, there is an intimacy to the human-automobile relationship. The car envelops its users in unique sensory experiences of sight, sound, touch, smell, and movement. That intimate, enclosed space can provide its occupants with a visceral sense of freedom, mobility, or adventure: precisely the qualities emphasized in automotive advertising. But for victims of disappearance in dictatorship-era Argentina, the car could be a suffocating and disorienting space, and a gateway into the nightmarish world of torture and detention. All these rich sensory and affective qualities also contributed to the automobile's significance as a carrier of memory, a kind of time machine linking past and present. Such memories could operate at both the individual and social level. In the case of the Ford Falcon, artists and activists working in the post-dictatorship era both represented and reinforced the Falcon's status as an object of collective, public memory. As anthropologist Antonius Robben has observed, artworks conveyed the "embodied dimension of trauma" in ways that documents and even testimonial accounts could not.[5] In this sense, the Falcon's fans and critics all pointed to that same defining quality: endurance. The old Falcons endured, both literally and metaphorically.

The story recounted here has pointed to other examples of endurance through Argentina's long dictatorship and post-dictatorship eras. It has highlighted the remarkable tenacity of activists like Pedro Troiani, who remained focused on his goal of achieving justice over more than four decades. Yet Troiani and his fellow survivors from Ford were up against other enduring forces. Take the example of José Rodríguez, who was backed by the anticommunist

American Institute for Free Labor Development when he assumed the leadership of the SMATA autoworkers' union in 1973. Rodríguez survived the dictatorship unscathed and emerged as one of the powerful bosses at the head of the CGT labor federation, maintaining his grip on SMATA for some thirty-six years until just before his death in 2009. Ford Argentina also weathered the economic storms of the dictatorship era and even recorded record profits through government contracts and financial speculation in the early 1980s. It survived the crisis in the local automotive sector and counted among the large firms that benefited from the last military junta's largesse when its corporate debt was absorbed by the state in 1983.

The laws imposed by the military juntas also endured well into the democratic era, as evidenced by the obstacles that frustrated the Ford survivors' labor court claims in the 1980s. In fact, some 417 laws decreed by the generals remained active well into the twenty-first century, accounting for nearly one-tenth of the laws governing the country.[6] Finally, the dictatorship left enduring economic and social wounds. Between 1976 and 1983, the ruling juntas successfully dismantled decades of labor gains and drove down employment and real incomes. Their policies hit especially hard in the suburban districts of Gran Buenos Aires, whose residents had benefited greatly from new employment opportunities after midcentury and who suffered intense surveillance and repression after March 24, 1976.

Still, history teaches that change is possible, and the Ford survivors have helped to change the legal framework governing corporate accountability for human rights violations. Although former Ford executives Pedro Müller and Héctor Sibilla appealed their convictions, the 2018 verdict in the Ford case set national and international precedents, counting as the first example of a criminal judgment against representatives of a multinational corporation in a domestic court of the Global South.[7] In fact, human rights scholars Leigh A. Payne, Gabriel Pereira, and Laura Bernal-Bermúdez highlighted the Ford plaintiffs' singular achievement in their 2020 book *Transitional Justice and Corporate Accountability from Below: Deploying Archimedes' Lever*. They even chose a photograph from the hearings in the San Martín criminal court to illustrate the cover. This comprehensive study of global corporate accountability efforts details the myriad obstacles faced by those who try to challenge companies for their involvement in human rights violations. Yet it cites the Ford survivors' success as a hopeful example of "civil society mobilization and institutional innovation."[8]

Conclusion

Typically, Pedro Troiani and Tomás Ojea Quintana did not rest after the 2018 criminal court decision. Instead, they petitioned the Inter-American Commission on Human Rights (IACHR) to take up Troiani's wrongful dismissal case against Ford Argentina that had been denied by the Argentine Supreme Court in the 1980s. The IACHR operates as an independent body within the Organization of American States charged with ensuring that member states uphold the standards laid out in the American Convention on Human Rights. It ruled in favor of Troiani's claim on March 23, 2021. Reviewing the evidence and outcome of the Ford case, the commission determined that "authorities and managers at Ford" had participated in the repression against the two dozen men disappeared in 1976 by providing security forces with information from their personnel files and with organizational and infrastructural support.[9] It also condemned the Argentine government for denying Troiani justice in his original labor claim against Ford Argentina. The commission even invited Troiani to help draft its recommendations to the Argentine government.

Unfortunately, Pedro Troiani died suddenly of a heart attack at the age of eighty on August 1, 2021, just before Argentina's Federal Criminal Appeals Court upheld the 2018 convictions in the Ford case, putting an end to the appeals process. On December 1, 2021, his widow, Elisa Charlín, and their son, Marcelo Norberto Troiani, took part in a ceremony to mark the Argentine government's acceptance of the IACHR report.[10] By signing that document, the Argentine government committed itself to enacting the commission's recommendations, which reflected, in part, Troiani's own hopes for the future. Those included, first, measures to ensure that the decision reached a broad audience. The government agreed to publicize the IACHR report widely by announcing the agreement in two national newspapers, posting the full document on the website of the federal Human Rights Secretariat, and sharing it with the SMATA autoworkers' union and with Argentina's two national labor federations: the CGT and the CTA. It committed to organizing a major public ceremony with the participation of high government officials and invitations to the leaders of those same labor organizations and to the top executives at Ford Argentina.

In the legal realm, the agreement annulled the application of the statute of limitations in the wrongful dismissals of the Ford workers who lost their jobs while imprisoned in 1976 and 1977. The Human Rights Secretariat committed itself to "further advancing" the men's "demand for justice" by creating an ad hoc tribunal to determine the government compensation owed to the Troiani family for the dismissal of Pedro's original claim, and by pursuing compensation from Ford for the victims and their families. The secretariat also promised to work with Ford Argentina to achieve the following goals: the opening of Ford's corporate archives to bring to light relevant documents from the dictatorship era; the adoption of human rights training for Ford personnel in Argentina; an official commitment from Ford to uphold the United Nations Guiding Principles on Corporations and Human Rights; and a financial commitment from the company to support further research on corporate responsibility for human rights crimes in Argentina.

Finally, the federal Human Rights Secretariat committed itself to "measures of symbolic restitution and the transmission of memory" relating to the specific events at Ford Argentina and to the broader persecution of labor activists during Argentina's last dictatorship. These included the promise to raise a new monument near the Pacheco factory with three pillars marked Memory, Truth, and Justice. The secretariat was also to undertake a training and information event with both national and international labor organizations to disseminate information about labor persecution during the dictatorship years; the surviving Ford workers and their family members were to be invited. Finally, it was to work with Argentina's national research council, Consejo Nacional de Investigaciones Científicas y Técnicas (CONICET), to further academic research into corporate responsibility in human rights crimes.

There are still no complete answers to the questions that compelled the Ford survivors to seek justice over several decades. Even Victoria Basualdo, the historian who has dedicated her career to the study of workplace repression and who supported the Ford plaintiffs through their trial as an expert witness, acknowledges that "the interpretations of the causes, meaning, and consequences of the dictatorship are still up for debate, not only in the historiography but also in public political and social spheres."[11] However, the dogged efforts of the Ford survivors helped to move that debate forward and to shed light on the widespread repression suffered by workers in Argentina's industrial neighborhoods. Their story underscores the perseverance and creativity that have been the hallmarks of Argentine civil society since the dictatorship's fall.

Notes

INTRODUCTION

1. Horacio Aizpeolea, "La despedida al último Falcon taxi," *Clarín*, February 9, 2004, https://www.clarin.com/ediciones-anteriores/despedida-ultimo-falcon-taxi_0_H1LZQmR1RFe.html.
2. Eduardo Pavlovsky, "El Ford Falcon," *Página/12*, February 23, 2004, Contratapa, https://www.pagina12.com.ar/diario/contratapa/13-31808-2004-02-23.html.
3. Robben, *Argentina Betrayed*. For some representative titles about these long-standing debates over memory and justice in Argentina, see Jelin, *Los trabajos de la memoria*; Jelin and Langland, *Monumentos, memoriales y marcas territoriales*; Kaiser, *Postmemories of Terror*; Carnovale, Lorenz, and Pittaluga, *Historia, memoria y fuentes orales*; Jelin, "Public Memorialization in Perspective"; Crenzel, *La historia política del Nunca Más*; Lvovich and Bisquert, *La cambiante memoria de la dictadura*; Feld and Stites Mor, *El pasado que miramos*; Memoria Abierta, *Memorias en la ciudad*; Crenzel, *Los desaparecidos en la Argentina*; Andriotti Romanin, "Decir la verdad, hacer justicia"; Allier Montaño and Crenzel, *Las luchas por la memoria en América Latina*; Feld, "Preservar, recuperar, ocupar"; and Brennan, *Argentina's Missing Bones*.
4. Robben, *Argentina Betrayed*, 2.
5. Claims for Relief and Demand for Jury Trial, Pulega et al. v. Ford Motor Company, no. CV04-0411AHM (C.D. Cal, January 23, 2004).
6. Ministerio de Justicia, *Responsabilidad empresarial*.
7. Daniel Politi, "Argentina Convicts Ex-Ford Executives for Abuses during Dictatorship," *New York Times*, December 11, 2018, https://www.nytimes.com/2018/12/11/world/americas/argentina-ford.html; Cassandra Garrison and Nicolás Misculin, "Ex–Ford Argentina Executives Convicted in Torture Case; Victims May Sue in U.S." Reuters, December 11, 2018, https://www.reuters.com/article/us-argentina-rights-ford-motor-idUSKBN1OA25H; and Victoria Basualdo, "The Ford Case, 40 Years Later," JusticeInfo.net,

Fondation Hirondelle, February 18, 2019, https://www.justiceinfo.net/en/40348-the-ford-case-40-years-later.html.

8. Luciana Bertoia, "Secuestros y torturas a 24 trabajadores de Ford: Confirmaron las condenas contra dos exdirectivos de la empresa," *Página/12*, September 30, 2021, https://www.pagina12.com.ar/371536-secuestros-y-torturas-a-24-trabajadores-de-ford-confirmaron-.

9. Payne, Pereira, and Bernal-Bermúdez, *Transitional Justice*, 255–59. The authors considered the Ford Argentina case so significant that they featured it on the cover of their book.

10. Smith, *Talons of the Eagle*.

11. Carlos Osorio and Kathleen Costar, eds., "Kissinger to the Argentine Generals in 1976: 'If There Are Things That Have to Be Done, You Should Do Them Quickly,'" National Security Archive, Electronic Briefing Book, no. 133, August 27, 2004, https://nsarchive2.gwu.edu/NSAEBB/NSAEBB133/index.htm.

12. Some key examples include Joseph and Spenser, *In from the Cold*; Grandin, *The Last Colonial Massacre*; Alegre, *Railroad Radicals in Cold War Mexico*; Sarzynski, *Revolution in the Terra do Sol*; Field, Krepp, and Pettinà, *Latin America and the Global Cold War*; and Chastain and Lorek, *Itineraries of Expertise*. Other fine examples from a slightly earlier era include Winn, *Weavers of Revolution*; and Brennan, *The Labor Wars in Córdoba*.

13. Elena, *Dignifying Argentina*, 5.

14. See, for example, Verbitsky and Bohoslavsky, *Cuentas pendientes*; and V. Basualdo, Berghoff, and Bucheli, *Big Business and Dictatorships in Latin America*.

15. E. Basualdo, *Estudios de historia económica argentina*, 53–76.

16. O'Brien, *The Century of U.S. Capitalism in Latin America*, 125.

17. O'Brien, *The Century of U.S. Capitalism in Latin America*, viii.

18. García Márquez, *Cien años de soledad*; Galeano, *Las venas abiertas de América latina*; and Dorfman and Mattelart, *Para leer al Pato Donald*.

19. I discuss this in detail in chapter 3.

20. In both Mexico and Brazil, for example, local fans similarly adopted the Volkswagen Beetle as a beloved "national" car. See Rieger, *The People's Car*.

21. On Henry Ford's stature and fame in Brazil, see Grandin, *Fordlandia*; and Wolfe, *Autos and Progress*, 61–69.

22. Downs, *Diego Rivera*.

23. Grandin, *Fordlandia*, 152.

24. Wolfe, *Autos and Progress*, 64.
25. Wolfe, *Autos and Progress*; and Bachelor, "Miracle on Ice."
26. Winn, *Victims of the Chilean Miracle*. See also Klein, *The Shock Doctrine*.
27. Shapley, *Promise and Power*, 39–46; and Brinkley, *Wheels for the World*, 497–506.
28. Shapley, *Promise and Power*, 53.
29. Brinkley, *Wheels for the World*, 587.
30. Shapley, *Promise and Power*, 55.
31. Shapley, *Promise and Power*, 37.
32. Brinkley, *Wheels for the World*, 595.
33. Shapley, *Promise and Power*, 61–62.
34. Ford Motor Company, "The Ford Family of Fine Cars . . . for 1960," Detroit Public Library (DPL), National Automotive History Collection (NAHC), Automobiles, folder "Ford, 1960 (Miscellaneous)."
35. Ford Motor Company, "Falcon has more of everything you want most in a compact car," DPL, NAHC, folder "Ford, 1960 (Catalogs)."
36. Ford Motor Company, "Ford Falcon and Falcon Wagons," DPL, NAHC, Automobiles, folder "Ford, 1960 (Miscellaneous)."
37. Brinkley, *Wheels for the World*, 597.
38. Frank, *The Conquest of Cool*, 47.
39. Filmways, *A Wonderful New World of Fords* (advertisement, 1960), Internet Archive, https://archive.org/details/Wonderfu1960.
40. Seiler, *Republic of Drivers*, 71.
41. Seiler, *Republic of Drivers*, 72.
42. For a critical examination of this myth of American expansion and movement, see Grandin, *The End of the Myth*.
43. George Stoney, dir., *The American Road* (MPO Productions, 1953), Internet Archive, https://archive.org/details/the-american-road-1953.
44. Russell Lynes, "How Customers Shape Birth of New Car" (Ford Motors advertisement), *New York Times*, October 4, 1959, section 11. DPL, NAHC, Automobiles, folder "Ford, 1960 (Miscellaneous)."
45. "The Engineering Revolution and the New Ford Cars," *New York Times*, advertising supplement, October 4, 1959.
46. Roger Butterfield, "Henry Ford's Three Great Revolutions Are Still Going On," *New York Times*, October 4, 1959, section 11.
47. Brinkley, *Wheels for the World*, 597; and R. Miller, *Falcon: The New-Size Ford*, 23.

48. Brinkley, *Wheels for the World*, 598.
49. Gill, *The School of the Americas*; Grandin, *Empire's Workshop*; Grandin and Joseph, *A Century of Revolution*; McSherry, *Predatory States*; Rabe, *The Killing Zone*; and Weld, *Paper Cadavers*. On French counterinsurgency influences in Latin America, see Robin, *Escadrons de la mort*. On far-right influences from Spain, see Weld, "Holy War."
50. Wilkins and Hill, *American Business Abroad*, 424.
51. Shapley, *Promise and Power*, 74.
52. Brinkley, *Wheels for the World*, 614.
53. On government policy relating to the automotive sector in Australia, see Conlon and Perkins, *Wheels and Deals*.
54. On the evolution of the Falcon design in Australia, see Rob Margeit, "How the Ford Falcon Was Sold to the Australian Public," Drive, July 17, 2023, https://www.drive.com.au/caradvice/how-the-ford-falcon-was-sold-to-the-australian-public/.
55. The total combined sales of Falcon sedans and station wagons (Falcon Rural) came to 494,209. See "Ventas del Falcon por año," Todo Falcon, https://www.todofalcon.com.ar/historia.htm. Annual vehicle sales reports for all Argentine automakers dating back to 1966 can be found at Asociación de Fabricantes de Automotores, Anuarios, https://adefa.org.ar/es/estadisticas-anuarios.
56. Key titles that have influenced my thinking include Clarsen and Veracini, "Settler Colonial Automobilities"; Flink, *The Car Culture*; Flink, *The Automobile Age*; Böhm et al., *Against Automobility*; Duffy, *The Speed Handbook*; Gartman, "Three Ages of the Automobile"; Gewald, Luning, and Van Walraven, *The Speed of Change*; Grandin, *Fordlandia*; D. Miller, *Car Cultures*; S. W. Miller, *The Street Is Ours*; Mom, *Atlantic Automobilism*; Norton, *Fighting Traffic*; Paterson, *Automobile Politics*; Rieger, *The People's Car*; Ross, *Fast Cars, Clean Bodies*; Sachs, *For Love of the Automobile*; Seiler, *Republic of Drivers*; Siegelbaum, *Cars for Comrades*; Siegelbaum, *The Socialist Car*; Featherstone, Thrift, and Urry, *Automobilities*; Volti, *Cars and Culture*; Wolfe, *Autos and Progress*; and Wollen and Kerr, *Autopia: Cars and Culture*.
57. Urry, "The 'System' of Automobility."
58. Paterson, *Automobile Politics*, 19–31.
59. Gilroy, "Driving While Black"; and Seiler, *Republic of Drivers*, 105–28.

60. See, for instance, Siegelbaum, *Cars for Comrades*; and Siegelbaum, *The Socialist Car.*
61. Gewald, "Missionaries, Hereros, and Motorcars."
62. Clarsen and Veracini, "Settler Colonial Automobilities."
63. Barthes, "The New Citroen."
64. Rieger, *The People's Car.*
65. D. Miller, *Car Cultures.*
66. Young, "The Life and Death of Cars."
67. D. Miller, *Car Cultures*, 2.
68. Auslander, "Beyond Words," 1020.
69. Auslander, "Beyond Words," 1016.
70. See the essays in Featherstone, Thrift, and Urry, *Automobilities.*
71. CONADEP, *Nunca Más*; Calveiro, *Poder y desaparición*; and Memoria Abierta, *Memorias en la ciudad.*

CHAPTER ONE

1. "Argentine Man Drives '81 Falcon Nearly 10,000 Miles to Ford Headquarters in Dearborn," *Grand Rapids (MI) Press*, May 30, 2008, http://blog.mlive.com/grpress/2008/05/argentine_man_drives_81_falcon.html.
2. "Close Up: Argentina's Love for the Ford Falcon," BBC News, December 12, 2010, https://www.bbc.com/news/av/world-latin-america-11968544/close-up-argentina-s-love-for-the-ford-falcon; and Fiona Ortiz, "Argentine Death Squad Cars Try for New Image," Reuters, May 4, 2007, https://www.reuters.com/article/us-argentina-falcons/argentine-death-squad-cars-try-for-new-image-idUSN0332251120070504?pageNumber=2&virtualBrandChannel=0.
3. Historian Ezequiel Adamovsky chose a publicity shot from *La familia Falcón* to illustrate the cover of his comprehensive history of the Argentine middle class. See Adamovsky, *Historia de la clase media argentina.* For a survey of Falcon advertisements, see González Peña, "Ford Falcon (1962–1991)."
4. Salvatore, "Yankee Advertising in Buenos Aires."
5. Rock, *Argentina, 1516–1982*, 162–72.
6. See Orlove, *The Allure of the Foreign*; and Bauer, *Goods, Power, History.*

7. García Heras, *Automotores norteamericanos, caminos y modernización urbana*, 9–27.
8. Wilkins and Hill, *American Business Abroad*, 57; and Alejandro Jasinski, "Abogados y algo más: El estudio O'Farrell y su rol en la represión de Ford," *El Cohete a la Luna*, September 16, 2018, https://www.elcohetealaluna.com/abogados-y-algo-mas/.
9. Wilkins and Hill, *American Business Abroad*, 92–95.
10. Ford Argentina, "Los primeros años de Ford en Argentina," https://www.ford.com.ar/acerca-de-ford/institucional/los-primero-anos/.
11. Salvatore, "Yankee Advertising in Buenos Aires," 219. For a promotional depiction of GM's global spread, see the Handy (Jam) Organization, *General Motors around the World* (1927), Internet Archive, https://archive.org/details/GeneralM1927.
12. "Chevrolet," Autohistoria: La Historia de la Industria Automotriz Argentina, https://autohistoria.com.ar/index.php/marcas-de-autos/chevrolet/.
13. Piglia, *Autos, rutas y turismo*, 29–33; and Salvatore, "Imperial Mechanics," 677.
14. Belini, "Negocios, poder y política industrial," 111.
15. García Heras, *Automotores norteamericanos, caminos y modernización urbana*, 14–17.
16. Flink, *The Automobile Age*, 95. On Argentina's rudimentary road network, see Ballent, "Kilómetro cero," 109.
17. Salvatore, "Yankee Advertising in Buenos Aires," 224.
18. "Between 1919 and 1930, leading figures in the automotive business sector held half the positions on the board of directors and occupied the presidency on four different occasions." Piglia, *Autos, rutas y turismo*, 29. See also Ballent, "Kilómetro cero," 111.
19. Piglia, *Autos, rutas y turismo*, 33.
20. *Automovilismo* 79 (May 1925), cited in Ballent, "Kilómetro cero," 112.
21. "Paseos saludables, económicos e instructivos," in *Femenil* 1 (September 14, 1925), cited in Ballent, "Kilómetro cero," 129.
22. Salvatore, "Imperial Mechanics," 676–78; Ballent, "Kilómetro cero," 112–14; and Piglia, *Autos, rutas y turismo*, 117–28.
23. Salvatore, "Yankee Advertising in Buenos Aires," 216–35.
24. Salvatore, "Yankee Advertising in Buenos Aires," 221. See also R. Davis, "Negotiating Local and Global Knowledge."
25. Salvatore, "Yankee Advertising in Buenos Aires," 228.

26. On anxieties about urban chaos and criminality in the interwar era, see Caimari, *While the City Sleeps*. On the rise of the *gauchesco* ideal, see Ludmer, *El género gauchesco*; Huberman, *Gauchos and Foreigners*; and Acree, *Staging Frontiers*.
27. Salvatore, "Yankee Advertising in Buenos Aires," 226.
28. Salvatore, "Yankee Advertising in Buenos Aires," 222; and Pierce, *Gringo-Gaucho*, 108.
29. Piglia, *Autos, rutas y turismo*, 72.
30. Archetti, *El potrero, la pista y el ring*, 73.
31. Archetti, *El potrero, la pista y el ring*, 70. Argentina's state promotion of long-distance racing fits well with the model of settler colonial automobility defined in Clarsen and Veracini, "Settler Colonial Automobilities." See also Clarsen, "Australia—Drive It Like You Stole It"; and Ballent, "Kilómetro cero."
32. Archetti, *El potrero, la pista y el ring*, 75–78. For a detailed popular history of Argentine motorsports, see Parga, *Historia deportiva del automovilismo*.
33. "De nuevo campeón, como una costumbre," in Parga, *Historia deportiva del automovilismo*, vol. 3, no. 43.
34. Ballent, "Kilómetro cero," 112.
35. Sourrouille, *El complejo automotor en Argentina*, 31.
36. Sourrouille, *El complejo automotor en Argentina*, 39.
37. Wolfe, *Autos and Progress*, 91–106.
38. On Peronism, see Elena, *Dignifying Argentina*; James, *Resistance and Integration*; Karush and Chamosa, *The New Cultural History of Peronism*; and Milanesio, *Workers Go Shopping in Argentina*. On Frondizi, see Altamirano, *Arturo Frondizi, o el hombre de ideas como político*; Rodríguez Lamas, *La presidencia de Frondizi*; Sikkink, *Ideas and Institutions*; and Szusterman, *Frondizi and the Politics of Developmentalism*.
39. Sikkink, *Ideas and Institutions*, 4.
40. Schvarzer, *La industria que supimos conseguir*, 164–68.
41. Brennan, *The Labor Wars in Córdoba*, 30.
42. Sikkink, *Ideas and Institutions*, 3.
43. Gadano, *Historia del petróleo en la argentina*, 691–94.
44. On Peronist social policy and ideals of working-class dignity, see Elena, *Dignifying Argentina*; and Milanesio, *Workers Go Shopping*.
45. Elena, *Dignifying Argentina*, 4.
46. Cited in Elena, *Dignifying Argentina*, 69.

47. On the mechanisms of mass consent developed by the Peronist regime, see Plotkin, *Mañana es San Perón*.
48. Piglia, *Autos, rutas y turismo*, 91–98.
49. Piglia, *Autos, rutas y turismo*, 94.
50. Sheinin, *Argentina and the United States*, 105.
51. Although Perón pressured Mercedes Argentina to follow through on its promised investment in a modern manufacturing facility, for its first years the company appears to have operated as a front funneling Nazis and Nazi money to South America. See Weber, *La conexión alemana*, 52–80; and Belini, "Negocios, poder y política industrial," 120–21.
52. Belini, "Negocios, poder y política industrial," 122–25.
53. Belini, "Negocios, poder y política industrial," 116–17.
54. Belini, "Negocios, poder y política industrial," 128.
55. S. F. Woodell to J. Speers, September 12, 1955, Duke University Library, Hartman Center, JWT Archive, Shirley F. Woodell papers, office files and correspondence, box 3.
56. Seveso, "Millions of Small Battles," 314–16.
57. Adamovsky, *Historia de la clase media argentina*, 327–39.
58. Cited in Adamovsky, *Historia de la clase media argentina*, 332.
59. Sikkink, *Ideas and Institutions*, 33.
60. Wolfe, *Autos and Progress*, 113–24.
61. Adamovsky, *Historia de la clase media argentina*, 342–44; and Schneider, *Los compañeros*, 113–15.
62. Rey, *¿Es Frondizi un nuevo Perón?*, 125, cited in Adamovsky, *Historia de la clase media argentina*, 347.
63. Sikkink, *Ideas and Institutions*, 36.
64. Translation of Argentine Presidency Decree no. 3696, "Plant Overview and Analysis Files—Argentina, 1961–1962," Benson Ford Research Center (BFRC), accession 1942.
65. Sourrouille, *El complejo automotor en Argentina*, 49.
66. Wolfe, *Autos and Progress*, 121–22; and Bachelor, "Miracle on Ice."
67. Rabe, *The Most Dangerous Area in the World*, 11.
68. "Terrenos para la nueva fábrica Ford," *Mundo Ford* 36, no. 412 (August 1959): 30.
69. The one exception was Mercedes-Benz, which located its truck and bus manufacturing facility near the capital during Perón's second term in office.

70. "Peugeot," Autohistoria: La Historia de la Industria Automotriz Argentina, https://autohistoria.com.ar/index.php/marcas-de-autos/peugeot/; and "Citroën," Autohistoria: La Historia de la Industria Automotriz Argentina, https://autohistoria.com.ar/index.php/marcas-de-autos/citroen/.
71. Alejandro Franco, "Autos Argentinos: Historia del Chevrolet Chevy (y su antecesor, el Chevrolet 400)," Autos de Culto, http://www.autosdeculto.com.ar/argentinos-chevrolet-chevy/.
72. Diego Durruty, "Torino, el auto argentino que se ganó el cariño de la gente en la calle y la pista," *Automundo*, July 15, 2022, https://automundo.com.ar/torino-argentina-historia/.
73. Hernán Oliveri, "Fiat 600: 60 años de un clásico argentino," *Clarín*, April 30, 2020, https://www.clarin.com/autos/fiat-600-60-anos-clasico-argentino_0_IAyuJ49qN.html.
74. Argentine Car Proposal, work papers, January 6, 1961, and M. H. Wiley to Mr. W. L. Kee, "Argentine Passenger Car Program," January 25, 1961, BFRC, accession 1942, box 3.
75. Henry Ford II, "Speech on Foreign Competition," 1961, quoted in Wilkins and Hill, *American Business Abroad*, 414.
76. "Ecos de un Agasajo," *Mundo Ford* 36, no. 412 (August 1959): 31. Under the dictatorship of 1976–1983, this rhetoric about Argentina's commitment to "Western civilization" would be used as a justification for military rule.
77. "Ford Motor Argentina S.A., inauguró su centro industrial," *Mundo Ford* 36, no. 430 (October 1961): 18.
78. "Fue presentado el Falcon 62 a las autoridades nacionales," *Mundo Ford* 36, no. 433 (February–March 1962): 1.
79. "A un doble acontecimiento dió lugar la presentación del Falcon en la concesionaria Ford de Oscar Gálvez," *Mundo Ford* 36, no. 433 (February–March 1962): 11.
80. Seiler, *Republic of Drivers*, 72.
81. "Operation Pan American" [sic], *Time* 71, no. 26 (June 30, 1958): 27.
82. Rabe, *The Most Dangerous Area in the World*, 9.
83. Kathryn Sikkink notes that the developmentalist reform programs in Argentina and Brazil predated the publication of key American modernization texts by Rostow and Albert Hirschman. Moreover, the South American developmentalists put more emphasis on economic planning and the promotion of heavy industry. See Sikkink, *Ideas and Institutions*, 12–14.

84. Arturo Frondizi, "Report to the President on Latin American Mission," cited in Brands, *Latin America's Cold War*, 44.
85. William H. Brubeck, "Memorandum for Mr. McGeorge Bundy, the White House, Public Support for the Alliance for Progress," August 10, 1962. Papers of John F. Kennedy, Presidential Papers, National Security Files 1962, July 3–August 7. File: Alliance for Progress, General, July 1962, JFKNSF-290-023. http://www.jfklibrary.org/Asset-Viewer/Archives/JFKNSF-290-023.aspx.
86. Schuhrke, "Comradely Brainwashing," 42–43.
87. Schuhrke, "Comradely Brainwashing," 54.
88. González Peña, "Ford Falcon (1962–1991)," 113–28.
89. "Publicidades, 1962," Todo Falcon, https://www.todofalcon.com.ar/Fotos/Pub_62_01.jpg.
90. "Publicidades, 1962," Todo Falcon, https://www.todofalcon.com.ar/Fotos/Pub_62_04.jpg.
91. "Publicidades, 1963," Todo Falcon, https://www.todofalcon.com.ar/Fotos/Pub_62_02.jpg.
92. "Publicidades, 1965," Todo Falcon, https://www.todofalcon.com.ar/Fotos/Pub_65_06.jpg.
93. "Publicidades, 1963," Todo Falcon, https://www.todofalcon.com.ar/Fotos/Pub_63_01.jpg.
94. "Publicidades, 1963," Todo Falcon, https://www.todofalcon.com.ar/Fotos/Pub_63_04.jpg.
95. "Publicidades, 1966," Todo Falcon, https://www.todofalcon.com.ar/Fotos/Pub_66_05.jpg.
96. "Publicidades, 1966," Todo Falcon, https://www.todofalcon.com.ar/Fotos/Pub_66_06.jpg.
97. Internal JWT communications relating to Ford television investments in this period can be found in Duke University Library, Hartman Center, Dan Seymour papers, boxes 30–34.
98. Richard Cass to Dan Seymour, April 17, 1962, Duke University Library, Hartman Center, Dan Seymour papers, box 31, Ford Motor Company, January–June 1962.
99. Sheinin, *Argentina and the United States*, 101–2.
100. Aguilar, "Televisión y vida privada," 255–58.
101. Aguilar, "Televisión y vida privada," 255–58.
102. González Peña, "Ford Falcon (1962–1991)," 119–20.

103. Unfortunately, only a handful of episodes are available online. See "La familia Falcón episodios completos (6)," YouTube, https://www.youtube.com/watch?v=jydNjhc3LxM.
104. Jorge Nielsen, "La familia Falcón," Teleficciones, July 24, 2017, https://teleficcionesdeljilguero.blogspot.com/search/label/La%20familia%20Falc%C3%B3n.
105. This complaint appears in a letter to the editor in the popular magazine *Radiolandia*, published on January 4, 1963. Cited in Aguilar, "Televisión y vida privada," 262n18.
106. Aprea and Soto, "De *La familia Falcón* a *Graduados*."
107. Manzano, *The Age of Youth in Argentina*.
108. "Publicidades, 1970," Todo Falcon, https://www.todofalcon.com.ar/Fotos/Pub_70_01.jpg.
109. "Publicidades, 1970," Todo Falcon, https://www.todofalcon.com.ar/Fotos/Pub_70_05.jpg.
110. "Operación veteranos," *Fordlandia* (1968), BFRC, accession 1942, box 3.
111. Brands, *Latin America's Cold War*, 56–58.
112. Sikkink, *Ideas and Institutions*, 104.
113. Sikkink, *Ideas and Institutions*, 118.
114. Hammond, "A Functional Analysis of Defense Department Decision-Making."
115. "Militares argentinos visitan Ford Motor Company en Estados Unidos," *Mundo Ford* 36, no. 433 (February–March 1962): 25.
116. Cited in CONADEP, *Nunca Más*, 475.
117. Sourrouille, *El complejo automotor en Argentina*, 53.
118. Arturo Frondizi's brother Silvio Frondizi was a leading figure in this Argentine New Left. Pozzi and Schneider, *Los setentistas*; Sigal, *Intelectuales y poder en Argentina*; Spinelli, *De antiperonistas a peronistas revolucionarios*; and Terán, *Nuestros años sesentas*.

CHAPTER TWO

1. Testimony of Adolfo Sánchez, Tigre, November 9, 2006, Memoria Abierta, Archivo Oral, AO0461.
2. Piglia, *Autos, rutas y turismo*, 96.
3. Interview with Arcelia Ortiz, San Fernando, Buenos Aires, July 10, 2005.

4. Interview with Pedro Troiani, Beccar, Buenos Aires, July 8, 2005.
5. Testimony of Adolfo Sánchez, Memoria Abierta.
6. Interview with Arcelia Ortiz.
7. Interview with Arcelia Ortiz.
8. The institution of the internal claims committee will be described in detail below. For a history of its evolution, see V. Basualdo, "Labor and Structural Change"; and V. Basualdo, "Shop-Floor Labor Organization in Argentina."
9. As I will discuss in detail in subsequent chapters, no one knows exactly how many Ford Argentina workers were disappeared during military rule, though twenty-two union activists who were abducted within the first three weeks of the dictatorship would later band together, along with two others disappeared later in 1976, to launch a judicial investigation into their detentions.
10. Testimony of Pedro Troiani, cited in Poder Judicial de la Nación, Tribunal Oral en lo Criminal Federal no. 1 de San Martín, Fundamentos Causas 2855 y 2358, March 15, 2019.
11. CONADEP, Nunca Más, 375.
12. V. Basualdo, "Complicidad patronal-militar en la última dictadura argentina"; Verbitsky and Bohoslavsky, *Cuentas pendientes*; Ministerio de Justicia, *Responsabilidad empresarial*; and V. Basualdo, Berghoff, and Bucheli, *Big Business and Dictatorships in Latin America*.
13. Gramsci, "Americanism and Fordism." Although the literature on Fordism is too vast to cite here, an accessible synthesis appears in Pizzolato, *Challenging Global Capitalism*, 19–45.
14. US industrial investment in Argentina more than tripled between 1955 and 1969, from $230 million to $789 million. Brennan, *The Labor Wars in Córdoba*, 15. On the economic impacts of desarrollismo, see E. Basualdo, *Estudios de historia económica argentina*, 25–107.
15. Silver, *Forces of Labor*, 41–74.
16. Silver, *Forces of Labor*, 45.
17. Silver, *Forces of Labor*, 64.
18. Silver, *Forces of Labor*, 64. On autoworkers as agents of democratization in Brazil, see Wolfe, *Autos and Progress*, 145–77.
19. Brennan, *The Labor Wars in Córdoba*, 85–86.
20. Ford Argentina SCA, *Ford: 90 años en la Argentina*, 47.
21. Ford Argentina SCA, *Ford: 90 años en la Argentina*, 47. "La Panamericana" is the nickname given to the suburban stretch of Route 9, which extends

all the way to the Bolivian border, connecting to other highways that make up the Pan-American Highway network.
22. Ford Argentina SCA, *Ford: 90 años en la Argentina*, 60.
23. Schneider, *Los compañeros*, 31.
24. Schneider, *Los compañeros*, 36.
25. Schneider, *Los compañeros*, 68–69.
26. Schneider, *Los compañeros*, 55–56.
27. "Nuestra historia," Mondelez International (formerly Terrabusi), https://ar.mondelezinternational.com/about-us/our-history.
28. Forni and Roldán, "Trayectorias laborales de residentes de areas urbanas pobres," 587.
29. Abós, *Las organizaciones sindicales*, 12–13.
30. Schneider, *Los compañeros*, 42.
31. Schneider, *Los compañeros*, 60–63.
32. Benedetti, "Evolución espacial y funcional."
33. Benedetti, "Evolución espacial y funcional," 23.
34. Memoria Abierta, *Reconocer Campo de Mayo*, 64–72.
35. A synthesis of the economic and social changes wrought by desarrollismo appears in Aroskind, "El país del desarrollo posible."
36. Frigerio, *Los trabajadores y el desarrollo nacional*, 3, cited in Schneider, *Los compañeros*, 114.
37. Doyon, "La organización del movimiento sindical peronista," 203–5.
38. Brennan, *The Labor Wars in Córdoba*, 6–13.
39. Doyon, "La organización del movimiento sindical peronista," 206–7; and James, *Resistance and Integration*, 10–11.
40. James, *Resistance and Integration*, 7–40.
41. V. Basualdo, "Los delegados y las comisiones internas"; V. Basualdo, "Labor and Structural Change"; and Schneider, *Los compañeros*.
42. V. Basualdo, "Labor and Structural Change," 45–50; and V. Basualdo, "Los delegados y las comisiones internas," 85–89.
43. V. Basualdo, "Labor and Structural Change," 6.
44. V. Basualdo, "Los delegados y las comisiones internas," 4–6.
45. V. Basualdo, "Los delegados y las comisiones internas," 91–94.
46. Confederación General Económica, "Primer congreso de organización y relaciones de trabajo," Buenos Aires, 1954, 70–71, https://biblioteca.csjn.gov.ar/cgi-bin/koha/opac-detail.pl?biblionumber=6483, cited in V. Basualdo, "Los delegados y las comisiones internas," 92.

47. Seveso, "Millions of Small Battles," 314–16; James, *Resistance and Integration*, 43–71; and Schneider, *Los compañeros*, 77–91.
48. This intelligence service went through several minor name changes, though it is best known as the DIPPBA. Comisión Provincial por la Memoria, "Historia institucional de la DIPPBA."
49. Schneider, *Los compañeros*, 257–303; and James, *Resistance and Integration*, 215–19.
50. Brennan, *The Labor Wars in Córdoba*, 16–19, 85–99; and James, *Resistance and Integration*, 215–48.
51. The US military began courting the loyalty of Argentine officers in the late 1940s at the Latin American Ground School, precursor to the infamous School of the Americas, by offering them privileges that set them apart from other Latin American trainees. Gill, *The School of the Americas*, 65–69.
52. Brennan, *The Labor Wars in Córdoba*, 13.
53. Evans, Hoeffel, and James, "Reflections on Argentine Auto Workers and Their Unions," 134.
54. Sourrouille, *El complejo automotor en Argentina*, 56.
55. Asociación de Fabricantes de Automotores, *1966: 1,000,000 de automotores argentinos*.
56. Sourrouille, *El complejo automotor en Argentina*, 55.
57. Brennan, *The Labor Wars in Córdoba*, 136.
58. Interview with Arcelia Ortiz.
59. Alejandra Dandan, "Años de plomo en sangre," *El Cohete a la Luna*, April 22, 2018, https://www.elcohetealaluna.com/anos-de-plomo-en-sangre/.
60. On production methods at Ford Argentina, see Lascano, Menéndez, and Vocos, "Análisis del proceso de trabajo"; and Alejandro Jasinski, "La clase: Un economista, una historiadora y un sociólogo, en una lección magistral en el Juicio a Ford," *El Cohete a la Luna*, October 21, 2018, https://www.elcohetealaluna.com/la-clase/.
61. Ministerio de Justicia, *Responsabilidad empresarial*, 1:458.
62. *Fordlandia* (1968), BFRC, accession 1942, box 3; and Iglesias, *Escuela Técnica Henry Ford*, 24–30.
63. "Quinchos," *Fordlandia* (1968), BFRC, accession 1942, box 3.
64. Lascano Warnes, "Cambios y continuidades," 40.
65. Brennan, *The Labor Wars in Córdoba*, 16.
66. Brennan, *The Labor Wars in Córdoba*, 16.

67. The secret policy was known as the Plan CONINTES, or "the State Plan for Internal Disturbance." Pontoriero, "Estado de excepción y contrainsurgencia"; and Marengo Hecker, "El enemigo político."
68. Sourrouille, *El complejo automotor en Argentina*, 15–17.
69. Brennan, *The Labor Wars in Córdoba*, 143–44.
70. A detailed reconstruction of early dependency debates appears in Packenham, *The Dependency Movement*.
71. Brennan, *The Labor Wars in Córdoba*, 145; and Anzorena, *Tiempo de violencia y utopía*, 42–43.
72. Brands, *Latin America's Cold War*, 97–104.
73. Anzorena, *Tiempo de violencia y utopía*, 66–67.
74. Mangiantini, "La agrupación Tendencia de Avanzada Mecánica," 6.
75. In Spanish, the suffix *-azo* can be added to a noun to indicate either a physical blow or strike (a *puñetazo* to indicate a blow with a fist, or *puño*) or an augmented size (a *bigotazo* to indicate a large mustache, or *bigote*). In twentieth-century Latin America, it became common to refer to large urban riots or insurrections by adding *-azo* to the name of the corresponding city. The Bogotazo of 1948 marked a political turning point for Colombia, as did the Cordobazo of 1969 for Argentina. Other Argentine uprisings of the late 1960s and early 1970s included three separate Tucumanazos (in Tucumán), and the Rosariazo (in Rosario).
76. Brennan, *The Labor Wars in Córdoba*, 151.
77. Brennan, *The Labor Wars in Córdoba*, 158.
78. Brennan, *The Labor Wars in Córdoba*, 155.
79. Brennan, *The Labor Wars in Córdoba*, 157–59.
80. Nassif, *Tucumanazos*; Nassif, "Las luchas obreras tucumanas"; and Bonavena and Millán, "El movimiento estudiantil rosarino."
81. Brennan, *The Labor Wars in Córdoba*, 177.
82. Brennan, *The Labor Wars in Córdoba*, 172.
83. Jelin and Torre, "Los nuevos trabajadores en América Latina," 19.
84. Brennan, *The Labor Wars in Córdoba*, 163.
85. Laclau, "Argentina: Imperialist Strategy and the May Crisis," 19.
86. Harari, "La burocracia peronista," 2–3.
87. Cited in Lascano Warnes, "Cambios y continuidades," 40.
88. Lascano Warnes, "Cambios y continuidades," 43–44.
89. Brennan, *The Labor Wars in Córdoba*, 163.

CHAPTER THREE

1. For an analysis of the military coup of 1976 as a response to this labor mobilization, see V. Basualdo, "Business and the Military in the Argentine Dictatorship."
2. In his comprehensive study of workplace organizing among metalworkers in the Zona Norte, historian Alejandro Schneider stresses that plant-level activists in the metalworkers' union were similarly motivated by concrete issues rather than abstract ideological positions, although some were radicalized by the experience of mobilization itself. See Schneider, *Los compañeros*, 25–26.
3. A detailed analysis of workplace repression during the last dictatorship appears in Ministerio de Justicia, *Responsabilidad empresarial*. See also V. Basualdo, Berghoff, and Bucheli, *Big Business and Dictatorships in Latin America*.
4. On the naturalization of violence in Argentine popular culture, see Carassai, *The Argentine Silent Majority*.
5. Grandin, "Living in Revolutionary Time," 2.
6. Grandin, "Living in Revolutionary Time," 2.
7. Interview with Carlos Alberto Propato, Tigre, July 20, 2006.
8. Testimony of Adolfo Sánchez, Tigre, November 9, 2006, Memoria Abierta, Archivo Oral, A00461.
9. Court testimony of Roberto Cantello, cited in Alejandra Dandan, "Años de plomo en sangre," *El Cohete a la Luna*, April 22, 2018, https://www.elcohetealaluna.com/anos-de-plomo-en-sangre/.
10. Dandan, "Años de plomo en sangre."
11. Interview with Pedro Troiani, Beccar, Buenos Aires, July 8, 2005; and Lascano Warnes, "Cambios y continuidades," 41–42.
12. Dandan, "Años de plomo en sangre."
13. Dandan, "Años de plomo en sangre."
14. According to sworn testimony by former Ford overseer Ángel Migliaccio, workers who wanted to leave their immediate section had to fill out a yellow form, where they recorded the reason for their movements, and obtain a signature from their supervisor. Cited in Tomás Ojea Quintana and Elizabeth Gómez Alcorta, "Alegato querella particular de los trabajadores," Tribunal Oral en lo Criminal Federal no. 1 de San Martín, causas no. 2855 y 2358, 2018, 150.

15. Testimony of Adolfo Sánchez, Memoria Abierta.
16. Testimony of Adolfo Sánchez, Memoria Abierta.
17. Lascano Warnes, "Cambios y continuidades," 42.
18. Pizzolato, "Workers and Revolutionaries at the Twilight of Fordism."
19. Pizzolato, *Challenging Global Capitalism*, 120.
20. Pizzolato, *Challenging Global Capitalism*, 120. Less organized interpersonal violence also increased in some auto plants because of these pressures. Milloy, *Blood, Sweat, and Fear*.
21. Pizzolato, *Challenging Global Capitalism*, 124.
22. Pizzolato, *Challenging Global Capitalism*, 124.
23. Pizzolato, *Challenging Global Capitalism*, 125.
24. Silver, *Forces of Labor*, 53.
25. Schlesinger and Kinzer, *Bitter Fruit*.
26. Ferrer, *Cuba: An American History*, 346–49.
27. On the AIFLD's history and presence in Argentina, see Pozzi, "El sindicalismo norteamericano"; Corrêa, "Looking at the Southern Cone"; and Schuhrke, "Comradely Brainwashing," 39–67.
28. Schuhrke, "Comradely Brainwashing," 64.
29. By 1969, the AIFLD claimed to have trained 128,515 Latin American unionists. Schuhrke, "Comradely Brainwashing," 40.
30. NACLA and Díaz, "AIFLD Losing Its Grip," 3.
31. The questionnaires used by the AIFLD for intelligence gathering are reproduced in NACLA and Díaz, "AIFLD Losing Its Grip," 11.
32. Pozzi, "El sindicalismo norteamericano," 19.
33. Corrêa, "Looking at the Southern Cone," 261.
34. Schuhrke, "Comradely Brainwashing," 60.
35. Eugene H. Methvin, "Labor's New Weapon for Democracy," *Reader's Digest*, October 1966, 21–22, cited in Schuhrke, "Comradely Brainwashing," 55.
36. Evans, Hoeffel, and James, "Reflections on Argentine Auto Workers and Their Unions," 138.
37. James, *Resistance and Integration*, 226–27; and Brennan, *The Labor Wars in Córdoba*, 217.
38. Brennan, *The Labor Wars in Córdoba*, 69.
39. Brennan, *The Labor Wars in Córdoba*, 142–55.
40. Brennan, *The Labor Wars in Córdoba*, 217–20.
41. Brennan, *The Labor Wars in Córdoba*, 217–20.

42. Schneider, *Los compañeros*, 315; and Brennan, *The Labor Wars in Córdoba*, 216.
43. *La Verdad* (Buenos Aires), no. 204 (November 10, 1969), cited in Schneider, *Los compañeros*, 315.
44. Historian Federico Lorenz has analyzed interactions between shop-floor organizers and leftist militants in his research on the Astarsa shipyard, which was also located in the Zona Norte. See Lorenz, *Algo parecido a la felicidad*. However, as labor historian Victoria Basualdo notes, the dynamics of labor and guerrilla organizing have generally been studied separately, and much research remains to be done. See V. Basualdo, "The Argentine Dictatorship and Labor," 16.
45. Brennan, *The Labor Wars in Córdoba*, 171.
46. James, *Resistance and Integration*, 223–24; and Ministerio de Justicia, *Responsabilidad empresarial*, 1:217.
47. Löbbe, "Las 'desmemorias' de José Rodríguez," 3, cited in Lascano Warnes, "Cambios y continuidades," 52.
48. Testimony of Adolfo Sánchez, Memoria Abierta. On political activists in the Ford plant, see Lascano Warnes, "Cambios y continuidades," 51.
49. Lascano Warnes, "Cambios y continuidades," 51–52.
50. Interview with Carlos Alberto Propato.
51. Anzorena, *Tiempo de violencia y utopía*, 93–122.
52. Anzorena, *Tiempo de violencia y utopía*, 105.
53. Carnovale, "Las 'cárceles del pueblo,'" 199.
54. Felipe Pigna, "El asesinato de Vandor," *El Historiador*, https://www.elhistoriador.com.ar/el-asesinato-de-vandor/.
55. Gillespie, *Soldiers of Perón*, 89–96.
56. Carnovale, "Las 'cárceles del pueblo,'" 223–27.
57. Collier and Sater, *A History of Chile*, 335.
58. Duke University Library, Hartman Center, JWT Archive, 1929–98 and undated, box 12, folder "Argentina: Presentation to Executive Committee," 1973, April 2.
59. Cited in Svampa, "El populismo imposible y sus actores," 405.
60. "Allende and Chile: 'Bring Him Down,'" National Security Archive, November 3, 2020, https://nsarchive.gwu.edu/briefing-book/chile/2020-11-06/allende-inauguration-50th-anniversary.
61. J. G. O. Webster to Don Johnston, Buenos Aires, April 29, 1974, Hartman Center, JWT Archive, Don Johnston Papers, box 23.

62. "Contra biografía," *El Descamisado* 1, no. 0 (May 8, 1973): 16.
63. Brennan, *Labor Wars*, 255.
64. "La agresión a los dos dirigentes de Ford," *La Nación*, May 23, 1973; "Resultaron heridos un ejecutivo y una alta empleada de la Empresa Ford," *La Opinión*, May 23, 1973, 9; and Graham-Yooll, *De Perón a Videla*, 258.
65. "Murió un dirigente de Ford que fue baleado," *La Nación*, June 26, 1973.
66. "Ford Begins Paying Out 'Social Welfare,'" *Buenos Aires Herald*, May 29, 1973, 9; "Entregó una empresa donaciones exigidas," *La Nación*, May 29, 1973; "Ford, ERP Agree on Terms," *Buenos Aires Herald*, May 25, 1973, 9; and "Una situación inaceptable," *La Nación*, June 6, 1973.
67. The term they used was *cipayos*, or "sepoys," which refers to soldiers who had served as proxy fighters for the British in colonial India.
68. "Death Threats: Ford Sends 22 Top Men Back to U.S.," *Buenos Aires Herald*, November 30, 1973, 1; "Dirigentes de Ford amenazados dejan el país," *La Nación*, November 30, 1973, 1; and "Trial by Terror," *Time*, January 14, 1974.
69. J. G. O. Webster to Don Johnston, Buenos Aires, August 7, 1974, Hartman Center, JWT Archive, Don Johnston Papers, Inter-Office Communication Subseries, 1969–82, box 23, file "Argentina."
70. Leighton N. Hardey to Don Johnston, August 29, 1974, Hartman Center, JWT Archive, Don Johnston Papers, Inter-Office Communication Subseries, 1969–82, box 23, file "Argentina."
71. Pedro Troiani, cited in Lascano Warnes, "Cambios y continuidades," 48.
72. Interview with Pedro Troiani.
73. Interview with Pedro Troiani and Carlos Alberto Propato, Beccar, Buenos Aires, July 16, 2006.
74. Novaro and Palermo, *La dictadura militar*, 72.
75. Published in *Mayoría*, May 24, 1973, 8, cited in Lascano Warnes, "Cambios y continuidades," 47.
76. Novaro and Palermo, *La dictadura militar*, 72.
77. For a critical view of this issue from the perspective of a former militant, see Calveiro, *Política y/o violencia*.
78. Besoky, "Violencia paraestatal y organizaciones de derecha."
79. Lascano Warnes, "Cambios y continuidades," 76.
80. Lascano Warnes, "Cambios y continuidades," 49.
81. Lascano Warnes, "Cambios y continuidades," 49.
82. Werner and Aguirre, *Insurgencia obrera en la Argentina*.

83. Löbbe, *La guerrilla fabril*, 114.
84. Lascano Warnes, "Cambios y continuidades," 53.
85. James, "October 17th and 18th, 1945."
86. Lascano Warnes, "Cambios y continuidades," 57.
87. Lascano Warnes, "Cambios y continuidades," 54.
88. Interview with Pedro Troiani and Carlos Alberto Propato.
89. Lascano Warnes, "Cambios y continuidades," 53.
90. Lascano Warnes, "Cambios y continuidades," 57.
91. Löbbe, "Las 'desmemorias' de José Rodríguez," 3.
92. The Ford organizers followed a pattern that has been detected among other supposedly mainstream Peronist union delegates. As historian Victoria Basualdo has noted, by the early 1970s "there were important sectors of the working class that, knowingly, or unknowingly, were questioning the cornerstone of the capitalist system, the capital-labor relationship." Cited in Ministerio de Justicia, *Responsabilidad empresarial*, 1:460–61.
93. V. Basualdo, "Labor and Structural Change," 293.
94. Ministerio de Justicia, *Responsabilidad empresarial*, 1:463.
95. Luis Degiusti, cited in Lascano Warnes. "Cambios y continuidades," 62.
96. Lascano Warnes, "Cambios y continuidades," 62.
97. "The union represented itself as a broker selling labor power and it expected the corporation to pay it a percentage. This means that the organization did not see itself as an association of workers convinced of the need to bargain collectively, but as a structure that demanded payment for supplying a service." Historian Valeria Ianni, cited in Lascano Warnes, "Cambios y continuidades," 56.
98. Cited in Lascano Warnes, "Cambios y continuidades," 55–56.
99. Lascano Warnes, "Cambios y continuidades," 55–56.
100. Löbbe, *La guerrilla fabril*, 144.
101. Lascano Warnes, "Cambios y continuidades," 73–74; Franco, *Un enemigo para la nación*, 254; and V. Basualdo, "Aportes para el análisis del papel de la cúpula sindical," 242.
102. "Industrial Terrorism: Guerrilla Warfare in the Factory," US Embassy in Buenos Aires to Department of Defense, December 2, 1975, cited in Lascano Warnes, "Cambios y continuidades," 76.
103. Dandan, "Años de plomo en sangre."
104. Testimony of Adolfo Sánchez, Memoria Abierta.

105. Testimony of Adolfo Sánchez, Memoria Abierta; and interview with Pedro Troiani.
106. Dandan, "Años de plomo en sangre."
107. Sworn testimony cited in Tomás Ojea Quintana and Elizabeth Gómez Alcorta, "Alegato querella particular de los trabajadores," Tribunal Oral en lo Criminal Federal no. 1 de San Martín, causas no. 2855 y 2358, 2018, 115–16.
108. Testimony of Pedro Troiani at the truth trials in La Plata, Buenos Aires, reproduced in "¿El óvalo de la muerte? Empresas y represión bajo el Proceso Militar: El caso Ford," *Razón y Revolución*, September 1, 2002, https://razonyrevolucion.org/el-ovalo-de-la-muerte-empresas-y-represion-bajo-el-proceso-militar-el-caso-ford/.
109. Novaro and Palermo, *La dictadura militar*, 19.
110. Interview with Pedro Troiani.
111. Testimony cited in Elizabeth Gómez Alcorta, "Los directivos de Ford llegan a juicio," *El Cohete a la Luna*, December 16, 2017. Lawyer Gómez Alcorta had joined Tomás Ojea Quintana on the Ford workers' legal team by 2017.
112. Ford union steward Pastor José Murúa would later testify that Marcos was "famous for his bullying" and had once nearly run over a group of workers in the factory die shop while driving a Ford Taurus. Testimony of Pastor José Murúa, Archivo Nacional de la Memoria, CONADEP file 7688, cited in Ministerio de Justicia, *Responsabilidad empresarial*, 1:471.
113. Testimony of Juan Carlos Amoroso, Archivo Nacional de la Memoria, CONADEP file 1638, cited in Ministerio de Justicia, *Responsabilidad empresarial*, 1:471.
114. Testimony of Adolfo Sánchez, Memoria Abierta.
115. Testimony of Juan Carlos Ballesteros, Archivo Nacional de la Memoria, CONADEP file 7692, cited in Ministerio de Justicia, *Responsabilidad empresarial*, 1:472.
116. Testimony of Adolfo Sánchez, Memoria Abierta.
117. Testimony of Juan Carlos Amoroso, cited in Ministerio de Justicia, *Responsabilidad empresarial*, 1:472.
118. Martín Prieto, "El general argentino Ramón Camps, condenado a 25 años por violación de los derechos humanos," *El País*, December 2, 1986, https://elpais.com/diario/1986/12/03/internacional/533948425_850215.html.

119. Unless otherwise noted, the details of the Ford disappearances are all drawn from testimony cited in the final judgment presented by judges Osvaldo Alberto Facciano, Mario Jorge Gambacorta, and Eugenio J. Martínez Ferrero in the resolution of the Ford case. See Poder Judicial de la Nación, Tribunal Oral en lo Criminal Federal no. 1 de San Martín, Fundamentos causas no. 2855 y 2358, March 15, 2019.
120. Testimony of Pastor José Murúa, cited in Poder Judicial de la Nación, causas no. 2855 y 2358.
121. Juan Carlos Ballesteros, Declaration to Ministerio Público Fiscal, June 30, 2014, cited in Ford "Fundamentos."

CHAPTER FOUR

1. Rodrigo Gutiérrez Hermelo, interview with Nelva Méndez de Falcone, La Plata, April 2006. See also Seoane and Ruiz Núñez, *La noche de los lápices*, 77–86.
2. Robben, *Argentina Betrayed*, 103.
3. Guzman Bouvard, *Revolutionizing Motherhood*.
4. Héctor Olivera and Daniel Kon, dirs., *La noche de los lápices* (Aries Cinematográfica Argentina, 1986).
5. G. Gutiérrez, "Falcon verde," 43.
6. Brands, *Latin America's Cold War*, 111–21.
7. On material objects as representations of specific forms of state power, see Auslander, "Beyond Words," 1023.
8. On associations between driving culture and individualism, see Seiler, *Republic of Drivers*; and Sachs, *For Love of the Automobile*.
9. On the use of the term "sucking" to describe forced disappearance, see Feitlowitz, *A Lexicon of Terror*, 54.
10. G. Gutiérrez, "Falcon verde," 42.
11. Möser, "The Dark Side of 'Automobilism.'"
12. Link, *Forging Global Fordism*.
13. Gewald, "Missionaries, Hereros, and Motorcars," 257–85.
14. M. Davis, *Buda's Wagon*, 32–37.
15. Grandin, "Living in Revolutionary Time," 4. See also Weld, *Paper Cadavers*.
16. Finchelstein, *The Ideological Origins of the Dirty War*, 113–14.

17. Finchelstein, *The Ideological Origins of the Dirty War*, 120. See also Novaro and Palermo, *La dictadura militar*, 80–83.
18. Quoted in Cox, *Dirty Secrets, Dirty War*, 64.
19. Cox, *Dirty Secrets, Dirty War*, 65.
20. Cited in Marcos and Novaro, *La dictadura militar*, 87. Historian and journalist Martin Edwin Andersen obtained a copy of Vilas's manuscript, which the military prohibited him from publishing. See Andersen, *Dossier secreto*, 346–47.
21. Ministerio de Justicia, *Responsabilidad empresarial*, 1:243.
22. Cited in Robben, *Political Violence*, 192. The dictatorship's command structure and territorial divisions were first described in detail by a former army captain who denounced the junta's betrayal of earlier ideals of military honor. See Mittelbach, *Informe sobre desaparecedores*.
23. Robben, *Political Violence*, 192–98.
24. Memoria Abierta, "Reconocer Campo de Mayo."
25. Finchelstein, *The Ideological Origins of the Dirty War*, 120.
26. CONADEP, *Nunca Más*; Calveiro, *Poder y desaparición*; and Feitlowitz, *A Lexicon of Terror*.
27. Brazil's National Truth Commission report documented 210 disappearances committed by the military between 1964 and 1990. In Chile, the Pinochet dictatorship that seized power in 1973 openly arrested roughly 30,000 people it considered to be "subversives" and disappeared roughly 1,200, according to recent estimates. Some 172 Uruguayans were disappeared between 1973 and 1985. See Dias et al., *Relatório*, 500; Wyndham and Read, "From State Terrorism to State Errorism," 31; and Centro de Estudios Legales y Sociales, *Derechos humanos en Argentina*, 102.
28. CONADEP, *Nunca Más*, 16.
29. Crenzel, "Políticas de la memoria," 4; and Carlos Osorio and Marcos Novaro, "On 30th Anniversary of Argentine Coup: New Declassified Details on Repression and U.S. Support for Military Dictatorship," National Security Archive, March 23, 2006, http://nsarchive.gwu.edu/NSAEBB/NSAEBB185/.
30. Finchelstein, *The Ideological Origins of the Dirty War*, 115–22; Robin, *Escadrons de la mort*; and Novaro and Palermo, *La dictadura militar*, 80–85.
31. McSherry, *Predatory States*; Mignone, *Iglesia y dictadura*; and Verbitsky and Bohoslavsky, *Cuentas pendientes*.

32. Horacio Verbitsky, "Usted no puede fusilar 7000 personas," *Página/12*, August 31, 2003, http://www.pagina12.com.ar/diario/elpais/1-24857-2003-08-31.html.
33. Seoane and Muleiro, *El dictador*, 215.
34. "Foreign Minister Guzzetti Euphoric over Visit to United States, October 19, 1976," National Security Archive, Electronic Briefing Book, no. 73, part 2, ed. Carlos Osorio, http://nsarchive.gwu.edu/NSAEBB/NSAEBB73/index3.htm. See also Cox, *Dirty Secrets, Dirty War*, 80.
35. D'Antonio and Eidelman, "El sistema penitenciario," 102.
36. Seoane and Muleiro, *El dictador*, 227.
37. Memoria Abierta, *Memorias en la ciudad*, 220.
38. Memoria Abierta, *Memorias en la ciudad*, 215–19.
39. A helpful overview of these policies appears in Menazzi Canese, "Ciudad en dictadura."
40. Menazze Canesi, "Ciudad en dictadura," 3.
41. Laura, *La ciudad arterial*; and Tavella, "El plan de construcción de autopistas."
42. Ignacio Ariel Wonsiak, "Densificar 'dedensificando,'" *Café de las Ciudades*, May 2018, https://cafedelasciudades.com.ar/articulos/densificar-desdensificando/. On the displacements, see Menase Canezzi, "Ciudad en dictadura," 6.
43. Stephan, "A Typology of the Collaboration," 249.
44. Verbitsky and Bohoslavsky, *Cuentas pendientes*; and Ministerio de Justicia, *Responsabilidad empresarial*.
45. Almirón, *Campo Santo*, 137–38.
46. Gaby Weber, *Milagros no hay: Los desaparecidos de Mercedes Benz* (Betacam, 2003).
47. Testimony of Omar Torres, Memoria Abierta, Fondo Luis Moreno Ocampo (hereafter FLMO), 1.1, box 6, folio 16, pages 3018–19.
48. Sebastián Abrevaya, "Escrache al fiscal Hermelo," *Página/12*, November 29, 2007. On Scilingo's confession, see Verbitsky, *Confessions of an Argentine Dirty Warrior*.
49. Quoted in Cox, *Dirty Secrets, Dirty War*, 88.
50. Testimony of Robert Cox, Memoria Abierta, FLMO, series 1, box 1, folio 3, page 408.

51. Testimony of Manuel Alberto Laprida, Memoria Abierta, FLMO, series 1, box 4, folio 10, page 1810. In the transcript, the guns were referred to as "Itakas."
52. Novaro and Palermo, *La dictadura militar*, 85.
53. Maxwell Chaplin to Washington, July 23, 1976, reproduced as Document 7, Subject: South America–Southern Cone Security Practices, July 23, 1976, National Security Archive, Electronic Briefing Book, no. 73, part 2, ed. Carlos Osorio, http://nsarchive.gwu.edu/NSAEBB/NSAEBB73/index3.htm.
54. On the performative qualities of state terrorism in Argentina, see Taylor, *Disappearing Acts*.
55. Caviglia, *Vivir a oscuras*, 19–21.
56. Thank you to Javier Mignone for sharing this story. Emilio Mignone had been targeted for openly denouncing the kidnapping attack on his daughter, Monica, on May 14, 1976. He went on to found one of Argentina's leading human rights organizations, the Center for Legal and Social Studies (CELS).
57. María Seoane, "La orden que dió la dictadura para la compra de falcon verdes sin patentes," *Clarín*, March 3, 2006.
58. Testimony of Ana María Careaga, Memoria Abierta, FMLO, series 1, box 4, folio 10, page 1862.
59. Testimony of Graciela Irma Trotta, Memoria Abierta, FMLO, series 1, box 4, folio 10, page 1936.
60. "Taxistas aseguran que Arroyo 'perteneció a la dictadura' y que miente sobre su pasado," *Diario la Capital* (Mar del Plata, Argentina), August 22, 2015, http://www.lacapitalmdp.com/noticias/La-Ciudad/2015/08/22/286706.htm. When I moved to Buenos Aires a decade after the dictatorship's fall from power, I was warned by friends to be careful about what I said in a taxi, because taxi drivers were still assumed to be police informants.
61. "'Somos derechos y humanos': Cómo se armó la campaña," *Clarín*, March 23, 2006, https://www.clarin.com/ediciones-anteriores/derechos-humanos-armo-campana_0_HyTgj9HyoFe.html.
62. On Brazil, see Weschler, *A Miracle, a Universe*; on Guatemala, see Weld, *Paper Cadavers*.
63. On Operation Condor, see McSherry, *Predatory States*.

64. Argentina's Archivo Nacional de la Memoria, incorporated in 2003, is the official repository of testimonies collected by the National Commission on the Disappearance of Persons, the Trial of the Military Juntas, and later judicial instances. The independent human rights archive Memoria Abierta has collected over seven hundred oral interviews with survivors and witnesses from the dictatorship era.
65. Testimony of Adriana Elba Arce, Memoria Abierta, FLMO, series 1, box 8, folio 22, page 4185.
66. Testimony of Guillermo Rolando Puerta, Memoria Abierta, FLMO, series 1, box 7, folio 19, page 3753.
67. Feitlowitz, *A Lexicon of Terror*, 59.
68. Testimony of Adriana Calvo de Laborde, Memoria Abierta, FLMO, box 1, folio 3, page 431.
69. Jorge Bianchini, *Mansión Seré* (Coruya Cine, 2013), https://www.youtube.com/watch?v=7bl7hSYaPog.
70. Memoria Abierta, *Memorias en la ciudad*, 98.
71. Testimony of Jorge Federico Watts, Memoria Abierta, FMLO, series 1, box 8, folio 23, page 4406.
72. This account of Laborde's detention draws on her testimony to the Juicio a las Juntas in 1985, and reports of her testimony to the Juicio a la Verdad in La Plata in 2000. See Testimony of Adriana Calvo de Laborde; and Victoria Ginzberg, "Lo más parecido a un campo nazi: Adriana Calvo testimonio en el Juicio a la Verdad de La Plata," *Página/12*, http://www.pagina12.com.ar/2000/00-02/00-02-17/pag13.htm. Laborde's testimony is also discussed in Robben, "Testimonies, Truths, and Transitions of Justice," 186–87.
73. Testimony of Adriana Calvo de Laborde, box 1, folio 3, page 430; and Ginzberg, "Lo más parecido a un campo nazi."
74. Testimony of Adriana Calvo de Laborde, box 1, folio 3, pages 444–45.
75. Testimony of Rubén Fernando Schell, Memoria Abierta, FLMO, series 1, box 2, folio 4, pages 836–37.
76. On the issue of civilian complicity, see Finchelstein, *The Ideological Origins of the Dirty War*, 124–25; and Sheinin, *Consent of the Damned*.
77. Sheinin, *Consent of the Damned*, 5–6.
78. In 1977, General Ramón Díaz Bessone proposed the creation of a "New Republic" in Argentina under military control that would last until at least 2000. Finchelstein, *The Ideological Origins of the Dirty War*, 141.

79. "1976. Nuevamente la Argentina encuentra su camino. 1977. Nuevo año de fe y esperanza para todos los argentinos de buena voluntad. Ford Motor Argentina y su gente comprometen su participación en el esfuerzo para la realización de los grandes destinos de la Patria. Nuevamente Ford le da más," *Clarín*, January 2, 1977 (page number illegible).
80. "Celebró Ford Motor Argentina los 65 años de su radicación," *La Nación*, August 11, 1978, 6.
81. "Prevé expandirse una fábrica de automotores," *La Nación*, August 13, 1978, 9. See also "Ford May Expand Argentine Facilities for $335 million," *Wall Street Journal*, August 18, 1978.
82. "Murió Juan Bautista Sasiaiñ, ex jefe de la federal durante la dictadura," *Clarín*, March 6, 2006, https://www.clarin.com/ediciones-anteriores/murio-juan-bautista-sasiain-ex-jefe-federal-dictadura_0_ByiMHAr1otx.html.
83. "Información de prensa: Iniciación de las obras de la planta de camiones Ford," May 13, 1980, in Pedro Norberto Troiani, "Solicitud de declaraciones indagatorias," case 18.018/02, Molinari, Antonio, vs. Ford Personnel, folio 712.
84. On the military's distortions of language and rhetoric, see Feitlowitz, *A Lexicon of Terror*.
85. Carassai, "The Dark Side of Social Desire," 45.
86. Carassai, "The Dark Side of Social Desire."
87. Ford Argentina SCA, *Ford: 90 años en la Argentina*, 81.
88. On the landscape tropes of the early twentieth century as they related to road building, see Ballent, "Kilómetro cero," 116–17.
89. Canal Mix, "Ford Falcon: Todas las publicidades," YouTube, December 26, 2018, https://www.youtube.com/watch?v=_PZABV6OvJs.
90. The original wording is: "por defender con todo lo que invertimos en él. Ford Falcon: está con todos." In Argentina, the term *gaucho* is used colloquially to mean noble and brave.
91. Testimony of Arnaldo "Lalo" Piñón, Memoria Abierta, Archivo Oral, Buenos Aires, 2010.
92. Testimony of Omar Torres, series 1, box 6, folio 16, page 3024.
93. Feinmann, *La sangre derramada*, 101.

CHAPTER FIVE

1. Alejandro Jasinski, "La lista de la Ford," *El Cohete a la Luna*, June 3, 2018, https://www.elcohetealaluna.com/la-lista-de-la-ford/.
2. Testimony of Elisa Charlín, Solicitud de declaraciones indagatorias efectuada por Pedro Troiani en la causa 18.018/02 caratulada "Molinari, Antonio—Personal Ford s/ privación ilegal de la libertad," Juzgado Federal en lo Criminal y Correccional no. 3, Secretaría no. 6 de Capital Federal, cited in Ministerio de Justicia, *Responsabilidad empresarial*, 1:480.
3. Testimony of Eduardo Norberto Pulega, Archivo Nacional de la Memoria, CONADEP file 7690, cited in Ministerio de Justicia, *Responsabilidad empresarial*, 1:486.
4. CONADEP, *Nunca Más*, 381.
5. Testimony of Adolfo Sánchez, Tigre, November 9, 2006, Memoria Abierta, Archivo Oral, AO0461.
6. Flor Alcaraz and Luciano Galende, dirs., *El peligroso oficio de ser trabajador* (Televisión Pública Argentina), YouTube, March 25, 2022, https://www.youtube.com/watch?v=S_QJm2CEJRM.
7. Details of the men's detention draw from causa 18.018/02 caratulada "Molinari, Antonio—Personal Ford s/ privación ilegal de la libertad," Juzgado Federal en lo Criminal y Correccional no. 3, Secretaría no. 6 de Capital Federal.
8. CONADEP, *Nunca Más*, 408.
9. In December 1977, for example, newly appointed US ambassador Raúl Castro met with the junta's interior minister, General Albano Harguindeguy, to discuss the Carter administration's concerns about the human rights situation. Harguindeguy assured Castro that he was planning a mass release of PEN prisoners in time for Christmas, adding that this gesture was "simply a speeding up of what all along has been the intention of the Argentine government: to cut as far as possible the numbers of persons held under the PEN." Unclassified US Department of State case no. 0-2016-16244, doc. no. C06281230, date: May 7, 2018, Argentina Declassification Project, https://www.intelligence.gov/argentina-declassification-project.
10. D'Antonio and Eidelman, "El sistema penitenciario," 98.
11. CONADEP, *Nunca Más*, 412.
12. CONADEP, *Nunca Más*, 409.

13. Adolfo Sánchez recounted in an oral history interview in 2006 that his wife, sister, and mother were all strip-searched and groped when they visited him in prison. Testimony of Adolfo Sánchez, Memoria Abierta.
14. Interview with Pedro Troiani, Beccar, Buenos Aires, August 12, 2006.
15. The National Commission on the Disappearance of Persons accumulated evidence in 1984 of 8,625 cases of prisoners detained under the PEN, 4,029 of whom were released from custody in less than a year. CONADEP, *Nunca Más*, 409.
16. Ministerio de Justicia, *Responsabilidad empresarial*, 1:487.
17. Comisión Provincial por la Memoria, El Archivo Dirección de Inteligencia de la Policía de la Provincia de Buenos Aires (hereafter Archivo DIPPBA), memorándum del jefe de la delegación DIPPBA, September 4, 1976, DIPPBA, departamento B, bibliorato 1/1, legajo 41, asunto: Ford SA, cited in Ministerio de Justicia, *Responsabilidad empresarial*, 1:487.
18. Archivo DIPPBA, Mesa "B," carpeta 117, legajo 34, tomo 1, caratulado Ford Motor Company Gral. Pacheco, "Situación en Establecimiento 'Ford Motors Argentina,' de Gral. Pacheco," April 12, 1976.
19. Archivo DIPPBA, Mesa "B," carpeta 117, legajo 34, tomo 1, caratulado "Ford Motor Company Gral. Pacheco," May 1, 1976.
20. Juan de Onis, "Businessmen under the Gun in Argentina," *New York Times*, February 22, 1976, F3.
21. Cited in Ministerio de Justicia, *Responsabilidad empresarial*, 1:488.
22. V. Basualdo, *Memoria en las aulas*, 5.
23. Anthropologist Lindsay DuBois uncovered similar stories during her fieldwork in Gran Buenos Aires. DuBois, *The Politics of the Past*, 89.
24. CONADEP, *Nunca Más*, 409–16.
25. Testimony of Adolfo Sánchez, Memoria Abierta.
26. Memoria Abierta, "Reconocer Campo de Mayo," 64–72.
27. Solicitud de declaraciones indagatorias efectuada por Pedro Troiani en la causa 19.018/02 caratulada "Molinari, Antonio—Personal Ford s/ privación ilegal de la libertad," Juzgado Federal en lo Criminal y Correccional no. 3, Secretaría no. 6 de Capital Federal, cited in Ministerio de Justicia, *Responsabilidad Empresarial*, 1:480.
28. Alcaraz and Galende, *El peligroso oficio de ser trabajador*.
29. On the economic "shock therapy" imposed by the Chilean and Argentine dictatorships, see Klein, *The Shock Doctrine*, 91–143. See also Winn, *Victims of the Chilean Miracle*.

30. Schorr, "La desindustrialización como eje del proyecto refundacional," 39.
31. Martínez de Hoz speech, cited in Sourrouille, *El complejo automotor en Argentina*, 71. My understanding of Martínez de Hoz's assault on the developmentalist project draws on E. Basualdo, "El legado dictatorial."
32. Cited in Sourrouille, *El complejo automotor en Argentina*, 71.
33. Stephan, "A Typology of the Collaboration," 247.
34. Bohoslavsky, "Banking Southern Cone Dictatorships," 188.
35. E. Basualdo, "El legado dictatorial," 91.
36. Schorr, "La desindustrialización como eje del proyecto refundacional," 37.
37. E. Basualdo, "El legado dictatorial," 83.
38. Walsh and his small team of journalists collected information from international radio transmissions and listened in on police radio frequencies; they also spoke with former detainees and police and army infiltrators. They circulated their reports by mail to embassies, media, and international organizations. McCaughan, *True Crimes*, 247–54.
39. One of Walsh's most famous books, *¿Quién mató a Rosendo?*, exposed the corruption and violence at the heart of the Peronist metalworkers' union, the Unión de Obreros Metalúrgicos (UOM).
40. Quoted in McCaughan, *True Crimes*, 289.
41. McCaughan, *True Crimes*, 288.
42. McCaughan, *True Crimes*, 282.
43. McCaughan, *True Crimes*, 283.
44. Years later, Adolfo Sánchez reported feeling the same suspicions toward other Ford activists who survived the dictatorship era unscathed. It was part of the general fear that no one knew exactly whom they were dealing with. Testimony of Adolfo Sánchez, Memoria Abierta. On survivor guilt and suspicion in general, see Crenzel, *La historia política del Nunca Más*, 42–44; and Park, *The Reappeared*.
45. Poder Judicial de la Nación, Tribunal Oral en lo Criminal Federal no. 1 de San Martín, Fundamentos Causas 2855 y 2358, March 15, 2019; and Lascano Warnes, "Cambios y continuidades," 94.
46. Interview with Estela Gareis, Buenos Aires, August 20, 2022.
47. Sociologist Francisco Delich noted that it was common practice during the dictatorship for employers to consult with security forces regarding any new hires. Cited in Abós, *Las organizaciones sindicales*, 11.
48. Cited in Lascano Warnes, "Cambios y continuidades," 94.

49. Testimony of Adolfo Sánchez, Memoria Abierta. On the widespread use of blacklists against labor activists, see Delich, "Después del diluvio, la clase obrera," 140.
50. Basualdo and Bona, "La deuda externa (pública y privada)," 12–18.
51. As Jennifer Adair notes, hunger was especially demoralizing, because urban workers in Argentina had historically eaten well. Adair, *In Search of the Lost Decade*, 15.
52. Adair, *In Search of the Lost Decade*, 16.
53. Abós, *Las organizaciones sindicales*, 86–87; and Lorenz, *¿De quién es el 24 de marzo?*, 67.
54. Sikkink, *The Justice Cascade*, 62.
55. "La Dictadura del '76 y la Deuda," Museo de la Deuda Externa, Facultad de Economía, Universidad de Buenos Aires, https://museodeladeuda.econ.uba.ar/la-dictadura-del-76-y-la-deuda/.
56. Crenzel, "La reconstrucción de un universo," 159.
57. Crenzel, *La historia política del Nunca Más*, 56–57.
58. Adair, *In Search of the Lost Decade*, 29–45.
59. Some key sources on the creative boom of the early 1980s include Longoni and Bruzzone, *El siluetazo*; Amado, *La imagen justa*; and Fortuna, *Moving Otherwise*.
60. Bobby Flores, "Pipo Cipolatti y Los Twist: Cómo hizo el éxito de 'Pensé que se trataba de cieguitos' y la llegada del humor al rock," Infobae, August 7, 2021, https://www.infobae.com/sociedad/2021/08/07/pipo-cipolatti-y-los-twist-como-hizo-el-exito-de-pense-que-se-trataba-de-cieguitos-y-la-llegada-del-humor-al-rock/.
61. José González Asturias, dir., *Ford Falcon, buen estado*, YouTube, 1985, https://www.youtube.com/watch?v=OcoMhJS569k. I owe my understanding of the film's impact to my husband, Rodrigo Gutiérrez Hermelo, who attended the original screening.
62. Néstor Sabatini, *De esto ni una palabra a nadie*, http://www.autores.org.ar/nsabatini/de_esto.htm. On the significance of anniversaries as moments of debate over memory, see Jelin, *Las conmemoraciones*.
63. The basic premise of this short film may have been inspired by the 1983 American horror film *Christine*, which was based on a Stephen King novel. Le Blanc and Odell, *John Carpenter*, 43–46.
64. Mortenson, "A Journey into the Shadows."

65. Sikkink, *The Justice Cascade*, 82.
66. See, for example, Crenzel, *La historia política del Nunca Más*; Lessa, *Memory and Transitional Justice*; and Wright, *State Terrorism in Latin America*.
67. Crenzel, *La historia política del Nunca Más*, 137–42.
68. Sikkink, *The Justice Cascade*, 70–76.
69. Interview with Pedro Troiani, 2006.
70. Adair, *In Search of the Lost Decade*, 89.
71. Testimony of Adolfo Sánchez, Memoria Abierta.
72. Testimony of Graciela Geuna, cited in CONADEP, *Nunca Más*, 377.
73. That period was later extended for three more months. See Crenzel, *La historia política del Nunca Más*, 67–68.
74. Interview with Pedro Troiani, 2006.
75. Crenzel, "La reconstrucción de un universo," 162.
76. The first survivors' group, known as the Association of Former Detained and Disappeared Persons (Asociación de Ex Detenidos Desaparecidos), was founded in October 1984 by Adriana Calvo, who was discussed in chapter 4. Crenzel, "La reconstrucción de un universo," 157.
77. Crenzel, *La historia política del Nunca Más*, 71.
78. Interview with Pedro Troiani, 2006.
79. Esteban Peicovich and Eduardo Meglioli, "Sobre antihéroes y tumbas: Análisis de Ernesto Sábato," *Revista Somos* (April 1985), http://www.magicasruinas.com.ar/revistero/argentina/ernesto-sabato.htm.
80. CONADEP, *Nunca Más*, 375–79.
81. Secret decree 504/77, "Continuation of the Offensive against Subversion," cited in CONADEP, *Nunca Más*, 375.
82. CONADEP, *Nunca Más*, 375.
83. In their testimony to the CONADEP, the men differed slightly regarding the date of that meeting. While Juan Carlos Amoroso recalled it as having occurred one day before the coup, on March 23, Pedro Troiani dated it to March 25, the day after the military took power and announced an end to union activities. Either way, they recalled it as occurring in late March, well before Ramón Camps was appointed as chief of the Buenos Aires provincial police in April.
84. Cited in CONADEP, *Nunca Más*, 381. The precise expression was "Devuelvan la pelota que la paleta la temenos nosotros, ahora."
85. Cited in CONADEP, *Nunca Más*, 381.
86. Crenzel, *La historia política del Nunca Más*, 20.

87. Crenzel, *La historia política del Nunca Más*, 17–20.
88. Crenzel, *La historia política del Nunca Más*, 66–69.
89. Cited in Crenzel, *La historia política del Nunca Más*, 66; emphasis in the original.
90. Cited in DuBois, *The Politics of the Past*, 92.
91. Interview with Pedro Troiani, 2006.
92. The details of this early claim are summarized in Comisión Interamericana de Derechos Humanos (CIDH), caso 11.159, "Pedro Norberto Troiani," article 63, p. 13.
93. The original wording is "El hecho fundamental que no se vivía en el país un estado de derecho." See Anexo 2, Sentencia Definitiva no. 35.866 de fecha 24 de febrero de 1986, dictada por la Sala V. de la Cámara Nacional de Apelaciones y Trabajo, escrito de la parte peticionaria de 23 de noviembre de 1998, cited in CIDH, caso 11.159, "Pedro Norberto Troiani," article 27, p. 7.
94. See "Conti Juan Carlos c/ Ford Motor Argentina S.A. s/ Cobro de Pesos," Sala VI, expediente no. 26.091, Juzgado no. 24, Buenos Aires (February 10, 1987), at Fallos para Constitucionalismo Social, https://constitucionalismosocial.blogspot.com/search?q=Conti.
95. "Conti Juan Carlos c/ Ford Motor Argentina S.A."
96. Interview with Pedro Troiani, 2006; and "Conti Juan Carlos c/ Ford Motor Argentina S.A."
97. In fact, the two Supreme Court judges who dissented in the rejection of Pedro's appeal made this very argument, that the precedent set in the Conti case should also be applied to Pedro's. See CIDH, caso 11.159, "Pedro Norberto Troiani," article 35, p. 9.
98. Anexo 2, Sentencia Definitiva no. 35.866 de fecha 24 de febrero de 1986, dictada por la Sala V. de la Cámara Nacional de Apelaciones y Trabajo, escrito de la parte peticionaria de 23 de noviembre de 1998, cited in CIDH, caso 11.159, "Pedro Norberto Troiani," article 64, p. 13.
99. Anexo 2, Sentencia Definitiva no. 35.866 de fecha 24 de febrero de 1986, dictada por la Sala V. de la Cámara Nacional de Apelaciones y Trabajo, escrito de la parte peticionaria de 23 de noviembre de 1998, cited in CIDH, caso11.159, "Pedro Norberto Troiani," article 65, pp. 12–13.
100. Interview with Pedro Troiani, 2006.
101. Adair, *In Search of the Lost Decade*, 99–100.
102. See Adair, *In Search of the Lost Decade*, 107–16.

103. Sourrouille, *El complejo automotor en Argentina*, 16.
104. Schvarzer, "La reconversión de la industria automotriz argentina," 7.
105. Schvarzer, "La reconversión de la industria automotriz argentina," 7.
106. Ministerio de Justicia, *Responsabilidad empresarial*, 1:459.
107. E. Basualdo and V. Basualdo, "Confronting Labor Power," 224.
108. E. Basualdo and V. Basualdo, "Confronting Labor Power," 226.
109. Acevedo, Basualdo, and Khavisse, *¿Quién es quién?*
110. Ortiz and Schorr, "La economía political del gobierno de Alfonsín," 462, cited in Adair, *In Search of the Lost Decade*, 112. On the long-term power of these economic groups, see Azpiazu, Basualdo, and Khavisse, *El nuevo poder económico*.
111. E. Basualdo, *Endeudar y fugar*. By 1983, Ford ranked fourth among Argentina's multinational firms in terms of its foreign debt accumulation, which amounted to US$80.42 million. See E. Basualdo and V. Basualdo, "Confronting Labor Power," 226.
112. Aroskind, "La hiperinflación de 1989."
113. Adair, *In Search of the Lost Decade*, 111.
114. On the political implications of food security during the Alfonsín years, see Adair, *In Search of the Lost Decade*.
115. On Peronist clientelism, see Auyero, *Poor People's Politics*.
116. Wright, *State Terrorism in Latin America*, 153–60.

CHAPTER SIX

1. Crenzel, *La historia política del Nunca Más*, 150–53.
2. Sergio Ciancaglini, "Qué nos preocupa a los argentinos," *Clarín*, June 5, 1994, cited in Crenzel, *La historia política del Nunca Más*, 251n274.
3. Robert and Gutiérrez Hermelo, "Argentina: Where Youth Is a Crime."
4. Crenzel, "Entre la historia y la memoria," 54–55.
5. Memoria Abierta, *Abogados, derecho y política*, 98–147.
6. An accessible discussion of universal jurisdiction appears in Roht-Arriaza, *The Pinochet Effect*, 6–8.
7. Payne, Pereira, and Bernal-Bermúdez, *Transitional Justice*.
8. The literature on these long-term debates over memory and justice in Argentina is vast. For some representative titles, see Jelin, *Los trabajos de la memoria*; Jelin and Langland, *Monumentos, memoriales y marcas territoriales*;

Carnovale, Lorenz, and Pittaluga, *Historia, memoria y fuentes orales*; Jelin, "Public Memorialization in Perspective"; Crenzel, *La historia política del Nunca Más*; Lvovich and Bisquert, *La cambiante memoria de la dictadura*; Feld and Stites Mor, *El pasado que miramos*; Memoria Abierta, *Memorias en la ciudad*; Crenzel, *Los desaparecidos en la Argentina*; Andriotti Romanin, "Decir la verdad, hacer justicia"; Allier Montaño and Crenzel, *Las luchas por la memoria en América Latina*; Feld, "Preservar, recuperar, ocupar"; Brennan, *Argentina's Missing Bones*; and Robben, *Argentina Betrayed*.

9. Grandin, "The Instruction of Great Catastrophe."
10. Crenzel, *La historia política del Nunca Más*, 127–29.
11. Robben, *Argentina Betrayed*, 96.
12. Crenzel, "Entre la historia y la memoria," 48–51; and Robben, *Argentina Betrayed*, 61–66.
13. A careful analysis of the document appears in Crenzel, *La historia política del Nunca Más*.
14. Grandin, "The Instruction of Great Catastrophe," 48.
15. "Ocho días para fabricarlo y una rifa: Así se despidió el último Falcon producido en Argentina," *Clarín*, November 23, 2021, https://www.clarin.com/autos/ocho-dias-para-fabricarlo-y-una-rifa-asi-se-despidio-el-ultimo-falcon-producido-en-argentina_0_dKi8_bvRV.html. The Autolatina merger lasted until 1995.
16. Adamovsky, *Historia de la clase media argentina*, 424–29.
17. Cosse, "Mafalda: Talisman of Democracy."
18. Fiona Ortiz, "Argentine Death Squad Cars Try for New Image," Reuters, May 4, 2007, https://www.reuters.com/article/us-argentina-falcons-idUSN0332251120070504.
19. Tom White, "Classic Falcon Fan? Don't Forget Your Argentine Cousins," *Cars Guide*, January 30, 2018, https://www.carsguide.com.au/oversteer/classic-falcon-fan-dont-forget-your-argentine-cousins-67000.
20. The Buenos Aires "Friends of the Falcon Club" (Club Amigos del Falcon) was founded in 1997 and ran a website (todofalcon.com) for several years. They are now on Facebook at https://www.facebook.com/clubdelfalcon/.
21. Ruiz, *Graffiti Argentina*, 8.
22. Robert and Gutiérrez Hermelo, "Argentina: Where Youth Is a Crime," 12–15.
23. Penn, "The Phenomenal Forms of Political Graffiti," 320. It is difficult to date this graffiti precisely or identify it with a specific artist. Emails to art

historian Ana Longoni and to the art collectives Grupo de Arte Callejero and BA Street Art turned up no leads on the graffiti's specific provenance.
24. Lorenz, ¿De quién es el 24 de marzo?
25. F. Gutiérrez, Treintamil – Secuela – Cosas del Río.
26. See Verbitsky, Confessions of an Argentine Dirty Warrior.
27. See, for example, Jelin, "The Politics of Memory."
28. Guzman Bouvard, Revolutionizing Motherhood, 73–75.
29. Longoni and Bruzzone, El siluetazo.
30. Testimony of Tomás Ojea Quintana, Memoria Abierta, Buenos Aires, August 28, 2006.
31. Memoria Abierta, Abogados, derecho y política. See also Sikkink and Walling, "Argentina's Contribution to Global Trends in Transitional Justice."
32. Roht-Arriaza, The Pinochet Effect, 99.
33. Rodríguez Pinzón, Martin, and Ojea Quintana, La dimensión internacional de los derechos humanos.
34. Starr, Global Revolt, 19–42.
35. V. Basualdo, Berghoff, and Bucheli, "Crime and (No) Punishment," 3–4.
36. Payne, Pereira, and Bernal-Bermúdez, Transitional Justice, 1.
37. Allyn Z. Lite, "Another Attempt to Heal the Wounds of the Holocaust," Human Rights Magazine, Spring 2000, https://www.americanbar.org/groups/crsj/publications/human_rights_magazine_home/human_rights_vol27_2000/spring2000/hr_spring00_lite/.
38. Billstein et al., Working for the Enemy; Imlay and Horn, The Politics of Industrial Collaboration; and Black, IBM and the Holocaust.
39. Filártiga v. Peña-Irala, 630 F.2d 876, 881 (2nd Cir. 1980), cited in Stephen P. Mulligan, "The Alien Tort Statute (ATS): A Primer," Congressional Research Service Report R44947, updated June 1, 2018, p. 6, https://crsreports.congress.gov/product/pdf/R/R44947.
40. Cited in Mulligan, "The Alien Tort Statute," 6.
41. This American principle of corporate personhood took shape in the last decades of the nineteenth century, when courts upheld arguments presented by business lawyers who claimed that private corporations should enjoy the same protections as individuals. Those protections had been laid out in the Fourteenth Amendment of the US Constitution, passed in 1868 to protect the rights of newly freed slaves. See Bakan, The Corporation.
42. Herz, "The Liberalizing Effects of Tort," 211–12. See also Chambers, "The Unocal Settlement," 14–16. In the long run, the ATS turned out to be less

effective than hoped as a tool of corporate human rights prosecutions. See Payne, Pereira, and Bernal-Bermúdez, *Transitional Justice*, 80–85.
43. "Iwanowa v. Ford Motor Co., 67 F. Supp. 2d 424, 443 (D. N.J. 1999)," Justia US Law, https://law.justia.com/cases/federal/district-courts/FSupp2/67/424/2375384/#:~:text=Ford%20Werke's%20forced%20laborers%2C%20including,Ford%20Werke%20between%201941%2D1945.
44. Weeramantry, "Time Limitation under the United States Alien Tort Claims Act," 627.
45. "Ford Contributes $13 Million to German Slave-Labor Fund," United Press International, March 29, 2000, https://www.upi.com/Archives/2000/03/29/Ford-contributes-13-million-to-German-slave-labor-fund/1614954306000/.
46. Claims for Relief and Demand for Jury Trial, Pulega et al. v. Ford Motor Company, no. CV04-0411AHM (C.D. Cal, January 23, 2004), 19.
47. For an analysis of corporate veto strategies, see Payne, Pereira, and Bernal-Bermúdez, *Transitional Justice*, 113–61.
48. EarthRights International, "Shock and Law: George W. Bush's Attack on Law and Universal Human Rights," EarthRights International Report, March 2005, 36, https://earthrights.org/wp-content/uploads/publications/shock-and-law.pdf.
49. Collingsworth, "'Corporate Social Responsibility' Unmasked."
50. Rosen, "The Alien Tort Statute," 628.
51. Rosen, "The Alien Tort Statute," 634.
52. Human Rights Watch, "Getting Away with Torture: The Bush Administration and Mistreatment of Detainees," July 12, 2011, https://www.hrw.org/report/2011/07/12/getting-away-torture/bush-administration-and-mistreatment-detainees.
53. Chambers, "The Unocal Settlement," 14.
54. Chambers, "The Unocal Settlement," 16. See also "Sosa v. Alvarez-Machain," Oyez, https://www.oyez.org/cases/2003/03-339.
55. In their comprehensive analysis of global corporate complicity cases, Leigh Payne, Gabriel Pereira, and Laura Bernal-Bermúdez "did not find even one judgment under the ATS against corporations for their complicity in authoritarian and armed conflict violence." See Payne, Pereira, and Bernal-Bermúdez, *Transitional Justice*, 82.
56. Andriotti Romanin, "Decir la verdad, hacer justicia."

57. V. Basualdo, "The Argentine Dictatorship and Labor," 12.
58. Andriotti Romanin, "Neoliberalismo y lucha sindical." The CTA changed its name in 1996 to the Argentine Workers' Central (Central de Trabajadores Argentinos).
59. Quoted in V. Basualdo, "Complicidad patronal-militar en la última dictadura argentina," 20.
60. The group even traveled to Spain to present their report to Judge Baltasar Garzón, who had initiated investigations into human rights violations in Chile and Argentina using Spanish law. Unfortunately, though he gave them a sympathetic hearing, Garzón was not able to pursue their legal demands in Spain. "A 18 años del testimonio de la CTA ante Baltasar Garzón," Asociación Trabajadores del Estado, March 22, 2016, https://ate.org.ar/a-18-anos-del-testimonio-de-la-cta-ante-baltasar-garzon/. For an overview of Baltasar's work and its impacts in Chile and Argentina, see Roht-Arriaza, *The Pinochet Effect*.
61. Roht-Arriaza, *The Pinochet Effect*, 106–8.
62. For a detailed description of the procedures used in these hearings, see Andriotti Romanin, "Decir la verdad, hacer justicia."
63. V. Basualdo, Ojea Quintana, and Varsky, "Los casos de Ford y Mercedes Benz," 194.
64. Weber, *Die Verschwundenen von Mercedes-Benz*.
65. The transcript of these proceedings can be found at "¿El óvalo de la muerte? Empresas y represión bajo el Proceso Militar: El caso Ford," *Razón y Revolución*, September 1, 2002, https://razonyrevolucion.org/el-ovalo-de-la-muerte-empresas-y-represion-bajo-el-proceso-militar-el-caso-ford/.
66. For a summary of Schiffrin's career, see Bautista Cañón, "Se declaró Ciudadano Ilustre post mortem al doctor Leopoldo Héctor Schiffrin," *Palabras del Derecho*, January 13, 2023, https://palabrasdelderecho.com.ar/articulo/4076/Se-declaro-Ciudadano-Ilustre-post-mortem-al-doctor-Leopoldo-Hector-Schiffrin.
67. These included Servicio Paz y Justicia, Centro de Estudios Legales y Sociales, Familiares de Detenidos y Desaparecidos por Razones Políticas, Asamblea Permanente por los Derechos Humanos, Madres de Plaza de Mayo línea Fundadora, and Fundación Memoria Histórica y Social. "Sobre Memoria Abierta," Memoria Abierta, http://memoriaabierta.org.ar/wp/sobre-memoria-abierta/.

68. Dora Schwarzstein, founding director of the Oral History Program of the Faculty of Philosophy and Letters at the University of Buenos Aires, is credited with spearheading the field of oral history in Argentina. See Carnovale, Lorenz, and Pittaluga, *Historia, memoria y fuentes orales*, 23–25.
69. Carnovale, Lorenz, and Pittaluga, "Memoria y política en la situación de entrevista," 32.
70. The interviews relating to the Ford case are catalogued at Memoria Abierta, Archivo Oral, "Represión, luchas obreras y organización sindical: El caso Ford," AR MA AO, C06, https://memoriaabierta.indice.ar/fondoserie/629-represion-luchas-obreras-y-organizacion-sindical-el-caso-ford.
71. Feitlowitz, *A Lexicon of Terror*.
72. Crenzel, "La reconstrucción de un universo," 151. See also V. Basualdo, "The Argentine Dictatorship and Labor," 14.
73. This was the response to my inquiries at SMATA headquarters. On the lack of union archives, see V. Basualdo, "The Argentine Dictatorship and Labor," 14.
74. Carnovale, Lorenz, and Pittaluga, *Historia, memoria y fuentes orales*, 11.
75. V. Basualdo, "The Argentine Dictatorship and Labor," 14.
76. Comisión Provincial por la Memoria, https://www.comisionporlamemoria.org/.
77. Carlos Osorio, ed., National Security Archive, Electronic Briefing Book, no. 73, part 1, National Security Archive, https://nsarchive2.gwu.edu//NSAEBB/NSAEBB73/.
78. "Argentina's Political Prisoners Situation," August 11, 1977, US Department of State Virtual Reading Room (hereafter DoSVRR), https://foia.state.gov/Search/Results.aspx?searchText=((*)%20AND%20(Argentina:%20Prison%20Population%20Profile))%20AND%20(8/11/1977)&collection=ARGENTINA.
79. "Labor Disappearances," April 11, 1978, DoSVRR, https://foia.state.gov/Search/Results.aspx?searchText=(*)%20AND%20(keeping%20the%20lid%20on%20labor)&collection=ARGENTINA.
80. "Worker Detainees and Disappeared," May 9, 1978, DoSVRR, https://foia.state.gov/Search/Results.aspx?searchText=(((*)%20AND%20(Argentina:%20Prison%20Population%20Profile))%20AND%20(8/11/1977))%20AND%20(Worker%20Detainees%20and%20disappeared)&collection=ARGENTINA.

Notes to pages 190-194

81. V. Basualdo, "The Argentine Dictatorship and Labor."
82. Some key titles include V. Basualdo and Lorenz, "Los trabajadores industriales argentinos"; Lorenz, *Los zapatos de Carlito*; Rodríguez, "Estrategias de lucha en industrias dinámicas"; and Schneider, "Ladran Sancho." A major compilation of such case studies appears in Ministerio de Justicia, *Responsabilidad empresarial*.
83. An early work to make this argument is Brennan, *The Labor Wars in Córdoba*.
84. Dinerstein, "¡Que se vayan todos!," 191.
85. Some key titles include Azpiazu, Basualdo, and Khavisse, *El nuevo poder económico*; E. Basualdo, *Deuda externa y poder económico*; E. Basualdo, *Estudios de historia económica argentina*; and E. Basualdo, *Endeudar y fugar*.
86. Cited in Naomi Klein, "Out of the Ordinary," *Guardian*, January 25, 2003, https://www.theguardian.com/world/2003/jan/25/argentina.weekend7.
87. Roht-Arriaza, *The Pinochet Effect*, 114. The case is known as Juzgado Federal en lo Criminal y Correccional no. 4, "Simón, J. H. y otros," resolución del 6 de marzo de 2001.
88. "Ford Lawsuit (re Argentina)," Business and Human Rights Resource Centre, February 24, 2006, https://www.business-humanrights.org/en/latest-news/ford-lawsuit-re-argentina-2/.
89. Robben, *Argentina Betrayed*, 238.
90. Crenzel, "La reconstrucción de un universo," 180; and Sikkink and Walling, "Argentina's Contribution to Global Trends in Transitional Justice," 317–18.
91. Cited in Andriotti Romanin, "En el nombre del pasado," 2.
92. United Nations Treaty Collection, "Status of Treaties," chapter 4: Human Rights, https://treaties.un.org/pages/ViewDetails.aspx?src=IND&mtdsg_no=IV-6&chapter=4&clang=_en.
93. On the operations and limitations of this archive, see Crenzel, "La reconstrucción de un universo," 182–89.
94. Néstor Kirchner, "Palabras del president Néstor Kirchner, en el acto de conmemoración del 'Día nacional de la memoria por la verdad y la justicia,' celebrado en el colegio militar de la nación," cited in Andriotti Romanin, "En el nombre del pasado," 4–5.
95. V. Basualdo, Ojea Quintana, and Varsky, "Los casos de Ford y Mercedes Benz," 190.
96. Solicitud de Declaraciones Indagatorias, causa no. 18.018/02, "Molinari, Antonio—Personal Ford s/privación illegal de la libertad," 2006.

97. V. Basualdo, Ojea Quintana, and Varsky, "Los casos de Ford y Mercedes Benz," 191.
98. Andriotti Romanin, "Decir la verdad, hacer justicia," 13–16.
99. Andriotti Romanin, "Decir la verdad, hacer justicia," 15–16; and Roht-Arriaza, *The Pinochet Effect*, 106–8.
100. Andriotti Romanin, "Decir la verdad, hacer justicia," 16.
101. Luciana Rosende, "Un tal Jorge Julio López," Política Argentina, September 17, 2016, https://www.politicargentina.com/notas/201609/16658-un-tal-jorge-julio-lopez.html.
102. On the Grandmothers, see Arditti, *Searching for Life*.
103. Interview with José Rossanigo, Tandil, Argentina, July 12, 2008.
104. On the controversies that surrounded ESMA's redefinition as the Space of Memory and Human Rights, see Andermann, "Returning to the Site of Horror"; and Feld, "Preservar, recuperar, ocupar." Although Rossanigo's work did not find a home in Buenos Aires, *Autores ideológicos* did eventually become part of the permanent collection at the Haroldo Conti Cultural Center for Memory at the former ESMA.
105. Interview with José Rossanigo.
106. The members of the collective were scupltors Omar Estela, Javier Bernasconi, Marcela Oliva, Marcelo Montanari, Luciano Parodi, and Margarita Rocha. Guillemont, "Art et mémoire."
107. Guillemont, "Art et mémoire," para. 11.
108. "*Autores ideológicos*," Centro Cultural de la Memoria Haroldo Conti, http://conti.derhuman.jus.gov.ar/2014/03/i-autores-ideologicos.php#:~:text=Autores%20ideol%C3%B3gicos%20es%20un%20cuestionamiento,pret%C3%A9rito%20y%20nuestro%20cuerpo%20presente. This site includes a link to a short video that recounts the Falcon's history in Argentina. El Conti, "Ford Falcon, de la represión a la obra de arte," YouTube, September 4, 2014, https://www.youtube.com/watch?v=WCQFmSmTRYg&t=15s.
109. Causa no. 4012/3, Tribunal Federal de San Martín, Province of Buenos Aires, May 20, 2013.
110. Alejandro Jasinski, "Inmortalizar las luchas obreras," *El Cohete a la Luna*, February 21, 2021, https://www.elcohetealaluna.com/inmortalizar-las-luchas-obreras/.
111. See, for example, E. Basualdo, *Deuda externa y poder económico*.

112. Ministerio de Justicia, *Responsabilidad empresarial*. Other relevant titles include V. Basualdo, "Complicidad patronal-militar en la última dictadura argentina"; V. Basualdo, "Los delegados y las comisiones internas"; V. Basualdo, *La clase trabajadora Argentina*; V. Basualdo, "Shop-Floor Labor Organization in Argentina"; and V. Basualdo, Ojea Quintana, and Varsky, "Los casos de Ford y Mercedes Benz."
113. Lascano, Menéndez, and Vocos, "Análisis del proceso de trabajo."
114. See Billstein et al., *Working for the Enemy*, 136; and Simon Reich, "Ford's Research Efforts in Assessing the Activities of Its Subsidiary in Nazi Germany," commentary on *Research Findings about Ford-Werke under the Nazi Regime* (Dearborn, MI: Ford Motor Company, December 6, 2001), https://www.jewishvirtuallibrary.org/jsource/Holocaust/Ford.pdf. On the Müller and Sibilla defense team's professional ties with the O'Farrell law firm, which had represented Ford Motors in Argentina since the early twentieth century, see Alejandro Jasinski, "Abogados y algo más: El estudio O'Farrell y su rol en la represión de Ford," *El Cohete a la Luna*, September 16, 2018, https://www.elcohetealaluna.com/abogados-y-algo-mas/.
115. Alejandro Jasinski, "La clase: Un economista, una historiadora y un sociólogo, en una lección magistral en el Juicio a Ford," *El Cohete a la Luna*, October 21, 2018, https://www.elcohetealaluna.com/la-clase/.
116. Victoria Basualdo, personal communication, December 19, 2018.
117. Alejandro Jasinski, "De la fábrica a la comisaría," *El Cohete a la Luna*, August 19, 2018, https://www.elcohetealaluna.com/de-la-fabrica-a-la-comisaria/.
118. "Juicios de lesa humanidad en tiempo real," Ministerio de Justicia y Derechos Humanos, Secretaría de Derechos Humanos, http://www.juiciosdelesahumanidad.ar/#!/. On grassroots initiatives organized by universities in the province of Buenos Aires, see Florencia Blanco, "Diario del juicio: Una iniciativa que repara," *Página/12*, March 25, 2021, https://www.pagina12.com.ar/331506-diario-del-juicio-una-iniciativa-que-repara.
119. Poder Judicial de la Nación, San Martín, 11 de diciembre de 2018, Registro Resol. no. 249, causas no. 2855 y 2358, Business and Human Rights Resource Centre, https://media.business-humanrights.org/media/documents/files/documents/veredicto_2855.pdf.
120. Poder Judicial de la Nación, Registro Resol. no. 249, causas no. 2855 y 2358.
121. Poder Judicial de la Nación, Registro Resol. no. 249, causas no. 2855 y 2358.

122. Victoria Basualdo, "The Ford Case, 40 Years Later," JusticeInfo.net, Fondation Hirondelle, February 18, 2019, https://www.justiceinfo.net/en/40348-the-ford-case-40-years-later.html.
123. Elizabeth Gómez Alcorta, "A pesar de todo," *El Cohete a la Luna*, December 16, 2018, https://www.elcohetealaluna.com/a-pesar-de-todo/.
124. Victorio Paulón, "Balance de un año de lucha," *El Cohete a la Luna*, December 16, 2018, https://www.elcohetealaluna.com/balance-de-un-ano-de-lucha/.
125. Video excerpt of Victorio Paulón's interview at Memoria Abierta, "Corporate Responsibility in Crimes against Humanity: Personal Reflections," Centro de Estudios Legales y Sociales, https://www.cels.org.ar/web/en/2017/03/corporate-responsibility-in-crimes-against-humanity-personal-reflections/. Paulón had been a lead organizer of the 1975 metalworkers' strike in the steel town of Villa Constitución and had spent six years in prison. He had resumed his labor activism after the end of the dictatorship. In 2016 he was also a board member at the Center for Legal and Social Studies (Centro de Estudios Legales y Sociales, or CELS), one of Argentina's most respected human rights organizations.
126. On the relationship between human rights trials and memory work in Argentina, see Kaiser, "Argentina's Trials."

CONCLUSION

1. Agustín Lafforgue, "TC: El primer triunfo del Falcon," *Solo TC*, April 24, 2020, https://www.solotc.com.ar/primer-triunfo-ford-falcon-turismo-carretera/#:~:text=El%2024%20de%20abril%20de%201966%2C%20en%20la%20Vuelta%20Pan,exitoso%20en%20la%20%E2%80%9Cm%C3%A1xima%E2%80%9D; and "Werner y la renovación en el TC: 'Si es el último año del Falcon, intentaremos despedirlo con un campeonato," *La Voz*, June 28, 2023, https://www.lavoz.com.ar/deportes/motores/werner-y-la-renovacion-en-el-tc-si-es-el-ultimo-ano-del-falcon-intentaremos-despedirlo-con-un-campeonato/.
2. Auto Historia, "La llegada del Ford Falcon al Turismo Carretera," YouTube, September 7, 2023, https://www.youtube.com/watch?v=-zaVn_tZdao.
3. Barthes, "The New Citroën."
4. Berdahl, "Go, Trabi, Go!"

5. Robben, *Argentina Betrayed*, 86.
6. Sin Fin and Memoria Abierta, *Las leyes de la dictadura*, https://www.lasleyesdeladictadura.com.ar/index.php?a=Start.
7. Payne, Pereira, and Bernal-Bermúdez, *Transitional Justice*, 121.
8. Payne, Pereira, and Bernal-Bermúdez, *Transitional Justice*, 223.
9. The original wording is "aporte de la estructura organizacional y de infraestructura territorial por parte de las autoridades y personal jerárquico de Ford a las fuerzas militares para la realización de los secuestros." See Comisión Interamericana de Derechos Humanos and Government of Argentina, "Acuerdo de cumplimiento de recomendaciones," caso 11.159, "Pedro Norberto Troiani," informe no. 22/21, 2, https://www.ohchr.org/sites/default/files/documents/issues/truth/nsa/2022-09-14/submission-NSAs-hrc51-state-argentina-4-es.pdf.
10. Ministerio de Justicia y Derechos Humanos, Secretaría de Derechos Humanos, "El Estado argentino firmará un acuerdo ante la Comisión Interamericana por el caso de un trabajador de Ford secuestrado en dictadura," November 30, 2021, https://www.argentina.gob.ar/noticias/el-estado-argentino-firmara-un-acuerdo-ante-la-comision-interamericana-por-el-caso-de-un#:~:text=secuestrado%20en%20dictadura-,El%20Estado%20argentino%20firmar%C3%A1%20un%20acuerdo%20ante%20la%20Comisi%C3%B3n%20Interamericana,de%20Ford%20secuestrado%20en%20dictadura&text=Al%20recuperar%20su%20libertad%20se,el%20pa%C3%ADs%20estaba%20en%20dictadura.
11. V. Basualdo, "The Argentine Dictatorship and Labor," 8.

References

ARCHIVES

Archivo DIPPBA, Comisión Provincial por la Memoria, La Plata
Benson Ford Research Center, Dearborn, Michigan
Detroit Public Library, National Automotive History Collection
Hartman Center for Sales, Advertising, and Marketing History, Duke University
Memoria Abierta, Buenos Aires
Papers of John F. Kennedy, Presidential Papers
US Argentina Declassification Project

NEWSPAPERS, MAGAZINES, AND NEWS AGENCIES

BBC News
Buenos Aires Herald
Cars Guide
Clarín (Buenos Aires)
El Cohete a la Luna
Diario la Capital (Mar del Plata, Argentina)
Grand Rapids (MI) Press
Guardian (London)
Human Rights Magazine
Mundo Ford
La Nación (Buenos Aires)
New York Times
La Opinión (Buenos Aires)
Página/12
El País (Madrid)
Razón y Revolución
Reader's Digest
Reuters

References

Revista Somos
Time
United Press International
La Verdad (Buenos Aires)
La Voz (Córdoba)
Wall Street Journal

BOOKS AND JOURNAL ARTICLES

Abós, Alvaro. *Las organizaciones sindicales y el poder militar (1976–1983)*. Buenos Aires: Centro Editor de América Latina, 1984.

Acevedo, Manuel, Eduardo M. Basualdo, and Miguel Khavisse. *¿Quién es quién? Los dueños del poder económico (Argentina 1973–1987)*. Buenos Aires: Editora/12, 1990.

Acree, William Garrett, Jr. *Staging Frontiers: The Making of Modern Popular Culture in Argentina and Uruguay*. Albuquerque: University of New Mexico Press, 2019.

Adair, Jennifer. *In Search of the Lost Decade: Everyday Rights in Post-Dictatorship Argentina*. Oakland: University of California Press, 2019.

Adamovsky, Ezequiel. *Historia de la clase media Argentina: Apogeo y decadencia de una ilusión, 1919–2003*. Buenos Aires: Planeta, 2009.

Aguilar, Gonzalo. "Televisión y vida privada." In *Historia de la vida privada en la Argentina*, vol. 3, *La Argentina entre multitudes y soledades: De los años treinta a la actualidad*, edited by Fernando Devoto and Marta Madero. Buenos Aires: Taurus, 1999.

Aguirre, Carlos, and Javier Villa-Flores, eds. *From the Ashes of History: Loss and Recovery of Archives and Libraries in Modern Latin America*. Raleigh, NC: Editorial A Contracorriente, 2015.

Alegre, Robert F. *Railroad Radicals in Cold War Mexico: Gender, Class, and Memory*. Lincoln: University of Nebraska Press, 2013.

Allier Montaño, Eugenia, and Emilio Crenzel, eds. *Las luchas por la memoria en América Latina: Historia reciente y violencia política*. Mexico City: Bonilla Artigas Editores, 2015.

Almirón, Fernando. *Campo Santo: Los asesinatos del ejército en Campo de Mayo; Testimonios del ex-sargento Víctor Ibáñez*. Buenos Aires: Editorial 21, 1999.

Altamirano, Carlos. *Arturo Frondizi, o el hombre de ideas como político.* Buenos Aires: Fondo de Cultura Económica, 1998.

Amado, Ana. *La imagen justa: Cine argentino y política (1980–2007).* Buenos Aires: Ediciones Colihue, 2009.

Andermann, Jens. "Returning to the Site of Horror: On the Reclaiming of Clandestine Concentration Camps in Argentina." *Theory, Culture and Society* 29, no. 1 (January 2012): 76–98.

Andersen, Martin Edwin. *Dossier Secreto: Argentina's Desaparecidos and the Myth of the "Dirty War."* Boulder, CO: Westview Press, 1993.

Andriotti Romanin, Enrique. "Decir la verdad, hacer justicia: Los Juicios por la Verdad en Argentina." *European Review of Latin American and Caribbean Studies*, no. 94 (April 2013): 5–23.

Andriotti Romanin, Enrique. "En el nombre del pasado: Política y luchas por la Memoria durante el gobierno de Kirchner." Paper presented at the XXVII Congreso de la Asociación Latinoamericana de Sociología, VIII Jornadas de Sociología de la Universidad de Buenos Aires, Asociación Latinoamericana de Sociología, Buenos Aires, 2009.

Andriotti Romanin, Enrique. "Neoliberalismo y lucha sindical (1989–1995): Creencias, memoria y tradición en el Congreso de Trabajadores Argentinos." *Trabajo y Sociedad* 10, no. 11 (2008): 1–15. https://www.redalyc.org/articulo.oa?id=387334683005.

Anzorena, Oscar. *Tiempo de violencia y utopía: Del golpe de Onganía (1966) al golpe de Videla (1976).* Buenos Aires: Ediciones Colihue, 1998.

Aprea, Gustavo, and Marita Soto. "De *La familia Falcón* a *Graduados*: 50 años de retratos cotidianos." *Revista de Ciencias Sociales*, no. 81 (August 2012): 84–89. https://www.studocu.com/es-ar/document/universidad-de-buenos-aires/semiotica-i/de-la-familia-falcon-texto-de-aproa-y-soto/26572605.

Archetti, Eduardo P. *El potrero, la pista y el ring: Las patrias del deporte argentino.* Colección Popular, no. 593. Buenos Aires: Fondo de Cultura Económica, 2001.

Arditti, Rita. *Searching for Life: The Grandmothers of the Plaza de Mayo and the Disappeared Children of Argentina.* Berkeley: University of California Press, 1999.

Aroskind, Ricardo. "La hiperinflación de 1989: Radiografía del país posdictatorial." *Espóiler: Revista de Política*, March 16, 2019.

References

http://espoiler.sociales.uba.ar/2019/03/16/la-hiperinflacion-de-1989-radiografia-del-pais-posdictatorial/.

Aroskind, Ricardo. "El país del desarrollo posible." In *Violencia, proscripción y autoritarismo (1955–1976)*, vol. 9 of *Nueva historia argentina*, edited by Daniel James, 63–116. Buenos Aires: Editorial Sudamericana, 2003.

Asociación de Fabricantes de Automotores. *1966: 1,000,000 de automotores argentinos*. Buenos Aires: Asociación de Fabricantes de Automotores, 1966.

Auslander, Leora. "Beyond Words." *American Historical Review* 110, no. 4 (October 2005): 1015–45.

Auyero, Javier. *Poor People's Politics: Peronist Survival Networks and the Legacy of Evita*. Durham, NC: Duke University Press, 2000.

Azpiazu, Daniel, Eduardo Basualdo, and Miguel Khavisse. *El nuevo poder económico en la Argentina de los años 80*. Buenos Aires: Siglo XXI, 2004.

Azpiazu, Daniel, Martín Schorr, and Victoria Basualdo. *La industria y el sindicalismo de base en la Argentina*. Buenos Aires: Atuel, 2010.

Bachelor, Steven J. "Miracle on Ice: Industrial Workers and the Promise of Americanization in Cold War Mexico." In *In from the Cold: Latin America's New Encounter with the Cold War*, edited by Gilbert M. Joseph and Daniela Spenser, 253–72. Durham, NC: Duke University Press, 2008.

Bakan, Joel. *The Corporation: The Pathological Pursuit of Profit and Power*. New York: Free Press, 2004.

Ballent, Anahí. "Kilómetro cero: La construcción del universo simbólico del camino en la Argentina de los años treinta." *Boletín del Instituto de Historia Argentina y Americana Dr. Emilio Ravignani*, no. 27 (January–June 2005): 107–37.

Barthes, Roland. "The New Citroën." In *Mythologies*, 88–90. Translated by Annette Lavers. New York: Hill and Wang, 1972.

Basualdo, Eduardo. *Deuda externa y poder económico en la Argentina*. Buenos Aires: Editorial Nueva América, 1987.

Basualdo, Eduardo, ed. *Endeudar y fugar: Un análisis de la historia económica argentina, desde Martínez de Hoz hasta Macri*. 2nd ed. Buenos Aires: Siglo XXI, 2020.

Basualdo, Eduardo. *Estudios de historia económica argentina: Desde mediados del siglo XX a la actualidad*. Buenos Aires: Siglo XXI, 2010.

Basualdo, Eduardo. "El legado dictatorial: El nuevo patrón de acumulación de capital, la desindustrialización, y el ocaso de los trabajadores." In *Cuentas pendientes: Los cómplices económicos de la dictadura*, edited by Horacio Verbitsky and Juan Pablo Bohoslavsky, 81–99. Buenos Aires: Siglo XXI, 2013.

Basualdo, Eduardo, and Victoria Basualdo. "Confronting Labor Power: Ford Motor Argentina and the Dictatorship (1976–1983)." In *Big Business and Dictatorship in Latin America: A Transnational History of Profits and Repression*, edited by Victoria Basualdo, Hartmut Berghoff, and Marcelo Bucheli, 215–36. Cham, Switzerland: Palgrave Macmillan, 2020.

Basualdo, Eduardo, and Leandro M. Bona. "La deuda externa (pública y privada) y la fuga de capitales durante la valorización financiera, 1976–2000." In *Endeudar y fugar: Un análisis de la historia económica argentina, desde Martínez de Hoz hasta Macri*, 2nd ed., edited by Eduardo Basualdo, 12–43. Buenos Aires: Siglo XXI, 2020.

Basualdo, Victoria. "Aportes para el análisis del papel de la cúpula sindical en la represión a los trabajadores en la década de 1970." In *Cuentas pendientes: Los cómplices económicos de la dictadura*, edited by Horacio Verbitsky and Juan Pablo Bohoslavsky, 235–55. Buenos Aires: Siglo XXI, 2013.

Basualdo, Victoria. "The Argentine Dictatorship and Labor (1976–1983): A Historiographical Essay." *International Labor and Working-Class History* 93 (Spring 2018): 8–26.

Basualdo, Victoria. "Business and the Military in the Argentine Dictatorship (1976–1983): Institutional, Economic, and Repressive Relations." In *Big Business and Dictatorship in Latin America: A Transnational History of Profits and Repression*, edited by Victoria Basualdo, Hartmut Berghoff, and Marcelo Bucheli, 35–62. Cham, Switzerland: Palgrave Macmillan, 2020.

Basualdo, Victoria, ed. *La clase trabajadora argentina en el Siglo XX: Experiencias de lucha y organización*. Buenos Aires: Cara o Ceca, 2011.

Basualdo, Victoria. "Complicidad patronal-militar en la última dictadura argentina: Los casos de Acindar, Astarsa, Dálmine Siderca, Ford,

Ledesma y Mercedes Benz." *Revista Engranaje*, no. 5 (March 2006): 1–21.

Basualdo, Victoria. "Los delegados y las comisiones internas en la historia argentina, 1943–2007." In *La industria y el sindicalismo de base en la Argentina*, by Daniel Azpiazu, Martín Schorr, and Victoria Basualdo, 81–157. Buenos Aires: Atuel, 2010.

Basualdo, Victoria. "Labor and Structural Change: Shop-Floor Organization and Militancy in Argentine Industrial Factories." PhD diss., Columbia University, 2010.

Basualdo, Victoria. *Memoria en las aulas*. No. 13, *La clase trabajadora durante la última dictadura militar argentina, 1976–1983*. La Plata, Argentina: Comisión Provincial por la Memoria.

Basualdo, Victoria. "Shop-Floor Labor Organization in Argentina from Early Peronism to the 'Proceso' Military Dictatorship." *WorkingUSA* 14, no. 3 (September 2011): 305–32.

Basualdo, Victoria, Hartmut Berghoff, and Marcelo Bucheli, eds. *Big Business and Dictatorships in Latin America: A Transnational History of Profits and Repression*. Cham, Switzerland: Palgrave Macmillan, 2020.

Basualdo, Victoria, Hartmut Berghoff, and Marcelo Bucheli. "Crime and (No) Punishment: Business Corporations and Dictatorships." In *Big Business and Dictatorship in Latin America: A Transnational History of Profits and Repression*, edited by Victoria Basualdo, Hartmut Berghoff, and Marcelo Bucheli, 1–34. Cham, Switzerland: Palgrave Macmillan, 2020.

Basualdo, Victoria, and Federico Lorenz. "Los trabajadores industriales argentinos en la primera mitad de la década del '70: Propuestas para una agenda de investigación a partir del análisis comparativo de casos." *Páginas: Revista Digital de la Escuela de Historia* 4, no. 6 (2012): 123–57.

Basualdo, Victoria, Tomás Ojea Quintana, and Carolina Varsky. "Los casos de Ford y Mercedes Benz." In *Cuentas pendientes: Los cómplices económicos de la dictadura*, edited by Horacio Verbitsky and Juan Pablo Bohoslavsky, 185–202. Buenos Aires: Siglo XXI, 2013.

Bauer, Arnold J. *Goods, Power, History: Latin America's Material Culture*. Cambridge: Cambridge University Press, 2001.

Belini, Claudio. "Negocios, poder y política industrial en los orígenes de la industria automotriz argentina, 1943–1958." *Revista de Historia Industrial* 15, no. 2 (December 2006): 109–35.

Benedetti, Julio César. "Evolución espacial y funcional del predio militar de Campo de Mayo y su entorno suburbano o periurbano." Unpublished graduate paper, Seminario de Investigación III, Universidad del Salvador, Buenos Aires, n.d. https://www.scribd.com/document/639063656/Untitled.

Berdahl, Daphne. "'Go, Trabi, Go!' Reflections on a Car and Its Symbolization over Time." *Anthropology and Humanism* 25, no. 2 (December 2000): 131–41.

Besoky, Juan Luis. "Violencia paraestatal y organizaciones de derecha: Aportes para repensar el entramado represivo en la Argentina, 1970–1976." *Nuevo Mundo Mundos Nuevos* 5 (2016). https://journals.openedition.org/nuevomundo/68974#quotation.

Billstein, Reinhold, Karola Fings, Anita Kugler, and Nicholas Levis. *Working for the Enemy: Ford, General Motors, and Forced Labor in Germany during the Second World War.* New York: Berghahn Books, 2000.

Black, Edwin. *IBM and the Holocaust: The Strategic Alliance between Nazi Germany and America's Most Powerful Corporation.* New York: Three Rivers Press, 2001.

Böhm, Steffen, Campbell Jones, Chris Land, and Matthew Paterson, eds. *Against Automobility.* Malden, MA: Blackwell, 2006.

Bohoslavsky, Juan Pablo. "Banking Southern Cone Dictatorships." In *Big Business and Dictatorships in Latin America: A Transnational History of Profits and Repression*, edited by Victoria Basualdo, Hartmut Berghoff, and Marcelo Bucheli, 185–214. Cham, Switzerland: Palgrave Macmillan, 2020.

Bonavena, Pablo, and Mariano Millán, "El movimiento estudiantil rosarino, antes y durante el Rosariazo de mayo de 1969." Paper presented at the VII Jornadas de Sociología, Facultad de Ciencias Sociales, Universidad de Buenos Aires, 2007. https://cdsa.aacademica.org/000-106/417.pdf?view.

Brands, Hal. *Latin America's Cold War.* Cambridge, MA: Harvard University Press, 2012.

References

Brennan, James P. *Argentina's Missing Bones: Revisiting the History of the Dirty War*. Oakland: University of California Press, 2018.

Brennan, James P. *The Labor Wars in Córdoba, 1955–1976: Ideology, Work, and Labor Politics in an Argentine Industrial Society*. Cambridge, MA: Harvard University Press, 1994.

Brinkley, Douglas. *Wheels for the World: Henry Ford, His Company, and a Century of Progress*. New York: Viking, 2003.

Caimari, Lila. *While the City Sleeps: A History of Pistoleros, Policemen, and the Crime Beat in Buenos Aires before Perón*. Translated by Lisa Ubelaker Andrade and Richard Shindell. Oakland: University of California Press, 2017.

Calveiro, Pilar. *Poder y desaparición: Los campos de concentración en Argentina*. Buenos Aires: Ediciones Colihue, 2008.

Calveiro, Pilar. *Política y/o violencia: Una aproximación a la guerrilla de los años setenta*. Buenos Aires: Editorial Norma, 2008.

Carassai, Sebastián. *The Argentine Silent Majority: Middle Classes, Politics, Violence, and Memory in the Seventies*. Durham, NC: Duke University Press, 2014.

Carassai, Sebastián. "The Dark Side of Social Desire: Violence as Metaphor, Fantasy and Satire in Argentina, 1969–1975." *Journal of Latin American Studies* 47, no. 1 (February 2015): 31–63.

Cardoso, Fernando Henrique, and Enzo Faletto. *Dependency and Development in Latin America*. Translated by Marjory Mattingly Urquidi. Berkeley: University of California Press, 1979.

Carnovale, Vera. "Las 'cárceles del pueblo': Los secuestros de la izquierda armada argentina." *Postdata* 25, no. 1 (April–September 2020): 199–239.

Carnovale, Vera, Federico Lorenz, and Roberto Pittaluga, eds. *Historia, memoria y fuentes orales*. Buenos Aires: Ediciones CeDInCI; Ediciones Memoria Abierta, 2006.

Carnovale, Vera, Federico Lorenz, and Roberto Pittaluga. "Memoria y política en la situación de entrevista: En torno a la constitución de un archivo oral sobre el Terrorismo de Estado en la Argentina." In *Historia, memoria y fuentes orales*, edited by Vera Carnovale, Federico Lorenz, and Roberto Pittaluga, 29–44. Buenos Aires: Ediciones CeDInCI; Ediciones Memoria Abierta, 2006.

Catalá-Carrasco, Jorge L., Paulo Drinot, and James Scorer, eds. *Comics and Memory in Latin America*. Pittsburgh: University of Pittsburgh Press, 2017.

Caviglia, Mariana. *Vivir a oscuras: Escenas cotidianas durante la dictadura*. Buenos Aires: Aguilar, 2006.

Centro de Estudios Legales y Sociales. *Derechos humanos en Argentina: Informe 2013*. Buenos Aires: Siglo XXI, 2013.

Chambers, Rachel. "The Unocal Settlement: Implications for the Developing Law on Corporate Complicity in Human Rights Abuses." *Human Rights Brief* 13, no. 1 (2005): 14–17.

Chastain, Andrea B., and Timothy W. Lorek, eds. *Itineraries of Expertise: Science, Technology, and the Environment in Latin America's Long Cold War*. Pittsburgh: University of Pittsburgh Press, 2020.

Clarsen, Georgine. "'Australia—Drive It Like You Stole It': Automobility as a Medium of Communication in Settler Colonial Australia." *Mobilities* 12, no. 4 (2017): 520–33.

Clarsen, Georgine, and Lorenzo Veracini. "Settler Colonial Automobilities: A Distinct Constellation of Automobile Cultures?" *History Compass* 10, no. 12 (2012): 889–900.

Collier, Simon, and William F. Sater. *A History of Chile, 1808–2002*. 2nd ed. Cambridge: Cambridge University Press, 2004.

Collingsworth, Terry. "'Corporate Social Responsibility' Unmasked." *St. Thomas Law Review* 16, no. 4 (Summer 2004): 669–86.

Comisión Nacional Sobre la Desaparición de Personas (CONADEP). *Nunca Más: Informe de la Comisión Nacional Sobre la Desaparición de Personas*. 6th ed. Buenos Aires: Editorial Universitaria de Buenos Aires, 2003.

Comisión Provincial por la Memoria. "Historia institucional de la DIPPBA: La inteligencia policial a través de sus documentos." La Plata, Argentina: Comisión Provincial por la Memoria, n.d. https://www.comisionporlamemoria.org/archivos/archivo/historia-institucional-dippba/historia-institucional-dippba.pdf.

Conlon, Robert, and John Perkins. *Wheels and Deals: The Automotive Industry in Twentieth-Century Australia*. Burlington, VT: Ashgate, 2001.

Corrêa, Larissa Rosa. "Looking at the Southern Cone: American Trade Unionism in the Cold War Military Dictatorships of Brazil and

Argentina." *International Review of Social History* 62, no. S25 (December 2017): 245–69.

Cosse, Isabella. "Mafalda: Talisman of Democracy and Icon of Nostalgia for the 1960s." In *Comics and Memory in Latin America*, edited by Jorge L. Catalá-Carrasco, Paulo Drinot, and James Scorer, 86–107. Pittsburgh: University of Pittsburgh Press, 2017.

Cox, David. *Dirty Secrets, Dirty War*. Charleston, SC: Evening Post Publishing Company, 2008.

Crenzel, Emilio, ed. *Los desaparecidos en la Argentina: Memorias, representaciones e ideas (1983–2008)*. Buenos Aires: Editorial Biblos, 2010.

Crenzel, Emilio. "Entre la historia y la memoria: A 40 años del golpe de Estado en la Argentina." *História: Questões & Debates* 64, no. 2 (July–December 2016): 39–69.

Crenzel, Emilio. *La historia política del Nunca Más: La memoria de las desapariciones en la Argentina*. Buenos Aires: Siglo XXI, 2008.

Crenzel, Emilio. "Políticas de la memoria: La historia del informe *Nunca Más*." *Papeles del Centro de Estudios sobre la Identidad Colectiva*, no. 61 (September 2010): 1–31. https://identidadcolectiva.es/pdf/61.pdf.

Crenzel, Emilio. "La reconstrucción de un universo: Desaparición forzada de personas en la Argentina." In *From the Ashes of History: Loss and Recovery of Archives and Libraries in Modern Latin America*, edited by Carlos Aguirre and Javier Villa-Flores, 145–96. Raleigh, NC: Editorial A Contracorriente, 2015.

D'Antonio, Débora, and Ariel Eidelman. "El sistema penitenciario y los presos políticos durante la configuración de una nueva estrategia represiva del estado argentino (1966–1976)." *Iberoamericana* 10, no. 40 (December 2010): 93–111.

Davis, Mike. *Buda's Wagon: A Brief History of the Car Bomb*. London: Verso, 2008.

Davis, Rhiannon. "Negotiating Local and Global Knowledge and History: J. Walter Thompson around the Globe 1928–1960." *Journal of Australian Studies* 36, no. 1 (2012): 81–97.

Delich, Francisco. "Después del diluvio, la clase obrera." In *Argentina hoy*, edited by Alain Rouquié, 129–50. Buenos Aires: Siglo XXI, 1982.

Dias, José Carlos, José Paulo Cavalcanti Filho, Maria Rita Kehl, Paulo Sérgio Pinheiro, Pedro Bohomoletz de Abreu Dallari, and Rosa Maria

Cardoso da Cunha. *Relatório*. Vol. 1. Brasília: Comissão Nacional de Verdade, 2014.

Dinerstein, Ana C. "¡Que se Vayan Todos! Popular Insurrection and the Asambleas Barriales in Argentina." *Bulletin of Latin American Research* 22, no. 2 (April 2003): 187–200.

Dirección Nacional del Sistema Argentino de Información Jurídica. *El Estado Mayor del Comando de Institutos Militares: Zona de Defensa IV*. Programa Verdad y Justicia. Buenos Aires: Editorial Ministerio de Justicia y Derechos Humanos de la Nación, 2015.

Dorfman, Ariel, and Armand Mattelart. *Para leer al Pato Donald*. Valparaíso, Chile: Ediciones Universitarias de Valparaíso, 1971.

Downs, Linda Bank. *Diego Rivera: The Detroit Industry Murals*. New York: W. W. Norton, 1999.

Doyon, Louise M. "La organización del movimiento sindical peronista, 1946–1955." *Desarrollo Económico* 24, no. 94 (July–September 1984): 203–34.

DuBois, Lindsay. *The Politics of the Past in an Argentine Working-Class Neighbourhood*. Toronto: University of Toronto Press, 2005.

Duffy, Enda. *The Speed Handbook: Velocity, Pleasure, Modernism*. Durham, NC: Duke University Press, 2009.

Elena, Eduardo. *Dignifying Argentina: Peronism, Citizenship, and Mass Consumption*. Pittsburgh: University of Pittsburgh Press, 2011.

Evans, Judith, Paul Heath Hoeffel, and Daniel James. "Reflections on Argentine Auto Workers and Their Unions." In *The Political Economy of the Latin American Motor Vehicle Industry*, edited by Rich Kronish and Kenneth S. Mericle. Cambridge, MA: MIT Press, 1984.

Featherstone, Mike, Nigel Thrift, and John Urry, eds. *Automobilities*. London: Sage Publications, 2005.

Feinmann, José Pablo. *La sangre derramada: Ensayo sobre la violencia política*. Buenos Aires: Editorial Seiz Barral, 2001.

Feitlowitz, Marguerite. *A Lexicon of Terror: Argentina and the Legacies of Torture*. Oxford: Oxford University Press, 1998.

Feld, Claudia. "Preservar, recuperar, ocupar: Controversias memoriales en torno a la ex-ESMA (1998–2013)." *Revista Colombiana de Sociología* 40, no. 1 (June 2017): 101–31.

Feld, Claudia, and Jessica Stites Mor, eds. *El pasado que miramos: Memoria e imagen ante la historia reciente*. Buenos Aires: Ediciones Paidós, 2009.
Ferrer, Ada. *Cuba: An American History*. New York: Scribner, 2021.
Field, Thomas C., Jr., Stella Krepp, and Vanni Pettinà, eds. *Latin America and the Global Cold War*. Chapel Hill: University of North Carolina Press, 2020.
Finchelstein, Federico. *The Ideological Origins of the Dirty War: Fascism, Populism, and Dictatorship in Twentieth Century Argentina*. Oxford: Oxford University Press, 2014.
Flink, James J. *The Automobile Age*. Cambridge, MA: MIT Press, 1988.
Flink, James J. *The Car Culture*. Cambridge, MA: MIT Press, 1975.
Ford Argentina SCA. *Ford: 90 años en la Argentina*. Buenos Aires: Ford Argentina SCA, 2003.
Forni, Floreal H., and Laura M. Roldán. "Trayectorias laborales de residentes de areas urbanas pobres: Un estudio de casos en el conurbano bonaerense." *Desarrollo Económico* 35, no. 140 (January–March 1996): 585–99.
Fortuna, Victoria. *Moving Otherwise: Dance, Violence, and Memory in Buenos Aires*. New York: Oxford University Press, 2019.
Franco, Marina. *Un enemigo para la nación: Orden interno, violencia y "subversión," 1973–1976*. Buenos Aires: Fondo de Cultura Económica, 2012.
Frank, Thomas. *The Conquest of Cool: Business Culture, Counterculture, and the Rise of Hip Consumerism*. Chicago: University of Chicago Press, 1997.
Frigerio, Rogelio. *Los trabajadores y el desarrollo nacional*. Buenos Aires: Sociedad Editora Argentina, 1939.
Gadano, Nicolás. *Historia del petróleo en la Argentina, 1907–1955: Desde los inicios hasta la caída de Perón*. Buenos Aires: Edhasa, 2006.
Galeano, Eduardo. *Las venas abiertas de América Latina*. Caracas: Siglo XXI, 1971.
García Heras, Raúl. *Automotores norteamericanos, caminos y modernización urbana en la Argentina, 1918–1939*. Buenos Aires: Libros de Hispanoamérica, 1985.
García Márquez, Gabriel. *Cien años de soledad*. Buenos Aires: Editorial Sudamericana, 1967.

Gartman, David. "Three Ages of the Automobile: The Cultural Logics of the Car." *Theory, Culture and Society* 21, nos. 4–5 (August–October 2004): 169–95.

Gewald, Jan-Bart. "Missionaries, Hereros, and Motorcars: Mobility and the Impact of Motor Vehicles in Namibia before 1940." *International Journal of African Historical Studies* 35, nos. 2–3 (2002): 257–85.

Gewald, Jan-Bart, Sabine Luning, and Klaas Van Walraven, eds. *The Speed of Change: Motor Vehicles and People in Africa.* Leiden: Brill, 2009.

Gill, Lesley. *The School of the Americas: Military Training and Political Violence in the Americas.* Durham, NC: Duke University Press, 2004.

Gillespie, Richard. *Soldiers of Perón: Argentina's Montoneros.* Oxford: Clarendon Press, 1982.

Gilroy, Paul. "Driving While Black." In *Car Cultures*, edited by Daniel Miller, 81–104. Oxford: Berg Publishers, 2001.

González Peña, Eduardo Pablo. "Ford Falcon (1962–1991): El mismo, pero mejor; Illusio, habitus y sentido práctico en el Campo Automotriz Argentino." Master's thesis, Universidad Nacional de San Martín, 2017.

Graham-Yooll, Andrew. *De Perón a Videla.* Buenos Aires: Editorial Legasa, 1989.

Gramsci, Antonio. "Americanism and Fordism." In *Selections from the Prison Notebooks of Antonio Gramsci*, edited by Quintin Hoare and Geoffrey Nowell Smith, 277–318. New York: International Publishers, 1971.

Grandin, Greg. *Empire's Workshop: Latin America, the United States, and the Rise of the New Imperialism.* New York: Henry Holt, 2006.

Grandin, Greg. *The End of the Myth: From the Frontier to the Border Wall in the Mind of America.* New York: Henry Holt, 2019.

Grandin, Greg. *Fordlandia: The Rise and Fall of Henry Ford's Forgotten Jungle City.* New York: Henry Holt, 2009.

Grandin, Greg. "The Instruction of Great Catastrophe: Truth Commissions, National History, and State Formation in Argentina, Chile, and Guatemala." *American Historical Review* 110, no. 1 (February 2005): 46–67.

Grandin, Greg. *The Last Colonial Massacre: Latin America in the Cold War.* Updated ed. Chicago: University of Chicago Press, 2011.

Grandin, Greg. "Living in Revolutionary Time: Coming to Terms with the Violence of Latin America's Cold War." In *A Century of Revolution: Insurgent and Counterinsurgent Violence during Latin America's Long Cold War*, edited by Greg Grandin and Gilbert M. Joseph, 1–44. Durham, NC: Duke University Press, 2010.

Grandin, Greg, and Gilbert M. Joseph, eds. *A Century of Revolution: Insurgent and Counterinsurgent Violence during Latin America's Long Cold War*. Durham, NC: Duke University Press, 2010.

Guillemont, Michèle. "Art et mémoire: Ce que désosser une Ford Falcon veut dire." *Amerika: Mémoires, identités, territoires*, no. 3 (December 10, 2010). https://journals.openedition.org/amerika/1443#text.

Gutiérrez, Fernando. *Treintamil – Secuela – Cosas del Río*. Buenos Aires: Centro Cultural de la Memoria Haroldo Conti, 2014.

Gutiérrez, Graciela B. "Falcon verde." In *Los lugares de la memoria*, by Silvia Nardi, Mabel Sampaolo, Andrea Trotta, et al., 73–86. Buenos Aires: Editorial Madreselva, 2009.

Guzman Bouvard, Marguerite. *Revolutionizing Motherhood: The Mothers of the Plaza de Mayo*. Lanham, MD: Rowman and Littlefield, 2004.

Hammond, Paul Y. "A Functional Analysis of Defense Department Decision-Making in the McNamara Administration." *American Political Science Review* 62, no. 1 (March 1968): 57–69.

Harari, Ianina. "La burocracia peronista: El sindicato automotriz argentino ante el auge de la lucha de clases, 1969–1976." *Revista Izquierdas* 3, no. 8 (December 2010): 1–19.

Herz, Richard L. "The Liberalizing Effects of Tort: How Corporate Complicity Liability under the Alien Tort Statute Advances Constructive Engagement." *Harvard Human Rights Journal* 21, no. 2 (2008): 207–39.

Huberman, Ariana. *Gauchos and Foreigners: Glossing Culture and Identity in the Argentine Countryside*. Lanham, MD: Lexington Books, 2011.

Ianni, Valeria Laura. "La relación capital-trabajo en la empresa Ford Motor Argentina (1959–1963)." Consejo Nacional de Investigaciones Científicas y Técnicas (CONICET), Instituto de Investigaciones Económicas, FCE-UBA, 2010. http://sedici.unlp.edu.ar/bitstream/handle/10915/107138/wLa_relaci%C3%B3n_capital-trabajo_en_la_empresa_Ford_Motor_Argentina__1959-1963_.5151.pdf-PDFA.pdf?sequence=1.

Iglesias, Federico. *Escuela Técnica Henry Ford: 50 años de historia*. Ricardo Rojas, Argentina: Ford Argentina, 2015.
Imlay, Talbot, and Martin Horn. *The Politics of Industrial Collaboration during World War II: Ford France, Vichy and Nazi Germany*. Cambridge: Cambridge University Press, 2014.
James, Daniel. "October 17th and 18th, 1945: Mass Protest, Peronism, and the Argentine Working Class." *Journal of Social History* 21, no. 3 (Spring 1988): 441–61.
James, Daniel. *Resistance and Integration: Peronism and the Argentine Working Class, 1946–1976*. Cambridge: Cambridge University Press, 1988.
James, Daniel, ed. *Violencia, proscripción y autoritarismo (1955–1976)*. Vol. 9 of *Nueva historia argentina*. Buenos Aires: Editorial Sudamericana, 2003.
Jelin, Elizabeth, ed. *Las conmemoraciones: Las disputas en las fechas "in-felices."* Buenos Aires: Siglo XXI, 2002.
Jelin, Elizabeth. "The Politics of Memory: The Human Rights Movement and the Construction of Democracy in Argentina." *Latin American Perspectives* 21, no. 2 (Spring 1994): 38–58.
Jelin, Elizabeth. "Public Memorialization in Perspective: Truth, Justice and Memory of Past Repression in the Southern Cone of South America." *International Journal of Transitional Justice* 1, no. 1 (March 2007): 138–56.
Jelin, Elizabeth. *Los trabajos de la memoria*. Vol. 1, *Colección memorias de la represión*. Buenos Aires: Siglo XXI, 2002.
Jelin, Elizabeth. "Victims, Relatives, and Citizens in Argentina: Whose Voice Is Legitimate Enough?" In *Humanitarianism and Suffering: The Mobilization of Empathy*, edited by Richard Ashby Wilson and Richard D. Brown, 177–201. Cambridge: Cambridge University Press, 2009.
Jelin, Elizabeth, and Victoria Langland, eds. *Monumentos, memoriales y marcas territoriales*. Colección memorias de la represion. Buenos Aires: Siglo XXI, 2003.
Jelin, Elizabeth, and Juan Carlos Torre. "Los nuevos trabajadores en América Latina: Una reflexión sobre la tesis de la aristocracia obrera." *Desarrollo Económico* 22, no. 85 (April–June 1982): 3–23.

Joseph, Gilbert M., and Daniela Spenser, eds. *In from the Cold: Latin America's New Encounter with the Cold War.* Durham, NC: Duke University Press, 2008.

Kaiser, Susana. "Argentina's Trials: New Ways of Writing Memory." *Latin American Perspectives* 42, no. 3 (May 2015): 193–206.

Kaiser, Susana. *Postmemories of Terror: A New Generation Copes with the Legacy of the "Dirty War."* New York: Palgrave Macmillan, 2005.

Kaiser, Susana. "Writing and Reading Memories at a Buenos Aires Memorial Site: The Ex-ESMA." *History and Memory* 32, no. 1 (Spring–Summer 2020): 69–99.

Karush, Matthew B., and Oscar Chamosa, eds. *The New Cultural History of Peronism: Power and Identity in Mid-Twentieth-Century Argentina.* Durham, NC: Duke University Press, 2010.

Klein, Naomi. *The Shock Doctrine: The Rise of Disaster Capitalism.* Toronto: Knopf Canada, 2007.

Kosacoff, Bernardo, and Daniel Azpiazu. *La industria argentina: Desarrollo y cambios estructurales.* Buenos Aires: Centro Editor de América Latina, 1989.

Kosacoff, Bernardo, and Adrián Ramos. *Cambios contemporáneos en la estructura industrial argentina (1975–2000).* Bernal, Argentina: Universidad Nacional de Quilmes, 2001.

Kronish, Rich, and Kenneth S. Mericle, eds. *The Political Economy of the Latin American Motor Vehicle Industry.* Cambridge, MA: MIT Press, 1984.

Laclau, Ernesto. "Argentina: Imperialist Strategy and the May Crisis." *New Left Review* I, no. 62 (July–August 1970): 3–21.

Lascano, Verónica, Fernando Menéndez, and Federico Vocos. "Análisis del proceso de trabajo en la planta de automóviles Ford." Working paper. Buenos Aires: Taller de Estudios Laborales, 1999. http://tel.org.ar/spip/descarga/ford.pdf.

Lascano Warnes, Marina Florencia. "Cambios y continuidades en la historia de los trabajadores industriales argentinos, 1973–1983: Una aproximación a través del caso de Ford Motor Argentina S.A." Master's thesis, Universidad Nacional de General Sarmiento, 2012.

Laura, Guillermo. *La ciudad arterial.* Buenos Aires: self-published, 1970.

Le Blanc, Michelle, and Colin Odell. *John Carpenter.* Harpenden, Herts., England: Kamera Books, 2001.

Lessa, Francesca. *Memory and Transitional Justice in Argentina and Uruguay: Against Impunity.* New York: Palgrave Macmillan, 2013.

Link, Stefan J. *Forging Global Fordism: Nazi Germany, Soviet Russia, and the Contest over the Industrial Order.* Princeton, NJ: Princeton University Press, 2020.

Löbbe, Héctor Eduardo. "Las 'desmemorias' de José Rodríguez." *El Aromo* 2, no. 15 (October 2004): 3.

Löbbe, Héctor. *La guerrilla fabril: Clase obrera e izquierda en la Coordinadora Interfabril de Zona Norte (1975–1976).* Buenos Aires: Ediciones RyR, 2006.

Longoni, Ana, and Gustavo Bruzzone. *El siluetazo.* Buenos Aires: Adriana Hidalgo Editora, 2008.

Lorenz, Federico. *Algo parecido a la felicidad: Una historia de la lucha de la clase trabajadora durante la década del setenta (1973–1978).* Buenos Aires: Edhasa, 2014.

Lorenz, Federico. *¿De quién es el 24 de marzo? Memoria, historia y política.* Buenos Aires: Editorial Sb, 2023.

Lorenz, Federico. *Los zapatos de Carlito: Una historia de los trabajadores navales de Tigre en la década del setenta.* Buenos Aires: Editorial Norma, 2007.

Ludmer, Josefina. *El género gauchesco.* Buenos Aires: Editorial Perfil, 2000.

Lvovich, Daniel, and Jaquelina Bisquert. *La cambiante memoria de la dictadura: Discursos públicos, movimientos sociales y legitimidad democrática.* Los Polvorines, Argentina: Universidad Nacional de General Sarmiento; Buenos Aires: Biblioteca Nacional, 2008.

Mangiantini, Martín. "La agrupación Tendencia de Avanzada Mecánica (TAM): Una experiencia de militancia entre los trabajadores automotrices de Buenos Aires (1968–1972)." Paper presented at the V Jornadas Nacionales de Historia Social, La Falda, Córdoba, 2015.

Manzano, Valeria. *The Age of Youth in Argentina: Culture, Politics, and Sexuality from Perón to Videla.* Chapel Hill: University of North Carolina Press, 2014.

Marengo Hecker, María Eugenia. "El enemigo político bajo la lupa del Plan Conintes (1958–1962)." *Socio Debate: Revista de Ciencias Sociales* 5, no. 8 (2019): 1–29.

McCaughan, Michael. *True Crimes: Rodolfo Walsh, the Life and Times of a Radical Intellectual.* London: Latin America Bureau, 2002.

McSherry, J. Patrice. *Predatory States: Operation Condor and Covert War in Latin America.* Lanham, MD: Rowman and Littlefield, 2005.

Memoria Abierta. *Abogados, derecho y política.* Buenos Aires: Memoria Abierta, 2010.

Memoria Abierta. *Memorias en la ciudad: Señales del terrorismo de estado en Buenos Aires.* Buenos Aires: Editorial Universitaria de Buenos Aires, 2009.

Memoria Abierta. *Reconocer Campo de Mayo: Relatos y trayectorias de la militancia y el terror estatal.* Buenos Aires: Memoria Abierta.

Menazzi Canese, Luján. "Ciudad en dictadura: Procesos urbanos en la ciudad de Buenos Aires durante la última dictadura militar (1976–1983)." *Scripta Nova: Revista Electrónica de Geografía y Ciencias Sociales* 17, no. 429 (February 10, 2013). https://revistes.ub.edu/index.php/ScriptaNova/article/view/14918.

Mignone, Emilio Fermín. *Iglesia y dictadura: El papel de la iglesia a la luz de sus relaciones con el régimen militar.* Buenos Aires: Ediciones del Pensamiento Nacional, 1986.

Milanesio, Natalia. *Workers Go Shopping in Argentina: The Rise of Popular Consumer Culture.* Albuquerque: University of New Mexico Press, 2013.

Miller, Daniel, ed. *Car Cultures.* Oxford: Berg Publishers, 2001.

Miller, Ray. *Falcon: The New-Size Ford.* Ford Road Series, 7. Oceanside, CA: Evergreen Press, 1997.)

Miller, Shawn William. *The Street Is Ours: Community, the Car, and the Nature of Public Space in Rio de Janeiro.* Cambridge: Cambridge University Press, 2018.

Milloy, Jeremy. *Blood, Sweat, and Fear: Violence at Work in the North American Auto Industry, 1960–80.* Vancouver: University of British Columbia Press, 2017.

Ministerio de Justicia y Derechos Humanos de la Nación, Secretaría de Derechos Humanos, Programa Verdad y Justicia, FLACSO Argentina, Centro de Estudios Legales y Sociales, and Sistema Argentino de Información Jurídica. *Responsabilidad empresarial en delitos de lesa humanidad: Represión a trabajadores durante el terrorismo de estado.* 2 vols. Buenos Aires: Editorial Ministerio de Justicia y Derechos Humanos de la Nación, 2015.

Mittelbach, Federico. *Informe sobre desaparecedores.* Buenos Aires: Ediciones de la Urraca, 1984.

Mom, Gijs. *Atlantic Automobilism: The Emergence and Persistence of the Car, 1895–1940*. New York: Berghahn Books, 2014.

Mortenson, Erik. "A Journey into the Shadows: *The Twilight Zone*'s Visual Critique of the Cold War." *Science Fiction Film and Television* 7, no. 1 (Spring 2014): 55–76.

Möser, Kurt. "The Dark Side of 'Automobilism,' 1900–1930: Violence, War, and the Motorcar." *Journal of Transport History* 24, no. 2 (September 2003): 238–58.

Nardi, Silvia, Mabel Sampaolo, Andrea Trotta, et al. *Los lugares de la memoria*. Buenos Aires: Editorial Madreselva, 2009.

Nassif, Silvia. "Las luchas obreras tucumanas durante la autodenominada Revolución Argentina (1966–1973)." PhD diss., Universidad de Buenos Aires, 2015. http://repositorio.filo.uba.ar/jspui/bitstream/filodigital/3003/1/uba_ffyl_t_2015_899550.pdf.

Nassif, Silvia. *Tucumanazos: Una huella histórica de luchas populares, 1969–1972*. Tucumán, Argentina: Universidad Nacional de Tucumán, Facultad de Filosofía y Letras, 2013.

North American Congress on Latin America (NACLA) and Carlos Díaz. "AIFLD Losing Its Grip." *NACLA's Latin America and Empire Report* 8, no. 9 (1974): 3–23.

Norton, Peter D. *Fighting Traffic: The Dawn of the Motor Age in the American City*. Cambridge, MA: MIT Press, 2008.

Nosiglia, Julio E. *El desarrollismo*. Buenos Aires: Centro Editor de América Latina, 1983.

Novaro, Marcos, and Vicente Palermo. *La dictadura militar, 1976–1983: Del golpe de estado a la restauración democrática*. Buenos Aires: Ediciones Paidós, 2003.

O'Brien, Thomas. *The Century of U.S. Capitalism in Latin America*. Albuquerque: University of New Mexico Press, 1999.

Orlove, Benjamin, ed. *The Allure of the Foreign: Imported Goods in Postcolonial Latin America*. Ann Arbor: University of Michigan Press, 1997.

Ortiz, Ricardo, and Martín Schorr. "La economía political del gobierno de Alfonsín: Creciente subordinación al poder económico durante la 'década perdida.'" In *Los años de Alfonsín: ¿El poder de la democracia o la democracia del poder?*, edited by Alfredo Raúl Pucciarelli, 291–333. Buenos Aires: Siglo XXI, 2006.

Packenham, Robert A. *The Dependency Movement: Scholarship and Politics in Development Studies*. Cambridge, MA: Harvard University Press, 1992.

Parga, Alfredo. *Historia deportiva del automovilismo argentino: Hombres, máquinas, circuitos*. 4 vols. Buenos Aires: La Nación, 1996.

Park, Rebekah. *The Reappeared: Argentine Former Political Prisoners*. New Brunswick, NJ: Rutgers University Press, 2014.

Paterson, Matthew. *Automobile Politics: Ecology and Cultural Political Economy*. Cambridge: Cambridge University Press, 2007.

Payne, Leigh A., and Gabriel Pereira. "Accountability for Corporate Complicity in Human Rights Violations: Argentina's Transitional Justice Innovation?" In *The Economic Accomplices to the Argentine Dictatorship: Outstanding Debts*, edited by Horacio Verbitsky and Juan Pablo Bohoslavsky, 29–46. Cambridge: Cambridge University Press, 2016.

Payne, Leigh A., Gabriel Pereira, and Laura Bernal-Bermúdez. *Transitional Justice and Corporate Accountability from Below: Deploying Archimedes' Lever*. Cambridge: Cambridge University Press, 2020.

Penn, Roger. "The Phenomenal Forms of Political Graffiti in Rome and Buenos Aires: A Comparison Based upon Detailed Descriptive Analysis." *Visual Studies* 33, no. 4 (2018): 313–25.

Pierce, Russell. *Gringo-Gaucho: An Advertising Odyssey*. Ashland, OR: Southern Cross Publishers, 1991.

Piglia, Melina. *Autos, rutas y turismo: El automóvil club argentino y el estado*. Buenos Aires: Siglo XXI, 2014.

Pizzolato, Nicola. *Challenging Global Capitalism: Labor Migration, Radical Struggle, and Urban Change in Detroit and Turin*. New York: Palgrave Macmillan, 2013.

Pizzolato, Nicola. "Workers and Revolutionaries at the Twilight of Fordism: The Breakdown of Industrial Relations in the Automobile Plants of Detroit and Turin, 1967–1973." *Labor History* 45, no. 4 (November 2004): 419–43.

Plotkin, Mariano Ben. *Mañana es San Perón: A Cultural History of Perón's Argentina*. Translated by Keith Zahniser. Lanham, MD: Rowman and Littlefield, 2002.

Pontoriero, Esteban Damián. "Estado de excepción y contrainsurgencia: El Plan CONINTES y la militarización de la seguridad interna en la

Argentina (1958–1962)." *Revista Contenciosa* 3, no. 4 (June 2015): 1–16.

Pozzi, Pablo. "El sindicalismo norteamericano en América Latina y en la Argentina: El AIFLD entre 1961–1976." *Herramienta: Revista de Debate y Crítica Marxista* 10 (July 1999): 1–24. https://www.herramienta.com.ar/el-sindicalismo-norteamericano-en-america-latina-y-en-la-argentina-el-aifld-entre-1961-1976.

Pozzi, Pablo, and Alejandro Schneider. *Los setentistas: Izquierda y clase obrera, 1969–1976*. Buenos Aires: Editorial Universitaria de Buenos Aires, 2000.

Pucciarelli, Alfredo Raúl, ed. *Empresarios, tecnócratas y militares: La trama corporativa de la última dictadura*. Buenos Aires: Siglo XXI, 2002.

Rabe, Stephen G. *The Killing Zone: The United States Wages Cold War in Latin America*. New York: Oxford University Press, 2011.

Rabe, Steven G. *The Most Dangerous Area in the World: John F. Kennedy Confronts Communist Revolution in Latin America*. Chapel Hill: University of North Carolina Press, 1999.

República Argentina, Junta Militar. *Documentos básicos y bases políticas de las fuerzas armadas para el proceso de reorganización nacional*. Buenos Aires: Imprenta del Congreso de la Nación, 1980.

Rey, Esteban. *¿Es Frondizi un nuevo Perón?* Buenos Aires: Ediciones Lucha Obrera, 1957.

Rieger, Bernhard. *The People's Car: A Global History of the Volkswagen Beetle*. Cambridge, MA: Harvard University Press, 2013.

Robben, Antonius. C. G. M. *Argentina Betrayed: Memory, Mourning, and Accountability*. Philadelphia: University of Pennsylvania Press, 2018.

Robben, Antonius C. G. M. *Political Violence and Trauma in Argentina*. Philadelphia: University of Pennsylvania Press, 2005.

Robben, Antonio C. G. M. "Testimonies, Truths, and Transitions of Justice in Argentina and Chile." In *Transitional Justice: Global Mechanisms and Local Realities after Genocide and Mass Violence*, edited by Alexander Laban Hinton, 179–205. New Brunswick, NJ: Rutgers University Press, 2011.

Robert, Karen, and Rodrigo Gutiérrez Hermelo. "Argentina: Where Youth Is a Crime." *NACLA Report on the Americas* 26, no. 3 (December 1992): 12–15.

Robin, Marie-Monique. *Escadrons de la mort, l'école française*. Paris: Éditions La Découverte, 2008.

Rock, David. *Argentina, 1516–1982: From Spanish Colonization to the Falklands War*. Berkeley: University of California Press, 1985.

Rodríguez, Florencia. "Estrategias de lucha en industrias dinámicas durante la segunda ISIS: Un análisis a partir del estudio de caso de Mercedes-Benz Argentina." In *La clase trabajadora argentina en el siglo XX: Experiencias de lucha y organización*, edited by Victoria Basualdo, 115–50. Buenos Aires: Cara o Ceca, 2011.

Rodríguez Lamas, Daniel. *La presidencia de Frondizi*. Biblioteca Política Argentina, no. 54. Buenos Aires: Centro Editor de América Latina, 1984.

Rodríguez Pinzón, Diego, Claudia Martin, and Tomás Ojea Quintana. *La dimensión internacional de los derechos humanos*. Washington, DC: Inter-American Development Bank, 1999.

Roht-Arriaza, Naomi. *The Pinochet Effect: Transnational Justice in the Age of Human Rights*. Philadelphia: University of Pennsylvania Press, 2005.

Rosen, Captain Mark E., JAGC, US Navy (Ret.). "The Alien Tort Statute: An Emerging Threat to National Security." *St. Thomas Law Review* 16, no. 4 (Summer 2004): 628–68.

Ross, Kristin. *Fast Cars, Clean Bodies: Decolonization and the Reordering of French Culture*. Cambridge, MA: MIT Press, 1996.

Ruiz, Maximiliano. *Graffiti Argentina*. London: Thames and Hudson, 2009.

Sachs, Wolfgang. *For Love of the Automobile: Looking Back into the History of Our Desires*. Translated by Dan Reneau. Berkeley: University of California Press, 1992.

Salvatore, Ricardo D. "Imperial Mechanics: South America's Hemispheric Integration in the Machine Age." *American Quarterly* 58, no. 3 (September 2006): 662–691.

Salvatore, Ricardo D. "Yankee Advertising in Buenos Aires: Reflections on Americanization." *Interventions: International Journal of Postcolonial Studies* 7, no. 2 (July 2005): 216–35.

Sarzynski, Sarah. *Revolution in the Terra do Sol: The Cold War in Brazil*. Stanford, CA: Stanford University Press, 2018.

Schlesinger, Stephen, and Stephen Kinzer. *Bitter Fruit: The Untold Story of the American Coup in Guatemala*. Rev. and exp. ed. Cambridge, MA: Harvard University, David Rockefeller Center for Latin American Studies, 2005.

Schneider, Alejandro. *Los compañeros: Trabajadores, izquierda y peronismo*. Buenos Aires: Imago Mundi, 2005.

Schneider, Alejandro. "'Ladran Sancho': Dictadura y clase obrera en la Zona Norte del Gran Buenos Aires." In *De la revolución libertadora al menemismo: Historia social y política argentina*, edited by Hernán Camarero, Pablo Pozzi, and Alejandro Schneider, 203–40. Buenos Aires: Imago Mundi, 2000.

Schorr, Martín. "La desindustrialización como eje del proyecto refundacional de la economía y la sociedad en Argentina, 1976–1983." *América Latina en la Historia Económica* 19, no. 3 (December 2012): 31–56.

Schuhrke, Jeff. "'Comradely Brainwashing': International Development, Labor Education, and Industrial Relations in the Cold War." *Labor: Studies in Working-Class History of the Americas* 16, no. 3 (September 2019): 39–67.

Schvarzer, Jorge. *La industria que supimos conseguir: Una historia política-social de la industria argentina*. Buenos Aires: Planeta, 2000.

Schvarzer, Jorge. "La reconversión de la industria automotriz argentina: Un balance a mitad de camino." *Ciclos de Historia Económica y Social* 5, no. 8 (1995): 5–27.

Sebreli, Juan José. *Buenos Aires, vida cotidiana y alienación, seguido de Buenos Aires, ciudad en crisis*. Buenos Aires: Editorial Sudamericana, 2003.

Seiler, Cotten. *Republic of Drivers: A Cultural History of Automobility in America*. Chicago: University of Chicago Press, 2008.

Seoane, María, and Vicente Muleiro. *El dictador: La historia secreta y pública de Jorge Rafael Videla*. Buenos Aires: Editorial Sudamericana, 2001.

Seoane, María, and Héctor Ruiz Núñez. *La noche de los lápices*. 2nd ed. Buenos Aires: Planeta, 1992.

Seveso, César. "Millions of Small Battles: The Peronist Resistance in Argentina." *Bulletin of Latin American Research* 30, no. 3 (July 2011): 313–27.

Shapley, Deborah. *Promise and Power: The Life and Times of Robert McNamara*. Boston: Little, Brown, 1993.

Sheinin, David M. K. *Argentina and the United States: An Alliance Contained*. Athens: University of Georgia Press, 2006.

Sheinin, David M. K. *Consent of the Damned: Ordinary Argentinians in the Dirty War*. Gainesville: University Press of Florida, 2012.

Siegelbaum, Lewis H. *Cars for Comrades: The Life of the Soviet Automobile*. Ithaca, NY: Cornell University Press, 2008.

Siegelbaum, Lewis H., ed. *The Socialist Car: Automobility in the Eastern Bloc*. Ithaca, NY: Cornell University Press, 2011.

Sigal, Silvia. *Intelectuales y poder en Argentina: La década del sesenta*. Buenos Aires: Siglo XXI, 2002.

Sigal, Silvia. *La Plaza de Mayo: Una crónica*. Buenos Aires: Siglo XXI, 2006.

Sikkink, Kathryn. *Ideas and Institutions: Developmentalism in Brazil and Argentina*. Ithaca, NY: Cornell University Press, 1991.

Sikkink, Kathryn. *The Justice Cascade: How Human Rights Prosecutions Are Changing World Politics*. New York: W. W. Norton, 2011.

Sikkink, Kathryn, and Carrie Booth Walling. "Argentina's Contribution to Global Trends in Transitional Justice." In *Transitional Justice in the Twenty-First Century: Beyond Truth versus Justice*, edited by Naomi Roht-Arriaza and Javier Mariezcurrena, 301–24. Cambridge: Cambridge University Press, 2006.

Silver, Beverly J. *Forces of Labor: Workers' Movements and Globalization since 1870*. Cambridge: Cambridge University Press, 2003.

Smith, Peter H. *Talons of the Eagle: Latin America, the United States, and the World*. 3rd ed. New York: Oxford University Press, 2007.

Sourrouille, Juan V. *El complejo automotor en Argentina: Transnacionales en América Latina*. Buenos Aires: Editorial Nueva Imagen, 1980.

Spinelli, María Estela. *De antiperonistas a peronistas revolucionarios: Las clases medias en el centro de la crisis política argentina (1955–1973)*. Buenos Aires: Editorial Sudamericana, 2013.

Starr, Amory. *Global Revolt: A Guide to the Movements against Globalization*. London: Zed Books, 2005.

Stephan, Meta. "A Typology of the Collaboration between Multinational Corporations, Home Governments, and Authoritarian Regimes: Evidence from German Investors in Argentina." In *Big Business* and *Dictatorships in Latin America: A Transnational History of Profits and Repression*, edited by Victoria Basualdo, Hartmut Berghoff, and Marcelo Bucheli, 237–62. Cham, Switzerland: Palgrave Macmillan, 2020.

Svampa, Maristella. "El populismo imposible y sus actores, 1973–1976." In *Violencia, proscripción y autoritarismo (1955–1976)*, vol. 9 of *Nueva historia argentina*, edited by Daniel James, 381–436. Buenos Aires: Editorial Sudamericana, 2003.

Szusterman, Celia. *Frondizi and the Politics of Developmentalism in Argentina, 1955–62*. Pittsburgh: University of Pittsburgh Press, 1993.

Tavella, Gabriela. "El plan de construcción de autopistas de la última dictadura militar argentina: Una aproximación desde La ciudad arterial." Paper presented at the XIII Jornadas Interescuelas/Departamentos de Historia, Departamento de Historia de la Facultad de Humanidades, Universidad Nacional de Catamarca, Catamarca, Argentina, 2011. https://cdsa.aacademica.org/000-071/337.pdf.

Taylor, Diana. *Disappearing Acts: Spectacles of Gender and Nationalism in Argentina's "Dirty War."* Durham, NC: Duke University Press, 1997.

Terán, Oscar. *Nuestros años sesentas: La formación de la nueva izquierda intelectual argentina, 1956–1966*. Buenos Aires: Siglo XXI, 2013.

Urry, John. "The 'System' of Automobility." *Theory, Culture and Society* 21, nos. 4–5 (October 2004): 25–39.

Verbitsky, Horacio. *Confessions of an Argentine Dirty Warrior: A Firsthand Account of Atrocity*. New York: New Press, 2005.

Verbitsky, Horacio, and Juan Pablo Bohoslavsky, eds. *Cuentas pendientes: Los cómplices económicos de la dictadura*. Buenos Aires: Siglo XXI, 2013.

Volti, Rudi. *Cars and Culture: The Life Story of a Technology*. Baltimore: Johns Hopkins University Press, 2006.

Walsh, Rodolfo. *¿Quién mató a Rosendo?* Buenos Aires: Editorial Tiempo Contemporáneo, 1969.

Weber, Gaby. *La conexión alemana: El lavado del dinero nazi en Argentina*. Buenos Aires: Edhasa, 2005.

Weber, Gaby. *Die Verschwundenen von Mercedes-Benz*. Hamburg: Assoziation A, 2001.

References

Weeramantry, J. Romesh. "Time Limitation under the United States Alien Tort Claims Act." *International Review of the Red Cross* 85, no. 851 (September 2003): 627–35.

Weld, Kirsten. "Holy War: Latin America's Far Right." *Dissent*, Spring 2020. https://www.dissentmagazine.org/article/holy-war-latin-americas-far-right.

Weld, Kirsten. *Paper Cadavers: The Archives of Dictatorship in Guatemala.* Durham, NC: Duke University Press, 2014.

Werner, Ruth, and Facundo Aguirre. *Insurgencia obrera en la Argentina, 1969–1976: Clasismo, coordinadoras interfabriles y estrategias de la izquierda.* Buenos Aires: Ediciones IPS, 2009.

Weschler, Lawrence. *A Miracle, a Universe: Settling Accounts with Torturers.* Chicago: University of Chicago Press, 1990.

Wilkins, Mira, and Frank Ernest Hill. *American Business Abroad: Ford on Six Continents.* Detroit: Wayne State University Press, 1964.

Winn, Peter, ed. *Victims of the Chilean Miracle: Workers and Neoliberalism in the Pinochet Era, 1973–2002.* Durham, NC: Duke University Press, 2004.

Winn, Peter. *Weavers of Revolution: The Yarur Workers and Chile's Road to Socialism.* New York: Oxford University Press, 1986.

Wolfe, Joel. *Autos and Progress: The Brazilian Search for Modernity.* New York: Oxford University Press, 2010.

Wollen, Peter, and Joe Kerr, eds. *Autopia: Cars and Culture.* London: Reaktion Books, 2003.

Wright, Thomas C. *State Terrorism in Latin America: Chile, Argentina, and International Human Rights.* Lanham, MD: Rowman and Littlefield, 2007.

Wyndham, Marivic, and Peter Read. "From State Terrorism to State Errorism: Post-Pinochet Chile's Long Search for Truth and Justice." *Public Historian* 32, no. 1 (February 2010): 31–44.

Young, Diana. "The Life and Death of Cars: Private Vehicles on the Pitjantjatjara Lands, South Australia." In *Car Cultures*, edited by Daniel Miller, 35–57. Oxford: Berg Publishers, 2001.

Index

ACA, 26–27; and Peronism, 32
Acindar: kidnapping of executives, 90; labor repression at, 115
Adair, Jennifer, 151
Advertising: and appeals to national values, 16–17, 27–29, 42, 131; and Cold War propaganda, 9–10; of Falcon sedan in Argentina, 22–23, 42–47, 131; of Falcon sedan in US, 11–12. *See also* Falcon sedan; Ford Argentina SCA; J. Walter Thompson
Agosti, General Orlando, 161
Aguilar, Gonzalo, 46
AIFLD. *See* American Institute for Free Labor Development
Alessandri, Jorge, 36
Alien tort Claims Act (ATCA). *See* Alien Tort Statute (ATS)
Alien Tort Statute (ATS): Ford Argentina survivors' claim, 180–81; Ford Werke case (Germany), 179–80; and human rights law, 178–81; resistance to, 180–81; Supreme Court (of USA) decision regarding, 181; UNOCAL case, 179
Alfonsín, Raúl: election of, 147; letter from Ford survivors, 151–52; theory of two demons, 168–69
Alfonsín government: amnesty laws passed by, 160; and economic crisis of 1989, 161–2; human rights and, 150–52; memory regime of, 168–69
Allende, Salvador, 91
Alliance for Progress, 40–42
Alsogaray, Álvaro, 34
American Institute for Free Labor Development (AIFLD), 41–2, 86–89; and Brazilian coup, 87; and SMATA, 86–87
Amnesty International, 155–56, 168

amnesty laws: overturned, 192; passed by Carlos Menem, 162–63; passed by Raúl Alfonsín, 160
Amoroso, Juan Carlos: disappearance, 105; letter to Raúl Alfonsín, 151–2; meeting with Ford management, 102–3; quoted in *Nunca Más*, 154; testimony to CONADEP, 152–53; wrongful dismissal claim against Ford, 157–59
Annichiarico, Ciro, 200
Aramburu, General Pedro Eugenio, 34
Arbenz, Jacobo, 85
Arce, Adriana Elba, 125
archives: corporate, 159, 178, 188–89; declassification of, 5, 189–90; destruction of PEN, 147, 152; of DIPPBA, 189; of Memoria Abierta, 187–88; and memory struggles, 189; of Ministry of the Interior, 122; National Archive of Memory, 193, 202; of oral testimony, 124; of Rodolfo Walsh, 188; of terror, 124; union, 188; US State Department declassification of, 189–90
Argentine Anticommunist Alliance (Triple A): assassinations, 95–96; and *grupos de tarea*, 116; union collaboration with, 95–96; use of unmarked cars, 113–14
Argentine Automobile Club (ACA), 26–27; and Peronism, 32
aristocracy of labor: autoworkers as, 58, 108, 137
Armando, Alberto J., 22
Asamblea Permanente de los Derechos Humanos (APDH): humanitarian framework of, 156, 168; interviewing methods of, 155; participation in truth trials, 185

285

Index

Association of Automotive Factories (ADEFA), 66
Association of Former Detained and Disappeared Persons, 126
assembly line: disappearances from, at Ford Argentina, 106–7, 185; discipline at Ford Argentina, 67; significance within Fordism, 15, 57, 83; union activism over pace and safety of, 78, 81, 83–85, 186
automobile manufacturers: and ADEFA, 66; Argentine, 33, 36, 66; and economic restructuring of 1970s, 160–61; multinational investments in Argentina, 32–33, 37–39. *See also* Fiat; Ford Argentina; General Motors; Industrias Kaiser Argentina (IKA); Kaiser Motors; Mercedes-Benz
automobiles: and bombings, 112–13; as carriers of memory, 17–18, 173–74, 210; as cultural artifacts, 17; and disappearances, 110–15, 122–28; and national identities, 16–17; and Peronism, 32–33; and sensory experiences, 17–18, 124–28, 132; as surveillance tools, 113–14
Automobility: authoritarian, 110–12, 118–24, 133–34; defined, 14–15, 207–10; and labor conditions, 83–85, 98; scholarship on, 15–18
Autores ideológicos, 198
autoworkers: and Cordobazo, 73–75; and crisis of Fordism, 83–85; at Ford Argentina, 76–77; political expecations of, 19, 56, 74; scholarship on, 57–58, 83–85; unionization of, 68. *See also* Ford Argentina SCA; Ford Argentina union activists; Sindicato de Mecánicos y Afines del Transporte (SMATA)

Barry de la Rín, Noemí, 93
Barthes, Roland, 16
Basualdo, Eduardo, 143; testimony in Ford case, 200

Basualdo, Victoria, 64, 213; testimony in Ford case, 200
Batista, Fulgencio, 36
Bellingeri, Claudia, 201
Benegas, Carlos Coll, 34
Bernal Bermúdez, Laura, 211
Bignone, General Reynaldo, 147
Bordaberry, Juan María, 91–92
Brazil: automotive policies, 30–36; military coup, 87
Brennan, James P., 74–75
Buenos Aires Herald, 114–21
Buenos Aires Provincial Police: and "Camps circuit," 103; detention of Ford workers, 103–7; Dirección de Inteligencia de la Policía de Buenos Aires (DIPPBA), 64–65; undercover presence at Pacheco plant, 89
Burson-Marstellar, 123
Bush, George W., 181

Cacciatore, Brigadier Osvaldo, 118–19
Calvo de Laborde, Adriana, 125–27
Campo de Mayo Army base, 60–62, 61, 141
Camps, General Ramón: 102–3; amnesty by Carlos Menem, 163
Cantello, Roberto, 67, 81–82
capital flight, 145, 191–92
Carassai, Sebastián, 130
car culture: *criollo*, 26–29, 48; global, 15–16; US influence on Argentina's, 23–26
Cardoso, Fernando Henrique, 70
Careaga, Ana María, 123
cars. *See* automobiles
Carter, Jimmy, 129, 142
Castro, Fidel, 36, 86
Castro, Raúl (US diplomat), 190
Chaplin, Maxwell, 121
Charlín, Elisa: 53, 54; at ceremony marking IACHR report, 212; communications with Ford management, 136; fears about Ford disappearances, 105; at hearings in Ford Argentina human rights

trial, 202; meeting with Lieutenant Colonel Molinari, 136
Ciancaglini, Sergio, 192
Cipolatti, Pipo, 148
citizenship, 6; in Alfonsín era, 151–52
clandestine detention centers: Automotores Orletti, 118; el Banco, 110; Campo de Mayo, 116; Escuela Superior de Mecánica de la Armada (ESMA), 118; Garage Azopardo, 118; el Olimpo, 118; la Perla, 130; el Pozo de Banfield, 127; el Pozo de Quilmes, 127; origins, 118; *quincho* at Pacheco plant (of Ford Argentina), 55, 104–7; el Vesubio, 126
Clinton, Bill, 189
Coggi, Juan Martín, 128
Cold War historiography, 5–7, 10
Collins, Mike, 94
Comisiones internas de reclamos. See internal claims committees
Comisión Provincial por la Memoria, 189
CONADEP (Comisión Nacional sobre la Desaparición de Peronas): disappearances of union activists recorded by, 153; disappearances recorded by, 116; interview methods of, 155–56; mandate of, 152; and National Archive of Memory, 193; *Nunca Más* report, 155–56, 169; risks surrounding work of, 132; testimony of Ford survivors, 152–54
Confederación General de Trabajo (CGT): and AIFLD, 86; and Carlos Menem, 162; founding of, 63; and José Rodríguez, 211; and Juan Perón, 63–65; left Peronist opposition to, 71
Confederación General Económica (CGE), 64
Congreso de Trabajadores de la Argentina (CTA), 183
Conti, Juan Carlos: disappearance of, 106; wrongful dismissal claim against Ford Argentina, 157–59

Córdoba: Cordobazo uprising, 73–76; industrialization under Perón, 37; labor dissent within SMATA, 87–88
Cordobazo, 73–76; in global context, 84–85; impacts in Argentina, 79, 88–89
corporate accountability: and Alien Tort Statute, 179–81; challenges facing, 205, 211; in human rights law, 177–81
corporate complicity: accusations against Ford Motor Company, 178–80; challenge of proving in court, 204–5, 211; in human rights law, 177–81; investigations in Argentina, 3; of Mercedes-Benz, 184; with Nazi regime, 177, 179–80; research on, 6; of UNOCAL, 179. *See also* Ford Argentine human rights case; Ford Argentina SCA
corporations, Argentine: and crisis of 2001, 192–93; profits during dictatorship, 145–46, 161–62
corporations, multinational: and Alliance for Progress, 41; and antiglobalization movement, 177; archives of, 188–89; and Argentine automotive policies, 36–37; attacks on, 74, 90; complicity with dictatorship, 120; concerns about anti-Americanism, 27–28; denounced as agents of imperialism, 6, 85–86; dependency theory critiques of, 70–71; investments in Latin America, 6; nationalizations of, 86, 91; in 1920s Argentina, 23–26; and television culture, 46; and human rights law, 177–81; *See also* corporate accountability; corporate complicity; Ford Argentina, SCA; Ford Motor Company; General Motors; J. Walter Thompson
Courard, Juan, 94, 128–30
Cox, Robert, 114, 121
Crenzel, Emilio, 168
Cuban Revolution, 36, 86

Index

Daverio Cox, Maud, 121
Davis, Mike, 112–13
declassified records. *See* archives
debt, external (Argentina), 142; during Alfonsín government, 161–62; during dictatorship, 146
de la Rúa, Fernando, 191
Delgado, Federico, 192
dependency theory, 70–71
desarrollismo (developmentalism), 34–36, 62, 68–69, 77; dismantling of, 142–44
Díaz Bessone, General Ramón, 117
Dirección de Inteligencia de la Policía de Buenos Aires (DIPPBA), 64–65, 89; archives, 189; records used in Ford Argentina case, 201
disappearances, 1–3, 116–18; by Argentine Anticommunist Alliance (Triple A), 113–14; artistic representations of, 148–50; cars used in, 110–15, 122–28; Falcon sedans associated with, 1, 109–15, 121–22, 128; of Ford union activists, 103–7, 226n9; of Jorge Julio López, 195; in other South American countries, 237n27; as public spectacles, 122–24; survivors of, 124–28; union activists as percentage of, 153–54
driving: identified with American Cold War freedom, 10
Due Obedience Law, 160

Economic Commission for Latin America and the Caribbean (Comisión Económica para América Latina y el Caribe), 31
economic development policies, 6–7, 30–32; and Alliance for Progress, 40–42; and automotive manufacturing, 16, 32–36
Eisenhower, Dwight D., 36, 40
El Broche, 197
Elena, Eduardo, 32
ESMA Museum and Site of Memory, 193

Etchecolatz, Miguel Osvaldo, 195
executives: complicity in human rights crimes, 3; targeted by guerrilla groups, 6, 90, 93–94. *See also* Ford Argentina SCA
extrajudicial kidnappings. *See* disappearances

Facciano, Judge Osvaldo, 203
Falcon sedan (Ford), 11–14, 170; advertisements, 9–10, 42–47, 128–32; as "Argentine classic," 28, 131; artistic representations of, 147–50, 172–75, 196–98; in Australia, 13–14; compared with Model T, 11–12, 40. 44; design, 8–9, 171–72; *La familia Falcón*, 45–47; fan clubs, 1, 170–72; and Ford survivors, 209; launch events, 39–40; and memory, 1–3, 18–20, 112; military purchase orders, 122; and nostalgia, 170–72; popularity in Argentina, 52–53; as symbol, 1–2, 5, 10, 48, 134; as tool of disappearances, 110–12; and Turismo Carretera, 207
Falcone, Jorge (son), 109–10
Falcone, Jorge Ademar, 109–10
Falcone, María Claudia, 109
Faletto, Enzo, 70
Falklands War (Guerra de Malvinas), 146
Fangio, Juan Manuel, 32
Farrell, General Edelmiro Julián, 63
Federal Appeals Court of La Plata, 182–87
Federal Criminal Appeals Court (of Argentina), 4
Federal Penitentiary Service (of Argentina), 117–18
Feinmann, José Pablo, 133
Fiat Concord: Argentine factories, 37; kidnappings of executives, 90; labor conflicts in Córdoba plants, 75; popularity of Fiat 600, 38; reduced Argentine investments in 1970s, 160–61
financial crises: of 1989, 162; of 2001, 191–92

Floriani, Carmen, 126
Ford, Henry II: and Falcon design project, 9; tour of Latin America, 37; views of Latin American automotive policies, 39
Ford Argentina human rights case: appeals in, 211; defendants in, 192–95; delays in, 199–200; resolution of, 200–203; significance of, 204–6
Ford Argentina SCA, 52; blacklist of union activists, 136, 141–42; buyout offer to activists, 100; commitment to Argentine industrial modernization, 39–40, 48; construction of Pacheco plant, 37; disappearances from, 103–8, 226n9; evacuation of US personnel, 94; founding of, 29; guerrilla attacks on executives, 93; impacts of dictatorship's economic reforms, 160–62; labor discipline at, 67, 230n14; layoffs, 140; lobbying of military dictatorship by, 139–41; public support for military dictatorship, 128–31; subsidiaries, 67; success during military dictatorship, 160–61; union activism at, 54–55, 76–83; wrongful dismissal claims against, 157–59. *See also* Falcon sedan; Ford Argentina human rights case; Ford Argentina union activists; Pacheco plant
Ford Argentina union activists: disappearances of, 103–7; fears about political violence, 94–98; and Ford buyout offer, 100; meeting with José Rodríguez, 101; organizing efforts, 76–77, 81–83, 96–99; pride in working at Ford, 51–54; and Rodrigazo protests, 96–97; tensions with SMATA leadership, 98–100. *See also* Ford Argentina SCA; Ford survivors
Ford Australia: Falcon manufacturing, 13
Ford Falcon, buen estado, 148–50
Ford Industrial Center. *See* Pacheco plant (of Ford)

Fordism: global crisis of, 83–85; vulnerability to labor activism, 56–58
Ford Motor Company: in Argentina, 23–26, 28–29; and Argentine motorsports, 28; assembly plant in La Boca, 25, 59; founding of Argentine subsidiary, 29; German human rights investigations of, 178–80; Latin American investments, 37; perceptions of in Latin America, 6–7; post-war recovery, 8; 3, 10–11. *See also* Ford Argentina SCA
Ford survivors: Alien Tort Statute claim against Ford Motor Company, 180–81; appeals to SMATA for help, 157–59; continued surveillance of, 144; as detainees under the Poder Ejecutivo Nacional (PEN), 138–41; employment struggles of, 144–45; and expansion of memory regimes, 166–69; and Ford Argentina human rights case, 193–94, 199–204; and human rights movement, 194; letter to Raúl Alfonsín, 151–52; quoted in *Nunca Más*, 154; release from prison, 141–42; secret detention of, 135, 138; sign raised outside Pacheco plant, 199; testimony to CONADEP, 152–54; as witnesses to labor repression, 137–38; wrongful dismissal claims against Ford, 157–59. *See also* Ford Argentina SCA; Ford Argentina union activists
Ford survivors' family members: abuse suffered by, 136, 139, 243n13; as activists, 135–38, 163; communications with Ford management, 136; at Ford Argentina human rights trial, 201–2, 204; interviews with Memoria Abierta, 188; petitions to military authorities, 136, 141–42; at Tigre police station, 135. *See also* Charlín, Elisa; Ortiz, Arcelia; Troiani, Marcelo Norberto

Index

Franco, General Francisco, 117
Frigerio, Rogelio, 62
Frondizi, Arturo and Frondizi government: and Alliance for Progress, 41; automotive policies, 35–36, 49; coup against, 49; desarrollismo and, 34–35; and Ford Motor Company, 38–39; and labor movement, 68–69
Fuerzas Armadas Peronistas (FAP), 90; assassination of Ford executive, 93–94
Full Stop Law, 160

Galarraga, Guillermo: death of, 200; as defendant in Ford Argentina human rights case, 194; and Ford disappearances, 104; meeting with Ford internal claims committee, 102, 154
Gálvez, Juan, 29
Gálvez, Oscar, 29, 40
Gambacorta, Judge Mario Jorge, 203
García Rey, Héctor, 99–100
Gareis, Carlos, 54, 106
Gauchos, 27
Gelbard, José Ber, 64
Gendarmería Nacional. *See* National Gendarmerie
General Motors: and Argentine nationalism, 27–28; Buenos Aires assembly plant, 24; Buenos Aires manufacturing plant, 37–38; competition with Ford, 37–38; labor conflicts at, 88–89; and motorsports, 28–29; withdrawal from Argentina, 161
Germany, corporate human rights investigations in, 177–78
Giovanelli, Luis V., 93
Gómez Alcorta, Elizabeth, 200
Gonzalez Asturias, José, 148–50
Graham-Yooll, Andrew, 114
Gramsci, Antonio, 56

Gran Buenos Aires: food riots in, 162; impacts of dictatorship's economic policies in, 143–46; industrialization of, 59; labor conflicts in, 88, 89; leftist activism in, 72; police and military surveillance of, 89, 115–16; political expectations of, 79; repression in, 156
Grandin, Greg, 79–80, 169
Grimoldi, Alberto Luis, 130
grupos de tarea (task groups): creation of, 115–16; disappearances by, 111, 122–28; Falcon sedans associated with, 1, 120–28
guerrilla fabril, 100
guerrilla movements: appeal to youth, 71–72; attacks on Ford Argentina, 93–94; kidnappings, 89–90
Guevara, Ernesto "Che," 49, 72
Gutiérrez, Fernando, 172–74
Gutiérrez, Graciela B., 112
Guzzetti, Admiral César, 117

habeus data, 182
Harguindeguy, General Álbano, 121; and Falcon purchase orders, 122
highway building: Autopista Panamericana, 59; National System of Interstate and Defense Highways, 10; under military rule, 119
Hill, Robert, 100
Hobsbawm, Eric, 76
Hoffman, Paul, 3, 180–81
housing, 54, 60; and AIFLD, 86–87; of Ford workers, 209
human rights investigations: of 1980s, 150–56, 159–60; of 2000s, 166, 192–95
human rights law: corporate, 4, 157, 177–81, 205; international, impacts in Argentina, 176–77; universal jurisdiction, 165
Human Rights Secretariat (of Argentina), 200, 212–13

Iacocca, Lee, 13
Ibáñez, Victor, 120
import substitution industrialization. *See* economic development policies
Industriales Argentinos Fabricantes de Automotores (IAFA), 37
Industrias Aeronauticas y Mecánicas del Estado (IAME), 33
Industrias Kaiser Argentina (IKA), 33; and television advertising, 46; Torino as rival to Falcon, 38; union affiliation with SMATA, 68
Inflation, 142–43; crisis of 1989, 160–63
Inter-American Commission on Human Rights, 123, 155–56; decision in Troiani wrongful dismissal claim, 212
internal claims committees: in Argentine labor law, 63–64; at Ford Argentina, 55, 81–82; resistance from employers to, 64–65
International Monetary Fund, 142, 162

J. Walter Thompson (JWT): appeals to Argentine national values, 27, 48; and Falcon advertising in Argentina, 9–10, 42–47, 128–31; first office in Argentina, 24, 91; and General Motors, 24–28; perspectives on Peronist manufacturing, 33; and political instability of early 1970s, 91–92, 94

Kaiser, Henry J., 32
Kaiser Motors: 32–33. *See also* Industrial Kaiser Argentina (IKA)
Kennedy, John F., 40–42
Kirchner, Néstor, 192–93
Kissinger, Henry, 92, 117
Kitterman, D. B., 39
Kloosterman, Dirck: and AIFLD, 86–87; murder of, 93; and SMATA leadership, 76–77
Krieger Vasena, Adalbert, 70, 75
Kubitschek, Juscelino, 30, 35–36; and Operation Pan America, 40

Labor Appeals Court (of Argentina), 158–59
Labor historiography, 190–91
labor laws: changes during the dictatorship, 139–41; passed by Juan Perón, 63–64
labor repression: at Acindar, 115; described in *Nunca Más* report, 55, 153–54; evidence of in declassified archives, 189–90; investigations of, 20, 183; at Mercedes-Benz, 184. *See also* Ford Argentina human rights case; Ford Argentina SCA; Ford Argentina union activists
labor unions. *See* unions
Laclau, Ernesto, 75–76
La Familia Falcón, 45–47, 219n3
La Matanza, 156
Lambuschini, Admiral Armando, 151
La Noche de los lápices, 109–10
Lanusse, General Alejandro, 91
La Plata prison (Unidad Penal No. 9), 141
Laprida, General Manuel Alberto, 121
Laura, Guillermo, 119
Le Corbusier, 119
Liwski, Norberto, 156
López, Jorge Julio, 195
López Echague, Carlos Rafael, 125
López Rega, José, 113
Lucas, Alberto, 1

Macri, Mauricio, 204
Martínez de Hoz, José Alfredo: amnesty by Carlos Menem, 163; as dictatorship's finance minister, 142–43, 145, 160–62
Martínez Ferrero, Judge Eugenio J., 203
Massey, Raymond, 11
Mayer, Arno, 80
McNamara, Robert, 8, 49–50
Meany, George, 42
Memoria Abierta, 187–88; interviews with Ford survivors, 188

Index

memory, 1–2; artistic representations of, 173–75; cars as carriers of, 17–18; conflicts over, 188–90; ESMA Museum and Site of Memory, 193; of Falcon sedan (Ford), 1–3; markers outside Ford Argentina's Pacheco plant, 199; National Archive of, 193, 202; regimes, 167–68; work, 167–68

Méndez de Falcone, Nelva Alicia, 109–10

Menem, Carlos, 162–63

Mercedes-Benz: and ADEFA, 66; contracts with government of Juan Perón, 32, 222n51; disappearances of workers from, 120, 184; guerrilla attacks on executives, 184; truth trial investigation of, 184

Metz, Heinrich, 184

Mexico: Ford Latin American headquarters relocated to, 94; Ford Motors investment in, 7, 36–37; Volkswagen Beetle popularity in, 17

middle class: and anti-Peronism, 34; in Falcon advertising, 42–47; and New Left, 71–72; and "new poor," 170–71

Migliaccio, Ángel, 106

Miguel, Lorenzo, 100

military dictatorship (1976–1983): civilian complicity with, 117, 151; coup events, 101–2; economic policies, 142–46, 160–62; Falcon sedan as emblem of, 1, 112, 134; fall of, 145–47; Ford Argentina support of, 128–31; laws, 110, 211; mass disappearance as strategy, 116–17; memory regimes of, 167–68; Process of National Reorganization, 110; Rodolfo Walsh's denunciation of, 143–44; US support of, 117. *See also* disappearances

Miller, Daniel, 17

Model T (Ford): in Argentina, 23–24; comparison with Falcon sedan, 11–12, 40, 44

modernization theory, 41

Molinari, Lieutenant Colonel Antonio Francisco, 136; death of, 200; as defendant in Ford Argentina human rights Ford case, 192–95; and Ford disappearances, 106, 141, 185; meetings with Ford workers' wives, 136, 141

Montoneros, 72; break with Perón, 91; death threat against Dirk Kloosterman, 93; Ford survivors as presumed, 152; kidnappings of executives, 89–90, 184; Rodolfo Walsh and, 143–44

Moore, Brigadier General Carlos R., 49

Moreno, Nahuel, 72

Möser, Kurt, 112

Moses, Robert, 119

Moser, Hugo, 47

Mothers of the Plaza de Mayo, 110, 175

Motorsports: Falcon sedan's success in, 207; and Peronism, 32; Turismo Carretera (TC), 38–39

Müller, Pedro: actions during Ford disappearances, 154, 185; appeal, 211; conviction of, 203; as defendant in Ford Argentina human rights case, 194, 199–201

Murúa, Pastor José: CONADEP testimony of, 152–54; disappearance of, 105; release from prison, 141; quoted in *Nunca Más* report, 154

National Archive of Memory, 193, 202

National Commission on the Disappearance of Persons (CONADEP). *See* CONADEP

National Gendarmerie: as security at Ford's Pacheco plant, 94, 101

National Security Doctrine, 49–50, 65

New Left, 70–72, 75–76

Nicolaides, General Cristino, 130

Nixon, Richard, 92

North, Alex, 11

Index

Nunca Más report, 55, 155; Ford disappearances recorded in, 153–54. *See also* CONADEP

O'Farrell, Santiago Gregorio, 24
Ojea Quintana, Rodolfo María, 175–76
Ojea Quintana, Tomás: interest in international human rights law, 176–77, 182; Memoria Abierta interview, 188; 192–194; outreach to Paul Hoffman, 180; participation in 2006 human rights march, 194; strategies in Ford Argentina human rights case, 192–94, 200–201; and Troiani petition to IACHR, 212
Olivera, Héctor, 110
Onganía, General Juan Carlos, 50; and "Argentine Revolution," 69–70; protests against, 73–75
Ongaro, Raimundo, 70
Ortiz, Arcelia, 51, 135–36, 141–42

Pacheco plant (of Ford Argentina): disappearances from, 79–80; judicial inspection of, 199; last Falcon produced, 170; left-wing activism, 89; military occupation of, 101–2, 106; *quinchos*, 55, 67, 83; recreational facilities, 67–68; sign raised by Ford survivors, 199; union organizing at, 81–83
Paladino, José, 188
Partido Revolucionario de los Trabajadores (PRT), 72
Partido Revolucionario de los Trabajadores – Ejército Revolucionario del Pueblo (PRT-ERP): attack on Ford Argentina, 93; founding, 72; kidnappings of executives by, 90
Paterson, Matthew, 15
Paulón, Victorio, 204–5
Pavlovsky, Eduardo "Tato," 1
Payne, Leigh A., 211
Percivaldi, Diego, 22
Pereira, Gabriel, 211

Permanent Assembly of Human Rights (APDH): humanitarian framework of, 156, 168; interviewing methods of, 155; participation in truth trials, 185
Perón, Isabel, 96; overthrow of, 102
Perón, Juan Domingo: automotive policies, 31–33; and CGT labor federation, 63; coup against, 34; and government of, 65; return from exile, 91
Perrotta, Francisco: testimony to CONADEP, 152–54; wrongful dismissal claim against Ford Argentina, 157–59
Pierce, Russell, 28
Pinochet, General Augusto, 92
Piñón, Arnaldo, 132
Pizzolato, Nicola, 83–85
Poder Ejecutivo Nacional (PEN): Ford survivors detained under, 138–39; prisoner releases, 242n9; records destroyed, 147
Poligiotto, Emilio Félix, 170
Portillo, Ismael, 53
Proceso de Reorganización Nacional, 110
Propato, Carlos Alberto: disappearance of, 106; and Ford Argentina human rights case, 200; inquiry at Interior Ministry, 152; interview at Memoria Abierta, 188; participation in 2006 human rights march, 194–95; union activism at Ford, 55, 89, 95, 97
Provincial Memory Commission, 189
Puerta, Guillermo, 125

Radical Civic Union Party, 34
Rafecas, Daniel, 192
Revolución Libertadora, 34
Riveros, General Santiago Omar, 159–60
Robben, Antonius, 2, 210
Rockefeller, Nelson, 117
Rodrigo, Celestino, 96–97

Index

Rodríguez, José: and AIFLD, 86–87; appointment as SMATA Secretary General, 94–95; conflicts with Ford labor activists, 98–100; Mercedes-Benz investigations, 184; refusal to support Ford survivors, 157–60; and SMATA elections, 76–77
Rosario, 59
Rossanigo, José Ambrosio, 196, 197
Rostow, Walt Whitman, 41

Sabatini, Néstor, 148
Sábato, Ernesto, 153–54
Salvatore, Ricardo, 26
Sánchez, Adolfo: buyout offer from Ford, 100; disappearance, 105; employment at Ford Argentina, 51–53; employment struggles after release, 145; inquiry at Interior Ministry, 152; meeting with Ford management, 102–3; Memoria Abierta interview, 188; quoted in *Nunca Más* report, 154; union activism at Ford, 55, 77–78, 81–82; testimony to CONADEP, 152–54
Saro-Wiwa, Ken, 177
Sasiaiñ, General Juan Bautista, 130
Schiffrin, Judge Leopoldo, 184–87
Schonbrun, Benjamin, 3, 180–81
Schuhrke, Jeff, 86
Scilingo, Adolfo, 121
Sebreli, Juan José, 22
Secuela, 174
Seiler, Cotten, 10
Sheinin, David, 128
Sibilla, Héctor Francisco, 107
silhouette protest, 175
Silva, Luiz Inácio "Lula" da, 58
Silver, Beverly, 57–58, 82–83
Sikkink, Kathryn, 150
Sindicato de Mecánicos y Afines del Transporte (SMATA), 42, 61; and AIFLD, 86–88; archives destroyed, 188; autoworkers assigned to, 68; collusion with Ford management, 99–100, 234n7; conflicts with Ford delegates, 82, 94, 98–99; and control of rank and file, 87–89, 96; and federal police, 93; Ford workers affiliated with, 76–77; Green List election, 76; harassment of Ford workers' family members, 136; and labor repression at Mercedes-Benz, 184; Montonero attack on, 93; refusal to help Ford survivors, 157, 159; and Triple A, 95–96. *See also* Ford Argentina union activists; Kloosterman, Dirck; Rodríguez, José
Site of Memory and Human Rights (ex-ESMA), 193
Sloan, Alfred P., 24
SMATA. *See* Sindicato de Mecánicos y Afines del Transporte
Standard Oil, 27
statute of limitations: and crimes against humanity, 193; in Ford Argentina human rights case, 200–201; in wrongful dismissal case against Ford Argentina, 158–59, 212. *See also* UN Convention on the Non-Applicability of Statutory Limitations to War Crimes and Crimes Against Humanity
Suárez Mason, General Guillermo, 120
Supreme Court (of Argentina), 158–59

Tandil, 196–98
task groups (*grupos de tarea*): creation of, 115–16; disappearances by, 111, 122–28; Falcon sedans associated with, 1, 120–28
television, 46
testimony: of Ford survivors to CONADEP, 152–54; of Pedro Troiani to La Plata truth trial, 184–87; of survivors of disappearance, 124–28, 183

Tigre, 59; Campo de Mayo army base, 60–61; detention of Ford workers in police station, 103–6, 135; US multinationals in, 60
Terrabusi, 60
Torres, Omar, 120, 132
Tosco, Agustín, 70
Treintamil, 173
Trial of the Military Juntas, 126–27, 159–60
Troiani, Marcelo Norberto, 212
Troiani, Pedro: employment at Ford Argentina, 51–54, 53; at hearings in Ford Argentina human rights trial, 202; letter to Raúl Alfonsín, 151–52; marriage to Elisa Charlín, 53, 54; petition for exile, 139; petition to IACHR, 212; press interviews, 194; testimony to CONADEP, 152–54; testimony to La Plata truth trial, 184–87; unemployment, 144–45; wrongful dismissal claim against Ford Argentina, 157–59
Trotta, Graciela Irma, 123
truth commissions, 169. *See also* CONADEP
truth trials: Federal Appeals Court of La Plata and, 182–87; resistance to, 195; Troiani testimony at, 184–87
Tupamaros, 71–72
Turismo Carretera (TC), 28–29; Falcon sedan in, 207

unemployment: of Ford survivors, 144–45; in Gran Buenos Aires, 145–146
union activists, 3; *clasistas*, 70; at Ford Argentina, 76–83. *See also* Sindicato de Mecánicos y Afines del Transporte (SMATA)
Unión de Obreros Metalúrgicos (UOM), 66
Unions: AFL-CIO, 42; archives of, 188; Peronist legal structures, 62–63. *See also* AIFLD; internal claims committees; Sindicato de Mecánicos y Afines del Transporte (SMATA)
United Nations, 31
United Nations Convention on the Non-Applicability of Statutory Limitations to War Crimes and Crimes Against Humanity, 193
United Nations, Economic Commission for Latin America and the Caribbean (CEPAL), 31, 70–71
United States: Alliance for Progress, 40–42; car culture, 10, 15, 26; foreign policy toward Latin America, 36, 40–42, 49–50; human rights law in, 178–180; investment in Argentina, 226n4; Latin American critiques of imperialism, 6, 27, 85–86; multinational investment in Latin America, 6; training for Latin American militaries, 113
United States Agency for Economic Development (USAID), 41
United States Department of State: American Institute for Free Labor Development (AIFLD) absorbed into, 42; declassified records, 189–90
Universal jurisdiction, 165
Urry, John, 14

Vandor, Augusto, 65–67
Vanguardia Peronista, 88
Vargas, Getúlio, 30
Vedio, Marta, 185–86
Vence, Judge Alicia, 199
Venezuela, 37
Videla, General Jorge, 117
Vilas, General Acdel, 114–15
Villa Constitución: military assault on, 115
villas miserias, 60, 119
Viola, General Roberto, 145
Vocos, Federico, 201
Volkswagen Beetle: advertising, 16; success in US market, 8; as transnational brand, 16–17

Walsh, Rodolfo, 143–44, 188, 244n38
Watts, Jorge Federico, 126
Weber, Gaby, 120, 184
Webster, J. G. O., 92
West, Henry H., 39
Willey, M. H., 39
Woodell, Shirley, 33
World Cup (1978): Falcon advertising campaign for, 131; preparations for, 119

Xerox, 74

Zona Norte, 61; Campo de Mayo army base, 61–62; guerrilla attacks in, 90; housing in, 60; industrialization of, 58–62; labor activism in, 96–97, 230n2; left-wing activism in, 72; as military priority, 115–16; repression in, 135–36, 200

www.ingramcontent.com/pod-product-compliance
Lightning Source LLC
Chambersburg PA
CBHW020942230426

43666CB00005B/129